An Introduction to Spanish for Health Care Workers

An Introduction to

Spanish

for Health Care Workers

Communication and Culture

FOURTH EDITION

Robert O. Chase and Clarisa B. Medina de Chase

Yale UNIVERSITY PRESS

NEW HAVEN & LONDON

Yale University Press books may be purchased in
quantity for educational, business, or promotional
use. For information, please e-mail sales.press@
yale.edu (U.S. office) or sales@yaleup.co.uk (U.K.
office).

Editor: Tim Shea
Publishing Assistant: Ashley E. Lago
Manuscript Editor: Deborah Bruce-Hostler
Production Editor: Ann-Marie Imbornoni
Production Controller: Katie Golden

Designed by James J. Johnson and set in Melior
Roman and TheSans types.
Set by Tseng Information Systems, Inc.
Printed in the United States of America.

*Library of Congress Cataloging-
in-Publication Data*

Chase, Robert O., 1955–
An introduction to Spanish for health care
workers : communication and culture / Robert O.
Chase, Clarisa B. Medina de Chase. — 4th ed.
p. cm.
Text in English and Spanish.
Includes index.

ISBN 978-0-300-18059-6 (pbk. : alk. paper)
1. Spanish language—Conversation and phrase
books (for medical personnel) 2. Spanish
language—Textbooks for foreign speakers—
English. I. Medina de Chase, Clarisa B., 1963–
II. Title.
PC4120.M3C43 2012
468.3'42102461—dc23
2012008234

A catalogue record for this book is available from
the British Library.

This paper meets the requirements of ANSI/NISO
Z39.48-1992 (Permanence of Paper).

10 9 8 7 6 5 4 3 2

We dedicate this edition to students and professionals who dare suspend beliefs, postpone judgment, and experience the world of their patients; to explorers who comfortably negotiate unfamiliar cultures and guide their patients to achieve new cultural and sociolinguistic competencies of their own.

To have another language is to possess a second soul.
CHARLEMAGNE

Contents

Chapter 5
La familia

COMMUNICATION GOALS
Ask about Family Constellation
Take Family Medical History

VOCABULARY
Family Members
More Family Members
Some Regular Verbs
Hereditary Illnesses

STRUCTURE
Regular Verbs Ending in *-ar, -er,* and *-ir*
The Personal *a*
Direct Object Pronouns
Pronunciation of *B* and *V*

VIDEO PROGRAM
Demostración: ¿Cuáles idiomas habla?
Trama: La historia clínica familiar

CULTURAL NOTE
La familia

Chapter 6
La farmacia

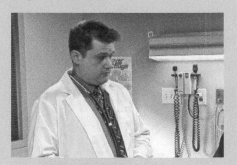

COMMUNICATION GOALS
Give Medication Instructions
Ask about Medication Allergies and
    Educate Patients about Allergic
    Reactions
Educate a Patient about Asthma
Ask Who Helps an Infirm Family
    Member
Explain How to Use a Pill Organizer

VOCABULARY
Forms of Medication
Dosing Instructions and Routes of
    Administration
Some Classes of Medications
Allergic Reactions

STRUCTURE
Commands with *favor de, hay que,* and
    tener que
Formal (*usted*) Commands
Demonstrative, Affirmative, and
    Negative Adjectives
Indirect Objects and the Verb *Dar*

VIDEO PROGRAM
Demostración: Cómo usar el inhalador
Trama: ¿Qué medicamentos toma?

CULTURAL NOTE
La confianza

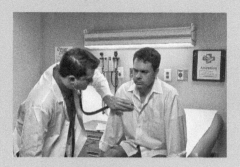

Chapter 9
«¿Qué pasó?»

COMMUNICATION GOALS
  Ask What Happened
  Give Test Results
  Conduct a Pre-surgery Interview
  Ask What Was Happening

VOCABULARY
  Times in the Past
  Pre-surgery
  Words of Reassurance

STRUCTURE
  The Preterit of Regular Verbs
  The Preterit of Some Irregular Verbs
  The Imperfect Mood of the Past Tense

VIDEO PROGRAM
  Demostración: Dolor terrible
  Trama: Memorias de México

CULTURAL NOTE
  Remedios caseros

Chapter 10
Padecimientos e historia médica

COMMUNICATION GOALS
  Ask about Current Medical Conditions
  Educate a Patient about Cancer
  Ask about Medical History
  Ask about Symptoms
  Educate a Patient about Tuberculosis
  Ask about Surgical History
  Educate a Patient about Vaccinations

VOCABULARY
  Illnesses and the Abbreviated History
  Illnesses and Review of Systems
  Infectious and Tropical Diseases
  Cancer
  General Symptoms
  Internal Organs and Glands
  Some Surgeries and Procedures
  Vaccinations

STRUCTURE
  The Verb *Padecer*
  The Present Perfect Tense
  Indefinite and Negative Pronouns
  The Verb *Ponerse* and Vaccinations

VIDEO PROGRAM
  Trama: La colecistitis
  Demostración: La sonografía

CULTURAL NOTE
  Feeling at Home Somewhere Else

Chapter 11
Internamientos, odontología y la salud mental

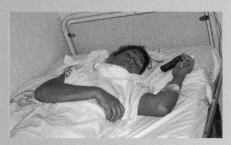

COMMUNICATION GOALS
Announce a Hospitalization
Discuss Activities of Daily Living
Plan a Hospital Discharge
Teach about Dental Hygiene
Conduct a Mental Status Exam
Address Addictions

VOCABULARY
Hospital Admission
Activities of Daily Living
Discharge Planning
The Dentist
Feelings
Mental Illnesses and Symptoms
Addictions

STRUCTURE
Reflexive Verbs
Se and Unplanned Events
The Verbs *Dormir* and *Poder*
The Verb *Sentirse*

VIDEO PROGRAM
Trama: La laparascopia
Demostración: At the Drop of a Hat

CULTURAL NOTE
Los nervios

Chapter 12
Maternidad y la protección sexual

COMMUNICATION GOALS
Confirm a Pregnancy
Teach about Possible Complications
Coach a Delivery
Promote Safer Sex

VOCABULARY
Pregnancy
Possible Complications
Delivery
Sexually Transmitted Diseases

STRUCTURE
Informal (*tú*) Commands

VIDEO PROGRAM
Trama: Mi hermano tiene SIDA
Atracción especial: What's My Line—
What's Your Temperature?

CULTURAL NOTES
Fathers and Childbirth
Communication about Sexual Matters

Preface

Effective communication is essential in health care, and communication is most effective when both parties share a common language. Ideally, patients articulate history, symptoms, and their understanding of diagnosis and treatment recommendations. Health care workers clarify this information, teach patients about treatment options, and obtain informed consent for procedures. In a series of exchanges, the practitioner and patient negotiate not only a correct understanding of factual information, but appreciation for broader issues of roles and expectations as well. This ideal exchange is often challenged by language and cultural differences.

When the patient and the health care provider do not speak the same language, the provider must accommodate the patient. Language accommodation increases health care access for a growing clientele of people with limited English proficiency. Providers who accommodate the patient's language elicit better information for diagnosis and treatment and inspire patients to follow recommendations, thus reducing delays in seeking care, enhancing quality of care, and improving treatment outcomes. When health care providers are able to include family and community members in communication, patients are more able to make use of these informal supports.

Language accommodation, also called language access services, helps to meet legal requirements and accreditation standards, increases patient satisfaction and retention, and may decrease malpractice claims. Good practice is the best inoculation against malpractice. The angry patient is the most likely to become litigious; to form satisfying relationships and invest in effective communication may help reduce exposure to costly judicial intervention.

Working in two languages is satisfying to health care givers as well. More than a competitive edge in the job market, bilingual health care workers gain the ability to directly communicate with patients with whom they otherwise would require an interpreter. Of course, qualified medical interpreters are essential for complex communication tasks that are beyond the language ability of the practi-

Acknowledgments

First a heartfelt thanks to you, the students, professors, institutions, and medical professionals who have used this book to enhance relationships and improve communication with patients. You deserve this new edition with its updated lexicon, refined pedagogy, and four-color embellishment. We recognize the American Council on the Teaching of Foreign Languages (ACTFL), whose publications and annual national conference provide us with fresh approaches to cultivating language acquisition. Professor Thomas Delventhal, Roger Negrón, Michael DiChello, and Central Connecticut State University's Schlock improvisation club proposed, clarified, and demonstrated *Drama imprevisto* exercises. Brave Tunxis Community College students tried and tested improvisation exercises including "The Host" and "Tangled Web." Our friends Juan Barrera of the *Universidad Autónoma de México* and Carlos Brito and Selene Cortés of *Ideal Escuela de Español* in Cuernavaca, Morelos, Mexico, guided us during treks that expanded our knowledge of Mexican culture. Alexandre Carré, MD, and Claudio Negrao, PhD, reviewed Cultural Notes, explained medical and psychological algorithms, and helped to assess the lexical and medical dialogue needs that underlie the book's specific communication goals. Karrie McCarter of Orthopedic Associates of Middletown, Connecticut, graciously provided digital bone images. Graphic artist Frank Dlugoleski, a member of our team since the first edition, moved us from monotony to color. Mike Zych gently and generously guided author-generated graphics. Karina Jiménez Rodríguez, our friend and favorite Latin jazz violinist, kindly loaned her musical voice to the audio program for this edition. Several friends shared enthusiasm and specific areas of expertise, including José Durán Toribio; Professor Karlene Ball; Harry Hernández; Dr. Jorge Amarante; and Dr. Hector Valerio Mena. Dr. Hans Lohman divulged his experiences as a medical intern at *el Hospital Morgan* in Santo Domingo. The following esteemed professors reviewed the third edition and graciously provided constructive criticism to improve this fourth edition: Rosa Chavez, the University of Georgia; María Francisca Sabló-Yates, Delta College; G. Helguero-Balcells, Nova Southeastern University; Alan Bruflat, Wayne

State College; Gerardo Cruz-Tanahara, Cardinal Stritch University; Susan Lister, De Anza College; Lisa Barboun, Coastal Carolina University; Patricia Davis, Darton College; Teresa Roig-Torres, University of Cincinnati – Raymond Walters College; David de Posada, Georgia College and State University; Jennifer Maxwell, Catholic University of America; Clementina E. Adams, Clemson University; and Teresia Taylor, Hardin-Simmons University. James Revillini and Stephen Lieberman informed and encouraged the innovative use of QR codes.

Introduction

An Introduction to Spanish for Health Care Workers facilitates better communication between health care providers and the growing Spanish-speaking community in the United States. It is not a phrase book or a translator. It is a first course in Spanish, progressively merging conversation and a health care lexicon in various medical contexts. Although it does not call for a prerequisite knowledge of Spanish, this book is also helpful to people who speak limited Spanish and aspire to apply their Spanish in a medical setting. Topics include building the patient-practitioner relationship, the patient's chief complaint, taking medical history, and defining current symptoms. We progress to injuries, pharmacotherapy, diet and nutrition, tests and procedures, diagnoses, and specialized topics such as hospitalizations, dentistry, illnesses, tropical and infectious diseases, mental health, palliative care, maternity, and sexual protection.

Prior to this edition, we solicited comments and suggestions from professors from all over the United States who had adopted the text, and from a group of professors who had not adopted the text. These led to the following refinements, including the addition of color for a more attractive presentation. We crafted many newer graphics that prompt conversation. There are 174 color illustrations. We updated the lexicon and expanded it to support talking about cancer, substance abuse, and additional tropical and infectious diseases. We condensed some grammar explanations and relocated them to topical areas where they were easily integrated into medical dialogue. We replaced translation exercises with target-language activities. To reduce the use of English, beginning in chapter 6, we wrote the instructions for most exercises and activities in Spanish. We clarified *Drama imprevisto* instructions without imposing excessive structure, and many of these were changed to more closely resemble actual, proven improvisation games that are used in theater classes. We added an audio program to the Web site, lengthened the online quizzes, and made some of the illustrations and classroom activity sheets available for download. We updated the links to World Wide Web sites that can be useful for research and post-communicative projects.

The crucial precepts of the book are context and communication. Vocabulary is organized by specific medical themes, and grammar lessons support the goal of conversing with patients. While sitting on a Cancún beach during spring break, no thirsty student thinks, "What an ideal place to use a stem-changing verb in the present tense!" Rather, the need to communicate trumps grammar; and the student ventures, "*Quiero una piña colada por favor.*" The message is first, and the student learns correct speech by using language for a purpose.

The text is divided into sections that are named for the practical communication goals, such as "Test a Patient's Orientation." This affirms the student's goal of learning the functional language that delivers health care in a patient's preferred language. Grammar appears in the context of specific communication tasks. For example, command forms are taught in the context of giving medication instructions. This is a guided, learn-by-doing approach in which students acquire language while using it in meaningful interaction.

The text is supported by a video program available at **yalebooks.com/medicalspanish**. There are twenty-four video clips that are brief enough to enhance "replay-ability" and not overwhelm the student. Video segments are called *La trama* (the plot) and *Demostración*. *La trama* is a series of interactions between the Flores family, Dr. Vargas, and nurse Rosmery. These closely follow the lexicon and structure as they develop in the book. *Demostración* is a segment that demonstrates a specific communication task in health care. For example, in chapter 4, Rosmery demonstrates taking telephone numbers, and students practice this skill while watching the video. The final two chapters present an *Atracción especial,* in which the cast performs improvisation exercises from chapters 11 and 12. Spanish subtitles can be toggled.

The companion Web site, **yalebooks.com/medicalspanish**, also supports the text with the audio program, tips for teachers and learners, and self-correcting quizzes to test skills while reinforcing medical vocabulary and related grammar. You'll be able to download helpful graphics such as the skeleton and the pain scale, and classroom activity sheets that support survey-taking communicative activities. The Web site also provides links to medical and language sites on the World Wide Web and the opportunity to download the audio program and video program's sound tracks to your personal digital audio player. You may access the audio program with quick response (QR) codes in the text. (These are three-dimensional UPCs.) Find the Web site at **yalebooks.com/medicalspanish.**

 A soccer goal icon identifies a broad communication goal, and heads a large section of material. This backward design in lesson planning calls for focus on what students soon will know how to do. With a goal in mind, we provide 275 learning experiences in the form of in-class activities that compel students to speak Spanish in the classroom, preparing them for the emotional and linguistic challenges of speaking to native-Spanish-speaking patients. These are organized under the headings *Hacia precisión,* which are the more mechanical exercises that promote accurate speech; and *Hacia fluidez,* which are the interaction activities that promote communication abilities in interpretive, interpersonal, and presentational modes.

A bicycle icon denotes *Ejercicios,* or directed mechanical activities that usually have one correct response and are intended to promote accuracy. There tend to be more *Ejercicios* in the first chapter, where everything may be new to you; and in the chapter about pharmacy, where accuracy is critical. Find an Answer Key to the *Ejercicios* at the end of the book; we have omitted from the Answer Key those exercises whose responses may vary.

An icon of faces identifies communicative *Actividades,* which are interactive and more open-ended. They call for students to use Spanish to complete a practical task that is typical to a medical setting. These require autonomous language production. The instructor provides coaching and consultation, and students practice with partners, play roles, and solve problems.

Two Greek drama masks signal unscripted improvisation activities, called *Drama imprevisto.* This cross-pollination of theater and language acquisition is a hyperextension of the communicative classroom. Improvisation requires spontaneous speech. During improvisation, you practice the Spanish that you know, and may clarify your message with gestures as needed. This helps to keep your thoughts in the target language and reduces the frustration of being a novice speaker. Improvisation exercises help groups of students to become supportive teams. When you improvise, you climb a scaffold of grammar and vocabulary and speak within a loosely prescribed social and lexical context. Of all the risks you'll take as a novice speaker, improvisation may be the most enjoyable. Improvisation is a fun way to build confidence. You can monitor and correct your own speech. Self-correction is more effective than instructor-originated correction, which is called recasting.

Where the video icon appears, students are prompted to watch a section of the video and to do activities based on the video program. To access the videos, click the Video program link at **yalebooks.com /medicalspanish**. When prompted, enter Password ROCHASE2012. At times, a student will not understand a video scene upon first viewing, although this will resolve after completing the corresponding chapter and reviewing the video. Each scene illustrates the structure, vocabulary, and communication goals of the chapter in which it appears. These are integrated into the text with activities based on the video. This allows students to observe good models interacting with patients, to check their comprehension, and to practice new skills while being coached by peers and the instructor.

When acquiring a second language, it is not possible to review too much. A three-arrow recycling icon appears next to *Reciclaje* activities that consolidate learning by showing new uses for previously learned vocabulary and structures. These first appear in chapter 3 and are placed at the end of each chapter prior to the Cultural Note feature.

The girder icon alerts you to a grammar explanation that is peppered with language examples. Grammar should be secondary to immersion and communication, but is a worthwhile shortcut to developing more accurate speech.

Earbuds let you know that the identified vocabulary list or conversation is available on the book Web site, from where you'll be able to download these files to your personal digital audio player. If you have a smartphone or other portable device with a QR code scanner and Internet connection, you'll be able to scan the code and listen to the audio without turning on your computer. The audio program transcript may be downloaded from the Web site as well.

A Cultural Note appears at the end of each chapter. These inform you on matters of immigration, acculturation, world views, diverse customs, communication styles, and language accommodation to support your development of an even more culturally-competent practice.

The medical information and illustrations included in the text are not intended to diagnose or treat illnesses. Although these dialogues, vignettes, and exercises are derived from lexical needs assessments and the authors' experiences interpreting for and observing diverse practitioners, they are included here for the sole purpose of teaching language.

Chapter 1
«Buenos días, soy el doctor»

Communication Goals

Vocabulary

Structure

Video

Cultural Note

By the time you finish this book you will be able to conduct essential medical interviews in Spanish, including patient registration, history-taking and physical examinations, common procedures, instructions for diet and pharmacotherapy, and health education. You will be able to talk about common illnesses, mental health, reproductive care, and safer sex practices. You will be more aware of some cultural dynamics of the healing relationship. With practice and experience, you will be able to communicate effectively in Spanish in your medical setting. By the end of this chapter you will be able to greet patients in Spanish, introduce yourself by name and profession, and describe people.

Greet Your Patient and Introduce Yourself

 Diálogo

The earbuds icon signals that this portion of text is included in this chapter's .mp3 file and is available for download from the Web site. You may also scan the QR code with your smartphone or other scanner-equipped audio player with Internet connection.

«Mucho gusto».

Dr. Vargas:	Buenos días. Soy el doctor Vargas.
Sr. Flores:	Buenos días, doctor. Soy Francisco Flores.
Dr. Vargas:	Mucho gusto.
Sr. Flores:	El gusto es mío. ¿Cómo está usted?
Dr. Vargas:	Bien, gracias, ¿y usted?
Sr. Flores:	Bien, bien, gracias.

Upside-down question marks and exclamation marks are written at the beginning of questions and exclamations.

 Vocabulario: Saludos y despedidas
(Greetings and Farewells)

Hola.	Hello.
Buenos días.	Good morning.
Buenas tardes.	Good afternoon.
Buenas noches.	Good evening; good night.
¿Cómo está usted?	How are you?
Estoy bien, gracias.	I am fine, thank you.
Muy bien.	Very well.

Me alegro.	I'm glad.
¿Y usted?	And you?
Estoy mal.	I'm ill.
Lo siento.	I'm sorry.
De nada.	You're welcome.
Mucho gusto.	Pleased to meet you.
Encantado/a.	Pleased to meet you.
El gusto es mío.	The pleasure is mine.
Igualmente.	Same here
Adiós.	Good-bye.
Hasta luego.	See you later.

Encantado/a: If you are female, say *encantada*.

Preguntas útiles

¿De dónde es usted?	Where are you from?
¿Cómo se llama usted?	What is your name?

Expresiones útiles

Soy el doctor Vargas.	I am Doctor Vargas.
Me llamo Francisco Flores.	My name is Francisco Flores.
Soy de Puerto Rico.	I am from Puerto Rico.
Soy puertorriqueño.	I am Puerto Rican.
Le presento a la doctora García.	I introduce you to Doctor García.

HACIA PRECISIÓN

1.1 Ejercicio

A bicycle signals a mechanical exercise, usually with one correct answer. Answers to most *ejercicios* may be found in the Answer Key at the end of the book.

Write two of the above expressions for each of the following language functions. Include accents and punctuation marks.

A. Greeting   *Buenos Tardes*

_____

B. Taking leave   *Adios*

_____

C. Introducing oneself   *yo soy Sarah*

yo soy enfemera Sarah

D. Expressing joy/sympathy   _Me Alegro   -I'm glad_

_____

E. Responding to an introduction   _Mucho Gusto_

_____

 ## 1.2 Ejercicio

The lines of the following dialogue are out of order. Work in small groups to put them in the correct order by numbering them in the spaces provided. Then take turns reading your finished product to the class.

_1_   Dr. Vargas: Buenos días. Soy el doctor Vargas.

_6_   Sr. Flores: Bien, bien, gracias. Doctor, le presento a mi esposa Marisol García de Flores.

_5_   Dr. Vargas: Muy bien, gracias, ¿y usted?

_4_   Sr. Flores: El gusto es mío. ¿Cómo está usted?

_3_   Dr. Vargas: Encantado.

_9_   Dr. Vargas: Soy de Puerto Rico.

¿dónde?
where?

_8_   Sra. Flores: Igualmente. Usted habla español. ¿De dónde es usted?

_7_   Dr. Vargas: Mucho gusto.

_2_   Sr. Flores: Buenos días, doctor. Soy Francisco Flores.

HACIA FLUIDEZ

A faces icon marks an activity in which students work with partners. Switch roles often and share your results with the class whenever prompted by the instructor.

 ## 1.3 Actividad

Repeat the greetings and farewells after the instructor. After the instructor demonstrates with several students, get up and move around the room, greeting each person. It is customary to shake hands when you greet someone. When finished, volunteer to act out for the class the best of your exchanges. Many people consider *hola* too casual for a first meeting. The letter *h* is silent in Spanish, as in *hola* (OH-la) and *hospital* (os-pi-TAL). (There are pronunciation notes at the end of each of the first five chapters.)

1.4 Actividad

From your places, take turns introducing yourselves to your neighbor by name.

Student 1: Buenas tardes. Me llamo Paul. ¿Cómo se llama usted?
Student 2: Buenas tardes. Me llamo Carol.
Class: Hola, Carol. ¿Cómo está usted?
Student 2: Bien, gracias. (*Then to student 3*) Buenas tardes. Me llamo Carol. ¿Cómo se llama usted?

Continue in this way until everyone has had a turn.

1.5 Actividad

Finish and act out the following conversations with a partner.

A. —Buenas tardes. Me llamo _____. ¿Cómo se llama usted?

—Me _____ .

—Mucho _____ .

— _____ .

B. —¿Cómo _____ ?

—Estoy muy bien, gracias.

—Me _____ .

—¿Y usted? ¿ _____ ?

—Estoy _____ .

C. —Hola, me llamo _____. ¿De dónde _____ ?

—Soy _____ .

—Hasta luego.

— _____ .

el enfermero   los enfermeros   la enfermera   las enfermeras

Estructura: El género y número de los nombres y artículos definidos (*Gender and Number of Nouns and Definite Articles*)

• In Spanish some nouns are masculine, like *el hospital* (the hospital), while others are feminine, like *la cama* (the bed). With some exceptions, nouns ending in *-o* are masculine, and nouns ending in *-a* are feminine. (*Día* is masculine, so we say *¡Buenos días! Mano* is feminine, so we say *la mano.*)

• Some nouns that refer to people change the last letter to become masculine or feminine. A male nurse is *el enfermero,* and a female nurse is *la enfermera.* Similarly, nouns indicating national origin or ethnicity, such as *norteamericano,* end in either *-o* or *-a* according to the gender of the person to whom they refer. Ethnicities are not capitalized.

> Soy Marcos. Soy enfermero. Soy argentino.
> La doctora García es cirujana. No es argentina, es mexicana.

• The nouns for professions ending in *-iatra* and *-ista,* such as *el/la pediatra* and *el/la ortopedista,* can be either masculine or feminine. In these cases the definite articles indicate gender. A male pediatrician is *el pediatra,* while a female pediatrician is *la pediatra,* and the same is true for *el ortopedista* and *la ortopedista.*

• When speaking about a third person and using a title with the last name, the definite article is placed before the title, as in *El doctor Brito es chileno.* The definite article is not used when addressing someone, as in *Buenas tardes, doctor Brito.*

• Nouns or adjectives ending in *-e,* such as *paciente* and *estudiante,* can be either masculine or feminine, depending on the gender of the person. A male student is *el estudiante,* while a female student is *la estudiante.* Words ending in *-ción,* such as *la infección,* are feminine. Most words ending in *-ma* or *-pa* are masculine and are of Greek origin: for example, *el mapa, el problema,* and *el sistema.*

• To make nouns plural in Spanish we add *-s* to nouns that end in vowels and *-es* to those ending in consonants. The articles and nouns must always agree in gender and number. The plural masculine article is *los,* and the plural feminine article is *las.*

Singular	*Plural*
el enfermero	los enfermeros
la enfermera	las enfermeras
el doctor	los doctores
la doctora	las doctoras
el hospital	los hospitales

HACIA PRECISIÓN

 1.6 Ejercicio

Change the nouns to agree with the gender of the person.

Modelo: El señor Nieves es secretario. / la señora Nieves
— El señor Nieves es secretario; la señora Nieves es secretaria.

> The letter *ñ* is pronounced like the "ni" in the word "onion."

A. El doctor Colón es neurólogo. / la doctora Palma
B. El doctor Aquino es odontólogo. / la doctora Losada
C. Ana es trabajadora social. / Tomás
D. El señor García es consejero. / la señora Marques
E. Leomara es farmacéutica. / Alfredo
F. El doctor Mena es psiquiatra. / la doctora Mariano

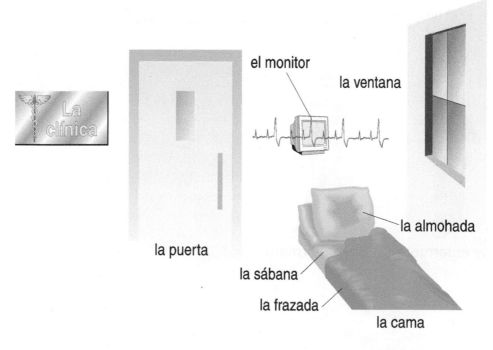

G. La doctora López es cardióloga. / el doctor López

H. La doctora Negrón es dentista. / el doctor José Peña Ortiz

 ## 1.7 Ejercicio

Give the plural of the following nouns and definite articles.

Modelo: la trabajadora social / las trabajadoras sociales

A. la clínica   _____

B. la puerta   _____

C. el monitor   _____

D. la cama   _____

E. la sábana   _____

F. la frazada   _____

G. la almohada   _____

H. el doctor   _____

I. el hospital   _____

Soy enfermera.   Soy enfermero.

Estructura: Los sujetos y el verbo *ser*
(*Subject Pronouns and the Verb* Ser)

• A sentence requires a subject and a verb. Subjects and verbs can be in the first, second, or third person. Speaking in the first person is to speak of oneself. Speaking in the second person is to ask about or tell about the person or persons whom you are addressing. Speaking in the third person is to ask or tell about someone else.

	Singular	*Plural*
First person	*yo* (I)	*nosotros* (we, mixed gender and masculine)
		nosotras (we, all feminine)
Second person	*tú* (you, informal)	*vosotros** (you, informal)
	usted (you, formal)	*ustedes* (you, formal)
Third person	*él* (he)	*ellos* (they, mixed gender and masculine)
	ella (she)	*ellas* (they, all feminine)

Vosotros is used in Spain and not presented in this text. Latin Americans generally understand this form but use *ustedes* for the second person plural.

• In the second person, note that *tú* is normally used when addressing a child or someone with whom you are on a first-name basis. With adults, using *tú* where *usted* would be proper may offend. Spanish-speakers from the Caribbean use the *tú* form with adults more readily than others, but one should use *usted* when in doubt. In the third person, note that *el* means "the" and *él* means "he."

• The plural masculine forms *nosotros* and *ellos* are used for a group of all males or a mixed group of males and females; the plural feminine forms *nosotras* and *ellas* are used with groups of all females.

• The verb *ser* means "to be." Use it to tell your name, occupation, characteristics, and national origin. As in English (I am, you are), the verb changes its form depending on its subject. Note that with the forms *soy* and *eres,* the pronoun is implied, but the form *es* can mean *you, she, he,* or *it* is. The subject and verb may be reversed to form a question: *¿Es usted doctor?*

yo **soy**	I am	**Soy** Manuel.
tú **eres**	you are	**Eres** inteligente.
usted, él, ella **es**	you are; he, she is	**¿Es** usted la madre?
nosotros, nosotras **somos**	we are	Tú y yo **somos** mexicanas.
ustedes, ellos, ellas **son**	you (plural), they are	Ellos **son** cardiólogos.

HACIA PRECISIÓN

1.8 Ejercicio

You work in an emergency room. In the spaces, indicate whether you would use *tú* or *usted* with the following people.

A. the Spanish-speaking nurse who usually works with you   _____

B. your patient, age five   _____

C. your new pediatric patient's mother   _____

D. the new cardiologist from Guatemala, whom you've not met   _____

E. a friend from the Spanish class who meets you for lunch   _____

F. your new patient, age forty-seven   _____

1.9 Ejercicio

Subject pronouns can substitute for the name of a person and act as the subject of the verb. Write which Spanish pronouns or subjects are implied by the following, and add the appropriate form of the verb *ser*. Note that the Spanish word *y* means "and," and is pronounced like "ee" in the English word "see."

    Modelo: Juan   ___él es___

A. el Sr. Romero _____   F. la clase y yo _____

B. Juan y yo _____   G. los doctores _____

C. Sergio y Ana _____   H. el doctor y el enfermero _____

D. las enfermeras _____   I. la clínica _____

E. la familia _____   J. usted, usted y usted _____

el obstetra

la doctora   el doctor

el pediatra

la secretaria

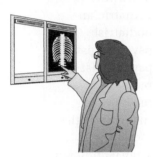

la radióloga

la cirujana

Vocabulario: Las profesiones (*Professions*)

el anestesiólogo, la anestesióloga	anesthesiologist
el asociado médico, la asociada médica*	physician's assistant
el audiólogo, la audióloga	audiologist
el/la ayudante de enfermero	nurse's aide
el cardiólogo, la cardióloga	cardiologist
el cirujano, la cirujana	surgeon
el comadrón, la comadrona	midwife
el consejero, la consejera	counselor
el/la dentista; el odontólogo, la odontóloga	dentist
el dermatólogo, la dermatóloga	dermatologist
el/la dietista	dietitian
el doctor, la doctora; el médico, la médica	doctor
el endocrinólogo, la endocrinóloga	endocrinologist
el enfermero, la enfermera	nurse
el/la estudiante de medicina	medical student
el farmacéutico, la farmacéutica	pharmacist
el ginecólogo, la ginecóloga**	gynecologist

el/la higienista dental	dental hygienist
el médico general, la médica general	general practitioner
el médico / la médica de cabecera	general practitioner
el médico internista, la médica internista	internist
el neumólogo, la neumóloga	pulmonologist
el neurólogo, la neuróloga	neurologist
el/la nutricionista	nutritionist
el/la obstetra	obstetrician
el oftalmólogo, la oftalmóloga	ophthalmologist
el oncólogo, la oncóloga	oncologist
el/la ortopedista	orthopedist
el otorrinolaringólogo, la otorrinolaringóloga	ENT doctor
el partero, la partera	midwife
el/la pediatra	pediatrician
el podólogo, la podóloga	podiatrist
el psicólogo, la psicóloga	psychologist
el/la psiquiatra	psychiatrist
el radiólogo, la radióloga	radiologist
el/la recepcionista	receptionist
el reumatólogo, la reumatóloga	rheumatologist
el secretario, la secretaria	secretary
el técnico de radiografía, la técnica de radiografía	x-ray technician
el terapeuta, la terapeuta	therapist
el/la terapeuta del habla	speech therapist
el terapeuta físico, la terapeuta física	physical therapist
el terapeuta respiratorio, la terapeuta respiratoria	respiratory therapist
el trabajador social, la trabajadora social	social worker
el urólogo, la uróloga	urologist

*The Spanish translation of "physician's assistant," *asociado médico,* was adopted by the American Academy of Physician Assistants in 1998 and reaffirmed in 2003. Due to its uniqueness to the United States, the nurse practitioner does not have a concise counterpart in Spanish. Depending on state laws, you may say, *un enfermero con licencia para diagnosticar y tratar padecimientos y recetar medicamentos* (a nurse who has a license to diagnose and treat ailments and prescribe medications).

**The letter *g* is like the English "h" when it precedes the vowels *e* and *i.* It is like the "g" in the English word "go" before the vowels *a, o,* and *u. Ginecólogo* contains an example of both. *J* is always pronounced like English "h," as in *cirujano.* Many words have accents that guide pronunciation.

Preguntas útiles

¿En qué trabaja usted?	What do you do for work?
¿Cuál es su especialidad?	What is your specialty?

HACIA PRECISIÓN

 ## 1.10 Ejercicio

Words that sound similar in two languages and have the same meaning are called "close cognates." Those that sound similar and have different meanings are called "false cognates" or "false friends," and may lead to misunderstanding. You'll safely assume the meaning of the following close cognates. Listen to the instructor read the following patient chief concerns, and refer him or her to the appropriate discipline. Some may have multiple correct responses.

Modelo: Profesor: Sufro de migrañas.
            Estudiantes: Usted necesita un neurólogo.

A. Necesito una inyección.
B. Sufro de problemas cardíacos.
C. Sufro de diabetes.
D. Necesito una operación.
E. Sufro de cáncer de los pulmones.
F. Sufro de cataratas.

G. Necesito una dieta especial.
H. Sufro de problemas emocionales.
I. Sufro de artritis.
J. Tengo la clavícula fracturada.
K. Sufro de psoriasis.
L. Mi bebé tiene fiebre.

• Spanish does not use the definite article *el* or *la* (the) or the indefinite article *un* or *una* (a, an) after the verb *ser* when stating a profession or nationality, unless the noun is modified.

Soy médico.   I am a doctor.
El Dr. Ortíz es un buen doctor. Dr. Ortíz is a good doctor.

• The definite article is used with titles. *Ella es la doctora Meléndez.* Such titles as *doctor* and *señor* are capitalized only when abbreviated (*Dr.* and *Sr.*)

HACIA FLUIDEZ

 ## 1.11 Actividad

It is time for a soirée! Find the Spanish name for your current—or future—profession. Next, move around the classroom introducing yourself and asking fellow students their occupations.

Modelo: —Buenas tardes. Soy Roberto. Soy enfermero.
          —Mucho gusto, Roberto. Soy Nancy.

—Encantado. ¿En qué trabaja usted?
—Soy médica.
—¿Cuál es su especialidad?
—Soy oftalmóloga.

Continue until you have spoken with everyone. When you have finished, take turns reporting your findings to the class. For example, *Ella es Nancy; es oftalmóloga. Él es William, es cirujano.* To make an introduction, say, *Clase, les presento a Nancy. Es oftalmóloga.*

 ## 1.12 Drama imprevisto

Let's play our first game of "The Host." Choose a host, who leaves the room for a moment while the class chooses five students and assigns each a medical profession from the vocabulary list. The host returns and is in the front of the room preparing a party. The chosen students take turns knocking on the door, entering the party, and exchanging small talk with each person while acting the role of their chosen profession using gestures, questions, and statements. Say anything but the name of your assigned profession. At the end, the host must guess each person's profession: *Zahra es odontóloga; Marek es ortopedista,* and so on. Then the instructor may interview students to demonstrate the forms of the verb *ser.* If one profession is assigned to more than one student, you'll be able to practice the plural forms as well (*Susan y Rashid son otorrinolaringólogos*).

¿Cuáles son las tres especialidades del Dr. Ernesto Córdova Ramos?

Vocabulario: Los países y las identidades nacionales (*Countries and Ethnicities*)

Región	País	Identidad nacional
Europa		
	España	español/española
América del norte		
	los Estados Unidos	estadounidense, norteamericano/a
	México	mexicano/a

El caribe

Cuba	cubano/a
la República Dominicana	dominicano/a
Puerto Rico	puertorriqueño/a

América central

Guatemala	guatemalteco/a
Honduras	hondureño/a
El Salvador	salvadoreño/a
Nicaragua	nicaragüense
Costa Rica	costarricense
Panamá	panameño/a

América del sur

Venezuela	venezolano/a
Colombia	colombiano/a
Ecuador	ecuatoriano/a
Perú	peruano/a
Bolivia	boliviano/a
Paraguay	paraguayo/a
Chile	chileno/a
Uruguay	uruguayo/a
Argentina	argentino/a

Preguntas útiles

¿De dónde es usted?	Where are you (formal) from?
¿De dónde eres?	Where are you (informal) from?

Expresiones útiles

Soy de Colombia.	I am from Colombia.
Soy colombiano.	I am Colombian.
La doctora es uruguaya.	The doctor is Uruguayan.

Puerto Rico has commonwealth status with the United States. Some ethnic groups have popular words for their national identity. For example, Puerto Ricans may call themselves *boricuas* or *borinqueños;* Dominicans, *quisque-yanos;* and Costa Ricans, *ticos.* Immigrants to the United States may add the extension *americano/a* to their national origin when they wish to, as in *co-lombianoamericano*

Ask Your Patient's Name

¿Cómo se llama usted? (*What Is Your Name?*)

Recall that *¿Cómo se llama usted?* means "What is your name?" Literally, it means, "How do you call yourself?" The letters *ll* are pronounced like the English letter "y." The reflexive pronouns *se* and *te* are discussed in chapter 11. Here are some variations.

¿Cómo se llama usted?	What is your name?
¿Cómo te llamas?*	What is your name?
Me llamo Arturo.	My name is Arturo.
¿Cómo se llama el (la) bebé?	What is the baby's name?
¿Cómo se llama el niño (la niña)?	What is the child's name?
Él se llama Armando.	His name is Armando.
Ella se llama Rosalinda.	Her name is Rosalinda.

*This is the familiar (*tú*) form, used with acquaintances and children.

HACIA PRECISIÓN

 ## 1.13 Actividad

With so many new friends from class, it is time to update your Rolodex. Ask students who sit near you their name, profession, and national origin. Fill in the directory cards that follow.

Nombre: _____

Profesión: _____

Nacionalidad: _____

Nombre: _____

Profesión: _____

Nacionalidad: _____

HACIA FLUIDEZ

 ### 1.14 Actividad

Role-play a case conference or morning rounds. Designate a student to be the patient, and take turns introducing yourself by name, occupation, and national origin.

> Modelo: —Hola. Me llamo Cristóbal. Soy dietista. Soy de los Estados Unidos.

When you have finished, test your memory by introducing all of the people in the room. For example, *Ella es Nancy; es trabajadora social. Él es Bill; es cirujano. Bill es estadounidense.* If you forget someone's personal information, ask for it again.

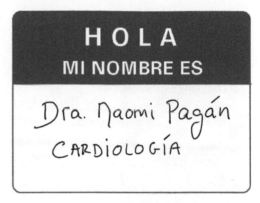

 ### 1.15 Drama imprevisto

Play *«¿Cómo te llamas?»* Form a circle. The first student points to another student anywhere in the circle and says *Me llamo* [*nombre*]. The student who was signaled then points to another student and says *Me llamo* [*nombre*]. Continue in this way until you know everyone's name. It is important to set a rhythm and follow it. This promotes concentration and the coveted dynamic of working as a team. Variations include *Mi nombre es* [*nombre*] and *Soy* [*nombre*].

 ### 1.16 Drama imprevisto

Ad lib a fib! Circulate in the classroom asking classmates for name, profession (or future profession), and national origin. This time, fib some of your information, and tell the truth about the rest. Tell the same fib or truth each time you are asked. After everyone has a turn interviewing each classmate, share what you have been told. For example, *Bill dice* (says) *que es de Puerto Rico.* Then the class will separate truth from fiction: *Bill no es de Puerto Rico, es de Florida.*

From the Web site you can listen to the audio tracks of the video or download them to your personal digital audio player.

Video «*Buenos días, soy el doctor Vargas*»

Here are some of the protagonists you'll meet in the video.

Mi nombre es Elsita. Mi papá se llama Francisco Flores, y mi mamá se llama Marisol García de Flores. Mi muñeca se llama Samantha. Ella está enferma. Le duelen los oídos. Necesita consultar con un otorrino-laringólogo.

Elsita Flores

Me llamo Francisco Flores. Soy casado. Mi esposa se llama Marisol García de Flores. Tenemos una hija. Ella se llama Elsita.

Francisco Flores

Soy Marisol García de Flores. Soy dominicana, de Santo Domingo. Mi padre tiene problema con la próstata, pero está bien, gracias a Dios. Vamos a consultar con un urólogo.

Marisol García de Flores

Soy el doctor Vargas. Soy de Puerto Rico. Soy médico generalista. No soy especialista. Trabajo con una variedad de problemas médicos.

Doctor Vargas

Watch the *Trama* for chapter 1. The script is provided here. Then do the activities that follow.

Sr. Flores:	Doctor, le presento a mi esposa Marisol García de Flores y a nuestra hija, Elsita.
Dr. Vargas:	Encantado.
Sra. Flores:	Igualmente. Usted habla español. ¿De dónde es usted?
Dr. Vargas:	Soy de Puerto Rico.
Sra. Flores:	Ah, usted es puertorriqueño. Soy dominicana, de la capital, Santo Domingo. ¿Cuál es su especialidad, doctor? ¿Es cardiólogo?
Dr. Vargas:	No, no soy cardiólogo. Los cardiólogos trabajan con problemas del corazón. Yo soy un médico generalista. Trabajo con una variedad de problemas médicos.
Sra. Flores:	Doctor, perdón, pero mi padre sufre de la próstata y no tiene doctor. Él necesita un médico, y usted es muy amable.
Dr. Vargas:	Si su padre tiene problema con la próstata, necesita un urólogo. Hay un buen urólogo en la clínica ambulatoria del hospital.
Sra. Flores:	Gracias. Doctor, otra pregunta. Elsita necesita un pediatra. ¿Hay algún pediatra bueno en la clínica también?
Dr. Vargas:	Sí. Los pediatras son especialistas que trabajan con los niños. ¿Cómo estás, Elsita?
Elsita:	Yo estoy bien, gracias, pero mi muñeca no está bien. Está enfermita. Le duelen los oídos. Le duelen mucho los oídos.
Dr. Vargas:	¿Cómo se llama tu muñeca?
Elsita:	Ella se llama Samantha.
Dr. Vargas:	Samantha es un nombre bonito. No te preocupes, Elsita. Samantha va a estar bien. Si le duelen los oídos, tiene que ir a un otorrinolaringólogo. Los otorrinolaringólogos son especialistas con los oídos, la nariz y la garganta.

HACIA PRECISIÓN

1.17 Ejercicio

Complete the following sentences with the correct words from those in parentheses, and read them aloud.

A. La esposa del Sr. Flores se llama (a. Elsita, b. Marisol, c. Francisca).
B. El doctor Vargas es de (a. Puerto Rico, b. La República Dominicana, c. México).
C. La familia Flores es de (a. Puerto Rico, b. La República Dominicana, c. México).
D. El doctor Vargas es (a. cardiólogo, b. urólogo, c. médico generalista).
E. El cardiólogo trabaja con problemas (a. del corazón, b. de los pulmones, c. del esqueleto).
F. Necesitas un urólogo si tienes problema con (a. la nariz, b. la próstata, c. los oídos).
G. Si te duele el oído, necesitas consultar con un (a. otorrinolaringólogo, b. pediatra, c. odontólogo).

HACIA FLUIDEZ

1.18 Drama imprevisto

Work in groups of three or four to spontaneously present a skit that is similar to the first meeting of Dr. Vargas and the Flores family. Choose a Dr. Vargas and a nurse. Other students are members of the Flores family and may substitute their own personal information. Don't worry about closely following the video script. Family members will speak of friends or relatives who suffer from various ailments, and Dr. Vargas and the nurse will suggest what medical professional should be consulted.

Describe People

Vocabulario: Características personales
(Personal Characteristics)

The verb *ser* is used to describe physical characteristics and personality traits. The following words are often used with *ser:*

gordo   bajo   alto y delgado

Above, left   Doña Gloria es dominicana y es morena. Su padre era de Haití.

Above, right   Don Samuel es rubio y anciano. Es muy delgado. Sus padres eran cubanos.

Left   Doña Otilia es de un pueblo de la región Mixe de Oaxaca, México. Es indígena y no habla español. Habla un dialecto precolombino.

rubio/a	blond(e), fair	**moreno/a***	brunette, dark
mayor, anciano/a	old	**joven**	young
grande	big	**pequeño/a**	small
alto/a	tall	**bajo/a**	short (height)
largo/a	long	**corto/a**	short (length)
mediano/a	medium	**gordo/a, obeso/a**	fat, obese
delgado/a	thin	**flaco/a**	skinny
bonito/a	pretty	**guapo/a**	handsome
feo/a	ugly	**bueno/a**	good
inteligente	intelligent	**simpático/a**	kind
amable	kind	**agradable**	pleasant

*There is regional variation in the use of the word *moreno/a,* which is often used to refer to black African Americans, people with black hair in Spain, and people with rather dark complexion in Spanish-speaking America.

Preguntas útiles

¿Cómo es Juan?   What is Juan like?

Estructura: La concordancia de adjetivos, sustantivos y artículos indefinidos
(Agreement of Adjectives, Nouns, and Indefinite Articles)

• Adjectives, like nouns, have gender (*género*) and number (*número*). Adjectives ending in *-o* change to *-a* to become feminine (e.g., *alto, alta*). Adjectives ending in a vowel add *-s* to become plural and those ending in a consonant add *-es*.

• When an adjective modifies a noun, it must agree with that noun in gender and number. In Spanish a descriptive adjective normally *follows* the noun.

el ojo infectado	the infected eye
los ojos infectados	the infected eyes
la herida infectada	the infected wound
las heridas infectadas	the infected wounds
El enfermero es alto.	The (male) nurse is tall.
La doctora es delgada.	The (female) doctor is thin.

• Adjectives ending in *-e* modify both masculine and feminine nouns.

El niño es amable.	The boy is nice.
La niña es inteligente.	The girl is intelligent.

• The indefinite articles, which correspond to "a," "an," and "some" in English, have both gender and number. They are *un, una, unos,* and *unas.* The indefinite article is generally not used after forms of the verb *ser,* unless the object is modified. Verbs do not have gender, but the articles, nouns, and adjectives must agree in both gender and number. When referring to a mixed group of males and females, the male forms are used.

Marco es enfermero.	Marco is a nurse.
Marco es un enfermero nuevo.	Marco is a new nurse.
Ana es neuróloga.	Ana is a neurologist.
Ana es una neuróloga buena.	Ana is a good neurologist.
Marco y Ana son altos.	Marco and Ana are tall.

HACIA PRECISIÓN

 ## 1.19 Ejercicio

The instructor will ask for the opposite of each of the following words. For example, *¿Cuál es el opuesto de flaco?* Students respond: *El opuesto de flaco es gordo.*

¿cuál? what?
opuesto opposite

A. alto	D. anciano	G. largo
B. delgado	E. grande	H. feo
C. bajo	F. corto	I. gordo

 ## 1.20 Ejercicio

Agree with the descriptions of the following people. Remember to use the correct indefinite article when the noun is followed by an adjective.

Modelo: La profesora es simpática.
           Sí, es una profesora simpática.

A. La doctora es inteligente.	E. El médico es alto.
B. Los estudiantes son interesantes.	F. Los pacientes son delgados.
C. La enfermera es joven.	G. Los doctores son mayores.
D. El profesor es guapo.	H. El neurólogo es simpático.

 ## 1.21 Ejercicio

To make a statement negative, place the word *no* before the verb. *Juan es alto* becomes *Juan no es alto.* When answering a question, you can use the word *no* twice. *¿Es alto Juan? No, Juan no es alto.* In this exercise, the first sentence tells you something about someone and the second sentence asks about his or her opposite. Notice that the gender also changes in each. Make the adjectives agree with their nouns.

Modelo: —Luis es alto. ¿Cómo es Guillermina?
  —Guillermina no es alta. Es baja.

A. Pedro es feo. ¿Cómo es Estrella?
B. Marta es gorda. ¿Cómo es Juan?
C. Miguel es alto. ¿Cómo es Rosa?
D. Ana es baja. ¿Cómo es Marco?
E. Doña María es anciana. ¿Cómo es José?
F. Carlos es guapo. ¿Cómo es Ana?
G. Luis es delgado. ¿Cómo es Estrella?
H. Juana es joven. ¿Cómo es Timoteo?

HACIA FLUIDEZ

 1.22 Actividad

Look at the chart that follows and state the similarities and the differences between the following people. For example, *Cristina Rojas y Samuel Ortiz son enfermeros.* Then, ask questions of classmates: *¿Cómo es el doctor Andino? Cuál es la especialidad de la doctora Droz?*

Nombre	Profesión	Nacionalidad	Características físicas
Cristina Rojas	enfermera	mexicana	joven, alta, delgada
Felipe Andino	cirujano	chileno	bajo, guapo
Carmen Machado	cirujana	mexicana	baja
Raquel Droz	obstetra	chilena	alta, delgada
Samuel Ortiz	enfermero	argentino	joven, alto, delgado

 1.23 Actividad

Describe the following people by drawing conclusions from the information presented in the chart. Note that while the titles *señor* and *señora* are used with the last name, the titles *don* and *doña,* which refer to seniors, are used with first names.

Nombre	Estatura (Height)	Peso (Weight)	Edad (Age)	
Doña Afortunada	5 pies	200 libras	68 años	**pies** feet
Don Amilcar	6 pies, 3 pulgadas	151 libras	72 años	**pulgadas** inches
Arturito	40 pulgadas	85 libras	5 años	
Aurelina	44 pulgadas	42 libras	5 años	

La pronunciación de las vocales
(*Pronunciation of Vowels*)

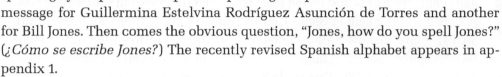

• For the most part, Spanish is pronounced as it is written. If you can spell it, you can say it. If you hear it spoken, you can write it. Imagine speaking by telephone to a Spanish-speaking receptionist. You leave one message for Guillermina Estelvina Rodríguez Asunción de Torres and another for Bill Jones. Then comes the obvious question, "Jones, how do you spell Jones?" (*¿Cómo se escribe Jones?*) The recently revised Spanish alphabet appears in appendix 1.

• Each vowel in Spanish has only one fundamental sound. Listen to and mimic native speakers, comparing your pronunciation to theirs. In class, practice exercises like *ma - me - mi - mo - mu* and *ta - te - ti - to - tu.*

Vowel	Like the English . . .		Examples from Spanish	
a	ah	mama	mano	mamograma
e	eh	way	vena	cerebro
i	ee	police	crisis	biopsia
o	oh	flow	droga	social
u	ooh	rude	pulso	músculo

• Two vowels together are pronounced separately unless they form a diphthong. Practice the following: *pie* (pi-E), *idea* (i-DE-a), *fiebre* (fi-E-bre), *luego* (lu-E-go), *heroína* (e-ro-I-na), and *codeína* (co-de-I-na). When unstressed *i* or *u* falls next to another vowel in a syllable, it unites with that vowel to form a diphthong. The vowels still sound the same, but they are pronounced as one syllable. Examples are *aire, seis, oigo,* and *pausa.*

• In spoken Spanish, vowels create linkages across word boundaries. For example, *mucho gusto* sounds like a single word. *¿Es usted la madre?* may sound like *¿esustedlamadre?* Practice the linkages in *los hospitales* and *la clínica.*

• Regressed students might practice this well-known refrain of fresh children: *A, E, I, O, U, ¡más sabe el burro que tú!,* which means, "A, E, I, O, U; a donkey knows more than you!" Courageous students might practice the following *trabalenguas,* or tongue-twisters.

Mi mamá me mima mucho.

Como poco coco como, poco coco compro.

Corto caña, caña corto; corto caña, caña corto; corto caña, caña corto.

Poquito a poquito Paquito empaca poquitas copitas en pocos paquetes.

Si Pancha plancha con cuatro planchas, ¿con cuántas planchas plancha Pancha?

Puerto Rican Independence Party seeks full independence from the United States to form a new sovereign nation. However, many voters fear they will lose their culture, language, and flag and will face an undesirable tax system and a loss of military protection and business incentives if Puerto Rico becomes a state.

The United States uses the name "American" for its citizens, but there are other Americas. People from the Caribbean, Central America, and South America have rights to the name as well. For this reason, people originating in the United States of America are often called *norteamericanos,* although Canadians and Mexicans also live in North America.

Consider the stress of leaving behind children and parents and working in a foreign place to support them economically.

Spanish-speaking countries continue to be a large source of immigration to the United States. Some people flee political oppression. Most of the people who immigrate do so not to sever ties with their beloved homelands. They are loyal family members who seek the opportunity to work and send financial support to those who remain behind. The move to a foreign land constitutes great personal sacrifice. In 2009 the population of the United States was 15 percent Hispanic (the term used by the census) and 12.4 percent black, making Hispanics the largest minority group there. By the year 2050, the breakdown will be roughly 50 percent white, 25 percent Hispanic, 15 percent black, and 10 percent Asian. The Association of Spanish Language Academies predicts that the United States will be home to the world's largest Spanish-speaking population by 2050, and that within three or four generations 10 percent of the world population will understand Spanish. The Hispanic population in the United States is growing rapidly because of immigration plus a tendency to have larger families (almost one in three Hispanic households has five or more people).

Chapter 2
«¿Cómo está usted?»

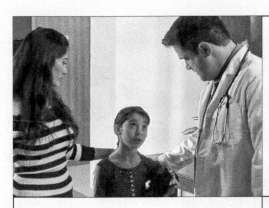

Communication Goals

Vocabulary

Structure

Video

Cultural Note

By the end of this chapter you will be able to ask patients how they feel and to ask questions to clarify various states of feelings. You will learn how to ask and give information about the location of people and places. You will know the difference between the two verbs that mean "to be" (*ser* and *estar*) and when to use each. You will learn the days of the week in Spanish, begin to talk about weekly schedules, and test whether the patient is oriented to person, place, and time.

Ask How Your Patient Is Feeling

Diálogo

«¿Qué te pasa, Elsita?»

Dr. Vargas:	Buenas tardes don Francisco. Buenas tardes doña Marisol. Hola Elsita.
Sr. Flores:	Buenas tardes, doctor.
Sra. Flores:	¿Cómo está usted?
Dr. Vargas:	Yo estoy bien, gracias a Dios. Y ustedes, ¿cómo están?
Sr. Flores:	Estamos un poco cansados, doctor. Elsita está enfermita.
Dr. Vargas:	Lo siento. ¿Qué te pasa, Elsita?

Sometimes in fast-paced North American society we ask, "How are you?" without waiting for an answer. In many cultures it is customary not only to wait for an answer but to ask about family as well. (Family relationships are treated in chapter 5.)

Vocabulario: Los sentimientos (*Feelings*)

bien	well, good	**mal**	not well, ill
feliz	happy	**triste**	sad
regular	okay	**así-así**	so-so
enfermo/a	ill, sick	**cansado/a**	tired
mejor	better	**peor**	worse
igual	the same	**más o menos**	so-so
nervioso/a	nervous	**preocupado/a**	worried

Preguntas útiles

¿Cómo está usted?	How are you (formal)?
¿Cómo estás?	How are you (informal)?
¿Qué tal?	How are you (informal)?
¿Cómo está la familia?	How is your family?

Expresiones útiles

Estoy bien, gracias.	I am fine, thank you.
Gracias a Dios.	Thank God.
Me alegro.	I am glad to hear it.
No estoy bien.	I don't feel well.
Lo siento.	I am sorry.
Estoy en la lucha.	I am hanging in there ("in the battle").

«Estoy enfermo».

Estructura: El verbo *estar* (*To Be*)

• The verb *estar*, like the verb *ser*, means "to be." Whereas *ser* is used to express time, origin, ethnicity, profession, possession, and physical or personality attributes, *estar* is used to express a state of being or condition, including how one feels and where someone or something is located. Thus *estar* is used to ask "How are you?" and "Where are you?"

• These are the forms of the verb *estar* in the present tense.

yo	**Estoy** cansado.
tú	¿**Estás** bien?
él, ella, usted	El paciente **está** mejor.
nosotros/nosotras	**Estamos** contentos.
ellos, ellas, ustedes	Los niños **están** enfermos.

El paciente está mejor.
La doctora está contenta.

Vocabulario: El dolor (*Pain*)

Use the verb *estar* to ask if the pain feels better or worse, and use the verb *ser* to describe the pain. You'll learn to talk more about pain in chapter 3.

¿Cómo está el dolor ahora?	How is the pain now?
¿Cómo es el dolor?	What is the pain like?
Señale el dibujo.	Point to the drawing.
No duele.	It doesn't hurt.
Duele un poco.	It hurts a little.
Es tolerable.	It is tolerable.
Duele mucho.	It hurts a lot.
Es intolerable.	It is not tolerable.
No aguanto el dolor.	I can't stand the pain.

The pain scale is available for download from the Web site.

¿Cómo está el dolor?
Señale el dibujo que corresponda.

0 1 2 3 4 5 6 7 8 9 10

No duele   Duele un poco   Tolerable   Duele mucho   Intolerable

HACIA PRECISIÓN

 ## 2.1 Ejercicio

Complete each sentence with the correct form of the verb *estar*. As an alternative, each student may make his or her own sentences on the classroom board, leaving a blank underline where the verb should go. Students then switch places to finish each other's sentences prior to a group editing session.

A. Mi mamá _____ enferma.

B. ¿_____ (tú) bien?

> *Tú* is implied by the verb form, as are *yo* and *nosotros*.

C. (Yo) _____ mucho mejor, gracias a Dios.

D. Mis pacientes _____ mejores.

E. Marisol y yo _____ preocupados por Elsita.

F. La clínica _____ en la Main Street.

HACIA FLUIDEZ

 ## 2.2 Actividad

Circulate in the classroom asking each student how he or she feels. Give appropriate group feedback to each response. Recall that you can use *me alegro* and *lo siento*.

Modelo: Class: Buenas tardes. ¿Cómo estás?
        Student 1: Buenas tardes. No estoy bien. Estoy enfermo/a.
        Class: ¿Estás mejor, igual o peor?
        Student 2: Peor.
        Class: Lo siento (pobre-c-i-i-i-t-o).

 ## 2.3 Actividad

Look at the illustration of a pain scale, *¿Cómo está el dolor?* In groups of two or three, take turns acting as if you were experiencing a particular intensity of pain. Ask, *¿Cómo está el dolor?* and instruct your partner, *Señale el dibujo que corres-*

¿Cómo está el dolor?
Señale el dibujo que corresponda.

ponda or *Señale con el dedo* ("Point with your finger"). Find out whether the pain is better, worse, or the same as before.

 ## 2.4 Drama imprevisto

Play another game of "The Host," which you learned in chapter 1. Choose a host, who leaves the room for a moment while the class chooses five students and assigns each a feeling from the vocabulary list. The host returns and is in the front of the room preparing a party. The chosen students take turns knocking on the door, entering the party, and exchanging small talk with each person while demonstrating the assigned feeling or emotion using gestures, questions, and statements. Say anything but the name of your assigned feeling. For example, student Paul receives *preocupado,* and circulates telling people with a worried expression, *Mi madre está enferma; mi padre está enfermo.* At the end of play, with the help of the remaining students, the host must guess each person's affective state, for example, *Paul está preocupado,* and so on.

 ## Ask Where People and Places Are Located

The verb *estar* is used to ask or say where a person, place, or thing is located. *¿Dónde está la clínica?* means "Where is the clinic?" Used in questions, interrogative words have written accents.

Vocabulario: ¿Dónde está? (*Where Is It?*)

a la derecha	on/to the right
a la izquierda	on/to the left
derecho	straight ahead
al final del pasillo	at the end of the hallway
en el primer piso/en la primera planta*	on the first floor

*In many countries, the ground floor of a building may be called *la planta baja,* and the next floor up may be called *el primer piso* or *la primera planta.* The numbers *primero* and *tercero* drop the final -*o* before a masculine singular noun, as in *el primer día.* As adjectives, the ordinal numbers have gender, as in *la segunda puerta a la izquierda.*

Preguntas útiles

¿Dónde está el laboratorio?   Where is the laboratory?

Expresiones útiles

Está a la derecha, al final del pasillo.   It is to the right, at the end of the hallway.

HACIA PRECISIÓN

 ## 2.5 Ejercicio

Complete each sentence with the correct form of the verb *estar.*

A. (Yo) _____ en casa.

The Spanish *en* is used for the English "in," "at," and "on."

B. ¿Dónde _____ usted?

C. ¿_____ (tú) en el baño?

D. Mis hijos y yo _____ en la cafetería.

E. El pediatra _____ en el consultorio hoy.

F. El doctor y la enfermera _____ en la clínica con un paciente.

HACIA FLUIDEZ

 ## 2.6 Actividad

Look at the elevator sign on page 36 and additional vocabulary. In groups of two or three, ask and tell where various areas of the hospital are located.

Departamento	Piso
Cirugía	Décimo
Maternidad	Octavo
Sala de espera	Noveno
Radiología	Séptimo
Laboratorio	Sexto
Consultorio del Dr. Vargas	Quinto
Habitaciones para los pacientes	Cuarto
Departamento de psiquiatría	Tercero
Inscripción de pacientes	Segundo
Departamento de urgencia	Primero

 2.7 Actividad

Think about the hospital or clinic with which you are most familiar. Draw the building elevations and a floor plan. Next, in small groups take turns asking and giving directions to specific places that are located on the drawings.

 Estructura: Haciendo preguntas (*Forming Questions*)

• To form a question, place the subject pronoun after the verb.

¿Está usted contento?	Are you happy?
¿Está el doctor en la clínica?	Is the doctor at the clinic?

• Spanish-speakers also may form a question from a statement by changing intonation.

¿Usted está contento?	You are happy?
¿El doctor está en la clínica?	The doctor is in the clinic?

• The expressions *¿no?*, *¿verdad?*, or *¿no es verdad?* may be placed at the end of a statement to form a question.

Juan está enfermo, ¿no?	Juan is ill, isn't he?
Juan está mejor, ¿verdad?	Juan is better, right?

Vocabulario: Los días de la semana (*Days of the Week*)

el lunes	Monday
el martes	Tuesday
el miércoles	Wednesday
el jueves	Thursday
el viernes	Friday
el sábado	Saturday
el domingo	Sunday
el fin de semana	weekend
todos los días	every day
de lunes a viernes	from Monday to Friday
Hoy es lunes.	Today is Monday.
mañana	morning, tomorrow
el lunes que viene	next Monday
el próximo martes	next Tuesday

Preguntas útiles

¿Qué día es hoy?	What day is it today?
¿Dónde está usted los lunes?	Where are you on Mondays?

Notice that the days of the week do not start with a capital letter. Notice, too, that the definite article is omitted with the days of the week when used after the verb *ser*. For example, *Hoy es lunes; mañana es martes.* When it is used, the definite article can differentiate between *this* Monday and *every* Monday. For example,

Estoy en el hospital *el lunes.*	I am at the hospital *this Monday.*
Estoy en el hospital *los lunes.*	I am at the hospital *on Mondays.*

HACIA PRECISIÓN

 ## 2.8 Actividad

Make up drills to practice the days of the week.

Modelo: Instructor: —Si hoy es lunes, ¿qué día es mañana?
           Class: —Si hoy es lunes, mañana es martes.

Hospital de cardiología
Horario de servicios

*«Estamos abiertos en las horas
más convenientes para usted.»*

Departamento	Horas
Farmacia	De lunes a sábado. Cerrada los domingos.
Laboratorio	De lunes a viernes. Cerrado los fines de semana.
Depto. de cirugía	Los martes y jueves.
Clínica ambulatoria	Todos los días de 8 a 6.

2.9 Actividad

The past participles *abierto* (open) and *cerrado* (closed) are used as adjectives and therefore must agree in gender with the noun they modify. For example, *El laboratorio está abierto* (open) *los martes; la clínica está abierta los domingos.* Refer to the *Horario de servicios del Hospital de Cardiología* and ask a partner whether specific departments are open or closed on specific days. Note that these questions are formed by placing the subject after the verb.

Modelo: —¿Está abierta la farmacia los domingos?
—No, la farmacia está cerrada los domingos.

Horario del doctor	
lunes	la clínica
martes	el hospital
miércoles	la clínica
jueves	el hospital
viernes	el consultorio
sábado	libre
domingo	libre

HACIA FLUIDEZ

 2.10 Actividad _____

Consult the *Horario del doctor*. Ask your partner where the doctor is on certain days; or when he is at the clinic, hospital, and so on.

> Modelo: —¿Dónde está el doctor los lunes?
> —Los lunes el doctor está en la clínica.
> —¿Cuándo (when) está en el hospital el doctor?
> —El doctor está en el hospital los martes y los jueves.

 2.11 Actividad _____

Take turns telling about your schedule for various days of the week. For example,

> Estoy en la clínica de lunes a viernes.
> Estoy en la clase los jueves.
> Estoy en casa los fines de semana.

 Estructura: *Ser* y *Estar* (*Choosing between* Ser *and* Estar)

• Recall the verb morphology of *ser* and *estar* in the present tense.

Sujeto	Ser	Estar
yo	soy	estoy
tú	eres	estás
él, ella, usted	es	está
nosotros/as	somos	estamos
ellos, ellas, ustedes	son	están

• *Ser* is used when speaking of origins (birthplaces), professions, and nationalities. It is also used with adjectives that describe inherent characteristics, such as tall and intelligent, and to tell the day, date, and time. It does not tell the location of things and people, but it tells the location of an event.

Origin:	Soy de Colombia.
Nationality:	Soy norteamericano.
Profession:	Mi esposa es secretaria.
Characteristics:	Ella es alta y delgada.
Telling time:	Mañana es sábado.
Location of an event:	El examen es en el consultorio.

• *Estar* is used in connection with locations of things or people and with adjectives that describe states of being, such as emotions, feelings, health, or conditions such as open, closed, broken, and swollen. Adjectives like *mejor* (better) and *cansado/a* (tired) describe conditions, so they are always used with *estar*.

Location:	Estoy en la clínica.
Emotions:	Gloria está deprimida.
Feelings:	¿Estás enfermo?
Conditions:	La clínica está abierta.

• Call it *Estar Wars,* but many adjectives can take on different meanings, depending on whether they are used with *ser* or with *estar*. The use of *ser* implies enduring traits. The use of *estar* implies there has been a recent change. Here are some examples.

Ser	*Estar*
Ella es feliz.	Ella está feliz.
(She is always happy.)	(She feels happy now.)
Eres delgado.	Estás delgado.
(You are thin.)	(You've lost weight.)
Miguel es listo.	Miguel está listo.
(Miguel is clever.)	(Miguel is ready.)
María es bonita.	María está bonita.
(María is beautiful.)	(María looks good today.)

Although the words *loco* (crazy) and *borracho* (drunk) are slang and you would not use them in connection with a patient, imagine the difference in meanings when *ser* and *estar* are used!

HACIA PRECISIÓN

 ## 2.12 Ejercicio

Read the following story. Choose between *ser* and *estar* and supply the correct form of the verb in the spaces provided.

Buenos días. Me llamo Hilda Rodríguez Portocarrero. _____

enfermera en el hospital Nuestra Señora de la Altagracia. El hospital

_____ grande y famoso. El hospital _____ en Lima, Perú.

Trabajo con la doctora Kathi Collins. La doctora Collins _____ norteamericana. Ella _____ en el hospital todos los días, pero yo

no. Los sábados _____ en la clínica y los domingos _____ en

casa. Los domingos la clínica _____ cerrada. La doctora _____

alta y delgada. Yo _____ baja y no muy delgada. La doctora y yo

_____ muy contentas.

2.13 Ejercicio

Here we place the answers first and the questions second. Like playing *Jeopardy,* complete the questions that would have elicited the following answers. Some will use *ser* and others will use *estar.*

A. Originalmente soy de Phoenix, Arizona.

—¿De dónde _____?

B. Estoy en el hospital de lunes a viernes.

—¿Cuándo _____ en el hospital?

C. Soy doctor de cabecera.

—¿Cuál _____ su profesión?

D. La enfermera es alta, morena y muy simpática.

—¿Cómo _____?

E. Estoy muy cansado.

—¿_____?

F. La doctora Marcelina Allende de Oviedo es la pediatra.

—¿_____?

¿Quién? Who?
¿Qué? What?
¿Cómo? How?
¿Dónde? Where?
¿De dónde? From where?

HACIA FLUIDEZ

2.14 Actividad

Play a *Jeopardy*-like guessing game using the personal descriptions from chapter 1. Use what you can observe as well as what you know about your classmates.

One person tells something about a classmate, and the rest of the class tries to guess the person's identity by asking the question that would have elicited that information. For example,

—Es una estudiante alta y rubia. —¿Cómo es Mary?
—Es de Nueva York. —¿De dónde es Phyllis?
—Él es dentista. —¿Quién es Vladimir? (*or*)
—Él es dentista. —¿Cuál es la profesión de Vladimir?

2.15 Drama imprevisto

Take turns in pairs sitting back-to-back in front of the classroom with cellular phones in hand. You and your partner have never seen each other before, and must share descriptions in order to connect when you meet at the airport (*el aeropuerto*). After greetings and introductions, one partner says, *Llego a las cuatro* (I arrive at four), and begins the exchange of self-descriptions. End with *Hasta las cuatro, entonces* (Until four o'clock, then).

Un chiste (*A Joke*)

Estudiante: ¿Cuál es correcto: Buenos Aires *está* en Brasil, o Buenos Aires *es* en Brasil?
Profesor: Buenos Aires *está* en Brasil.
Estudiante: ¡No profesor, Buenos Aires está en Argentina!

Test a Patient's Orientation

Health care workers at times must assess whether a patient is oriented to person, place, and time. You can do this in Spanish with three questions you have already learned.

¿Cómo se llama usted?
¿Qué día es hoy?
¿Dónde estamos?

You'll learn to ask the date and the time in chapter 4. The question, *¿Dónde está usted?* does not always work well with patients who think concretely. Such patients tend to answer, *Estoy aquí* (I am here). *¿Dónde estamos?* or multiple choices may be more effective. For example, *¿Estamos en una casa, una escuela o una clínica?*

 Video: *La orientación*

Watch the *Demostración* segment of video for chapter 2 and do the activity that follows.

«Señor Flores, ¿sabe usted dónde estamos?»

Dr. Vargas:	Buenas tardes.
Sr. Flores:	Buenas tardes.
Dr. Vargas:	¿Cómo se llama usted?
Sr. Flores:	Me llamo Francisco Flores.
Dr. Vargas:	Señor Flores, ¿sabe usted dónde estamos?
Sr. Flores:	Estamos en el consultorio.
Dr. Vargas:	Bueno, ¿en qué ciudad estamos?
Sr. Flores:	New Haven.
Dr. Vargas:	¿Cuál es el nombre de este lugar?
Sr. Flores:	No sé.
Dr. Vargas:	¿Estamos en una escuela, una clínica o una casa?
Sr. Flores:	Estamos en una clínica.
Dr. Vargas:	¿En qué año estamos?
Sr. Flores:	En el dos mil nueve.
Dr. Vargas:	Bien. ¿En qué mes estamos?
Sr. Flores:	Agosto.
Dr. Vargas:	Perfecto. ¿Qué día es?
Sr. Flores:	Hoy es lunes.
Dr. Vargas:	Muy bien. Gracias.

¿Sabe usted? Do you know?
la ciudad the city
el lugar the place
No sé. I don't know.

HACIA FLUIDEZ

   ## 2.16 Actividad

In small groups, demonstrate determining whether other group members are oriented to the three spheres of person, place, and time.

Vocabulario: Las especialidades (*Specialties*)

In chapter 1, we learned the names for various professions. Here, you'll notice a pattern in the formation of most of the names for specialties and the adjective forms that indicate *what kind* of evaluation, procedure, or operation. Think of them as fun to say. The instructor will help you with the pronunciation of accents. A guide to pronouncing accents follows this section.

Profesión	*Especialidad*	*Adjetivo*
el/la audiólogo/a	la audiología	audiológico/a
el/la cardiólogo/a	la cardiología	cardiológico/a
el/la dermatólogo/a	la dermatología	dermatológico/a
el/la endocrinólogo/a	la endocrinología	endocrinológico/a
el/la gastroenterólogo/a	la gastroenterología	gastroenterológico/a
el/la ginecólogo	la ginecología	ginecológico/a
el/la neurólogo/a	la neurología	neurológico/a
el/la obstetra	la obstetricia	obstétrico/a
el/la odontólogo/a	la odontología	odontológico/a
el/la oftalmólogo/a	la oftalmología	oftalmológico/a
el/la oncólogo/a	la oncología	oncológico/a
el/la ortopeda	la ortopedia	ortopédico/a
el/la otorrinolaringólogo/a	la otorrinolaringología	otorrinolaringológico/a
el/la pediatra	la pediatría	pediátrico/a
el/la psicólogo/a	la psicología	psicológico/a

el/la psiquiatra	la psiquiatría	psiquiátrico/a
el/la pulmonólogo/a	la pulmonología	pulmonológico/a
el/la radiólogo/a	la radiología	radiológico/a
el/la reumatólogo/a	la reumatología	reumatológico/a
el/la urólogo/a	la urología	urológico/a

The adjective forms are often used with the following nouns. Recall that adjectives must agree in gender and number with the nouns that they modify, for example, *El hospital psiquiátrico* and *La clínica psiquiátrica*. Words that end in *-ción* are always feminine.

Masculino	*Femenino*
el hospital	la clínica
el examen	la examinación
el procedimiento	la operación
el tratamiento	la evaluación

HACIA PRECISIÓN

 ### 2.17 Actividad

Ask where various professionals are, and answer using the adjective form for the profession, preceded by the noun *clínica* or *hospital,* as in the example.

Modelo: —¿Dónde está el oftalmólogo?
—El oftalmólogo está en la clínica oftalmológica.

2.18 Actividad

Tell people what kind of evaluation they need, where, and with whom, as in the example. The place can be a hospital or a clinic. To indicate the hospital or the clinic, you may use either the name for the specialty, as in *la clínica de psiquiatría,* or its adjective form, as in *la clínica psiquiátrica.*

Modelo: Sr. Ramos, una evaluación psiquiátrica
—Sr. Ramos, usted necesita una evaluación psiquiátrica.
—¿Dónde?
—En el hospital psiquiátrico.
—¿Con quién?
—Con el psiquiatra.

¿Con quién?
With whom?

A. Señora Camacho, una operación cardíaca
B. Doña Olga, un examen ginecológico
C. Señor Durán, un examen neurológico
D. Don Alfredo, un procedimiento urológico
E. Señora Quiñones, un tratamiento oftalmológico
F. Don Roberto, una evaluación psicológica

HACIA FLUIDEZ

2.19 Actividad

Make brief conversations based on the following ailments, whose names are close cognates with English. Tell people what kind of evaluation or procedure they need, and where to get it. After using the ailments below, propose your own to the class.

Modelo: *prostatitis*
—Sufro de prostatitis (*I suffer from prostatitis*).
—Necesita consultar con un urólogo. Hay un buen urólogo en la clínica de urología.

A. cáncer   D. dermatitis
B. glaucoma   E. ataques epilépticos
C. angina   F. esquizofrenia

2.20 Drama imprevisto

Play *¿Quién es usted?* A student leaves the room, and the class chooses a medical specialty from the vocabulary list, so that everyone knows it except the student who left. The student returns to the room and stands facing the instructor, who asks questions including *¿Quién es usted? ¿Cuál es su especialidad? ¿Por qué está aquí?* One or two students stand a distance behind the instructor, looking toward the student and miming the chosen specialty. (If the instructor looks back at them, they must pretend they were not helping.) The student answers the questions based on clues from the mimes until the correct specialty is stated. Play several rounds.

La pronunciación del acento prosódico y el acento ortográfico (*Pronunciation of Stress and the Written Accent*)

The oral stress point or prosody of a word is sometimes indicated by an acute accent. For example, the word *está* is stressed on the last syllable, and the word *clínica* is stressed on the first syllable. In the absence of a written accent mark, there are two rules.

• In words that end with a vowel, the letter *n,* or the letter *s,* the oral stress is on the next-to-last syllable. Examples are *plaza, mano, pulso, hablan, examen,* and *epidermis.* The instructor will help you with the pronunciation of these words.
• In words ending with consonants other than *n* or *s,* the oral stress or accent is on the last syllable, as in *hospital, general,* and *regular.*
• Written accent marks are used when a word will otherwise break these two rules, as in *pulmón, útil,* and *sábado.* Written accent marks are also used when the spoken accent is before the penultimate syllable, as in *clínica, estómago,* and *odontólogo.* To know whether to use a written accent mark, you first must know how to pronounce the word properly.
• In summary, a written accent mark is required when a word ending in a vowel, *n,* or *s* is stressed on the last syllable, when a word ending in any other consonant is stressed on any syllable but the last, and wherever two or more syllables remain after the syllable that receives the oral stress.
• There are other circumstances that require written accent marks. For example, when certain vowels are pronounced separately, as in *odontología;* and when two homonyms have different meanings, as in *mi* (my) and *mí* (me). We'll point these out later, because if you can do the following exercises, you are off to a great start.

HACIA PRECISIÓN

  2.21 Ejercicio

With help from the instructor, practice saying the following words and tongue-twister.

amigo	farmacia	ambulancia
aspirina	natural	social
hablar	colon	gastritis
diurética	resucitación	antibiótico

Trabalengua: El otorrinolaringólogo está en el hospital de otorrinolaringología para una operación otorrinolaringológica.

 2.22 Ejercicio

Listen to your instructor say the following words. Then, write written accent marks where needed. Use a pencil, in order to make corrections when finished.

A. facil

B. dificil

C. abril

D. cafe

E. perone

F. sabado

G. oncologo

H. final

Cultural Note: Attitudes and Ourselves

Exploring our attitudes toward groups that differ from our own is an essential step in learning a new language. There are two common outcomes when groups coexist in society. When *pluralism* prevails, groups retain and preserve their unique cultural characteristics, such as foods, language, and traditions. When there is *assimilation,* the norms, values, and practices of the majority culture are embraced. Although Latinos tend to assimilate by the third generation in the United States, many have rejected the melting pot image of the late nineteenth century. One Spanish-speaking immigrant sported a t-shirt that read, *¡Estás en América, habla español!* Some non-English-speaking Latinos go to their own neighborhood grocers and churches, watch television in Spanish, and fill out government forms in their native language. How do you feel about pluralism and assimilation?

Cortesía del humorista Pepe Angonoa, used with permission.

Some United States citizens today remind us that their immigrant parents or ancestors learned English. Indeed, many European immigrants of the last century were able to escape ethnic discrimination by learning English and adopting customs of the host culture. Nonetheless, a study by the Pew Hispanic Center revealed that Spanish-speakers learn English at a rate that is similar to that of immigrants who arrived a century ago. The first-generation immigrant retains native-speaker proficiency for their original language; bilingualism peaks in the second generation; and Spanish fades during the third generation.

Many consider it to be especially controversial to impose English on people of Puerto Rican heritage, who are not considered immigrants. They are born United States citizens, serve in the United States military, and speak Spanish as their native tongue. These are among the arguments advanced by some Latinos for bilingual government services.

It may take five years or more for an immigrant to become proficient in English as a second language. Individuals who do not have native language literacy may learn English less quickly than those who are literate in their pri-

Discrimination based on skin tone is common to many societies.

mary language. Because of advances in communication and transportation, Spanish-speakers who immigrate to the United States today are more likely to maintain close ties to their native countries than the immigrants of two generations ago. This makes them more likely to keep speaking their native language.

There seems to be a basic human tendency to "fill in the blanks," by assuming that we can perceive more about a person than what is apparent by appearance alone. Thus, we are prone to make generalizations based on skin tone, ethnicity, socioeconomic situation, and accent and English proficiency. The illogical aspects of such stereotypes are that they over-emphasize both the similarities between members of a group and the differences between groups. Stereotypes and over-generalized beliefs, when combined with judgment about what is favorable, constitute prejudice. It can be argued that most of us hold some prejudicial views. Discrimination, on the other hand, is the unfair *treatment* of another person based on prejudice. When we become aware of our beliefs, we can strive to keep them from causing us to treat others unfairly.

We can observe ourselves for signs of unhealthy attitudes. Complete the following sentences. (Do not share your answers.)

1. My parents think that Spanish-speakers are . . .
2. I like Spanish-speakers who . . .
3. I am suspicious of Spanish-speakers who . . .
4. Latino men tend to be . . .
5. Latina women tend to be . . .
6. Immigrants generally . . .
7. Undocumented aliens usually . . .
8. Government forms ought to be in English because . . .

Do your answers betray either positive or negative generalizations, or both? Even a positive stereotype, for example that Latinos like to hug, respect doctors, and value family, tend to rob individuals of their individuality. How might your generalizations influence your treatment of others? Recall that in the Diaspora there are Hispanic people who speak only Spanish, those who speak only English, and those who are bilingual or multilingual. Most are United States citizens, others are resident aliens, and some are without documents. There are those whose skin tones resemble those of their white European ancestors, and those who have the physical characteristics of the West African people who were enslaved and traded to the Spanish colonies. There are indigenous Indians from Latin America, some of whom do not speak Spanish but have their own native languages, and many shades and mixtures of all races. The Hispanic individual may face discrimination based on diverse prejudices involving race, ethnicity, language, customs, immigration, legal status, or socioeconomic situation.

Chapter 3
«¿Qué le pasa?»

«Tengo gripe».

By the end of this chapter you will be able to ask patients what symptoms and how much pain they are experiencing. You will know the complaints associated with the colds and flu season, and how to ask whether a patient feels hot, cold, hungry, thirsty, or sleepy. You will be familiar with the Spanish names for parts of the body and for injuries like cuts, burns, swelling, infections, and broken bones.

Discuss Colds and Influenza

Vocabulario: ¿Qué tiene? (*What Is the Matter?*)

Preguntas útiles

¿Qué tiene?	What is the matter?
¿Qué tiene el niño?	What is the matter with the child?
¿Qué le pasa?	What is happening (with you, him, or her)?
¿Qué síntomas tiene?	What symptoms do you have?
¿Qué problema tiene hoy?	What problem do you have today?

Expresiones útiles

Tengo gripe.	I have the flu.
Estoy resfriado/a.	I have a cold.
No tengo nada.	There's nothing wrong with me.

¿Qué tiene? means literally, "What do you have?" and elicits a description of symptoms. If nothing is wrong, say, *No tengo nada.* The double negative is neces-

sary in Spanish. After reviewing the verb *tener,* we shall learn a group of the most common complaints: cold and flu symptoms.

Estructura: El verbo *tener* (To Have)

yo	**Tengo** gripe.	I have the flu.
tú	¿Qué síntomas **tienes**?	What symptoms do you have?
él, ella, usted	¿**Tiene** usted fiebre?	Do you have a fever?
nosotros/as	Juan y yo **tenemos** diarrea.	Juan and I have diarrhea.
ellos, ellas, ustedes	Los niños **tienen** fiebre.	The children have fever.

HACIA PRECISIÓN

3.1 Ejercicio

Form sentences by choosing a subject pronoun from column **A**, supplying the correct form of the verb *tener* from column **B**, and an object or object phrase from column **C**. For example, *Juan tiene gripe.* The vocabulary follows this exercise.

A	B	C
Juan	tengo	fatiga.
Ana	tienes tiene	gripe.
Yo	tenemos	diarrea.
Tú	tienen	escalofrío.
La niña		dolor de cabeza.
Nosotros		una gripe terrible.
Los pacientes		catarro y dolor de garganta.
Mi madre		una fiebre de cuarenta grados.

Vocabulario: Los síntomas de la gripe
(Colds and Flu Symptoms)

Note that these are often used with the verb *tener* and without the direct object pronoun. An exception is *Estoy resfriado/a* (I have a cold).

«Tengo un dolor de cabeza horrible.
Me duele mucho la cabeza».

El resfriado / El resfrío (*Common Cold*)

la alergia	allergy
la influenza	influenza
el virus	virus
la gripe	flu, common cold
el resfrío, el resfriado	common cold
el catarro	mucus, common cold, congestion
la monga	common cold (Puerto Rico)
la gripa	common cold (Colombia)

El plural de *el virus* es *los virus.*

Los síntomas (*Symptoms*)

la congestión nasal	stuffy nose
la nariz tapada	stuffy (blocked) nose
el goteo post-nasal	post-nasal drip
la flema verdosa	greenish sputum
la fiebre	fever
la náusea	nausea
el vómito	vomit, vomiting
la tos	cough
el estornudo	sneeze
el mareo	dizziness
el escalofrío	chill
los sudores nocturnos	night sweats

la falta de aire	shortness of breath
la dificultad para respirar	shortness of breath
la fatiga	fatigue
la diarrea	diarrhea
el estreñimiento	constipation
el malestar general	malaise

El dolor (*Pain*)

el dolor de cabeza	headache
el dolor en el cuerpo	body ache
el dolor de garganta	sore throat

Preguntas útiles

¿Tiene mareo?	Are you dizzy (lightheaded, faint)?
¿Está usted mareado/a?	Are you dizzy (lightheaded, faint)?
¿Tose mucho?	Do you cough a lot?
¿Es una tos seca?	Is it a dry cough?

Gripe, resfrío, resfriado, and *catarro* are interchangeable. However, an old adage says, *Gripe les da a los ricos; catarro a los pobres* (the rich get the flu, and the poor get mucus). A similar refrain says, *Alergia les da a los ricos; raquiña a los pobres* (the rich get allergies, and the poor get itching). Latinos may be prone to the belief that exposure to the cold, such as leaving a window open at night, may allow *frío* to enter the body, resulting in illness.

 ## Video: *¿Qué le pasa?*

Watch the *Trama* for chapter 3, in which Marisol Flores consults with Dr. Vargas because of cold symptoms. Then do the activity.

Dr. Vargas:	Buenas tardes. ¿Cómo está usted, señora Flores?
Sra. Flores:	No me siento bien. Estoy enferma.
Dr. Vargas:	Lo siento. ¿Qué tiene?
Sra. Flores:	Tengo gripe. Estoy resfriada.
Dr. Vargas:	¿Qué síntomas tiene?
Sra. Flores:	Me duele la cabeza. Tengo dolor de garganta. Me pican los ojos. Me pican los oídos. La nariz la tengo congestionada.
Dr. Vargas:	¿Tose mucho?
Sra. Flores:	Sí, tengo una tos seca. Cuando toso, me duele mucho la garganta.

Dr. Vargas:	¿Tiene fiebre?
Sra. Flores:	En la noche. Cuando me da fiebre, me da escalofríos.
Dr. Vargas:	¿Tiene náusea o vómitos?
Sra. Flores:	No, pero no tengo hambre y casi no como.
Dr. Vargas:	¿Tiene diarrea?
Sra. Flores:	No.
Dr. Vargas:	Vamos a mirarle los oídos, la nariz y la garganta. Abra la boca y diga a-a-h.
Sra. Flores:	A-a-h. ¿Necesito un antibiótico?
Dr. Vargas:	No. Usted tiene un resfrío. Es un virus. Los antibióticos curan las infecciones bacterianas. Los antibióticos no curan los resfriados. Los resfriados duran una o dos semanas. Debe tomar muchos líquidos como té con limón y sopa de pollo. Debe tomar dos aspirinas o dos pastillas de ibuprofeno cada cuatro o seis horas si necesita para la fiebre y el dolor. Debe llamarme si tiene una fiebre persistente o dolor en el pecho.
Sra. Flores:	Gracias doctor Vargas.
Dr. Vargas:	Va a estar bien pronto.

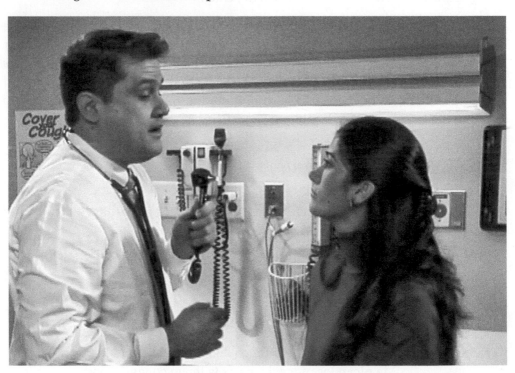

HACIA FLUIDEZ

 ## 3.2 Actividad

Ask a partner the following comprehension questions about the video.

    A. ¿Cómo está la señora Flores?
    B. ¿Qué tiene ella?
    C. ¿Le duelen los ojos?
    D. ¿Qué pasa cuando la Sra. Flores tose?
    E. ¿Tiene náusea o vómito?
    F. ¿Necesita la Sra. Flores un antibiótico?
    G. ¿Cuándo debe llamar al doctor o a un profesional médico?

 ## 3.3 Actividad

This worksheet is available for download from the Web site.

Conduct medical research. Find out what symptoms classmates have when they have a cold. Using the questionnaire, move about the classroom asking, *Cuando estás resfriado/a, ¿qué síntomas tienes?* Report the results of your study to the class: *Los síntomas más comunes del resfriado son . . .* and, *William tiene dolor de garganta cuando está resfriado.*

Cuestionario de síntomas	
Síntoma	*Nombre de compañero/a*
Fiebre	
Catarro	
Goteo post-nasal	
Dolor de cabeza	
Congestión nasal	
Malestar general	
Una tos seca	
Falta de aire	

3.4 Actividad

Take turns tastefully acting out the symptoms of colds and flu, while other students guess which you are miming. The interchange might go like this:

Clase:	¿Cómo estás, William?
Estudiante:	No muy bien. Estoy enfermo.
Clase:	¿Qué te pasa?
Estudiante:	(*Mime a symptom.*)
Clase:	¡Tienes _____!
Estudiante:	¡Sí! Tengo _____ (*or*) No, no tengo _____.

«Tengo una gripe terrible».

 ## 3.5 Actividad

Observe the two pictures of Marina, who suffers from a common cold. Identify the symptoms that she currently demonstrates.

Lectura: *El resfriado común*

Follow the text as the instructor reads about the common cold. Then answer the questions that follow. You will be able to guess the meaning of some of the new verbs. Less familiar verbs include *durar* (to last), *tomar* (to take), *fumar* (to smoke), *bajar* (to lower), *aliviar* (to relieve), and *descansar* (to rest).

Un virus causa el resfriado. Hay casi doscientos virus que causan el resfriado. Los síntomas incluyen catarro, dolor de garganta, tos, dolor de cabeza y malestares. El resfriado dura una o hasta dos semanas. Los niños normalmente tienen resfriado hasta seis veces al año. Los adultos usualmente tienen dos o tres resfriados cada año.

hasta	up to
remedios caseros	home remedies
debe	you should

Existen varios remedios caseros para el resfriado. Por ejemplo, debe tomar muchos líquidos como el agua o jugo (*juice*) para aliviar la congestión de la nariz. La sopa de pollo o una infusión (un té) de limón, jengibre y canela (*ginger and cinnamon*) son muy buenos para aliviar el frío del cuerpo. Debe usar un vaporizador en la casa. No debe fumar. La aspirina, el ibuprofeno y el acetaminofén bajan la fiebre y alivian los dolores. Los niños con fiebre no deben tomar aspirina. Es muy importante descansar.

Los antibióticos no curan el resfriado, pero el resfriado a veces causa una infección bacteriana como la bronquitis, la sinusitis o la pulmonía. Los antibióticos son para curar las infecciones bacterianas. Debe llamar al médico o a la clínica si tiene síntomas de una infección bacteriana como una fiebre alta, fiebre con escalofrío, fiebre persistente, dolor en el pecho cuando tose o esputo amarillo verdoso o de un color oscuro.

amarillo verdoso	yellow-greenish
oscuro	dark

HACIA FLUIDEZ

 ## 3.6 Actividad

Ask a partner the following reading comprehension questions.

A. ¿Qué causa los resfriados?
B. ¿Cuánto tiempo dura un resfriado?
C. ¿Curan el resfriado los antibióticos?
D. ¿Cuáles son los remedios caseros y para qué son?
E. ¿Cuáles son los síntomas de las infecciones bacterianas?
F. ¿Cuáles son los remedios que alivian la congestión nasal?
G. ¿Cuáles son los remedios que bajan la fiebre y alivian los dolores?
H. ¿Qué debo hacer si tengo una fiebre persistente?

3.7 Actividad

You are a doctor who is treating a patient who is suffering from a common head cold. Your partner is your patient, who believes that he or she needs an antibiotic. Educate your patient and negotiate the treatment, while your partner insists that you are not doing your duty.

 ## Ask Whether a Patient Feels Comfortable

Vocabulario: La comodidad (*Comfort*)

• *Tener* is also used to express hunger, thirst, sensations of heat and cold, and sleepiness. These expressions are translated for meaning, not word for word.

> ¿Tiene usted **hambre**?   Are you hungry?

• Drive states such as hunger and thirst are used as nouns and do not change their spelling to agree with the gender of the person.

> Miguel tiene **sueño**.
> María tiene **sueño**.

• Here are some idiomatic expressions using *tener* to practice in the exercises that follow.

Tengo **hambre**.	I am hungry.
¿Tiene **sed**?	Are you thirsty?
No tengo **calor**.	I don't feel like it is hot.
Los niños tienen **frío**.	The children feel like it is cold.
¿Tiene **sueño**?	Are you sleepy?
¿Tiene **prisa**?	Are you in a hurry?
¿Tiene **miedo** el niño?	Is the child afraid?
Usted tiene **razón**.	You are right.

• Recall that the verb *estar* is used with the adjectives *contento* (happy) and *cansado* (tired). *El niño está caliente* means the child has a fever (is hot to the touch). *El niño tiene calor* refers to the child's subjective experience of feeling that the day or the room is hot.

HACIA PRECISIÓN

 ### 3.8 Ejercicio

To aid your memorization, associate the following cues with one or more of the *tener* idioms, as in the examples. *Buenísimo/a* means "exceptionally good."

el café   El café es buenísimo cuando tengo sueño.
las frutas   Las frutas son buenísimas cuando tengo hambre.

A. una cama
B. un carro deportivo (*a sports car*)
C. una frazada
D. un osito de peluche (*a stuffed bear*)
E. una hamburguesa
F. un ventilador (*a fan*)
G. un vaso de agua (*a glass of water*)
H. una discusión (*an argument*)

HACIA FLUIDEZ

 ### 3.9 Actividad

If classroom space allows, divide large areas of the board into the categories *hambre, sed, frío, calor*, and so on. In the appropriate areas, draw and label the items or environs that you associate with these feelings, and create sentences from your drawings. This "semantic graffiti" helps create memory cues that are not English.

 ### 3.10 Actividad

The instructor will hand out index cards, each with one of the *tener* idioms on it. Take turns miming the idiom on your card. Ask, *¿Qué tengo?* The rest of the class will report, *¡Tienes _____!* Perhaps the instructor will add a few trick cards, like *Tengo dolor de cabeza* or *Tengo catarro*.

 ### 3.11 Drama imprevisto

This worksheet is available for download from the Web site.

Circulate in the classroom with the following *cuestionario* and ask classmates whether they are hungry, thirsty, and so forth. After gathering your data, report your findings to the rest of the class. For example, *Susan tiene frío cuando está en el hospital y yo no.*

Circunstancia	Nombre de compañero/a sí o no
Tener razón siempre	
Tener frío cuando está en el hospital	
Tener miedo de las inyecciones	
Tener prisa por la mañana	
Tener sueño a las ocho de la noche	
Tener hambre a medianoche	
Tener calor cuando está en la clase	

 Video: *La comodidad*

Elsita Flores, enfermera extraordinaria

Watch the *Demostración* for chapter 3, in which Elsita plays nurse and cares for her mother Marisol. Then do the activity that follows. Note that the informal (*tú*) form is used in this parent-child interaction.

Elsita:	Mami, soy enfermera.
Sra. Flores:	Eres enfermera. Qué linda. ¿Cómo te llamas?
Elsita:	Soy la enfermera Elsita.
Sra. Flores:	Mucho gusto enfermera Elsita.
Elsita:	¿Tienes sed?
Sra. Flores:	No, no tengo sed ahora. Tengo hambre. Tengo mucha hambre.
Elsita:	¿Tienes hambre? ¿Quieres un chocolate? Es delicioso.
Sra. Flores:	O, sí, muchas gracias. Me encanta el chocolate.
Elsita:	¿Tienes calor?
Sra. Flores:	No, tengo frío. Tengo mucho frío.
Elsita:	¿Tienes frío? ¿Quieres una sábana?

Sra. Flores:	O sí, muchas gracias. Eres una buena enfermera, Elsita. Ya no tengo frío, gracias.
Elsita:	¿Tienes miedo?
Sra. Flores:	Un poquito.
Elsita:	Acá está mi muñeca. No te preocupes. Todo va a estar bien.
Sra. Flores:	Qué linda. Ya no tengo miedo. Gracias.

3.12 Actividad

Ask a partner the following questions.

A. ¿Tiene sed la Sra. Flores?

B. ¿Tiene hambre la Sra. Flores?

C. ¿Tiene frío o calor la Sra. Flores?

D. ¿De qué tiene miedo la Sra. Flores?

E. Y tú, ¿tienes miedo a los doctores?

F. ¿Tienes miedo a las inyecciones?

Vocabulario: Las partes del cuerpo (*Parts of the Body*)

This section requires some memorization. Practice the following Spanish ana-tomical words during the next week while you are bathing, drying yourself, dress-ing, and so on. Name it as you dry it, so that kinesthesia cues memory as well. If you make index cards for studying, write the names in Spanish only. If needed, add a sketch of the body. This will help you avoid depending on English cues. Share with the class your techniques for memorization. Rote memory is a slow and tedious process. It is more helpful to elaborate on the new vocabulary, making drawings, sentences, and other associations.

La cabeza (*Head*)

el cráneo	cranium
el cabello, el pelo	hair

La cara (*Face*)

la frente	forehead
el ojo	eye
el pómulo, la mejilla	cheekbone, cheek
la nariz	nose
el seno frontal/ paranasal	frontal/ paranasal sinus

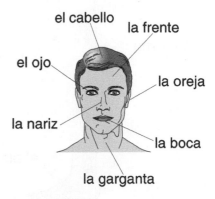

La cabeza

la oreja	ear (outer)
el oído	ear (inner)
la mandíbula	jaw
la barbilla	chin
la garganta	throat

La boca (*Mouth*)

el labio	lip
la lengua	tongue
el diente	tooth
la muela	molar
la encía	gum

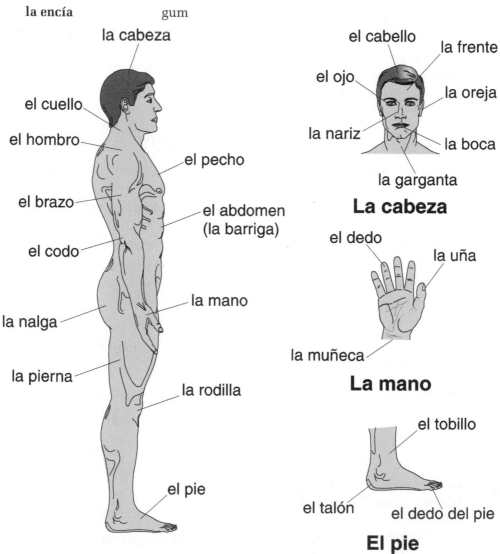

la cabeza

el cabello

la frente

el ojo

la oreja

el cuello

la nariz

el hombro

la boca

el pecho

la garganta

La cabeza

el brazo

el abdomen
(la barriga)

el dedo

la uña

el codo

la mano

la nalga

la muñeca

la pierna

La mano

la rodilla

el tobillo

el pie

el talón

el dedo del pie

El pie

El cuerpo humano

Las partes del cuerpo (*Parts of the Body*)

el pecho, el tórax	chest
el pecho, el seno	breast, mammary gland
el brazo	arm
la mano	hand
el dedo	finger
la uña	fingernail
el abdomen, la barriga	abdomen
el ombligo	navel
el recto, el ano	rectum
el pene	penis
el escroto	scrotum
la vagina	vagina
el gluteo	buttock
la nalga, el pompis (*popular*)	buttock
la pierna	leg
el muslo	thigh
el pie	foot
el talón	heel
el dedo del pie	toe
la uña del dedo del pie	toenail

Las coyunturas (*Joints*)

la coyuntura, la articulación	joint
el cuello	neck
la espalda	back
la espina dorsal	spine
la vértebra	vertebra
el hombro	shoulder
el codo	elbow
la muñeca, el radio	wrist
el nudillo	knuckle
la cadera	hip
la rodilla	knee
el tobillo	ankle

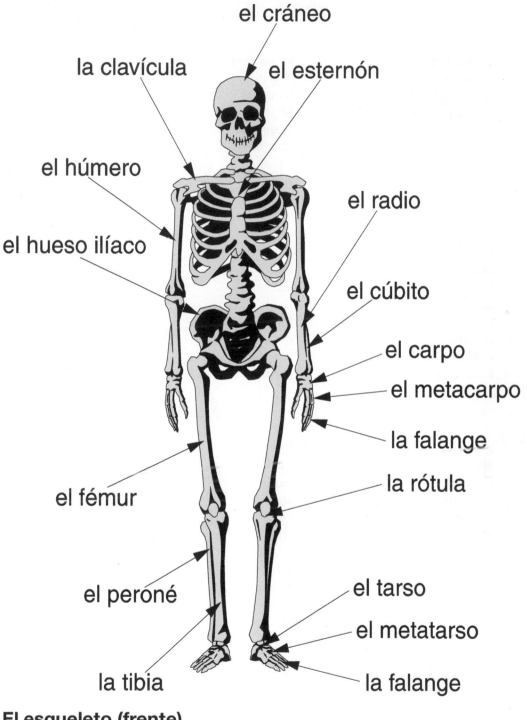

el cráneo

la clavícula

el esternón

el húmero

el radio

el hueso ilíaco

el cúbito

el carpo

el metacarpo

la falange

la rótula

el fémur

el peroné

el tarso

el metatarso

la tibia

la falange

El esqueleto (frente)

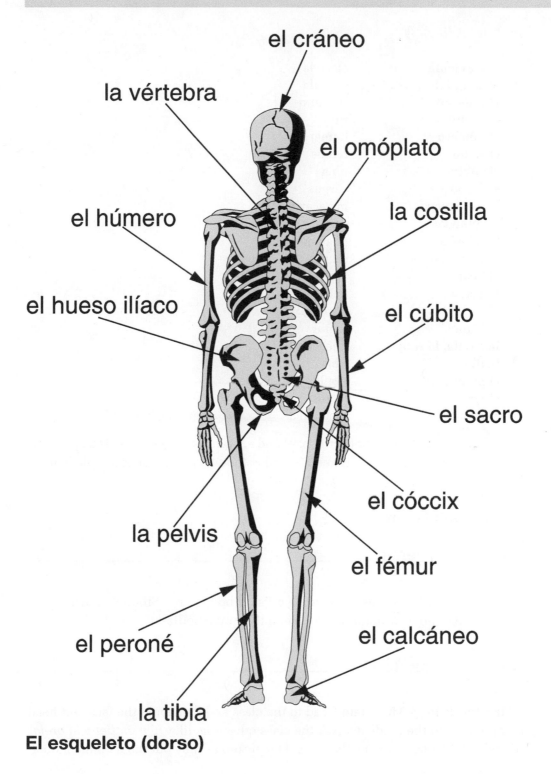

el cráneo

la vértebra

el omóplato

la costilla

el húmero

el hueso ilíaco

el cúbito

el sacro

el cóccix

la pelvis

el fémur

el peroné

el calcáneo

la tibia

El esqueleto (dorso)

Los huesos (*Bones*)

la clavícula	clavicle
el omóplato	scapula
el esternón	sternum
la costilla	rib
el húmero	humerus
el radio	radius
el cúbito	ulna
el carpo	carpus
el metacarpo	metacarpus
carpiano/a	carpal
la falange	phalange
el sacro	sacrum
el íleon	ilium
la pelvis	pelvis
el cóccix	coccyx
el fémur	femur
la patela, la rótula	kneecap
la tibia	tibia
el peroné	fibula
el tarso	tarsus
el metatarso	metatarsus

Note that although *la nalga* (Caribbean) and *el pompis* (Mexico, Central America) are not clinical terms, they are readily understood and their use is not likely to be offensive.

HACIA PRECISIÓN

 ### 3.13 Ejercicio

A leader can drill the class by reading a list of body parts. Students must repeat the word and move or point to the part on their own bodies.

 ### 3.14 Ejercicio

Instructor: Bring a Mr. Potato Head to the class and distribute the face and head components to the students. Ask the class questions like *¿Quién tiene la oreja?* Students take turns naming the parts they picked as they put them on the model.

HACIA FLUIDEZ

 3.15 Actividad

Students take turns as "police artist," drawing a face on the blackboard according to a description by other class members. Guidance may include, for example, *tiene la nariz grande; las orejas son pequeñas* (small); *y no tiene dientes.* Later, describe the various sketches while pointing to each aspect.

 3.16 Actividad

The instructor may obtain a Halloween skeleton and disassemble it. Distribute the bones to students, who must name the parts as they receive them. The instructor can lead in a drill by asking questions such as *¿Qué tiene Ana?* or *¿Quién tiene la cabeza?* Another idea is to make a variation of "pin-the-tail-on-the-donkey" by attaching a large cardboard person to the wall, or drawing one on the board. Distribute needed body parts drawn on paper. Students take turns naming the parts they were given and placing them on the model with tape or push pins. Blindfolded, anyone?

 3.17 Actividad

Play *Simón dice* like the game "Simon Says." Students stand while one class member chooses parts of the body and says, *Simón dice mueva la cabeza* or *No mueva las caderas.*

 3.18 Drama imprevisto

Play "Foot Bone Connected To." Form a circle. The first student points to another student anywhere in the circle and says, *el dedo del pie.* The student who was signaled then points to another student and says, *el pie.* Continue in this way until you have named parts of the body from toe to head. Include the joints, for example, *el tobillo* and *la rodilla.* It is important to set a rhythm and follow it. This promotes concentration and the coveted dynamic of working as a team. Variations include the head only, head to toe, and the bones of the skeleton.

Discuss Pain

Estructura: El verbo *doler* (*To Hurt, Ache*)

• In chapter 2 you learned that "pain" in Spanish is *el dolor*.

Tengo dolor de cabeza.	I have a headache.
¿Tiene dolor?	Do you have pain?
¿Dónde está el dolor?	Where is the pain?
Enséñame dónde duele.	Show me where it hurts.

• The verb *doler* means "to hurt." The third person (*duele* or *duelen*) is used because a part (or parts) of the body *does* the hurting. For example, *Me duele la cabeza* is literally "The head hurts me," and translated for meaning, "My head hurts." Spanish-speakers use the indirect article *me* to indicate who feels the hurt. They avoid redundancy by saying *la cabeza*.

• The indirect objects—*me, te, le, nos,* or *les*—are placed before the verb and represent the person who is in pain. *Le* represents "you," "him," and "her."

Me duele el cuerpo.	My body hurts.
¿Le duele la garganta?	Does your throat hurt?
¿Qué le duele?	What hurts you (him, her)?
¿Qué le duele a Roberto?	What hurts Roberto?

• When the subject (what hurts) is plural, the verb must also be plural.

Me duele el ojo izquierdo.	My left eye hurts.
Me duelen los ojos.	My eyes hurt.
Me duelen las coyunturas.	My joints hurt.

HACIA FLUIDEZ

3.19 Actividad

This is a guessing game. One student thinks of a body part that is hurting, and classmates guess. Whenever you say the name of a body part, point to that part of yourself while saying the word and you'll learn the vocabulary more quickly.

Modelo: —¿Le duele la cabeza?
— No, no me duele la cabeza.

Take turns guessing until the student says, *¡Sí, eso es!* (Yes, that is it!). Then start over with a new student.

 ## 3.20 Drama imprevisto

This is an elimination game. The instructor makes index cards or slips of paper with the Spanish name (or a drawing) of a body part written on each and distributes them to all students but the designated leader. Students form a circle, and the leader names parts of the body from memory. For example, the leader may state *hombro.* If no student was assigned this body part, students may ask each other, *¿Te duele el hombro?* just to be certain. If a student has been assigned this body part, he or she dramatically says, *¡El hombro me duele mucho!* and is eliminated from the game. When everyone has been eliminated, try to recall who experienced pain where: *A Paul le duele el/la _____.*

 ### Vocabulario: El dolor (*Pain*)

¿Cómo está el dolor?	How is the pain?
¿Le duele mucho?	Does it hurt a lot?
Me duele muchísimo.	It hurts a great deal.
. . . mucho	. . . a lot
. . . un poco	. . . a little
. . . un poquito	. . . a tiny bit
Está peor.	It's worse.
Está igual.	It's the same.
Está regular.	It's so-so.
Está mejor.	It's better.
¿Cuál es el brazo que le duele?	Which is the arm that hurts?
Es el brazo izquierdo/derecho.	It is the left/right arm.
Señale con el dedo.	Point with your finger.
¿Cómo es el dolor?	What is the pain like?
¿Es un dolor sordo?	Is it a dull ache?
. . . agudo/punzante	. . . sharp
. . . quemante/ardiente	. . . burning
. . . pesado	. . . crushing
. . . un dolor que corre	. . . a radiating pain

The verb *estar* refers to the state of the pain (*El dolor **está** igual*), and the verb *ser* is used to describe the pain (***Es** un dolor pesado*). "Right" and "left" are adjectives and must agree in gender with the noun they modify (*Me duele la pierna derecha y el brazo izquierdo*). Use articles and not the possessive adjectives with parts of the body (*Me duele el brazo*).

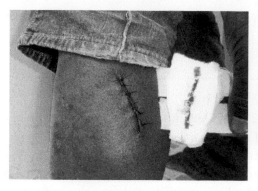 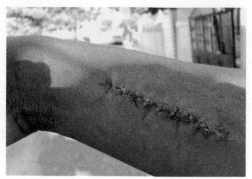

La pierna de Digo está cortada. ¿Qué tiene Lucas?

Diagnose Injuries

Vocabulario: Las heridas (*Injuries*)

Las heridas

el golpe	bump
la laceración	laceration
la cortada, el tajo	cut
la cortadura	bad cut
la quemadura	burn
la herida de bala	gunshot wound
la puñalada	stab wound
la infección	infection
la hinchazón	swelling

Tipos de fracturas

la fractura abierta (compuesta)	open (compound) fracture
la fractura conminuta	comminuted fracture
la fractura espiral	spiral fracture
la fractura oblicua	transverse fracture
la fractura simple	simple fracture

Expresiones útiles

Aplíquese crema antibiótica.	Apply antibiotic cream.
Aplíquese hielo.	Apply ice.

Necesita puntos.   You need stitches.
Necesita un yeso.   You need a cast.
Necesita una venda.   You need a bandage.

 ## Estructura: El participio pasado
(*The Past Participle*)

• The preceding vocabulary words are nouns and are often used with *tener*.

Usted tiene una infección.   You have an infection.
Tengo un golpe en la cabeza.   I have a bump on my head.

• In addition, you may use a past participle as an adjective that modifies the injured part of the body. To form the past participle in Spanish, add -*ado* to the stems of verbs that end in -*ar*, and -*ido* to the stems of verbs that end in -*er* or -*ir*. For example, the verb *quebrar* (to break) changes to *quebrado* (and *quebrada*) and *torcer* (to twist, sprain) changes to *torcido/a* (twisted, sprained). Note that *romper* is irregular in the past participle (*roto*), and less clinical-sounding than *quebrar*. Here is a mnemonic device: if you can pinch an inch, it must be *hinchazón*!

cortar	to cut	→	**cortado/a**	cut
quemar	to burn	→	**quemado/a**	burned
hinchar	to swell	→	**hinchado/a**	swollen
torcer	to sprain	→	**torcido/a**	sprained
infectar	to infect	→	**infectado/a**	infected
inflamar	to inflame	→	**inflamado/a**	inflamed
quebrar	to break	→	**quebrado/a**	broken
fracturar	to fracture	→	**fracturado/a**	fractured
romper	to break	→	**roto/a**	broken

• When the past participle is used as an adjective, it must follow the noun and agree with it in gender and number.

el brazo quebrado   the broken arm
la pierna quebrada   the broken leg
los ojos infectados   the infected eyes

• The past participle can be used with the verb *estar* as well as with the verb *tener*.

El brazo está fracturado.   The arm is fractured.
José tiene el brazo fracturado.   José has a fractured arm.

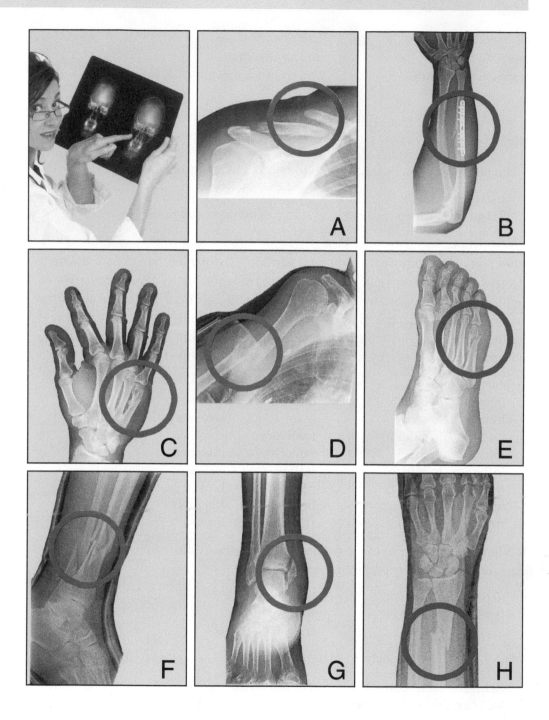

HACIA PRECISIÓN

 ### 3.21 Ejercicio

With a partner, read the x-ray images. Then identify the diagnosis of a broken bone as if to a patient. Remember that gender and number must agree when you use a past participle as an adjective. Vary your sentences by using the verb *tener* as in, *Usted tiene el brazo quebrado* and the verb *estar* as in, *El brazo está quebrado.*

 ### 3.22 Ejercicio

Tell the patient that the body part is sprained but not broken.

> Modelo: la muñeca   —La muñeca no está quebrada, gracias a Dios; está torcida.

A. la rodilla
B. los tobillos
C. el cuello
D. las muñecas

E. el dedo
F. la espalda
G. el tobillo izquierdo
H. la muñeca derecha

 ### 3.23 Ejercicio

Give some more good news. Say that the indicated part of the body is swollen but not infected.

> Modelo: el dedo   —El dedo está hinchado, pero no está infectado.

A. la encía
B. los labios
C. la rodilla
D. los tobillos

E. el dedo del pie
F. el codo izquierdo
G. la lengua
H. el ojo derecho

HACIA FLUIDEZ

 ### 3.24 Actividad

Speak Spanish continuously—and test your memory—during this activity. The first student says, *Miguel tuvo* (had) *un accidente automovilístico, el pobrecito.*

Tiene el brazo quebrado. The class repeats the report from the beginning. The next student adds yet another medical complaint, for example, *También tiene los tobillos hinchados.* The class repeats the entire report from the beginning before the next student adds to the list of injuries, and so on.

También Also

 ## 3.25 Drama imprevisto

When you have finished *actividad* 3.24, act out (or overact) a conversation with Miguel's parent or sibling in which you let him or her know what injuries Miguel sustained in the accident. The family member, repeating each portion of news, reacts with hyperbolic disbelief or anxiety, while you are a calming influence. Words of disbelief include *¡No puede ser!* (It can't be!). Words of assurance include *No se preocupe; todo va a estar bien* (Don't worry, everything is going to be all right).

 ## 3.26 Drama imprevisto

Play *Enfermero con tres cabezas.* Three students stand arm-in-arm and give a shift report to the class as if they were one person. Taking turns, each student tells only one word of the report at a time. For example, *El-paciente-en-la-habitación-tres-tiene-el-brazo-infectado* and so on. Keep track of the agreement of nouns and adjectives. Do not plan ahead. The results may be hilarious.

la habitación room

 ## 3.27 Reciclaje

Role-play a basic interview. Do not use English! Think of a set of cold symptoms or an ailing part of the body. Take turns in front of the class as *el/la paciente* while members of the class conduct an interview. The interview should elicit enough information to move from the patient's chief complaint to a finer definition of the problem and of the pain. As a frustrating but more challenging variation, try this exercise with a patient who answers only *Sí* or *No*.

Pronunciación de *G, C, J* y *H*
(*Pronunciation of* G, C, J, *and* H)

• The letter *g* is pronounced almost as the English "h" when it precedes the vowels *e* and *i*. It is a fricative sound, which means that to produce it, air passes through a slightly constricted airway. Examples are *general, género,* and *ginecología.* It is pronounced as the English "g" in "go" before consonants and the vowels *a, o,* and *u.* Examples are *gracias, gripe, garganta, gordo,* and *gusto.* To preserve this "g" sound before the vowels *e* and *i*, the letter *u* is inserted in the written word, as in *guerra* (war), *guitarra,* and the family name *Rodríguez.*

• The letter *c* is pronounced like the English "c" in "cent" when it precedes the vowels *e* and *i*. Examples are *cerebro* and *cirugía*. It is pronounced like the English "c" in "coin" before the vowels *a, o,* and *u,* and before consonants. Examples are *cansado, catarro, cortar, codo, Cuba, clínica,* and *recto.*

• *J* is pronounced like the English "h," as in *ojo, oreja,* and *jueves*. Spanish *h* is always silent, as in *herida, hambre,* and *hospital.* Note that the *g* is soft in the Spanish word for surgery, *cirugía,* because it is followed by *i.* To preserve the soft sound, the word for surgeon is written with a *j* (*cirujano*) as a spelling accommodation.

 ### 3.28 Reciclaje

Recall that in chapter 2 we learned to ask about pain. We asked, *¿Estás mejor, igual o peor?* Add this new information to what you know. Ask a partner about his or her pain, and prepare a skit you can perform for the class. Begin with *¿Qué le duele?* and then work toward a more specific description, as in the example. You may also want to use the pain scale from chapter 2, which appears again following this exercise. For example,

—¿Qué le duele?
—Me duele la mano.
—¿Cuál es la mano que le duele?
—Me duele la mano izquierda.
—¿Cómo está el dolor? ¿Está peor, igual o mejor?
—Está un poco mejor, gracias.
—¿Cómo es el dolor?
—Es un dolor sordo.

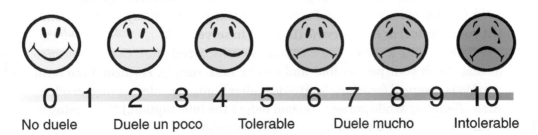

Chapter 4
El recepcionista

Communication Goals
Tell a Patient His or Her Vital Signs   84
Take a Telephone Message   88
Make and Negotiate Dates for Future
   Appointments   92
Conduct a Registration or Admissions
   Interview   96

Vocabulary
Numbers from Zero to 1,000   84
The Month, the Date, and the Time   92
Age   96
Personal Information   96

Structure
Possession   89
Forming Questions   90
Pronunciation of Ñ, R, RR, LL, and Y   100

Video
Demostración: Los números de
   teléfono   88
Trama: La recepcionista   98

Cultural Note
What's in a Name?   102

By the end of this chapter you will know the vocabulary that is used when receiving patients for admission at a medical office or hospital. You will be able to count to a thousand, report vital signs, and take telephone numbers. You will be able to negotiate with patients the dates and times of follow-up appointments. You'll be able to ask the patient's name, address, date of birth, insurance, and other information critical to the admissions process. In the cultural note, you will learn why Latinos have two last names.

 ## Tell a Patient His or Her Vital Signs

Vocabulario: Los números del cero al 1.000
(*Numbers from Zero to 1,000*)

Practice saying aloud the numbers from zero to ten. Build rhythm and fluency.

0	cero	4	cuatro	8	ocho
1	uno	5	cinco	9	nueve
2	dos	6	seis	10	diez
3	tres	7	siete		

Emphasize eleven through fifteen and the multiples of ten. The rest of the numbers to ninety-nine will be intuitive.

11	once	21	veintiuno	31	treinta y uno
12	doce	22	veintidós	32	treinta y dos
13	trece	23	veintitrés	33	treinta y tres
14	catorce	24	veinticuatro	34	treinta y cuatro
15	quince	25	veinticinco	35	treinta y cinco
16	dieciséis	26	veintiséis	36	treinta y seis
17	diecisiete	27	veintisiete	37	treinta y siete
18	dieciocho	28	veintiocho	38	treinta y ocho
19	diecinueve	29	veintinueve	39	treinta y nueve
20	veinte	30	treinta	40	cuarenta

Notice the patterns. Sixteen to twenty-nine are spelled as one word. After thirty, such numbers are spelled as three words. *Sesenta* has an *s* like *seis*. *Setenta* has a *t* like *siete*. Whether one word or three, native pronunciation usually involves linking the words as if they were one. (Recall how fast you counted when playing hide-and-seek as a child.) Heed the spelling of *quinientos, setecientos,* and *novecientos.*

50	cincuenta	190	ciento noventa
51	cincuenta y uno	199	ciento noventa y nueve
52	cincuenta y dos	200	doscientos
60	sesenta	225	doscientos veinticinco
70	setenta	300	trescientos
80	ochenta	351	trescientos cincuenta y uno
90	noventa	400	cuatrocientos
100	cien	500	quinientos
101	ciento uno	600	seiscientos
102	ciento dos	700	setecientos
130	ciento treinta	800	ochocientos
135	ciento treinta y cinco	900	novecientos
150	ciento cincuenta	1.000	mil

HACIA PRECISIÓN

 ### 4.1 Ejercicio

Take turns with a fellow student asking questions. *¿Cuántos?* and *¿cuántas?* mean "how many?" and must agree in gender and number with the nouns they precede.

Modelo: piernas
—¿Cuántas piernas tienes?

A. costillas
B. dedos
C. vértebras

D. orejas
E. dedos de los pies
F. hermanos (*siblings*)

Now as a larger group, ask how many of the following there are. *Hay* means "there is" and "there are." Add additional questions ad lib.

las vértebras
7 verticales
12 dorsales
5 lumbares

Modelo: días en la semana
—¿Cuántos días hay en una semana?

G. escritorios (*desks*) en la clase
H. solteros (*singles*) en la clase
I. libros (*books*) en la clase

J. ventanas (*windows*) en la clase
K. vegetarianos (*vegetarians*) en la clase
L. estudiantes de enfermería en la clase

4.2 Ejercicio

Ask your partner what your body temperature is, starting over and taking turns for each of the following readings. The decimal point is expressed *punto,* as in *noventa y ocho punto ocho grados* (98.8 degrees). (This may frighten a patient who normally uses the metric system, in which 37 degrees is normal and 40 is a high fever!)

Modelo: 98.0 —¿Cómo está mi temperatura?
            —Su temperatura está en noventa y ocho grados.

A. 98
B. 100.8
C. 97.4
D. 103

E. 104.2
F. 98.9
G. 101.2
H. 100.3

 ## 4.3 Ejercicio

Likewise, ask about blood pressure. The word "over" is *sobre,* as in *ciento veinte sobre ochenta* (120/80). *Presión arterial* may also be expressed *presión sanguinea.*

Modelo: (120/80) —¿Cuál es mi presión arterial?
                  —Su presión arterial está en ciento veinte sobre ochenta.

A. 110/68
B. 166/110
C. 134/80
D. 128/70

E. 122/84
F. 118/92
G. 106/74
H. 120/80

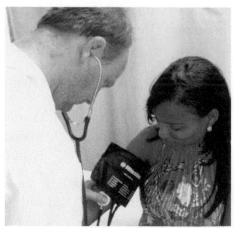

«Su presión arterial está en ciento veinte sobre ochenta. Es normal».

HACIA FLUIDEZ

 4.4 Actividad

It will be more fun than tedious, so you'll enjoy playing *¿Cuántos dulces hay?* The instructor will bring a small glass jar of candies such as M&Ms to class for counting. Pass it around and record names and guesses on the board. Then count the candies aloud to determine the winner.

 4.5 Actividad

Using the vital signs record, talk with a partner about the patients listed. The following questions may help start your conversation.

    A. ¿Quién tiene la presión alta?
    B. ¿Quién tiene taquicardia?
    C. ¿Quién tiene la presión baja?
    D. ¿Quién tiene fiebre?
    E. ¿Quiénes no tienen fiebre?
    F. ¿Quién tiene los signos normales?

Paciente	Presión arterial	Pulso	Temperatura
Sr. Bosch	128/78	90	103.8
Sr. García	160/110	160	98.9
Sra. Álvarez	90/55	84	98.7
Sra. Allende	120/70	68	97.9

 4.6 Drama imprevisto

Play "One to Twenty," which is like "Foot Bone Connected To," from chapter 3. Form a circle. The first student points to another student anywhere in the circle and says *uno*. The student who was signaled then points to another student and says *dos*. Continue in this way until you reach the desired goal. It is important to set a rhythm and follow it. This promotes concentration and the coveted dynamic of working as a team. Variations include starting from a higher number and counting backwards.

Take a Telephone Message

Los números telefónicos (*Telephone Numbers*)

«¿Cuál es su número de teléfono?»

Telephone numbers may be expressed orally using individual numbers. However, where ten-digit numbers are used, they are often organized as a single number followed by three groups of two-digit numbers. For example, 828-7932 is said 8-28-79-32, or *ocho-veintiocho, setenta y nueve, treinta y dos*. Zeros can change things. The number 679-7000 is *seis-setenta y nueve, siete mil,* and the number 305-7001 is *tres-cero-cinco, setenta-cero-uno*. When a double number, such as 77 appears, you may hear *doble siete.* Practice saying your work number or another frequently used telephone number. Take turns saying yours to the class to see how many can write it down correctly. Here is some additional vocabulary.

En este momento no está.	He or she is not here right now.
¿Quiere dejar un mensaje?	Would you like to leave a message?
¿Quién llama?	Who is calling?
¿Cuál es su número de teléfono?	What is your telephone number?
Mi número de teléfono es. . .	My telephone number is . . .

 ## Video: *Los números de teléfono*

Watch the *Demostración* for chapter 4 and do the activities that follow. In the video, Rosmery the nurse takes several telephone messages, and you have the opportunity to take notes along with her and then check your accuracy.

La enfermera Rosmery es mexicana, de Guadalajara, y es muy amable.

HACIA FLUIDEZ

 ### 4.7 Actividad

The instructor may dictate several telephone numbers for you to write in your notebook. Then the instructor will write them on the board so that you can check your results. Next, students may take turns telling work or other important phone numbers. Check your work after each number.

 ### 4.8 Actividad

The instructor may pass out index cards with telephone numbers written on them. Each card will have an exact double. Students circulate in the classroom exchanging telephone numbers until they have paired with the student who has the same number. Speak only Spanish, and don't show your card to anyone!

 ### 4.9 Actividad

In pairs, prepare a telephone conversation that you can demonstrate for the class. You are the receptionist. Your partner calls to leave telephone messages for a practitioner in the office. These may be similar to the demonstration that you saw on the video.

 ## Estructura: Posesión (*Possession*)

• English employs an "apostrophe ess" to indicate possession, as in "the doctor's office." One way to indicate possession in Spanish is with the formula *de* + noun, as in *el consultorio del doctor*.

la casa de Juan	Juan's house
la casa de los padres de Juan	Juan's parents' house
el departamento de psiquiatría	the psychiatry department

• Spanish also uses possessive adjectives, which like all adjectives must agree in gender and number with the nouns that they modify. The formula *de* + noun is the clearest way to express possession, because the terms *su* and *sus* have a surplus of meanings in Spanish.

mi, mis	my
tu, tus	your (informal)
su, sus	your (formal), his, her, its, their
nuestro/a/os/as	our

• Take note of the agreement of gender and number in the following examples.

Mi casa es su casa.	My house is your house.
Mis padres están vivos.	My parents are alive.
Nuestro hospital es bueno.	Our hospital is good.
Nuestras ideas son buenas.	Our ideas are good.

HACIA PRECISIÓN

 ## 4.10 Ejercicio

Read the following phrases aloud, saying the appropriate possessive adjective where indicated.

Modelo: la casa de Miguelito   <u>su</u> casa

A. las sábanas de Elsa   _____ sábanas

B. la cama de usted   _____ cama

C. las frazadas de nosotros   _____ frazadas

D. las camas de José y Rosa   _____ camas

E. la silla de la doctora   _____ silla

F. el consultorio de la doctora López   _____ consultorio

G. el estetoscopio de mí   _____ estetoscopio

 ## Estructura: Haciendo preguntas (*Forming Questions*)

• Intonation may turn a spoken statement into a question. For example, pitch is essential when asking aloud, *¿Su cita es a las cuatro?* When questions are written, however, two question marks signal the event. Placing the subject after the verb also makes the question more obvious. *¿Es su cita a las cuatro?*

• You learned in chapter 2 that another way to ask a question is to make a statement followed by a marker such as *¿no?, ¿verdad?,* or *¿cierto?* For example, *Su cita es a las cuatro, ¿no?*

• To solicit more than a yes-or-no answer, use an interrogative word. These have an accent mark when used in a written question.

¿dónde?	where?	¿adónde?	to where?
¿de dónde?	from where?	¿cómo?	how?
¿cuándo?	when?	¿quién/quiénes?	who?
¿cuál/cuáles?	which?	¿qué?	what?
¿cuánto/a?	how much?	¿cuántos/as?	how many?
¿a qué hora?	at what time?		

• Here are some examples.

¿Dónde vive?	¿De dónde es usted?
¿Cómo está usted?	¿Cuándo es su cita?
¿Quién es su doctor?	¿Cuál es el tobillo hinchado?
¿Qué le duele?	¿Cuántos años tiene?
¿Qué hora es?	¿A qué hora es la cita?

• *¿Qué?* and *¿cuál?* are not always interchangeable. *¿Qué?* requests a definition or an explanation, and *¿cuál?* asks for a choice. For example,

¿Qué es la pulmonía?	What is pneumonia?
¿Qué le duele?	What hurts you?
¿Cuál es el hombro que le duele?	Which is the arm that hurts you?
¿Cuál es su número de teléfono?	What is your telephone number?

HACIA FLUIDEZ

 ### 4.11 Actividad

Speak with other students. Practice several ways to ask for students' and their doctors' names (circumlocution helps build flexibility).

¿Quién es su doctor?
¿Cómo se llama su doctor?
¿Cuál es el nombre de su doctor?

 ### 4.12 Drama imprevisto

Play an "answer-and-question" game show. Working privately, students or pairs should write fairly well-known questions and answers. The instructor may circulate in the "audience" pretending to have a microphone and asking for *respuestas,* or answers. Any student can state the answer to his or her question, and then another student will volunteer to state the question that would have elicited that answer. Here are some examples.

Respuesta	Pregunta
Me llamo Rafael.	¿Cómo te llamas?
Es un doctor para el corazón.	¿Qué es un cardiólogo?
Guadalajara está en México.	¿Dónde está Guadalajara?
Es una inflamación del pulmón.	¿Qué es la pulmonía?

Make and Negotiate Dates for Future Appointments

Vocabulario: El mes, la fecha y la hora
(The Month, the Date, and the Time)

Los meses del año *(The Months of the Year)*

enero	January	julio	July
febrero	February	agosto	August
marzo	March	septiembre	September
abril	April	octubre	October
mayo	May	noviembre	November
junio	June	diciembre	December

1900 mil novecientos	1960 mil novecientos sesenta
2000 dos mil	2013 dos mil trece

Spanish does not identify the year as in the English "nineteen ninety-six."

La fecha *(The Date)*

It is best to write out the name of the month. Using numbers can be confusing, because Spanish-speakers normally write the day before the month. Hence, October 15, 2008, is written 15-10-08. In countries that use roman numerals for the month, this date would be 15-X-08. In the United States, writing the date 6-8-2015 might be understood as either August 6, 2015, or June 8, 2015, depending on the individual's degree of acculturation. In Spanish, write *el 6 de agosto de 2009*. (Months of the year are not written with an initial capital letter.) The first of the month has special treatment: *Hoy es el primero de mayo*.

¿Qué día es?	What day is it?
Hoy es jueves.	Today is Thursday.
¿Cuál es la fecha de hoy?	What is today's date?

Hoy es el cinco de febrero.   Today is February 5.
¿Cuál es su fecha de nacimiento?   What is your birth date?

 La hora (*Telling Time*)

Notice that *y* is used for the first thirty minutes after the hour, while *menos* is used for the twenty-nine minutes that precede the following hour. With the worldwide proliferation of digital watches, some Spanish-speakers now use digital time. For example, 10:45 in digital time is *Son las diez, cuarenta y cinco;* however, the traditional analog method is common.

¿Qué hora es?   What time is it?
Es la una.   1:00
Son las dos.   2:00
Son las tres.   3:00
Son las tres y cinco.   3:05
Son las seis y media.   6:30
Son las siete y cuarto (y quince).   7:15
Son las diez menos cinco.   9:55
Son las diez de la mañana.   It is 10:00 in the morning.
a las cuatro de la tarde   at 4:00 in the afternoon
a las diez de la noche   at 10:00 at night

> *Es la una* is singular, while *Son las dos* is plural. *Cuarto* means "quarter."

HACIA PRECISIÓN

 4.13 Ejercicio

Look at the clock faces and say the times, first as analog, and then as digital.

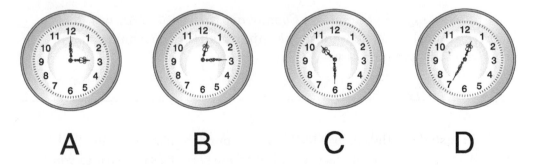

A   B   C   D

4.14 Ejercicio

Say the following times, translating from the digital form to traditional analog Spanish. Afterwards, say them in Spanish digital time.

A. 10:45 a.m.   C. 8:30 p.m.   E. 3:56 p.m.
B. 6:15 a.m.   D. 11:55 p.m.   F. 6:05 p.m.

4.15 Ejercicio

To say, "You have an appointment with the doctor at 10:15," use *Usted tiene una cita con el doctor a las diez y cuarto.* Tell a partner about the following appointments in Spanish. When you have finished, switch roles.

A. You have an appointment with the dentist on Thursday, December 14 at 3:30 in the afternoon.
B. You have an appointment in the clinic on Tuesday, January 22 at 10:15 in the morning.
C. You have an appointment with Doctor Contreras Medina on Friday, February 28 at 6:45 in the evening.
D. Your mother has an appointment with the neurologist, Dr. Solano, on Wednesday, May 30 at 1:00 in the afternoon.

HACIA FLUIDEZ

4.16 Actividad

Take turns asking fellow students, *¿Cuántos años tiene usted?* Answer, *Tengo ____ años.* (It's all right to stretch—or shrink—the truth!) Continue until you find a student who is the same age as you.

4.17 Actividad

Ask fellow students their date of birth. Move around the classroom and find someone born in the same month as you and someone born the same year as you.

4.18 Actividad

Play "Time Aerobics." Space permitting, the instructor stands with his or her back to the class, positions his or her hands like the hands of a clock, and chants the

time represented. Students, who are standing as well, copy the instructor's position and repeat the time.

▶◀ 4.19 Actividad

The instructor may bring a cardboard clock with movable hands or a plastic "Will
be back at . . ." clock from an office supplies store to use as a prop in the classroom
for practice in asking and telling the time.

▶◀ 4.20 Actividad

Look at the doctor's appointment book. With your partner, role-play the receptionist calling patients to remind them about their appointments. When you have
finished, switch roles.

MARTA DURÁN LÓPEZ, MD
LUNES, 2 DE JULIO
1:00 Sr. Julio Ortiz
1:15 Sra. Acevedo
1:30 Anita Negrón
1:45 José Durán
2:00 Sra. Elsa Morel
MARTES, 3 DE JULIO
10:00 Srta. Paola Castro
10:15 Sra. Ana Dejesús
10:30 Sr. Pedro García
10:45 Alberto Gómez

Vocabulario: La edad (*Age*)

Use the verb *tener* to express age. Thus the literal translation of *Tengo cincuenta años* is "I have fifty years," but its meaning in Spanish is clear. Never forget the importance of pronunciation. *Año* (pronounced "anyo") means "year," and *ano* you know from chapter 3!

¿Cuántos años tiene?	How old are you?
Tengo treinta años.	I am 30 years old.
¿En qué año estamos?	What year is this?
¿En qué año nació usted?	In what year were you born?
Nací en el año 2000.	I was born in the year 2000.

Nació and *nací* are from the past tense of the verb *nacer.*

HACIA PRECISIÓN

4.21 Ejercicio

It may be more comfortable to talk about someone else's age! Refer to the list of names and birthdates and ask a partner, for example, *¿Cuántos años tiene don Samuel?*

Nombre	*Fecha de nacimiento*
don Samuel	el 3 de octubre de 1945
Sara	el 14 de marzo de 1983
doña Olga	el 2 de mayo de 1931
Elsita	el 5 de febrero de 1995
el Sr. Arroyo	el primero de junio de 1968

Conduct a Registration or Admissions Interview

Vocabulario: Los datos personales
(*Personal Information*)

¿Cuál es su . . . ?	What is your . . . ?
nombre	name
apellido	last name
fecha de nacimiento	date of birth
número de Seguro Social	Social Security number
número de teléfono	telephone number
dirección	address

estado civil	marital status
soltero/a	single
casado/a	married
separado/a	separated
divorciado/a	divorced
viudo/a	widower/widow
¿Dónde vive usted?	Where do you live?
¿Qué . . . ?	What . . . ?
calle	street
número	number
ciudad	city
pueblo	town
¿Tiene usted plan médico?	Do you have health insurance?
¿Tiene seguro médico?	Do you have health insurance?
el Medicare	Medicare
el Medicaid	Medicaid
la asistencia pública	public assistance
¿Tiene la tarjeta?	Do you have the card?
¿A quién llamamos en caso de emergencia?	Whom do we call in case of emergency?
¿Tiene usted la custodia legal?	Do you have legal custody?
¿Es usted el tutor / la tutora legal?	Are you the legal guardian?
Favor de firmar el permiso para el tratamiento.	Please sign the consent to treatment form.

Another way to ask whether the patient is married is to ask, *¿Está usted casado/a?* Asking *¿Tiene pareja?* ("Do you have a partner?") removes the marriage implication. Note that *¿Es usted señorita?* may imply a question about virginity.

El Medicare es un plan médico público en los Estados Unidos para las personas que tienen sesenta y cinco años o más o que son discapacitadas. El Medicaid es un plan médico público para las personas que son pobres y tienen hijos o que son discapacitadas.

Video: *La recepcionista*

La enfermera
Rosmery y
don Francisco

Watch the *Trama* for chapter 4, which you may use as a model for *actividad* 4.22, which follows.

Rosmery: Buenas tardes. Me llamo Rosmery. Soy enfermera y trabajo con el doctor Vargas.

Sr. Flores: Mucho gusto. Soy Francisco Flores. Usted habla español. ¿De dónde es usted?

Rosmery: De México. De Guadalajara. Pero hace muchos años que vivo aquí en los Estados Unidos. Y usted, ¿de dónde es?

Sr. Flores: Soy de la República Dominicana, de Santo Domingo.

Rosmery: Dominicano. Excelente. La comida dominicana es deliciosa. ¿Usted tiene cita con el doctor hoy?

Sr. Flores: Sí, a las tres de la tarde. Para un examen físico.

Rosmery: Son las tres en punto. Es puntual. Muy bien. Gracias. Okay, nombre, Francisco Flores. ¿Es usted casado?

Sr. Flores: Sí, mi esposa se llama Marisol García de Flores.

Rosmery: ¿Cuál es su dirección?

Sr. Flores: Calle Main número quince, segundo piso.

Rosmery: ¿En qué pueblo vive?

Sr. Flores: Aquí en New Haven.

Rosmery: ¿Cuál es su número de teléfono?

Sr. Flores: Cinco, cuarenta y ocho, treinta y seis, veinticuatro.

Rosmery: ¿Cuál es su fecha de nacimiento?

Sr. Flores: El cinco de mayo del mil novecientos setenta y nueve.

Rosmery: ¿Tiene plan médico?

Sr. Flores: Sí. Aquí está la tarjeta.

Rosmery: Gracias. ¿En caso de emergencia, a quién debemos llamar?

Sr. Flores: A mi esposa, Marisol Flores, al cinco, cuarenta y ocho, treinta y seis, veinticuatro.

Rosmery: Vamos a confirmar el número. Cinco, cuarenta y ocho, treinta y
seis, veinticuatro. ¿Correcto?

Sr. Flores: Sí, correcto. Ella tiene celular. Su número es nueve, setenta y
siete, cuarenta y nueve, ochenta y siete.

Rosmery: Vamos a confirmar el celular. Nueve, setenta y siete, cuarenta y
nueve, ochenta y siete. ¿Verdad?

Sr. Flores: Sí, preciso.

Rosmery: Vamos a tomarle la temperatura. Su temperatura está en noventa
y ocho punto ocho. Muy bien. No tiene fiebre.

Sr. Flores: Me siento bien. Gracias a Dios.

Rosmery: Tome asiento allí por favor. El doctor viene pronto.

Sr. Flores: Gracias.

HACIA FLUIDEZ

 4.22 Actividad

Work with a partner to admit each other to the services of the Clínica Abreu using
the form that appears here.

Clínica Abreu
Formulario de inscripción del paciente

Nombre y apellidos: _____

Idioma: _____

Dirección: _____

Teléfono: _____

Fecha de nacimiento: _____

Número de seguro social: _____

Estado civil: _____

Plan médico: _____

Contacto de emergencia:

Nombre y apellidos: _____

Teléfono: _____

This *Formulario de inscripción*
is available for download from
the Web site.

4.23 Drama imprevisto

Review the advertisement for the dental office of *la doctora Dolores D. Repente.* Take turns acting out telephone calls between a patient and the receptionist at the dental office. Choose the service that you need, and work to set up an appointment and another for six months later. Create—or randomly assign to other students— specific challenging scenarios. For example, you are experiencing a lot of pain, and the doctor's office is very busy; or the doctor's office does not seem to be very busy until you reveal that you do not have insurance.

Dra. Dolores D. Repente
Servicios dentales para toda la familia

Limpiezas   **Extracciones**
Examinaciones   **Implantes**
Dentaduras   **Coronas**
  —completas y parciales   —de oro y de porcelana

Para más información, llame al (809) 356-8090
Abierto de lunes a jueves desde las 9 hasta las 4

Primera consulta gratis
Hablamos español e inglés
Aceptamos la mayoría de los planes dentales

Pronunciación de Ñ, R, RR, LL y Y
(*Pronunciation of* Ñ, R, RR, LL, *and* Y)

• The Spanish alphabet (*el alfabeto* or *el abecedario*) has twenty-seven letters (see appendix 1). The letter that appears in Spanish but not in English is the letter *ñ,* although some grammars include *rr* in the alphabet.
• The letter *ñ* (called *eñe*) is pronounced like the "ni" in "onion." Some examples are: *uña, señor, doña, año, sueño,* and *niño.*
• The letter *r* is pronounced by tapping the palate softly with the tip of the tongue, almost as in the English "tt" in "butter" or the "dd" in "ladder." When *rr* appears, it is trilled. Listen to good models and copy them. Practice saying *pero* (but) and *perro* (dog). Do not be discouraged. There are regions where a dialect calls for a more throaty sound. Those who can, however, may trill the letter *r* when it starts a word. Pronouncing the Spanish *r* like an English retroflex "r" can be irritating

to a native speaker. Practice saying *diarrea, catarro, carrera, roto, regular*, and *ró-tula*. Then try these tongue-twisters (*trabalenguas*):

Perro raro, pero perro al fin (An odd dog, but a dog after all).
Qué rápido corren los carros del ferrocarril (How fast the rail cars run).

• The letters *ll* when together are pronounced like English "y." The letter *y* (*ye*) is pronounced likewise, except when it stands alone in the word *y*, which is pronounced like Spanish *i*. Some examples are: *llamar, llegar, rodilla, yo, mayo*, and *yodo*. Caribbean Americans often give an English "j" sound to both *y* and *ll*. Some South Americans give them more of a "zsh" sound.

4.24 Reciclaje

In chapter 2 you learned how to determine whether a patient is oriented as to person, place, and time. Now you have expanded your repertoire to be able to ask about the date as well. Work with a partner to role-play for the class an interview to elicit whether a patient is oriented to three spheres, including the year, month, and day in the time sphere.

4.25 Reciclaje

Integrate what you have learned in the first four chapters. Set up a small clinic in the front of the classroom. Students volunteer to play the part of patient, patient family member, receptionist, and practitioner. The receptionist registers the patient, the practitioner enters the room, and introductions are made. Work out a situation in which the patient's diagnosis will be a sprained joint or a fractured bone, and schedule a follow-up visit with an orthopedist.

B y the end of this chapter you will be able to name the various members of a family and to ask about basic family medical history. In the process you will greatly expand your repertoire of words that narrate action.

Hay tres generaciones: abuela, hija y nieta.

Ask about Family Constellation

Vocabulario: Los familiares
(*Family Members*)

el padre, papá	father	**la madre, mamá**	mother
el esposo, el marido	husband	**la esposa, mujer**	wife
el hijo	son	**la hija**	daughter
el hermano	brother	**la hermana**	sister
el abuelo	grandfather	**la abuela**	grandmother
el nieto	grandson	**la nieta**	granddaughter
el tío	uncle	**la tía**	aunt
el sobrino	nephew	**la sobrina**	niece
el primo	male cousin	**la prima**	female cousin
el padrino	godfather	**la madrina**	godmother

Hijos means sons, but as a plural word it can refer to sons and daughters. *Hijas* refers only to daughters. In the same way, *padres* refers to parents, but *padre* only to father; and *hermanos* can refer to brothers and sisters or to brothers only.

¿Tiene hijos?
Sí, tengo dos hijos: un hijo y una hija.

Do you have children?
Yes, I have two: a son and a daughter.

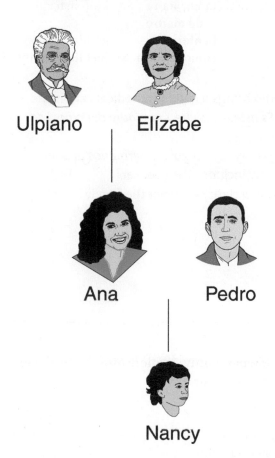

Ulpiano   Elízabe

Ana   Pedro

Nancy

La familia de Ana. ¿Quiénes son? Por ejemplo, Ana es la madre de Nancy.

Hola. Soy Ana. Soy hija única de mi papá y mamá. No tengo hermanos. Soy madre. Tengo una hija. Ella se llama Nancy y tiene cinco años de edad. Mi esposo se llama Pedro. Aquí está un diagrama de mi familia.

único/a only

Vocabulario: Más familiares (*More Family Members*)

el tío abuelo	great-uncle	**la tía abuela**	great-aunt
el/la bisabuelo/a	great-grandparent	**el/la bisnieto/a**	great-grandchild
el suegro	father-in-law	**la suegra**	mother-in-law
el yerno	son-in-law	**la nuera**	daughter-in-law
el cuñado	brother-in-law	**la cuñada**	sister-in-law
el padrastro	stepfather	**la madrastra**	stepmother
el hijastro	stepson	**la hijastra**	stepdaughter
el hermanastro	stepbrother	**la hermanastra**	stepsister

el hermano de padre	half-brother	**la hermana de padre**	half-sister
el hermano de madre	half-brother	**la hermana de madre**	half-sister
el ahijado	godson	**la ahijada**	goddaughter
hijo de crianza	foster child	**como familia**	just like family

• To establish whether a caretaker who brings a child for medical care is the child's parent, ask *¿Es su hijo/a?* or *¿Es usted el padre / la madre del niño / de la niña?*

• A Spanish-speaker with two siblings may say *Tengo dos hermanos* or *Somos tres hermanos.* The latter more explicitly includes the speaker.

• The adjectives *paterno/a* and *materno/a* clarify whether the family member is related by father or by mother.

HACIA PRECISIÓN

 ### 5.1 Ejercicio

Quiz a classmate by asking for the following family relationships, as in the example. Make up some additional questions on your own.

> Modelo: el padre de mi abuela
> —¿Quién es el padre de mi abuela?
> —El padre de su abuela es su bisabuelo.

A. la esposa de mi hermano
B. el hijo de mi hijo
C. el hijo de mi padrastro
D. la hermana de mi madre

E. el hijo de mi tía
F. la hermana de mi primo
G. la madre de mi esposa
H. el hijo de mi esposa y su exesposo

 ### 5.2 Ejercicio

Fill in the blanks with the names of family relationships based on the diagram of Arturo Martínez Mendoza's family.

Hola. Me llamo Arturo. Mi _____ se llama Juan Martínez. Él tiene

una _____ que se llama Carmen y es mi _____. También

tiene un _____que se llama Pedro y es mi _____. Soy el

_____de mi tía Carmen y mi tío Pedro. Tío Pedro tiene dos hijos.

Ellos son mis _____. El padre de mi padre es mi _____

Javier Martínez. La esposa de mi abuelo es mi _____.

Mi Familia
por Arturo Martínez Mendoza

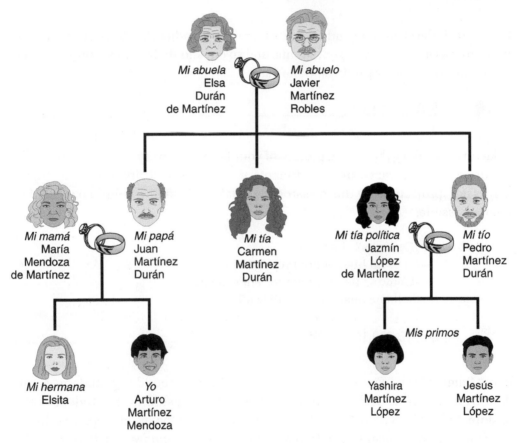

Mi abuela
Elsa
Durán
de Martínez

Mi abuelo
Javier
Martínez
Robles

Mi mamá
María
Mendoza
de Martínez

Mi papá
Juan
Martínez
Durán

Mi tía
Carmen
Martínez
Durán

Mi tía política
Jazmín
López
de Martínez

Mi tío
Pedro
Martínez
Durán

Mi hermana
Elsita

Yo
Arturo
Martínez
Mendoza

Mis primos

Yashira
Martínez
López

Jesús
Martínez
López

HACIA FLUIDEZ

 ### 5.3 Actividad

Refer to the diagram *Mi familia, por Arturo Martínez Mendoza* and make as many questions and statements as you can about the family relationships. Ask, for example, *¿Tiene hermanos Yashira?* or *¿Quién es doña Elsa?* Note that the titles *señor* and *señora* are used with last names, and the titles *don* and *doña* are used with first names.

 ### 5.4 Actividad

Circulate in the classroom and ask class members whether they have children, siblings, nieces and nephews, godparents, and so on, and their names and ages. Take notes, and report your findings to the class.

 ### 5.5 Actividad

Take turns showing the class a picture of your family. Identify and describe family members. With advance notice, students may e-mail or bring these on thumb drives for projection in the classroom. Break into spontaneous conversation where possible.

> Modelo: —¿Quién es? ¿Es su hija?
> —Sí, es mi hija menor (youngest).
> —¿Cómo se llama y cuántos años tiene?
> —Se llama Susan y tiene diez años.

 ### 5.6 Drama imprevisto

Play "Tangled Web." Five or six students form a circle around one student. A student from the circle declares his or her family relationship to the student in the middle, for example, *Soy tu madre,* and the student in the middle declares his or her consequential relationship to that student: *Eres mi madre, soy tu hijo/a.* The next student then does the same with the student in the middle and with each student who has gone before. When you feel ready, suppose someone in the group divorced (*Soy tu exmarido*) and married a person with children.

Estructura: Los verbos regulares terminados con
-ar, -er e *-ir* (*Regular Verbs Ending in* -ar, -er, *and* -ir)

• So far you have learned the three verbs *ser, estar,* and *tener.* Each morphs, or changes its form according to the subject of the sentence (the doer of the action). These three verbs are considered irregular, because their forms are idiosyncratic.

• Thankfully, there are regular verbs that share common morphology. These are divided into three groups, those whose infinitive forms end in *-ar,* in *-er,* and in *-ir.* Each group has a consistent set of forms.

• This is the morphology of the regular verb *hablar* (to talk or to speak):

yo	**Hablo** inglés y un poquito de español.
tú	¿**Hablas** inglés?
él, ella, usted	Mi mamá no **habla** inglés.
nosotros/as	En casa, **hablamos** español.
ellos, ellas, ustedes	Mis hijos **hablan** inglés, pero soy bilingüe.

• Regular verbs that end in *-er* have a consistent morphology. Here is the regular verb *comer* (to eat):

yo	En un restaurante italiano **como** espaguetis.
tú	¿**Comes** arroz con pollo?
él, ella, usted	Mi hijo **come** mucho y es gordito.
nosotros/as	Mi esposa y yo **comemos** a las seis.
ellos, ellas, ustedes	Los empleados **comen** en la cafetería.

• Regular verbs that end in *-ir* also have a consistent morphology. These differ from those that end in *-er* only in the first person plural (*nosotros/as*). Here is the regular verb *vivir* (to live):

yo	**Vivo** en una casa grande.
tú	¿Dónde **vives**?
él, ella, usted	Mi hija **vive** en una casa pequeña.
nosotros/as	**Vivimos** cerca del (*near the*) hospital.
ellos, ellas, ustedes	Mis hijos **viven** en Florida.

Video: *¿Cuáles idiomas habla?*

La enfermera Rosmery
y Elsita

Watch the *Demostración* for chapter 5, in which Rosmery and Elsita explore their emerging bicultural identities. Listen for the forms of the -*ar* verb *hablar* and the -*ir* verb *vivir*.

Rosmery: Elsita, ¿hablas inglés?

Elsita: Sí. Hablo inglés y español. Mi padre habla inglés y español también, pero mi mamá sólo habla español. Ella no habla inglés.

Rosmery: Tú hablas dos idiomas. Es muy bueno hablar dos idiomas. Tienes mucha suerte.

Elsita: En casa siempre hablamos español, pero en la escuela hablo inglés porque mis profesoras y mis amigos no hablan español. Cuando estamos de vacaciones en Santo Domingo, hablo español con mis primos. Todos mis primos hablan español.

Rosmery: ¿Te gusta jugar con tus primos?

Elsita: Sí. Claro. Pero toditos viven en Santo Domingo, y mis padres y yo vivimos aquí en New Haven. A veces mi mamá está muy triste porque vivimos muy lejos de mi abuela, mis tíos y mis primos.

Rosmery: Sí, es una pena cuando nuestros seres queridos viven lejos. Mi mamá vive en México y me hace mucha falta. Todos los meses le mando plata.

Elsita: ¿Plata?

Rosmery: «Plata» es dinero en Centroamérica.

Elsita: Mami dice que vivimos en los Estados Unidos porque papá tiene un buen trabajo y porque mi escuela es buena. Ella quiere vivir en Santo Domingo porque mi abuela está enferma. Mi abuela no tiene dinero. Cuando estamos en Santo Domingo mis padres le compran su medicina.

Rosmery: Tus padres quieren mucho a tu abuela.

Elsita: Sí. Y yo la quiero mucho también. Y quiero a mis primos. Quiero jugar con ellos hoy, pero tengo que esperar porque vamos de vacaciones en agosto.

Rosmery: Qué bueno. Me alegro mucho.

Vocabulario: Algunos verbos regulares
(Some Regular Verbs)

Verbos terminados en -*ar*

ayudar	to help	**llegar**	to arrive
caminar	to walk	**necesitar**	to need
cocinar	to cook	**practicar**	to practice
comprar	to buy	**preguntar**	to ask a question
cuidar	to care for	**recetar**	to prescribe
enseñar	to teach, show	**tomar**	to take, drink
estudiar	to study	**trabajar**	to work
examinar	to examine	**usar**	to use
llamar	to call	**visitar**	to visit

Verbos terminados en -*er*

aprender	to learn	**comer**	to eat
beber	to drink	**leer**	to read

Verbos terminados en -*ir*

abrir	to open	**sufrir de**	to suffer from
escribir	to write	**vivir**	to live

HACIA PRECISIÓN

 ### 5.7 Ejercicio

Identify the phrase or object in parentheses that is more likely to appear with each verb.

A. llegar (a las seis, por tres horas)

B. recetar (una hamburguesa, medicina para el colesterol)

C. caminar (en el parque, en la ambulancia)

D. leer (las instrucciones, los pacientes)

E. comprar (el doctor, el medicamento)

F. escribir (el radio, una receta)

G. cocinar (vegetales, las sábanas)

H. sufrir de (una enfermera, una enfermedad)

5.8 Ejercicio

To actively and visually demonstrate how verbs change form depending on the subject of the verb, or who does the action, use two cellular phones. Two students who hold the phones should stand and chat in Spanish. Then as a class, talk about the action. For example,

¿Con quién hablas, Tom?	Hablo con Bill.	Tom habla con Bill.
Tom y yo hablamos.	¿Quiénes hablan?	Tom y Bill hablan.

Seek food objects to illustrate *comer*. To illustrate *vivir*, pass around drawings of a house and of an apartment building, and ask, *¿Dónde vives?* and *¿Vives en un departamento o en una casa particular?*

5.9 Ejercicio

Complete the following sentences based on the photo collage.

A. Mi abuelo _____ vegetales para la familia.

B. Juan Miguel _____ al hospital para trabajar todos los días.

C. Tú _____ libros en inglés y español.

D. Los doctores _____ los medicamentos.

E. Marisol y su hermana _____ por teléfono todos los sábados.

F. Yo _____ mucha ensalada porque tiene fibra y muchas vitaminas.

G. Una enfermera _____ a mi abuela en su casa una vez a la semana.

H. Luisito _____ un vaso de _____ porque tiene _____.

I. Miguelina _____ libros por Internet con su tarjeta de crédito.

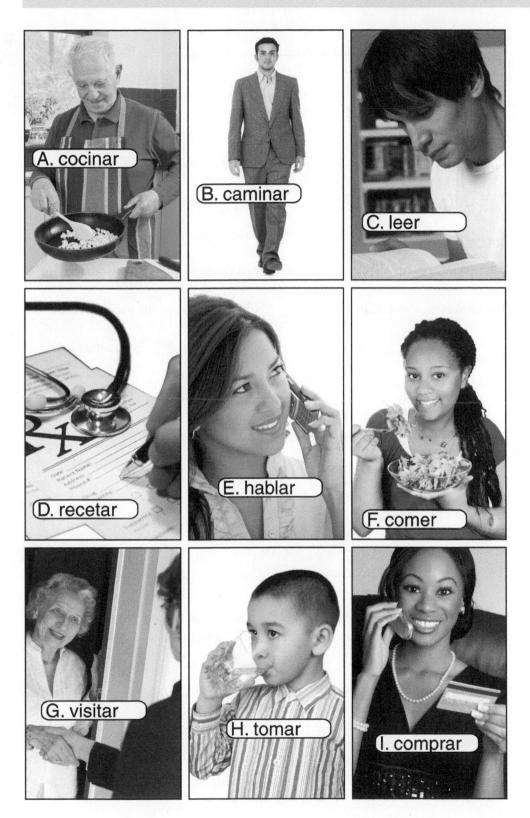

A. cocinar

B. caminar

C. leer

D. recetar

E. hablar

F. comer

G. visitar

H. tomar

I. comprar

5.10 Ejercicio

Complete this paragraph with the correct form of the verbs.

Me llamo Shawn. _____ (ser) enfermero y _____ (trabajar) en

la clínica de lunes a viernes. No _____ (vivir) lejos de la clínica y

_____ (caminar) a la clínica todos los días. La clínica _____

(abrir) a las ocho de la mañana. La doctora Valerio _____ (trabajar) en

la clínica también. Ella y yo _____ (cuidar) a nuestros pacientes. La

doctora _____ (examinar) a los pacientes y _____ (recetar) los

medicamentos. Yo _____ (enseñar) a los pacientes cómo tomar sus

medicamentos. Los pacientes _____ (comprar) sus medicamentos

en la farmacia y _____ (visitar) la clínica cuando están enfermos o

_____ (necesitar) más medicamento.

HACIA FLUIDEZ

5.11 Actividad

Work with a partner to ask and respond in full sentences to the following questions. Use the familiar (*tú*) form, as you are talking with a classmate.

Modelo: sufrir de
—¿Sufres de migrañas?
—No, no sufro de migrañas, gracias a Dios.

A. caminar   ¿Caminas a la clase?
B. llegar   ¿A qué hora llegas a la clase?
C. tomar   ¿Tomas antiácidos por la noche?
D. trabajar   ¿Qué días de la semana trabajas?

E. abrir   ¿Abre la clínica todos los días?
F. practicar   ¿Con quién practicas el español?
G. leer   ¿Lees el libro de español por la noche?
H. beber   ¿Bebes bebidas alcohólicas todos los días?
I. estudiar   ¿Cuántas horas estudias los fines de semana?

 5.12 Actividad _____

Circulate in the classroom asking classmates which languages (*idiomas*) they speak and which are spoken by members of their family. Identify bilingual and polyglot (multilingual) individuals and report your findings. (In Spanish, names of languages do not begin with a capital letter.)

> Modelo: —¿Qué idiomas habla tu familia en casa?
> —Nosotros hablamos inglés.
> —¿Qué idioma hablan tus abuelos?
> —Mis abuelos hablan italiano.

español	Spanish	**inglés**	English
francés	French	**italiano**	Italian
alemán	German	**portugués**	Portuguese
chino	Chinese	**japonés**	Japanese
árabe	Arabic	**polaco**	Polish

 5.13 Actividad _____

The verb *tomar* means "to drink" and "to take," as in taking a bus, a class, or a medication. Ask whether classmates drink coffee, tea, milk, or chocolate (*café, té, leche o chocolate*) in the morning and how many cups or glasses (*cuántos tazas o vasos*). In report afterwards, use various morphologies.

> Modelo: Cheryl y Bill toman café por la mañana. Susan y yo no tomamos café.

5.14 Actividad _____

Conduct the following survey (*¡sólo español, por favor!*). Write the names of classmates in spaces according to the frequency with which they eat at various places. Then discuss your results with the class. Key: *a veces* (occasionally), *a menudo* (frequently), and *siempre* (always).

Comer . . .	A veces	A menudo	Siempre
. . . en casa			
. . . en la cafetería			
. . . en un restaurante			
. . . en casa de los padres			
. . . en el trabajo (at work)			

5.15 Drama imprevisto

The instructor places items on a table in front of the room. These are common household objects that may be associated with the list of verbs we are studying. These may include, for example, a snack (*comer*), coins (*comprar*), a drink (*beber*), a book (*leer, enseñar,* and *estudiar*), and a cellular phone (*hablar* and *llamar*). Two students stand at the table and either act out a story as the class tells it or act out a story for the class to tell. For example, *Susan compra café y Bill toma mucho.*

5.16 Drama imprevisto

Play another game of "The Host." Choose a host, who leaves the room while a small group is assigned verbs from our new repertoire. The host returns and is in the front of the room preparing a party. The chosen students take turns arriving at the party, exchanging small talk, and demonstrating the assigned action word using gestures, questions, and statements. Say anything but the name of your verb. At the end, the host must guess each person's verb: *Sarah toma café, Paul examina a un paciente,* and so on. Prior to dismantling the scene, interview each player in order to demonstrate various subject-verb morphologies.

Estructura: La *a* personal (*The Personal* a)

• When a person receives the action of the verb directly, a preposition called the personal *a* is placed after the verb.

Visito **a** mi mamá todos los días.
La enfermera cuida **a** sus pacientes muy bien.

• The preposition *a* and the masculine definite article *el* form the contraction *al* (*a* + *el* = *al*).

Llamo **al** doctor cuando estoy enfermo.

• The personal *a* is not needed when a person is not the direct object of the verb.

Practico español en la comunidad.
Necesito aspirina para el dolor de cabeza.

HACIA PRECISIÓN

 ## 5.17 Ejercicio

Choose which of these sentences require the inclusion of the personal *a* and which do not, and write them in the provided spaces as needed.

A. Aprendo ___ español rápidamente.

B. Enseño inglés ___ mis padres.

C. Mi esposa y yo hablamos ___ español en casa.

D. Cuido ___ mis padres en la casa.

E. Visito ___ mi mamá todas las semanas.

F. Llamo ___ mi hermana por teléfono los domingos.

G. Mi hermano come ___ una hamburguesa al mediodía.

H. Mi tío bebe ___ tres tazas de café por la mañana.

 # Take Family Medical History

 ## Vocabulario: Las enfermedades hereditarias
(Hereditary Illnesses)

el alcoholismo	alcoholism
el asma	asthma
el cáncer	cancer
la depresión	depression

la diabetes	diabetes
la distrofia muscular	muscular dystrophy
la enfermedad de Alzheimer	Alzheimer's disease
la enfermedad de Huntington	Huntington's disease
la hemofilia	hemophilia
la hipertensión	hypertension
la presión alta	high blood pressure
los problemas cardíacos	cardiac problems
los problemas emocionales	emotional problems
el síndrome de Down	Down syndrome

Expresiones útiles

Su padre tiene la presión alta.	Your father has high blood pressure.
Mi madre tuvo cáncer.	My mother had cancer.
Mi padre murió.	My father died.
Mi padre está muerto.	My father is dead.

Preguntas útiles

¿Están vivos sus padres?	Are your parents alive?
¿Qué enfermedades tenían?	What illnesses did they have?
¿De qué murió su madre?	From what did your mother die?
¿Hay asma en la familia?	Is there asthma in the family?
¿Qué enfermedades hay en su familia?	What illnesses are there in your family?

Asma, like *agua,* is a feminine word that uses the masculine article *el* and a feminine adjective, for example, *el asma crónica, el asma aguda. Vivo* and *muerto* are adjectives meaning "alive" and "dead." The definite article (*el, la*) is not used after *hay,* as in *¿Hay asma en la familia?* To say that someone *had* an illness, use the past tense *tuvo,* which we'll present in chapter 9.

HACIA FLUIDEZ

 ### 5.18 Actividad

Form small groups and ask each other whether various relatives are living, as in the example. Ask about the cause of death, which may prompt you to refer to the glossary that appears at the end of this text. (Recall that the adjectives must agree in gender and number.)

Modelo: —¿Está vivo su abuelo?
            —Sí, mi abuelo está vivo (or) No, mi abuelo murió.

(*if negative*) —¿De qué murió?
        —Mi abuelo murió de un infarto cardíaco.

 ## 5.19 Actividad

In the same small groups, ask about several aspects of medical history, using the preceding vocabulary.

Modelo: —¿Hay asma en su familia?
        —No, no hay asma (or) Sí, mi madre tiene asma.

 ## Estructura: Los complementos directos
(*Direct Object Pronouns*)

• The direct object pronoun represents the person or thing that directly receives the action of the verb. It can be used to replace the direct object noun. It sounds natural and reflects economy of language. These are the direct object pronouns.

me	¿Me necesitas?	Do you need me?
te	Te necesito.	I need you.
lo/la	Lo/la visito.	I visit you/him/her/it.
nos	Ellos nos esperan.	They are waiting for us.
los/las	Los cuido.	I take care of them.

• Direct object pronouns must agree in gender and number with the object noun. They are used when the object noun has been mentioned or is understood. For example, here the object noun is mentioned in the question and replaced by the direct object in the answer.

—¿Usa usted insulina?	—Sí, *la* uso dos veces al día.
—¿Necesita el inhalador?	—No, no *lo* necesito.
—¿Tiene los supositorios?	—No, no *los* tengo.
—¿Tomas café?	—Sí, pero no *lo* tomo por la tarde.
—¿Cuándo visitas a tu mamá?	—*La* visito los domingos.

HACIA FLUIDEZ

 ## 5.20 Actividad

Notice the efficiency of the direct object pronoun. Take turns asking members of the class about what they drink. Use the direct object pronoun (*lo/la* or *los/las*) to answer the questions.

Modelo: —¿Tomas café?
            —Sí, lo tomo por la mañana.
            —¿Tomas cerveza (*beer*)?
            —Sí, pero la tomo solamente los sábados.

A. el té   E. las bebidas alcohólicas
B. el vino (*wine*)   F. el jugo de naranja (*orange juice*)
C. el agua (*f*)   G. el jugo de ciruela (*prune juice*)
D. la leche   H. el té de manzanilla (*chamomile tea*)

 ## 5.21 Actividad

Vary the verbs. Ask a partner the following questions. Use the direct object pronoun when answering. The symbols (*m*) and (*f*) are provided to indicate the gender of the direct object noun. You'll know whether they are singular or plural.

Modelo: —¿Toma aspirina (*f*) todos los días?
            —Sí, la tomo (*or*) No, no la tomo.

A. ¿Toma antibióticos (*m*) cuando tiene resfriado?
B. ¿Usa insulina (*f*) para la diabetes?
C. ¿Usa el inhalador (*m*) cuando tiene fatiga?
D. ¿Usa lentes (*m*) para leer?
E. ¿Visita a sus hermanos (*m*) en Puerto Rico?
F. ¿Necesita medicamento (*m*) para el dolor?
G. ¿Bebe bebidas alcohólicas (*f*)?
H. ¿Ayuda a sus padres (*m*) en la casa?

 ## Video: *La historia clínica familiar*

Watch the *Trama* for chapter 5 and do the activity that follows. In the video, Dr. Vargas takes Mr. Flores's medical history.

Dr. Vargas:	Buenas tardes, señor Flores.
Sr. Flores:	Buenas tardes, doctor.
Dr. Vargas:	Usted está aquí para un examen físico. ¿No?
Sr. Flores:	Sí, pero me siento bien, gracias a Dios.
Dr. Vargas:	Muy bien. Usted está casado y tiene una hija, ¿verdad?

Sr. Flores:	Sí, usted conoce a mi esposa Marisol y a nuestra hija Elsita.
Dr. Vargas:	Claro. ¿Cómo están ellas?
Sr. Flores:	Bien, bien gracias.
Dr. Vargas:	¿Cuántos años tiene Elsita ahora?
Sr. Flores:	Tiene diez años.
Dr. Vargas:	Diez años. Es una muchacha muy lista.
Sr. Flores:	Gracias.
Dr. Vargas:	Vamos a hablar de su historia médica familiar. ¿Están vivos sus padres?
Sr. Flores:	No. Están muertos. Mi padre murió el año pasado y Mamá murió hace ya cinco años.
Dr. Vargas:	¿De qué murieron sus padres?
Sr. Flores:	Mi mamá murió de cáncer del seno, y metástasis en el cerebro. Cuando murió Mamá, mi papá tuvo una depresión muy grande.
Dr. Vargas:	¿Qué otros problemas médicos tenía su padre?
Sr. Flores:	Mi padre tenía hipertensión y diabetes. Al final murió de un ataque al corazón.
Dr. Vargas:	Lo siento. Es muy triste.
Sr. Flores:	Hay que seguir adelante.
Dr. Vargas:	Eso es verdad. ¿Tiene hermanos?
Sr. Flores:	Somos cuatro hermanos. Dos hermanos y dos hermanas. Tengo un hermano menor y dos hermanas mayores.
Dr. Vargas:	Son cuatro hermanos entonces. ¿Cómo están ellos de salud?
Sr. Flores:	Todos están bien, gracias a Dios. Pero mi hermano menor, Pablito, padece del asma y usa una pompa. Cuando está muy mal, usa la máquina para nebulizar el medicamento.
Dr. Vargas:	Y usted, ¿tiene algún problema médico?
Sr. Flores:	Tengo tres enfermedades. Diabetes, la presión alta y el colesterol alto.
Dr. Vargas:	¿Usa insulina?
Sr. Flores:	No. No la necesito. Tomo una pastilla dos veces al día.
Dr. Vargas:	¿En qué trabaja usted?
Sr. Flores:	Soy contable y trabajo para un banco internacional.
Dr. Vargas:	¿Toma café?
Sr. Flores:	Sí. Tomo una taza por la mañana y una a como las tres de la tarde.
Dr. Vargas:	¿Toma bebidas alcohólicas?
Sr. Flores:	Tomo cerveza.
Dr. Vargas:	¿Cuánto toma y con qué frecuencia?
Sr. Flores:	Nada los días laborales. Los fines de semana tomo como dos o tres botellas de cerveza al día.
Dr. Vargas:	¿Fuma?

Sr. Flores: No, no fumo. Me disgusta el olor de los cigarrillos.

Dr. Vargas: ¿Fuma marihuana o usa alguna droga ilegal como la cocaína o la heroína?

Sr. Flores: No, doctor. Nada de eso.

Dr. Vargas: Muy bien.

HACIA FLUIDEZ

 ### 5.22 Actividad

Work with a partner to ask each other the following comprehension questions based on the video.

A. ¿Están vivos los padres del Sr. Flores?

B. ¿De qué murieron?

C. ¿Tiene hermanos el Sr. Flores?

D. ¿Sufre el Sr. Flores de algún problema médico?

E. ¿Necesita el Sr. Flores usar insulina?

F. ¿En qué trabaja él?

G. ¿Toma bebidas alcohólicas el Sr. Flores?

H. ¿Fuma el Sr. Flores?

 ### 5.23 Actividad

Improvise skits in which a practitioner interviews a patient to determine his or her family medical history, personal history, current conditions, and habits with regard to alcohol and tobacco. If desired, assign unusual roles, such as a hypochondriac or a "heart attack waiting to happen."

 ### 5.24 Drama imprevisto

Play the game show "Competitive Hypochondriac." Choose a panel of students. Each contestant tells of his or her aches, pains, injuries, and personal and family medical history. The object of the game is to amplify your own complaints while minimizing those of your opponents. A host should keep score using hyperbole in the assignment of points.

La pronunciación de *B* y *V* (*Pronunciation of* B *and* V)

• The letters *b* and *v* are pronounced very similarly, both spoken a little more softly than the English "b," and neither quite like the English "v." Prior to 2010 in many geographical regions, their names in Spanish were *be* and *ve*. Because the letters and their names sounded alike, Spanish-speakers would request clarification by asking, *¿«V» de vaca, o «b» de burro?* or *¿«V» corta o «b» larga?* To help with this, in 2010 the *Real Academia Española* confirmed that the letter *v* should be called *uve*, and the letter *w* should be called *doble uve*. The complete Spanish alphabet appears in appendix 1.

 vaca COW

• Practice the following words, and then try a pair of *trabalenguas*.

biopsia	fiebre	aborto
varicela	viruela	vivir

Veinte viudas con venas varicosas viven en una vivienda vieja.
¿Qué bebe el bebé? El bebé bebe leche buena de un biberón blanco.

♻ 5.25 Reciclaje

Here's a description of *tío* Alfredo and why he is important: *Mi tío Alfredo es rubio. Es alto y delgado. Trabaja como profesor y siempre llega tarde a la escuela. Es muy importante porque cuida a mi tía.* Describe *tía* Mercedes.

Tío Alfredo

Tía Mercedes

5.26 Reciclaje

Take a blank sheet of paper and pretend it is a family photo or bring your own family photo. Use adjectives from chapter 1 as well as your new verbs to describe family members and to say why they are important to you. Note that in the list that follows, we have replaced *gordo/a* with the more clinical adjective *sobrepeso/a*. It is used with the verb *estar,* because it is a state or condition.

rubio/a	moreno/a	anciano/a	joven
alto/a	bajo/a	delgado/a	mediano/a
sobrepeso/a	bonito/a	guapo/a	bueno/a
inteligente	simpático/a	amable	agradable

 ## 5.27 Reciclaje

Recycle the names for injuries from chapter 3 and the names for family relationships. You are an emergency room nurse, and your partner plays the roles of various family members, changing his or her voice as needed. Role-play a skit in which you call the home of a patient who was in an accident. You wish to speak with a parent, however the phone gets passed around to other family members who ask about the situation but are not parents.

Cultural Note: *La familia*

In North America an agrarian, extended family was typical prior to the industrialization that occurred between the world wars. As people in search of work moved farther from their parents, this multigenerational family shrank to a smaller, idealized nuclear family composed of father, mother, brothers, and sisters.

Often the Latino family is an extended family. Speaking of *mi familia,* one may have in mind aunts, uncles, and cousins as well as brothers, sisters, and in-laws. This is no surprise to health care workers who have had the responsibility of limiting the number of visitors at the bedside. In some countries, a family member must stay with a hospi-

Un grupo de hermanos celebra un cumpleaños.

talized patient for the purpose of delivering food, providing personal care, and making trips to a local pharmacy to purchase medications.

A *padrino* (godfather) or *madrina* (godmother) has almost equal standing with a parent, having promised to raise the child in the event the parents cannot. The child is expected to respect a godparent as a parent, although godparents count primarily as a support to the parents, or *compadres.* A hospital security guard outside the intensive care unit of a North American hospital once told a family member that visits were restricted to "immediate family only," to which the visitor replied, "I am his godfather."

Although children are highly valued and well cared for, they are not always the center of attention at family gatherings. In times past, an old saying dictated that *los muchachos hablan cuando las gallinas orinan* ("children talk when chickens urinate," which meant, "children should be seen and not heard").

Family boundaries are flexible. Even a neighbor can be considered part of the family. A close friend might be called *primo,* or cousin. People say of these relationships, *Somos como familia,* or "We're just like family." This may lead to misunderstanding.

The Latino family is a strong, primary support network for its members. Immigrants to the United States who are separated from family and homeland may suffer a profound sense of loss—greater than a clinician from a (now typical) North American nuclear family might expect. Many who emigrate leave their family reluctantly to work abroad and send money to support those who remain. They may leave behind children in the care of other relatives. This personal sacrifice is often misunderstood by people whose culture defines the family more narrowly. Individuals separated from their family through unresolved conflict or family dysfunction may have a heightened sense of shame, loneliness, or abandonment.

Some Spanish-speakers say, *Tengo tres hermanos;* others say, *Somos cuatro hermanos.* The latter demonstrates a cultural view that includes oneself in the count, unlike the concept of sibling rivalry. This is an example of the relation between worldview and language.

When working with a Latino family, a helper must assess the degree to which the family has retained, for its members, its highly influential cultural value. Family boundaries may be vague. Policies regarding confidentiality of a patient vis-à-vis the family may be misunderstood. What the broad family system believes about the nature of the distress itself will be a powerful factor in the patient's view of the problem being treated. The worth of the family to the individual and of the individual to the family must never be underestimated.

Chapter 6
La farmacia

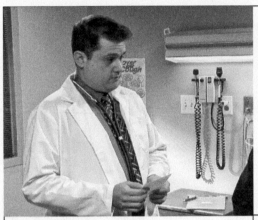

Communication Goals

Vocabulary

Structure

Video

Cultural Note

By the end of this chapter you will be able to write and explain basic instructions for taking medicines. You will be able to ask about drug allergies and educate patients about side effects and allergic reactions. You will know how to make polite and direct commands and to use these when educating patients about medication regimens, the management of asthma, and the use of pill organizers.

From here on, instructions for exercises and activities will appear in Spanish. This key will get you started. The verbs are used as formal commands, which you'll learn in this chapter.

agregue	add
colabore	collaborate
complete	complete
conteste	answer
escoja	choose
escriba	write
exponga	present
hable con compañeros/as	talk with classmates
haga oraciones completas	make complete sentences
identifique	identify
observe, vea	observe, see

Give Medication Instructions

In some areas, the pharmacist is the most accessible health care provider. Many people will consult a pharmacist prior to going to see a doctor. The pharmacist may dispense a medication that would be controlled elsewhere. Many countries are trying to end this practice because of the emergence of treatment-resistant infections. Mexico, for example, recently required that antibiotics be dispensed only with a prescription. In response, larger pharmacy chains offered free medical consultations on premises.

The noun *receta,* which is used for "prescription," also means "recipe," revealing some history of pharmacotherapy. The verb *recetar* means "to prescribe." While medicines were traditionally called *medicamentos,* the expression *medicina* has become common as well.

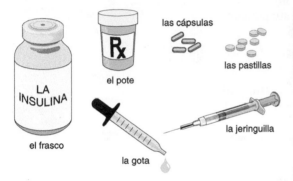

Formas de medicamentos

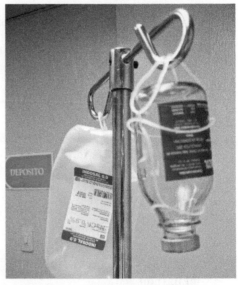

El suero es una solución de cloruro de sodio para hidratar al paciente por vía intravenosa.

Vocabulario: Formas de medicamento
(*Forms of Medication*)

Las tabletas

la tableta, la pastilla	tablet, pill
la píldora, el comprimido	tablet, pill
masticable	chewable

media tableta   half of a tablet
la cápsula, la gragea   capsule
el frasco, la botella   pill bottle, bottle

Las inyecciones e infusiones

la inyección   injection
la jeringuilla   syringe
el suero, el intravenoso   IV
el suero central   central IV line

Los líquidos

el jarabe   syrup
el elíxir   elixir
la suspensión   suspension

Los medicamentos tópicos

la crema   cream, ointment
el ungüento   ointment, balm

The *ü* in *ungüento* is pronounced like English "w."

Otras formas

el aerosol   aerosol
el gel   gel
la gota   drop
el inhalador, la pompa (*slang*)   inhaler
la inhalación   inhalation
el nebulizador (la máquina)   nebulizer (machine)
el parche   patch
el supositorio   suppository

Preguntas útiles

¿Es usted alérgico/a a algún medicamento?   Are you allergic to any medication?
¿Tiene usted alergia a algún medicamento?   Do you have an allergy to any medication?
¿Toma algún medicamento todos los días?   Do you take any medicine every day?
¿Necesita una receta nueva?   Do you need a new prescription?

Expresiones útiles

Hay que darle dos pastillas.   You must give him/her two pills.

La farmacia está abierta.

La Furoxona CP
es una suspensión
antidiarreica.

HACIA PRECISIÓN

   6.1 Ejercicio

Identifique las formas comunes de los siguientes (*following*) medicamentos. Por ejemplo,

la aspirina —pastilla y pastilla masticable

A. la nicotina
B. la leche de magnesia
C. el Pepto Bismol
D. la Visene
E. la insulina
F. el albuterol

G. la guaifenesina
H. la hidrocortisona 2%
I. el paregórico
J. la compazina
K. la vacuna para la varicela
L. el ibuprofeno

   6.2 Ejercicio

Haga oraciones completas con la forma correcta del verbo *tomar*.

A. Usted _____ (tomar) antiácidos por la noche.

B. Doña Violeta _____ (tomar) una aspirina todos los días.

C. Tú _____ (tomar) medicamento para los ataques epilépticos.

D. Mi esposa y yo _____ (tomar) la vitamina B 12 («be doce») por la mañana.

E. El señor Altamirano _____ (tomar) un diurético para quitar el agua.

F. Los padres de Juan _____ (tomar) medicamento para la hipertensión.

G. Los pacientes _____ (tomar) antibióticos para curar las infecciones bacterianas.

6.3 Actividad

This worksheet is available for download from the Web site.

Haga una encuesta (*survey*). Hable con cinco compañeros/as y en los espacios, escriba los nombres de los/las compañeros/as que toman aspirina, vitaminas o antiácidos, las horas que los toman y su preferencia de analgésico. Después, hable de los resultados.

Modelo:　¿Toma usted una aspirina todos los días?
　　　　　¿A qué hora la toma?
　　　　　¿Qué toma cuando tiene dolor de cabeza?

Nombre de compañero/a	Aspirina, sí o no y la hora	Vitamina, sí o no y la hora	Antiácido, sí o no y la hora	Preferencia de analgésico

Estructura: Los imperativos con *favor de, hay que* y *tener que* (*Commands with* favor de, hay que, *and* tener que)

• There is a gentle way to make a request. Use *favor de* and a verb infinitive (the *-r* form).

Favor de sentarse.　　　　Please sit down.
Favor de llamar a la clínica.　Please call the clinic.

• For a less personal request, use *hay que* or *es importante* and an infinitive. (*Hay* rhymes with the English word "buy" and means "there is" and "there are.") This tells something that ought to be done.

> Hay que tomar la medicina (*One ought to take the medicine*).
> Es importante tomar mucha agua con el medicamento.
> Hay que tomar el medicamento a la misma hora todos los días.

• A stronger or more direct command is to tell the patient that he or she "has to" do something. For this, you may use *tener que* and an infinitive. In such two-verb combinations, the first verb is conjugated and the second verb is not.

> Tienes que tomar la tableta.   You have to take the pill.
> Usted tiene que ir al laboratorio.   You have to go to the laboratory.

• To clarify whether the patient understood the instruction, choose content-related questions that cannot be answered with "yes" or "no."

> ¿A qué hora toma el ibuprofeno?
> ¿Cuántas pastillas toma a las nueve?

HACIA PRECISIÓN

6.4 Ejercicio

Escoja la forma apropiada para dar las siguientes instrucciones. Escoja entre *favor de, hay que* y *tener que.* Por ejemplo,

> Usar la nitroglicerina cuando le duele el pecho.
> —Tiene que usar la nitroglicerina cuando le duele el pecho.

> A. Llamar a la clínica mañana.
> B. Esperar por cinco minutos.
> C. Comer más frutas y vegetales.
> D. Tomar una aspirina de 81 miligramos todos los días.
> E. Usar la insulina después de comer (*after eating*).
> F. Tomar 2 acetaminofén cuando le duele la cabeza.
> G. Hacer una cita en la clínica ambulatoria.
> H. Usar el inhalador y llamar al 9-11 cuando tiene un episodio agudo del asma.

Vocabulario: Instrucciones para la dosificación y vías de administración
(Dosing Instructions and Routes of Administration)

La dosis *(Dosage)*

pastilla o tableta	pill
cucharadita	teaspoonful
cucharada	tablespoonful
miligramo	milligram
mililitro	milliliter

La vía de administración *(Route of Administration)*

tomar, poner, inyectar, aplicar	to take, to put, to inject, to apply
por vía intravenosa, por suero	intravenously
por vía oral, por la boca	by mouth
por vía intramuscular	intramuscularly
por vía subcutánea	subcutaneously
por inhalación	by inhalation
debajo de la lengua	under the tongue
en el ojo derecho/izquierdo	in the right/left eye
en el oído derecho/izquierdo	in the right/left ear
por la nariz	in the nose
por el ano, por el recto	in the anus, in the rectum
por la vagina	in the vagina
en el área afectada	to the affected area

La frecuencia *(Frequency)*

una vez al día, diario	once per day, daily
. . . veces al día	. . . times a day
cada . . . horas	every . . . hours
a las 9 de la mañana/noche	at 9 a.m. / p.m.
por la mañana/noche	in the morning / at night
al acostarse	at bedtime
un día sí, un día no; en días alternos	every other day
todos los días	every day
por . . . días	for . . . days
media hora antes de comer	a half hour before eating
una hora después de comer	an hour after eating
con las comidas	with meals
con leche	with milk

con mucha agua	with plenty of water
cuando sea necesario	as needed
sin falta	without fail

El propósito (*Purpose*)

para el dolor	for pain
para dormir	for sleep
para la fatiga	for shortness of breath
para quitar la picazón	to take away the itching
para bajar el colesterol	to lower cholesterol
para aliviar la ansiedad	to relieve anxiety
para eliminar el agua	to eliminate water
para evitar el embarazo	to avoid pregnancy

Dra. María Peña Robles de Jiménez
Calle del sol 3759
Cuernavaca, Morelos, México

Rx   Por 60 cc
         frasco #2

Amoxicilina Suspensión
     250 mg / 5 ml
USO: Tome 5cc por vía oral
    cada 8 horas por 5 días

Licencia número 5632145

Estructura: El imperativo formal
(*Formal* [usted] *Commands*)

• You learned several ways to give commands in the context of the pharmacy. These were versatile and uncomplicated, because the verb representing the action remained in its infinitive form.

Favor de + infinitivo	Favor de llegar a tiempo.
Hay que + infinitivo	Hay que tomar la tableta con mucha agua.
Es importante + infinitivo	Es importante tomar el antibiótico por 5 días.
Tener que + infinitivo	Tiene que tomar la medicina con comida.

• Spanish-speakers also use direct commands, which are especially useful when a concise imperative is appropriate. When stitching a laceration, you might say, "Don't move!" During a physical exam you might say, "Breathe deeply!" and during an x-ray you might say, "Don't breathe."

• Here is how to make a formal (*usted*) command. Remove the *-o* from the first person singular form of the present tense and then add *-e* for verbs that end in *-ar* and *-a* for verbs that end in *-er* or *-ir*.

respirar	¡Respire profundamente!	Breathe deeply!
toser	¡Tosa! / ¡No tosa!	Cough! / Don't cough!

• This formula accommodates verbs that have an irregular first person singular (*yo*) form, such as *poner*. To say "Put the nitroglycerine under your tongue," think in two steps. The first person singular of *poner* ("to put") is *pongo;* and as the verb infinitive ends in *-er,* the formal command is *ponga.*

Ponga la nitroglicerina debajo de la lengua.

• Of course native and fluent speakers do not have to think first about construction. For novices, however, this shortcut may help: "Think *yo* and use the wrong letter." In chapter 12 you'll learn informal commands, which are used with children.

 Video: *Cómo usar el inhalador*

Vea la *Demostración* del capítulo 6, donde el doctor Vargas usa los imperativos formales para explicar cómo usar un inhalador.

HACIA PRECISIÓN

 6.5 Ejercicio

Esta es una transcripción de la demostración *Cómo usar el inhalador*. En los siguientes espacios, escriba los imperativos formales correctos de los siguientes verbos.

agitar	to shake	**inhalar**	to inhale
quitar	to remove	**oprimir**	to press

exhalar	to exhale	**contener***	to contain
mantener*	to maintain	**retirar**	to retire
abrir	to open	**enjuagar*** *	to rinse
poner	to put		

*Mantener and contener are like tener (the yo form ends in -go).
**Enjuagar requires an added u to maintain its g sound. ¡Enjuague!

Quiero enseñarles cómo usar el inhalador para recibir el máximo beneficio

del medicamento. Primero, _____ (agitar) bien el inhalador. Así.

_____ (quitar) la tapa protectora. _____ (exhalar) completamente

a través de su nariz y _____ (mantener) la boca cerrada. _____

(abrir) la boca completamente y _____ (poner) la boquilla a una o dos

pulgadas de su boca. Así. _____ (inhalar) lentamente y profundamente

y, al mismo tiempo, _____ (oprimir) la parte de abajo del envase para

rociar el medicamento en la boca. Así. _____ (contener) el aliento

durante cinco a diez segundos, _____ (retirar) el inhalador y _____

(exhalar) lentamente a través de la nariz o boca. Así. _____ (poner) la

tapa protectora en el inhalador. Después de cada tratamiento, _____

(enjuagar) su boca con agua o enjuague bucal.

6.6 Ejercicio

Favor de dar las siguientes instrucciones en español. Use el imperativo formal en vez de (*instead of*) el infinitivo. Por ejemplo,

Tomar 2 pastillas dos veces al día para eliminar el agua.
—Tome 2 pastillas dos veces al día para eliminar el agua.

A. Tomar 1 pastilla cada 4 horas.
B. Tomar 1 cucharadita por la mañana y 2 al acostarse.
C. Tomar el medicamento con leche.

D. Tomar 1 pastilla 4 veces al día por 10 días.

E. Tomar mucha agua con el medicamento.

F. Tomar 1 cucharada por la mañana.

G. Tomar 2 pastillas cada 4 horas cuando sea necesario para el dolor.

H. Poner 2 gotas en cada ojo 2 veces al día.

I. Aplicar la crema por la mañana y por la noche.

J. Inyectar 2 cc («ce ce») por vía intramuscular 1 vez al mes.

 ## 6.7 Ejercicio

Use el imperativo formal para dar las siguientes instrucciones en español. Es importante escribir números árabes (1, 2, 3) en vez de palabras. Por ejemplo,

Ibuprofen 600 mg, take 1 tablet by mouth 3 times a day.
—Ibuprofeno 600 mg, tome 1 tableta por la boca 3 veces al día.

A. Take the medicine every day without fail.

B. Amoxicilina (250 mg/5 ml), take 1 teaspoonful 3 times a day for 5 days.

C. Guaifenesina, take 1 tablespoonful 4 times a day for congestion.

D. Salbutamol, take 1 puff (*inhalación*) every 4 to 6 hours as needed for shortness of breath.

E. Donepezilo, take 10 mg by mouth once a day in the morning.

F. Acetaminofén, take 2 tablets every 4 to 6 hours as needed for pain.

G. Mylanta, take 2 tablespoonfuls at bedtime.

H. Isoniazid, take 1 tablet every day in the morning.

I. Phenytoin 100 mg, take 1 capsule 3 times a day.

J. Loperamide, take 1 capsule every 2 to 3 hours as needed for diarrhea.

Video: *¿Qué medicamentos toma?*

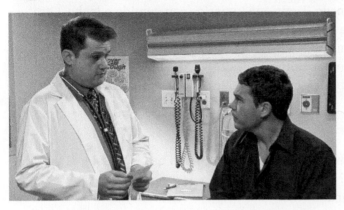

Vea la *Trama* del capítulo 6, donde el doctor Vargas habla con el señor Flores sobre sus alergias de medicamentos y sus medicamentos actuales.

Dr. Vargas: Señor Flores, ¿es usted alérgico a algún medicamento?

Sr. Flores: No tengo ninguna alergia.

Dr. Vargas: No tiene alergia a nada.

Sr. Flores: Perdón. Creo que soy alérgico a la penicilina.

Dr. Vargas: ¿Qué pasa cuando toma la penicilina?

Sr. Flores: La penicilina me da problemas con la piel. Cuando la tomo me pican los brazos.

Dr. Vargas: Cuando toma la penicilina, ¿se le hincha la cara o los labios o tiene dificultad para tragar?

Sr. Flores: No.

Dr. Vargas: Cuando toma la penicilina, ¿tiene dificultad para respirar?

Sr. Flores: No, gracias a Dios.

Dr. Vargas: ¿Toma algún medicamento todos los días?

Sr. Flores: Sí, aquí está la lista de mis medicamentos.

Dr. Vargas: A ver. El lisinopril. Es para la presión arterial. ¿Cuánto toma?

Sr. Flores: Del lisinopril tomo una pastilla de cinco miligramos dos veces al día. Una por la mañana con el desayuno y la otra en la noche antes de acostarme.

Dr. Vargas: ¿Tiene efectos secundarios, como hinchazón de la cara o la garganta?

Sr. Flores: No.

Dr. Vargas: La hidroclorotiazida. Es también para la hipertensión, como el lisinopril. Es un diurético, para eliminar el líquido del cuerpo. ¿Cuánta hidroclorotiazida toma?

Sr. Flores: Tomo cincuenta miligramos al día. Las pastillas son de veinticinco miligramos, y tomo dos pastillas por la mañana.

Dr. Vargas: El lisinopril y la hidroclorotiazida pueden provocar problemas con el estómago. Tiene que tomarlos con comida o leche. Otra vez a la lista . . . La metformina es para la diabetes tipo dos. ¿Cuánta toma?

Sr. Flores: Tomo quinientos miligramos dos veces al día.

Dr. Vargas: ¿Tiene algunos efectos secundarios como náusea o vómitos?

Sr. Flores: No.

Dr. Vargas: ¿Diarrea?

Sr. Flores: No.

Dr. Vargas: Bien. Finalmente, el salbutamol. ¿Usted usa la tableta, el líquido o el aerosol?

Sr. Flores: Es una pompa.

Dr. Vargas: El inhalador, entonces. ¿Con qué frecuencia lo usa?

Sr. Flores: Como dos veces al día, pero sólo cuando tengo fatiga.

Dr. Vargas: Bien. Lisinopril, hidroclorotiazida, metformina y salbutamol. Usted toma cuatro medicamentos. Toma tres medicamentos todos los días y sólo usa el inhalador cuando tiene dificultad para respirar. ¿Siempre toma los medicamentos todos los días?

Sr. Flores: Sí. Mi esposa Marisol insiste.

> **insistir**   to insist
> **de acuerdo**   agreed

Dr. Vargas: Me alegro. Es muy importante tomar todos los medicamentos de la manera indicada. Llámame si tiene un problema con los medicamentos.

Sr. Flores: Está bien. De acuerdo.

HACIA PRECISIÓN

 ## 6.8 Ejercicio

> This blank prescription is available for download from the Web site.

Escriba las recetas para renovar (*to renew*) los medicamentos del Sr. Flores por un mes. Escríbalas aquí o en el formulario que puedes descargar de nuestro *Web site*.

A. _____

B. _____

C. _____

D. _____

Dr. Mario Solano Cruz
Calle del Sol 35
Cuernavaca, Morelos

Rx

Lic. 16874688

HACIA FLUIDEZ

 ### 6.9 Actividad

Hágale a un/a compañero/a las siguientes preguntas basadas en el video.

A. ¿Es el señor Flores alérgico a algún medicamento? ¿Qué le pasa cuando lo toma?
B. ¿Cuáles medicamentos toma el Sr. Flores todos los días?
C. ¿De cuáles enfermedades crónicas sufre el Sr. Flores?
D. ¿Tiene el Sr. Flores efectos secundarios de la metformina?
E. ¿Usa el Sr. Flores un medicamento de alivio rápido para el asma?
F. ¿Con qué frecuencia usa el inhalador?

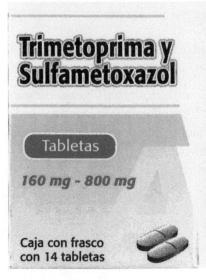

Trimetoprima y Sulfametoxazol

Tabletas

160 mg - 800 mg

Caja con frasco
con 14 tabletas

FORMULA:
Cada tableta contiene:
Trimetoprima .... 160 mg
Sulfametoxazol .... 800 mg
Excipiente cbp .... 1 tableta

VIA DE ADMINISTRACION: Oral.
DOSIS: La que el médico señale.
Consérvese el frasco bien tapado a temperatura ambiente a no más de 30°C y en lugar seco. Protéjase de la luz. Su venta requiere receta médica. No se administre durante el embarazo, lactancia, ni en niños menores de 3 meses. Este medicamento no deberá administrarse por períodos prolongados sin estricta vigilancia médica. No se deje al alcance de los niños.
Reg. No. 0310M79 SSA IV

La combinación de trimetoprima y sulfametoxazol es un antibiótico para combatir infecciones en el tracto urinario, el sistema digestivo y las vías respiratorias.

Vocabulario: Algunas clases de medicamentos
(*Some Classes of Medications*)

el analgésico, el calmante	analgesic
el antiácido	antacid
el antialérgico, el antihistamínico	antihistamine
el antibiótico	antibiotic
el anticoagulante	anticoagulant
el anticolinérgico	anticholinergic
el anticonvulsivo	anticonvulsive
el antidepresivo	antidepressant
el antidiarreico	antidiarrheal
el antiespasmódico	antispasmodic
el antigripal	cold reliever
el antihipertensivo	antihypertensive
el antiinflamatorio no esteroide (AINES)	nonsteroidal antiinflammatory drug (NSAID)
el antipirético, el antitérmico	antipyretic
el antitusígeno	cough suppressant
el barbitúrico	barbiturate
el broncodilatador	bronchodilator
el descongestionante	decongestant
el diurético	diuretic
el esteroide	steroid
el expectorante	expectorant
el laxante	laxative
la pastilla anticonceptiva	birth-control pill
la pastilla para bajar de peso	diet pill
la pastilla para dormir	sleeping pill
el sedante, el calmante	sedative
el tranquilizante	tranquilizer
la vitamina	vitamin

The NSAIDs can be called *calmante, analgésico,* or *antipirético,* depending on the use. Some immigrants may not be familiar with brand names for certain medicines. They may be more familiar with generic names like *acetaminofén* or *ibuprofeno,* because pharmaceutical companies in the patient's country of origin may have their own brand names or may import generic medications. Paracetamol is a universal generic name for acetaminophen.

HACIA PRECISIÓN

 ## 6.10 Ejercicio

Identifique la forma y la clase de medicamento o el propósito de los siguientes productos. Favor de usar oraciones completas. Por ejemplo,

Maalox

—Maalox es una suspensión. Es un antiácido. Es para aliviar
la acidez estomacal.

A. Advil
B. Proventil
C. Bactrim
D. Coumadin
E. Tylenol
F. Valium

G. Ex-Lax
H. Benadryl
I. One-a-Day
J. Pepto Bismol
K. Robitussin DM
L. la crema hidrocortizona 2 por ciento

HACIA FLUIDEZ

 ## 6.11 Drama imprevisto

The instructor will hand out two index cards to each student. On card one, write the class of a medication, e.g., *antibiótico*. On the other card, write a symptom or illness that might respond to that medication, e.g., *una infección en los oídos*. Next, the instructor should collect and redistribute the cards containing symptoms or illnesses. Students will then circulate in the room, speaking only Spanish, until they locate the student with the appropriate treatment for their condition. For example,

—Tengo una infección en los oídos. ¿Qué medicamento tienes?
—Tengo un antibiótico.

Here are some ideas for cards.

Card 1	Card 2	Card 1	Card 2
antidiarreico	diarrea	antigripal	gripe
analgésico	dolor de cabeza	antihipertensivo	hipertensión
antiácido	acidez	antitusígeno	tos
antihistamínico	alergia	laxante	estreñimiento
anticonvulsivo	convulsiones	pastilla para dormir	insomnia

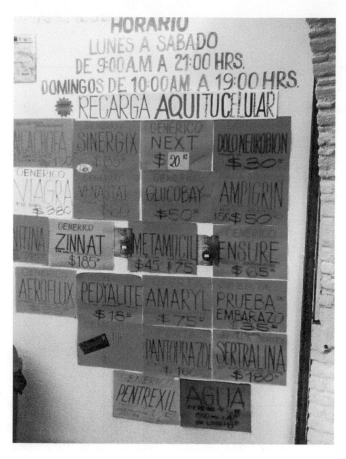

¿Para qué son algunos de estos medicamentos? ¿Cuánto cuestan (en pesos mexicanos)?

Estructura: Los adjetivos demostrativos y los adjetivos afirmativos y negativos
(*Demonstrative, Affirmative, and Negative Adjectives*)

• The demonstrative adjectives specify a particular person or thing. These are demonstrative adjectives.

	Singular	*Plural*	*Inglés*
Masculino	este	estos	this, these
Femenino	esta	estas	this, these

• The demonstrative adjective must agree in gender and number with the noun that it modifies.

Este medicamento es para el dolor.
Estos supositorios son para la nausea.
Esta inyección es para quitar (no escuchar) las voces.
Estas pastillas son para la diarrea.

- These adjectives may be used in affirmative and negative sentences:

	Singular	*Plural*	*Inglés*
Masculino	alguno, algún	algunos	some, any
	ninguno, ningún*		not any
Femenino	alguna	algunas	some, any
	ninguna*		not any

*The negative adjectives are almost always used in the singular form.

- *Alguno* and *ninguno* drop the *-o* before a masculine singular noun, but *alguna* and *ninguna* keep the final *-a.*

> ¿Es usted alérgico a algún medicamento?
> No. No soy alérgico a ningún medicamento.
> ¿Sufre usted de alguna enfermedad?

- The double negative is necessary. Think in terms of agreement. In an affirmative sentence, use the affirmative adjective. In a negative sentence, use the negative adjective.

> ¿Toma algún medicamento todos los días?
> No, no tomo ningún medicamento.

HACIA PRECISIÓN

 ## 6.12 Ejercicio

Use el adjetivo demostrativo apropiado (*este, estos, esta, estas*) para explicarle a don Ignacio los beneficios anticipados de sus medicamentos.

Don Ignacio, es muy importante usar _____ medicamentos en la

manera indicada. _____ crema es para aliviar el dolor de la quemadura.

En caso de fiebre, _____ pastillas son para quitar la fiebre. Si tiene

mucho dolor, _____ pastillas son para el dolor. _____ jarabe es

para la tos. Si está peor mañana, favor de llamar a _____ número

de teléfono. Finalmente, _____ recetas son para comprar más

medicamentos.

Ask about Medication Allergies and Educate Patients about Allergic Reactions

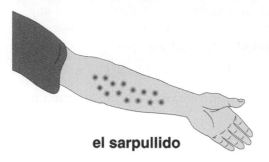

el sarpullido

Vocabulario: Las reacciones alérgicas
(Allergic Reactions)

la alergia	allergy
la anafilaxis	anaphylactic shock
el eccema	eczema
la epenefrina, la adrenalina	epinephrine, adrenaline
la erupción (manchas rojas)	rash (red marks)
la falta de aire	shortness of breath
la hinchazón	swelling
el jadeo	gasping
la picazón, la comezón	itch, itching
la raquiña (*slang*)	itching
el sarpullido, las ronchas	hives
el silbido	wheeze

Lectura: Los efectos secundarios
(Side Effects and Adverse Reactions)

Los doctores recetan los medicamentos para los beneficios de curar enfermedades o aliviar síntomas. Muchos medicamentos también tienen efectos secundarios. A veces los efectos secundarios son molestos pero desaparecen con el tiempo o con bajar la dosis. Los efectos secundarios incluyen náusea, mareo, indigestión, vómito, estreñimiento, diarrea, sequedad en la boca, dolor de cabeza, insomnio, irritabilidad y el sueño.

molesto bothersome
sequedad dryness

Muchas veces los efectos secundarios son benignos, pero algunas personas tienen una reacción alérgica. La reacción alérgica ocurre cuando el sistema inmunológico responde al medicamento. La reacción alérgica más severa es la anafilaxis. Los síntomas de una reacción alérgica incluyen hinchazón, picazón, manchas rojas, inflamación en la garganta, asma, ritmo cardíaco irregular y/o dificultad para respirar. La dificultad para respirar siempre es una emergencia médica. Hay que llamar al doctor o al hospital inmediatamente si tiene una reacción alérgica después de tomar un medicamento.

Educate a Patient about Asthma

 Lectura: El asma (*Asthma*)

El asma es una enfermedad crónica de los bronquios que causa inflamación en los pulmones y las vías respiratorias. Es una patología frecuente en la infancia, pero solo un 4 por ciento persiste con asma a los dieciocho años. El asma no es contagiosa. Durante un ataque (un episodio agudo) del asma, el paciente sufre de dificultad para respirar. Otros síntomas incluyen:

la crisis de tos	coughing spell
los jadeos	gasping, panting
los silbidos	wheezing
la falta de aire	shortness of breath
la dificultad para respirar	shortness of breath
el pecho apretado	tight chest
la respiración silbante	wheezing
la dificultad para hablar	difficulty speaking
la comezón en la barbilla o garganta	itching in the chin or throat

El asma no tiene cura pero es posible controlar los síntomas con medicamentos que un doctor receta. Es necesario tener un cuidado médico continuo para controlar el asma. Todas las personas que sufren de asma necesitan un medicamento de alivio rápido para usar durante un ataque. Muchas personas necesitan también usar todos los días un medicamento preventivo. Los medicamentos son en forma líquida, en forma de tableta o cápsula y en aerosol (para inhalar). Los antiinflamatorios son medicamentos preventivos y los broncodilatadores son para el tratamiento de episodios agudos.

También hay que evitar las cosas que provocan los ataques. Algunas de las cosas que provocan los ataques son:

el polen y el polvo	pollen and dust
los ácaros del polvo	dust mites
las cucarachas	cockroaches
el moho	mold
la caspa de animal	animal dander
el humo	smoke
las alergias	allergies

las alfombras	carpets
los perfumes	perfumes
el frío	cold weather
el ejercicio físico	physical exercise
las infecciones virales	viral infections

Algunos episodios o ataques de asma son severos y son una emergencia médica de vida o muerte. Es necesario llamar al doctor o a la clínica si el efecto del medicamento de alivio rápido dura menos de cuatro horas (o si no quita la tos o la respiración silbante). Es importante tener un plan para ir al hospital cuando el medicamento no alivia los síntomas y la respiración está rápida y difícil.

HACIA FLUIDEZ

 6.13 Actividad

Haga y conteste estas preguntas con un/a compañero/a para confirmar su comprensión.

A. ¿Son todos los efectos secundarios una emergencia médica?
B. ¿Cuál es la reacción alérgica más severa?
C. ¿Cuáles son los síntomas de la anafilaxis?
D. ¿Qué tienen en común un ataque de asma y una reacción alérgica?
E. ¿Es el asma una enfermedad contagiosa?
F. ¿Cuáles son algunos de los alérgenos que provocan el asma?
G. ¿Qué es un medicamento de alivio rápido?
H. ¿Cuándo es necesario usar un medicamento de alivio rápido?
I. ¿Cuándo es necesario llamar al doctor o a la clínica?
J. ¿Cuándo es necesario ir rápidamente al hospital?

 6.14 Drama imprevisto

Work with a partner to make a skit in which a practitioner educates the parent of a child with asthma about the disease and ways to control it. Discuss an emergency plan for when rescue medication (*un medicamento de alivio rápido*) does not resolve an acute episode. Instead of acting out your skit with your partner, switch partners in order to demonstrate a less-scripted and more spontaneous version for the class. Parents of the child may choose to play the role of an exceptionally nervous parent or a parent who minimizes the possible dangers.

Ask Who Helps an Infirm Family Member

Estructura: Los complementos indirectos y el verbo *dar* (*Indirect Objects and the Verb* Dar)

• Unlike direct objects, which represent the person or thing that directly receives the action of the verb, indirect objects indicate to whom or for whom something is done. They are almost always necessary, as they indicate the beneficiary of a transitive verb.

• The indirect objects are *me, te, le, nos,* and *les*.

Me duele el brazo.	My arm hurts (me).
Te cuido al niño.	I take care of the child for you.
Le escribo una receta.	I write you/him/her a prescription.
El radiólogo **nos** lee la placa.	The radiologist reads the film for us.
Les compro la medicina.	I buy the medicine for them.

• The indirect object *le* is both masculine and feminine, and therefore less specific than *me, te,* and *nos. Le* can mean to or for "you," "him," or "her." It is often clarified by using *a* and a more specific designation of the beneficiary of the action.

La ortopedista **me** examina la rodilla.
El doctor **le** receta un medicamento **a Javier**.

• Study the following sentences, and note that the direct object pronouns represent the direct receiver of the action, and the indirect object pronouns represent the person to whom or for whom the action is being done.

Indirect Objects	*Direct Objects*
El doctor **le** pone puntos **al niño**.	El doctor **lo** cuida bien.
Le examino los oídos **a usted**.	**Los** examino ahora.
Le pongo una inyección **a José**.	**La** pongo ahora.

El acetaminofén pediátrico es para los niños con dolor o con fiebre. No les dé aspirina para la fiebre.

• Dar (*to give*) takes an irregular form in the first person singular, and is a verb that is frequently used in the context of the pharmacy. *Dar* commonly uses an indirect object to represent the person to/for whom something is given.

Le doy acetaminofén al bebé.	I give acetaminophen to the baby.
¿**Le das** comida sólida al bebé?	Do you give solid food to the baby?
¿**Le da** leche del pecho al bebé?	Do you give the baby breast milk?

• With instructions that use an infinitive form of the verb, you may attach the indirect object (as a suffix) to the infinitive. As before, where increased clarity is needed, add *a* and identify the person to whom the action is to be done.

Hay que **darle al niño** el jarabe cada cuatro horas sin falta.
Usted tiene que **darle a su madre** la insulina después de comer.

• Direct and indirect objects may be used together. The indirect object always goes first. The objects may be placed before a conjugated verb or as a suffix to a verb infinitive. It makes no difference which way you do this.

La enfermera tiene que inyectar**me** la insulina.
La enfermera **me la** tiene que inyectar.
La enfermera tiene que inyectár**mela**.

• Never use two objects beginning with *l* together. When the indirect object *le* or *les* appears before the direct object *lo, la, los,* or *las,* change the indirect object to *se.* For example, "You have to give it to him every six hours."

Se lo tiene que dar cada seis horas.
Tiene que dár**selo** cada seis horas.

HACIA PRECISIÓN

 ## 6.15 Ejercicio

Agregue el complemento indirecto apropiado a las siguientes oraciones. Por ejemplo,

Receto un medicamento para su padre.
—Le receto un medicamento para su padre.

A. Receto un medicamento para sus hijos.
B. Escribo una carta a usted.
C. Llamo una ambulancia para la paciente.

D. Enseño español a los estudiantes.

E. Contesto el teléfono por la secretaria.

F. Leo el libro a usted.

G. La doctora contesta la pregunta para nosotros.

 ## 6.16 Ejercicio

Complete las oraciones con el complemento indirecto y la forma correcta del verbo indicado.

Modelo: La enfermera _____ (tomar) la temperatura (a mí).
—La enfermera __me toma__ la temperatura.

A. El doctor _____ (recetar) un medicamento para Juan.

B. La doctora _____ (preguntar) su historia médica a él.

C. Yo _____ (escribir) una carta al plan médico.

D. La anestesióloga _____ (explicar) el procedimiento (a mí).

E. El enfermero _____ (hablar) español a los pacientes.

F. Usted _____ (comprar) la medicina para sus padres.

G. La pediatra _____ (recetar) un antibiótico para mi bebé.

HACIA FLUIDEZ

6.17 Actividad

La abuela de su compañero/a está enferma y necesita ayuda. Pregúntele quién le ayuda con lo siguiente.

Modelo: cocinar
¿Quién le cocina a tu abuela?
—Mi madre le cocina todos los días.

A. ayudar con la casa
B. comprar la comida
C. hacer las citas médicas
D. recetar los medicamentos
E. enseñar a usar la insulina
F. examinar los pies para ver si hay úlceras
G. llamar al consultorio para hacer una cita con el doctor

 ### 6.18 Actividad

Observe el horario para los medicamentos de Juancito. Usted es enfermero y su compañero/a es el padre o la madre de Juancito. Pregúntale si le da los medicamentos y a qué hora se los da. Por ejemplo,

—¿Le da a Juancito la amoxicilina tres veces al día?
—Sí. Se la doy a las nueve de la mañana, la una de la tarde y las nueve de la noche.

	Hora de administración			
Medicamento	9	1	5	9
Amoxicilina, 1 cucharadita	X	X		X
Acetaminofén, 2 cucharaditas	X			X
Robitussin, 1 cucharada	X	X	X	X
El inhalador, 2 inhalaciones	X			X

 ### 6.19 Actividad

Colabore con un/a compañero/a para planear y exponer un diálogo a la clase. Estas son algunas ideas.

A. Pregúntele a su compañero/a si toma algún medicamento diario y si tiene alergia a algún medicamento.
B. Su compañero/a es alérgico/a a la penicilina. Pregúntele qué le pasa cuando toma la penicilina.
C. Explíquele a su compañero/a cómo usar un medicamento específico. Explíquele los posibles efectos secundarios.
D. Explíquele a su compañero/a los posibles problemas asociados con beber bebidas alcohólicas cuando toma un medicamento específico.

E. Explíquele a su compañero/a la vacuna para la gripe (*the flu vaccine*) y pregúntale si es alérgico/a a los huevos (*eggs*).

6.20 Drama imprevisto

El profesor debe traer un paquete grande de M&M's o Skittles. En este drama, los dulces son pastillas y cada color es un medicamento específico. Usted es enfermero y su compañero/a es paciente. Con su compañero/a, prepare y exponga un diálogo donde le explica al paciente cómo tomar el medicamento. Debe incluir el nombre del medicamento, el propósito de tomarlo, la dosis, la vía de administración, la frecuencia, los posibles efectos secundarios y qué debe hacer si tiene preguntas o problemas con el medicamento. Debe aprender los colores en español.

los rojos	the red ones	**los anaranjados**	the orange ones
los amarillos	the yellow ones	**los verdes**	the green ones
los azules	the blue ones	**los morados**	the purple ones
los marrones	the brown ones	**claros/oscuros**	light/dark

Explain How to Use a Pill Organizer

Lectura: El recordatorio de pastillas (Pill Organizer)

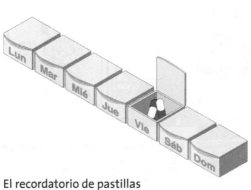

El recordatorio de pastillas

Watch for the following verbs in this description of how to use a pill organizer:

olvidar	to forget	**vender**	to sell
usar	to use	**preparar**	to prepare
poner	to put	**corresponder**	to correspond

caja box

El recordatorio de pastillas (también se llama el organizador de pastillas) es una caja que tiene siete compartimientos, uno para cada día de la semana. El recordatorio es para no olvidar tomar el medicamento. Las farmacias los ven-

titioners should consider the possible adverse effects of maintaining strict relationship boundaries on their relationships with customers from other cultures. Perhaps there is some personal information one might disclose—in the interest of making a relationship feel more natural to the patient—while not violating a necessary parameter of self-disclosure.

Many new Latino immigrants find it difficult to adjust to the time pressures of the managed care system in the United States. Returning home from the doctor's office, one new arrival began to list the questions she had wanted to ask the doctor. "It is not like my country," she said. "Here they do not sit down and talk to you; they hurry out." Courtesy and "small talk" are more conventional in Latino culture than in the managed care system, where time and efficiency may be measured in patients per hour. It may take time to warm up. One often asks about the patient's family. The Spanish-speaking patient may not mention his or her most urgent health concern first. He or she may wait until after discussing a subordinate concern and sensing the *confianza* needed before talking of more important or more intimate problems. It must be established that the practitioner has time to listen.

Communication styles may affect *confianza*. For example, Latinos tend to be "high-context" communicators. That is, they tend to focus as much on the nonverbal cues and context of a conversation as on the content. Saying coolly, "If you do not take the medication, you will get sick," without appropriate affect may dilute the message. The patient may think unconsciously, "He told me I'd get sick, but he did not appear very worried, so it may not be so important." A precept of successful cross-cultural communication is to learn the way that a particular patient population may wish to be treated, and to strive to treat people that way.

Many Latinos who are proficient in English will prefer Spanish for talking about intimate and personal feelings or topics like sexuality. This is in part due to speaking Spanish at home or having spoken Spanish as a child. They may speak Spanish in times of distress. Coping mechanisms like "self talk" may be inseparable from one's native language. Some patients have denied that they speak English at all in the hopes of being assisted by a Spanish-speaking helper in whom they may sense more *confianza.* When English is a second language and the patient becomes psychotic, proficiency in English may diminish or disappear because of the psychotic disorganization. (Conversely, the concentration used in speaking a second language may temporarily repress the psychosis.) As the patient improves, the use of English also improves and can be a cognitive sign of recovery. Brain damage, as from a stroke, has been known to disable a second language while leaving the first language intact.

Chapter 7
La nutrición y las dietas

By the end of this chapter you will know the names of common foods in Spanish and be able to ask patients about their dietary habits and preferences. You will be able to give basic instructions for low-fat, low concentrated sugar, weight-reducing, and clear-liquids diets.

Ask Patients about Food Preferences

A Naura le gustan los vegetales. Foto cortesía del Dr. Jorge Amarante, nutriólogo clínico.

Vocabulario: Mi Plato del USDA
(*The USDA* Mi Plato)

Granos: «Consuma la mitad en granos integrales»

el pan	bread
las pastas	pasta
el arroz, el arroz integral	rice, whole-grain rice
el cereal cocido	cooked cereal
el cereal seco	dry cereal
la tortilla	tortilla

> In Mexico a *tortilla* is an unleavened corn cake. In the Caribbean region it is an omelet.

Verduras: «Varíe sus vegetales»

los vegetales, las verduras	vegetables, green vegetables
el ají, el pimiento	pepper
la calabaza	squash
la cebolla	onion
los guisantes	peas

la lechuga	lettuce
la plátano de cocinar	plantain
el repollo	cabbage
el tomate, el jitomate	tomato
la zanahoria	carrot

Frutas: «Enfoque en las frutas»

la banana, el guineo, el banano, el plátano*	banana
la ciruela	prune
la manzana	apple
el melón	melon
la naranja, la china (Caribe)	orange
la piña	pineapple
la toronja	grapefruit
la uva	grape

*The fruit that is eaten raw (excluding el *plátano de cocinar*) may be *el guineo* in Puerto Rico and the Dominican Republic; *el banano* in Central America and Colombia; and *el plátano* in Cuba.

Enfoque en las frutas. Hay piña, melón, papaya, naranja y banana.

Leche: «Coma alimentos ricos en calcio»

el mantecado, el helado	ice cream
la leche baja en grasa	low-fat milk
la leche descremada	fat-free (no-fat) milk
el queso bajo en grasa	low-fat cheese
el yogur bajo en grasa	low-fat yogurt

Carnes y frijoles: «Escoja proteínas bajas en grasa»

la carne de res	beef
el cerdo	pork
los frijoles, las habichuelas	beans, pea beans
el huevo	egg
la mantequilla de cacahuate	peanut butter
el pescado	fish
el pollo	chicken

The nutrition charts *Mi Plato* and *Mi Pirámide* are available for download from the Web site.

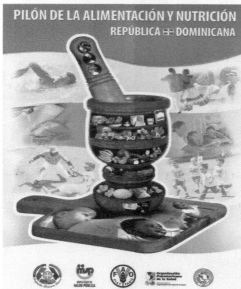

«El pilón nutricional» es símbolo de la educación pública para la nutrición en la República Dominicana.

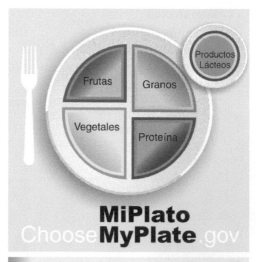

"Choose My Plate" has replaced the USDA pyramid.

Aceites: «Los aceites no son un grupo de alimentos, pero son parte de una buena dieta»

el aceite	oil
el aceite de maíz, de oliva, de soja	corn, olive, soybean oil
las grasas	fats
la manteca	lard
la mantequilla	butter
la margarina	margarine
la mayonesa	mayonnaise

Expresiones útiles

Debe comer más vegetales.	You should eat more vegetables.
Debe comer menos grasa.	You should eat less fat.
No debe usar mucha sal.	You should not use a lot of salt.
En vez de comer dulce, coma frutas.	Instead of eating candy, eat fruit.

 Estructura: Verbos como *gustar* (*Verbs like* Gustar)

• The verb *disgustar* means "To disgust." Like the verb *doler,* which you know from chapter 3, it is most frequently used in the third person (singular and plural), and it is used with indirect objects (*me, te, le, nos, les*). For example,

Me disgustan las arañas.	Spiders disgust me.
A Luisa le disgustan las anchovas.	Anchovies disgust Luisa.

• The verb *gustar* is the opposite of *disgustar* and means "to please." It may be confusing because the meaning-based translation of *Me gusta el café* is "I like coffee." The literal translation, "Coffee pleases me" explains why we use the form *gusta.*

Me gusta el café.	I like coffee.
¿Te gusta el café?	Do you like coffee?
A Luisa le gusta la leche.	Luisa likes milk.
No nos gusta la cerveza.	We don't like beer.
A mi papá le gusta la cerveza.	My dad likes beer.

• If the subject (that which pleases) is plural, use the third person plural form of the verb.

Me gustan las comidas.	I like the meals.
¿Le gustan las uvas?	Do you like grapes?

• We can also express our opinion of an activity by following the verb *gustar* with a verb infinitive.

No me gusta cocinar.   I do not like to cook.
¿Qué le gusta comer?   What do you like to eat?

• Other verbs that are used like *gustar* include, for example,

interesar (*to interest*)   Me interesa la medicina.
importar (*to matter*)   Nos importan los pacientes.
aburrir (*to bore*)   Me aburre la televisión.
fascinar (*to fascinate*)   A Juan le fascina comer.

Vocabulario: Más alimentos y bebidas
(*More Foods and Beverages*)

El desayuno (*Breakfast*)

el huevo	egg
el pan tostado, la tostada	toast
el tocino	bacon
el panqueque	pancake
la salchicha	sausage
la fruta	fruit
el cereal	cereal
la toronja	grapefruit
la avena	oatmeal

El almuerzo (*Lunch*)

el emparedado, **el sándwich** (Caribe)	sandwich
el jamón	ham
el queso	cheese
la sopa	soup
la ensalada	salad
las papas fritas	french fries

La cena (*Supper, Dinner*)

el arroz	rice
la papa	potato
el pan	bread
las pastas	pasta
la carne	meat
las habichuelas	beans
el pollo	chicken
la carne de res	beef

el cerdo	pork
el pescado	fish
el vegetal, la verdura	vegetable

Las bebidas (*Beverages*)

el café	coffee
el té	tea
la leche	milk
el refresco, la gaseosa	soft drink
el chocolate	hot cocoa
el agua*	water
el jugo de naranja, de china (Caribe)	orange juice
el jugo de manzana	apple juice
el jugo de ciruela	prune juice
el jugo de tomate	tomato juice
la cerveza	beer
el vino	wine

Agua and *azúcar* (sugar), like *asma* and *área*, are feminine nouns that are used with the masculine definite article (*el*). Adjectives take their feminine form, however (*el agua está fría; mi azúcar está alta*).

Preguntas útiles

¿Toma usted bebidas alcohólicas?	Do you drink alcoholic beverages?
¿Toma café descafeinado?	Do you drink decaffeinated coffee?

HACIA PRECISIÓN

 ## 7.1 Ejercicio

Complete las siguientes oraciones con el vocabulario nuevo.

A. _____ (pollo, carne de res) es carne roja.

B. _____ (el pescado, el cacahuate) es del océano.

C. _____ (el mantecado, el melón) es rico en calcio.

D. La avena es buena para _____ (la fibra, la picazón).

E. Para consumir bacteria beneficiosa, coma _____ (yogur, cerdo).

F. Para tener más fibra en la dieta, coma _____ (pan, pan integral).

G. Para tener más vitamina A, coma _____ (carne de res, zanahoria).

H. Un ingrediente principal de la ensalada es _____ (lechuga, manteca).

I. _____ (la ciruela, el huevo) es posible futuro madre o padre de

familia.

7.2 Ejercicio

Complete las frases siguientes en una manera lógica como el modelo.

Modelo: A mí **me gustan** (gustar) las frutas.

A. A mí _____ (aburrir) trabajar en una oficina.

B. A mis padres _____ (fascinar) cuidar a su nieto.

C. A mí _____ (interesar) cocinar sin mucha grasa.

D. A los estudiantes _____ (fascinar) aprender el español.

E. A nuestro profesor _____ (importar) hablar dos idiomas.

F. A mi mejor amigo _____ (gustar) comer arroz con pollo y ensalada.

el cereal   la leche

la mantequilla

el pan tostado

Jugo de naranja

el jugo de naranja

el café

el tocino

la salchicha

el huevo

¿Qué le gusta comer para el desayuno? (¿Con qué le gusta desayunar?)

7.3 Ejercicio

En el diagrama, escriba algunos de los alimentos que usted asocia con el desayuno, el almuerzo y la cena. Organícelos (*organize them*) por sus grupos alimenticios.

	Desayuno	*Almuerzo*	*Cena*
Granos	_____	_____	_____
	_____	_____	_____
Verduras	_____	_____	_____
	_____	_____	_____
Frutas	_____	_____	_____
	_____	_____	_____
Leche	_____	_____	_____
	_____	_____	_____
Carnes y frijoles	_____	_____	_____
	_____	_____	_____

HACIA FLUIDEZ

7.4 Actividad

Entreviste (*interview*) a sus compañeros/as. Circule en la clase y pregúntales a sus compañeros/as sobre sus gustos y disgustos. Después comparta los resultados de la encuesta.

Modelo: tomar café por la mañana
—¿Te gusta tomar café por la mañana?
—Sí, me gusta tomar café por la mañana.
(o)
—No, no me gusta el café. No lo tomo por la mañana.

A. tomar jugo de ciruela con el desayuno
B. tomar jugo de naranja por la mañana
C. comer una banana con el almuerzo

D. comer un emparedado para el almuerzo

E. tomar cerveza con la cena

F. tomar bebidas alcohólicas todos los días

G. tomar café por la tarde

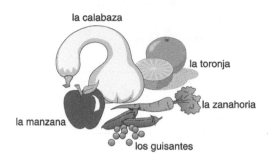

la calabaza

la toronja

la zanahoria

la manzana

los guisantes

Varíe sus verduras y enfóquese en las frutas.

Estructura: Los verbos *querer* y *preferir* para expresar gustos y preferencias (*The Verbs* Querer *and* Preferir *to Express Likes and Preferences*)

• "I like coffee" is *Me gusta el café.* "I want coffee" is *Quiero café. Querer* is an irregular *-er* verb. The first *e* changes to *ie* except in the first person plural.

yo	**Quiero** una ensalada.
tú	¿**Quieres** un vaso de leche?
él, ella, usted	¿**Quiere** usted una taza de café?
nosotros/as	**Queremos** comer una dieta balanceada.
ellos, ellas, ustedes	Mis padres **quieren** bajar de peso.

• Like *gustar,* the verb *querer* can precede a noun or another verb. The second verb is not conjugated.

Quiero tomar un vaso de agua.

¿Quieres cenar en la cafetería?

• The phrase, *Si Dios quiere* means "God willing." Some Spanish-speakers may prefer this over a more direct "yes" or "no" when talking about plans.

• *Preferir* is an irregular *-ir* verb. Like *querer,* the first *e* changes to *ie* except in the first person plural. Also like *querer,* it can precede a verb.

yo	**Prefiero** el arroz a las papas.
tú	¿**Prefieres** el arroz o las papas?
él, ella, usted	Sandra **prefiere** el refresco a la leche.
nosotros/as	Sergio y yo **preferimos** beber leche.
ellos, ellas, ustedes	Mis padres **prefieren** tomar té.

HACIA FLUIDEZ

  7.5 Actividad

Practique el vocabulario nuevo. Ofrezca (*offer*) alimentos específicos a un/a compañero/a. Su compañero/a decide qué le gusta comer y qué quiere comer para el desayuno, el almuerzo y la cena.

> Modelo: desayuno, huevos
> —Para el desayuno, ¿quiere huevos?
> —Sí, quiero huevos (Sí, los quiero).
> (o)
> —No me gustan los huevos. Quiero pan tostado y café.

  7.6 Actividad

Use el verbo *preferir* para preguntarle a un/a compañero/a sobre sus preferencias.

> Modelo: café o té
> —¿Prefiere usted café o té?
> —Bueno, me gusta el café, pero prefiero el té.

A. la leche fría o el chocolate   E. la sopa o la ensalada
B. el pollo o la carne de res   F. el vino o la cerveza
C. las papas o el arroz   G. las frutas o los vegetales
D. el tocino o la salchicha   H. el pescado o el cerdo

  7.7 Drama imprevisto

Con un/a compañero/a, prepare un drama para exponer a la clase. La última línea (*last line*) debe ser, «Para una buena hambre no hay pan duro» (*For a good hunger, there's no such thing as stale bread*).

> Modelo: Carlos: Tengo hambre. Necesito comer.
> María: ¿Quieres arroz con habichuelas?
> Carlos: No me gusta el arroz. Prefiero comer una hamburguesa.
> María: No hay hamburguesa en la casa. ¿Quieres una ensalada?
> Carlos: No me gusta la ensalada. Prefiero papas fritas.
> María: Carlos, coma la ensalada. Para una buena hambre no hay pan duro.

Video: *Para una buena hambre no hay pan duro*

Vea la *Demostración* del capítulo 7, donde la enfermera Rosmery comparte su almuerzo con la Sra. Flores.

Rosmery:	Hablando de dietas me da mucha hambre. ¿Tienes hambre?
Sra. Flores:	Ay, sí. Tengo mucha hambre.
Rosmery:	Tengo mi almuerzo aquí. Vamos a ver qué podemos compartir.
Sra. Flores:	Eres muy amable Rosmery.
Rosmery:	Gracias, pero antes de llamarme amable, vamos a ver qué tenemos para comer.
Sra. Flores:	Para una buena hambre no hay pan duro.
Rosmery:	Del grupo de las frutas, presento, una banana y unas uvas. ¿Te gustan las bananas?
Sra. Flores:	Sí, me gustan las bananas, pero prefiero las uvas.
Rosmery:	Quieres las uvas entonces. Te las doy. Del grupo de los granos, tenemos pan.
Sra. Flores:	Sí, el pan me gusta. Cuando hace frío, me encanta comer pan con mantequilla y tomar una taza de chocolate caliente. Pero a Francisco no le doy ni mantequilla ni chocolate. Tú sabes, la dieta.
Rosmery:	Hablando de chocolate. ¿Sabes qué?
Sra. Flores:	No, dime.
Rosmery:	Mi esposo está un poco gordito, así que para ayudarle con su dieta, cuando compramos chocolate, yo me lo como primero. Así él sigue con su dieta y evita el chocolate.
Sra. Flores:	Eres simpática y generosa, Rosmery.

 ## Educate Patients about Special Diets

Vocabulario: Las comidas y las dietas (*Meals and Diets*)

la nutrición	nutrition	**la dieta**	diet
comer	to eat	**ayunar**	to fast

Las comidas (*Meals*)

el desayuno	breakfast	**desayunar**	to eat breakfast
el almuerzo	lunch	**almorzar**	to eat lunch
la cena	supper, dinner	**cenar**	to eat supper, dinner
la comida	dinner, meal	**la merienda**	snack
la bebida	beverage	**el alimento**	food

Las dietas (*Diets*)

seguir	to follow	**la dieta balanceada**	balanced diet
la sal	salt	**el sodio**	sodium
la grasa	fat	**el colesterol**	cholesterol
el azúcar	sugar	**la fibra**	fiber
la proteína	protein	**el almidón**	starch
el carbohidrato	carbohydrate	**el calcio**	calcium
la libra	pound	**la onza**	ounce
la caloría	calorie	**el gramo**	gram

Preguntas útiles

¿Come bien el niño?	Does the child eat well?
¿Cuánto pesa usted?	How much do you weigh?
¿Ha bajado de peso recientemente?	Have you lost weight recently?
¿Ha subido de peso recientemente?	Have you gained weight recently?

Debe comer más frutas y vegetales
para la fibra y las vitaminas.

Estructura: El verbo *deber* (*Should, Ought To*)

The verb *deber* is a regular verb ending in *-er*. It is useful for discussing diets because it expresses what one should or should not do.

yo	**Debo** comer porciones más pequeñas.
tú	No **debes** comer mucha grasa.
él, ella, usted	Usted no **debe** comer comida rápida.
nosotros/as	**Debemos** comer una dieta balanceada.
ellos, ellas, ustedes	Los pacientes no **deben** comer mucha sal.

Coma de cuatro a cinco porciones del grupo de verduras diaria. Hay zanahoria, ají, calabaza, coliflor, bróculi, chayote y berenjena.

Lectura: Un plan para bajar de peso (*A Weight-Reducing Diet*)

Para tener una dieta saludable y balanceada, debe comer todos los días comidas de cada grupo de alimentos. También es importante tener un equilibrio entre lo que come y su actividad física. Una dieta balanceada tiene de siete a ocho porciones del grupo de los granos, de cuatro a cinco porciones del grupo de las verduras, de cuatro a cinco porciones del grupo de las frutas, de dos a tres del grupo de la leche, dos o menos porciones del grupo de la carne y no mucha grasa. Cada día se debe comer por lo menos cinco porciones de frutas y vegetales.

Para bajar de peso, es importante comer una dieta balanceada, hacer ejercicio regularmente, comer menos calorías y no comer mucha grasa ni azúcar. Para comer menos calorías, debe comer menos porciones, o comer porciones más pequeñas.

Datos nutricionales		
Tamaño por porción 1 taza (236 ml)		
Porciones por envase 1		
Cantidad por porción		
Calorías 120 Calorías de grasa 45		
		% Valor diario*
Grasa total 5g		8%
Grasa saturada 3g		15%
Ácido grasoso *Trans* 0g		
Colesterol 20mg		7%
Sodio 120 mg		5%
Carbohidrato total 11mg		4%
Fibra dietética 0g		
Azúcares 11g		
Proteínas 9g		17%
Vitamina A 10%	•	Vitamina C 4%
Calcio 30% • Hierro 0% • Vitamina D 25%		
*Los porcentajes de valores diarios están basados en una dieta de 2,000 calorías.		

Lectura: La dieta baja en grasa y colesterol
(*Low-Fat, Low-Cholesterol Diet*)

Una persona con el colesterol alto no debe comer mucha grasa. La carne y la grasa de animal tienen colesterol. Las personas con el colesterol alto deben tomar leche descremada o baja en grasa. No deben comer más de tres huevos a la semana. Los alimentos que son permitidos incluyen los panes y cereales, las tortillas de maíz, el arroz, los frijoles y todas las frutas, vegetales y verduras. El coco (*coconut*) tiene mucha grasa. No coma la carne de res más de tres veces a la semana. Coma porciones pequeñas y quite la grasa antes de cocinarla. También quite la piel del pollo antes de cocinarlo. Debe comer pescado grasoso, como el atún y el salmón. Las grasas permitidas son el aceite de maíz, el aceite de oliva y el aceite de soja. El aceite de maíz puede bajar el colesterol.

Lectura: La dieta baja en azúcares concentradas
(Diet Low in Concentrated Sugars)

Las personas que tienen un nivel alto de triglicéridos en la sangre y las personas que sufren de la diabetes deben seguir una dieta baja en azúcares concentradas. La diabetes es una enfermedad que afecta el metabolismo del cuerpo, o la capacidad de procesar la comida. El comer azúcar no causa la diabetes, pero las personas que tienen diabetes tienen demasiada (*too much*) azúcar en la sangre. No hay cura para la diabetes, pero es posible controlarla. Para controlar la diabetes hay que hacer ejercicio regularmente, comer una dieta balanceada, controlar el peso y evitar las azúcares concentradas. También, si el doctor o enfermero receta una medicina, hay que tomarla en la manera indicada. Con respecto a la dieta, no debe dejar de comer ninguna de las comidas (*Don't skip meals*). Coma las comidas a la misma hora y la misma porción todos los días, especialmente si usa medicamento para bajar el azúcar. Coma alimentos ricos en fibra como granos, verduras y frutas. Debe usar menos sal, grasa, azúcar y alcohol. Los siguientes alimentos tienen mucha azúcar. Evítelos (*Avoid them*).

el azúcar de caña	cane sugar
el dulce	candy
la miel de abeja	honey
el almíbar, el sirope	syrup
la torta, el bizcocho (Caribe)	cake
la leche condensada	condensed milk
la gaseosa, el refresco (Caribe)	pop, soda, soft drink

HACIA PRECISIÓN

7.8 Ejercicio

El señor López tiene el colesterol muy alto. Quiere seguir la dieta baja en grasa y tiene varias preguntas. Contéstele las siguientes preguntas.

A. ¿Debo cocinar con manteca?　　No, no debe _____.

B. ¿Debo comer pollo y pescado?　　Sí, debe _____.

C. ¿Debo comer mucho coco?　　_____.

D. ¿Debo tomar leche baja en grasa?　　_____.

E. ¿Debo comer queso bajo en grasa?　　_____.

F. ¿Debo comer papas fritas?　　_____.

G. ¿Debo usar aceite de maíz?　　_____.

H. En vez de la carne de res, ¿qué debo comer?　　_____.

I. ¿Cómo debo preparar el pollo para cocinar?　　_____.

7.9 Ejercicio

El señor Vega tiene diabetes y los triglicéridos altos. Quiere seguir la dieta baja en azúcares concentradas y tiene muchas preguntas. Contéstele las siguientes preguntas.

A ¿Debo usar mucha azúcar cuando cocino?　　No, no debe _____.

B. ¿Debo comer ensalada?　　Sí, debe _____.

C. ¿Debo beber vino?　　_____.

D. ¿Debo comer muchos dulces?　　_____.

E. ¿Debo comer frijoles? _____.

F. ¿Debo usar leche condensada? _____.

G. ¿Debo tomar refrescos dietéticos? _____.

H. ¿Debo usar azúcar artificial? _____.

HACIA FLUIDEZ

7.10 Actividad

Escriba una dieta balanceada y compártala con sus compañeros/as.

El desayuno

_____

_____

_____

_____

El almuerzo

_____

_____

_____

_____

La cena

_____

_____

_____

_____

La merienda (Snack)

_____

_____

_____

_____

Teach Patients How to Prepare for a Colonoscopy

Vocabulario: La colonoscopia y la dieta de líquidos claros (*Colonoscopy and the Clear-Liquids Diet*)

el agua	water
los refrescos claros (no rojos)	clear soda (not red)
el café o té sin leche	coffee or tea without milk
el jugo de manzana	apple juice
el caldo	broth
la gelatina	gelatine
los laxantes	laxatives
el citrato de magnesio	magnesium citrate
el bisacodilo	bisacodyl
evitar	to avoid
la aspirina	aspirin
los anticoagulantes	anticoagulants

A soft diet may be indicated as an intermediate step between a clear-liquids diet and a regular diet or for persons who require choking precautions. This vocabulary will help.

la dieta blanda, la dieta de puré	soft diet (puree diet)
la dieta corriente	regular diet
los frijoles majados	mashed beans
el puré de papa, arroz, manzana	puree of potato, rice, apple

HACIA PRECISIÓN

7.11 Ejercicio

Complete estas instrucciones para una colonoscopia. Incluya ejemplos de lo que debe y no debe comer y tomar. Comparta sus instrucciones con sus compañeros/as.

Su colonoscopia es el _____. No _____ (tomar)

aspirina después del _____. El día anterior, _____

(tomar) bisacodilo 5 mg, 4 comprimidos por vía _____ a las ocho de la

mañana y siga una dieta de _____ _____. No _____ (comer)

nada y no _____ (tomar) ningún producto lácteo. A las seis de la tarde,

_____ (tomar) diez onzas de citrato de magnesio. A las nueve de la

noche, tome otras diez onzas de _____ de _____. Siga una dieta

de _____ _____ toda la _____. No tome nada por dos horas

antes de la colonoscopia.

HACIA FLUIDEZ

 ### 7.12 Actividad

Consulte la lista de las compras y aconseje (*advise*)
a los siguientes pacientes sobre lo que deben y no
deben comprar.

> Modelo: Señora Acevedo, la dieta baja en sal
> —Señora Acevedo, usted debe comprar
> las zanahorias pero no compre las
> salchichas. Coma frutas y vegetales
> frescos.

A. Señora Blanco Peña, la dieta baja en grasa y
colesterol
B. Pedrito Jiménez, la dieta de líquidos claros
C. Señora Medina Ortiz, la dieta para bajar
de peso
D. Doña Olga, la dieta baja en azúcares
concentrados

La lista de las compras

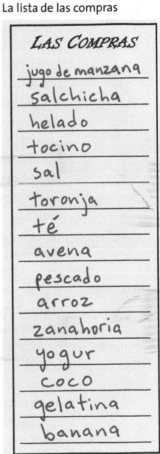

LAS COMPRAS
jugo de manzana
salchicha
helado
tocino
sal
toronja
té
avena
pescado
arroz
zanahoria
yogur
coco
gelatina
banana

 Video: *Cómo bajar de peso*

Vea la *Trama* del capítulo 7, donde la enfermera Rosmery le explica a la Sra. Flores
cómo seguir una dieta para bajar de peso.

Rosmery: ¿Cómo está usted Sra. Flores?
Sra. Flores: Marisol. Llámame Marisol.

Rosmery:	Marisol es un nombre bonito. Mi mamá se llama Marisol. ¿Cómo estás?
Sra. Flores:	Bien. Bueno, un poco preocupada por Francisco. Tiene diabetes, el colesterol alto y la presión alta.

Rosmery: Bueno, son problemas crónicos, es verdad, pero hay tratamiento, y podemos ayudar a tu esposo.

Sra. Flores: ¿Qué podemos hacer? Dicen que si no controla el azúcar, la presión arterial y el colesterol, le puede dar un ataque al corazón, un derrame cerebral o quedarse ciego.

Rosmery: Ay, pobrecita, estás asustada porque lo quieres mucho. Pero no debes preocuparte tanto. Vamos a hablar de cómo lo podemos ayudar. Primero, ¿tienen un plan de alimentación para controlar la diabetes?

Sra. Flores: ¿Un plan de alimentación?

Rosmery: Sí, un plan de alimentación es decir una dieta especial para la diabetes.

Sra. Flores: Bueno, tratamos de evitar el azúcar. Compramos refresco dietético, pero Francisco no puede tomarse un café sin echarle tres cucharaditas de azúcar.

Rosmery: Bueno, es importante evitar el azúcar, pero más importante es controlar el peso. Don Francisco tiene diabetes tipo dos. Ese tipo de diabetes muchas veces mejora cuando bajamos de peso.

Sra. Flores: Es difícil bajar de peso.

Rosmery: Difícil, sí; pero imposible, no. Hablando en general, hay que comer porciones pequeñas y comer alimentos saludables que no tienen mucha grasa o azúcar. Frutas y verduras, pescado, las carnes que no tienen mucha grasa, frijoles, y la leche baja en grasa son buenos. Si come poco, y come alimentos saludables, puede controlar el peso. Y si baja de peso, se puede controlar mucho mejor el colesterol, la presión arterial y la diabetes.

Sra. Flores: Francisco no come mucho. Le hago arroz, habichuelas y carne casi todos los días, pero uso la pechuga de pollo porque dicen que la pechuga tiene menos grasa.

Rosmery: Excelente.

Sra. Flores: Bueno, sí, pero a Francisco le gusta comer su pollo frito y su salami. Sí, tienen mucha grasa, pero quiero hacerle la comida que a él le gusta.

Rosmery: Eres una buena esposa, Marisol. Explíquele a don Francisco que le estás preparando comida saludable para que estén más años juntos.

Sra. Flores: Me gusta la idea de estar más años juntos.

Rosmery: Muy bien. Y, ¿es físicamente activo don Francisco?

Sra. Flores: Allí está el otro problema. Francisco trabaja en una oficina, donde tiene mucho estrés y hace poco ejercicio.

Rosmery: Para bajar de peso, hay que tener un equilibrio entre lo que comemos y la actividad física. Es bueno hacer ejercicio. Debe hacer media hora a una hora de actividad física casi cada día. ¿Qué le gusta hacer?

Sra. Flores: A él le gusta caminar, pero siempre dice que no tiene tiempo.

Rosmery: ¿Por qué no caminan en la tarde, después de la cena? Sería un buen momento para hablar. Incluso hasta sería romántico.

Sra. Flores: Ahora estamos hablando el mismo idioma.

HACIA FLUIDEZ

 ### 7.13 Drama imprevisto

It is dinner time at the Flores's house later that night. Play the parts of Francisco, Marisol, and Elsita discussing what is for dinner. You may choose to play a more cooperative—or a less cooperative—Francisco. For example, *Pero mi amor, me gustan los dulces.*

 ### 7.14 Drama imprevisto

Play the game *Afortunadamente, desafortunadamente.* Take turns adding to a string of statements. Start with *Tengo hambre* or *Tengo sed.* The next statement begins with *afortunadamente,* the statement after that begins with *desafortunadamente,* and so on.

Modelo: —Tengo sed.
    —Afortunadamente, tenemos café.
    —Desafortunadamente, el café está frío y no me gusta el café frío.
    —Afortunadamente, hay cerveza.
    —Desafortunadamente, tengo que trabajar.

7.15 Drama imprevisto

Con un/a compañero/a, prepare un drama sobre las dietas para presentar a la clase. La última línea debe ser, «Por la boca muere el pez» (*The fish dies through his mouth*). Aquí hay un ejemplo.

Modelo: Carlos: María, ¿qué quieres comer?
María: Quiero comer helado.
Carlos: Pero mi amor, tienes diabetes y no debes comer dulces.
María: Quiero comer salchicha.
Carlos: Pero tienes el colesterol alto y no debes comer grasa.
María: No me importa la dieta.
Carlos: Por la boca muere el pez.

7.16 Reciclaje

Food and drink can be comforting, which can make dieting little more than wishful shrinking. Recycle the comfort idioms that use the verb *tener*. Find out what a partner likes or prefers to eat or drink when he or she feels hungry, thirsty, hot, cold, afraid, or in a hurry. For example,

—¿Qué prefieres tomar o comer cuando tienes miedo?
—Cuando tengo miedo prefiero tomar café descafeinado y comer espinacas como Popeye.

above: La yuca

above right: El plátano

right: La banana («el guineo» en Puerto Rico y la República Dominicana)

Cultural Note: Balancing Diet and Exercise

Hispanic cuisine has many starchy vegetables. In some areas, this may be due to their availability as compared to other foods. Although they are like vegetables in their vitamin content, their carbohydrate content is more similar to bread than to vegetables. These include rice, lima beans (*habas*), corn, and winter squash (*calabaza*). *Yuca* and *plátano* are two starchy vegetables that you may not know. *Yuca* is a root that may be boiled (and topped with sautéed onions!) or grated, pressed, mixed with spices, and fried. It is one of the oldest foods in America. Before Columbus arrived in the "New World," the native people made a cake called *casave* by grating and pressing the *yuca,* adding salt, and cooking it on a hot rock. (To make *casave* at home, grate the *yuca,* press out the juice with cheesecloth, add salt, and cook it in a dry cast-iron pan. The raw juice contains cyanide, which is toxic.) The colonists took *casave* back to Spain because it did not spoil on the long voyages. *Plátano* is a vegetable that looks like a large, fat banana but has a flavor of its own (although when very ripe it tastes like a sweet potato). Prior to ripening, fry, crush, and refry transverse slices to make *tostones,* a real favorite in the Caribbean, but not good for low-fat diets. When very ripe, sauté thin, longitudinal slices in olive oil. Other roots and tubers like *batata, yautía, malanga coco,* and *ñame* are carbohydrates that are boiled alone or in sauces and stews. People on a strict diabetic diet who use a system of exchanges or *intercambios* might be instructed to be consistent with carbohydrates and to use certain of these foods in place of bread.

Epidemiologically, Latinos born outside of the United States have lower incidents of obesity and obesity-exacerbated illnesses such as hypertension and type two diabetes mellitus. After five years in the United States, however, they begin to close the gap with Latinos born in the United States and with a sample of all native-born North Americans. A study found that Latinos here less than five years had a 16 percent rate of obesity, and after five years in the United States, this had increased to 22 percent. Latinos born in the United States and U.S. citizens in general had a 30 percent rate of obesity. There were similar progressions for hypertension and type two diabetes.

For some natives of the United States, it is a challenge to find the right balance between calories taken in and calories burned, or between eating and exercise. One Latina proposed this explanation, "Before I moved to the United States, I ate a big breakfast and a heavy lunch to get enough calories for a long day at work. When I bought food from a street vendor, it was either fruit or corn on the cob. Sweet, fatty snacks were not as common as they are here, where anything placed on the table at the office disappears by lunchtime. I got substantial exercise walking to and from the bus stop. Here there is a surplus of food, and I drive everywhere because either there is no public transportation or it's too cold to walk. Since I do not burn as many calories, I have to eat much smaller portions and be especially careful not to eat too many of my favorite carbohydrates, like rice and yucca."

Para la merienda, vamos a comer frutas. Hay papaya, piña y melón.

Chapter 8
El examen físico

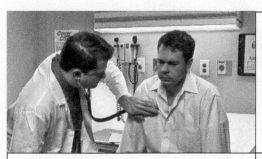

By the end of this chapter you will know the Spanish terms necessary to conduct the physical exam portion of a history and physical. You will be able to ask how long various symptoms have been present, to ask what makes things better or worse, to describe bowel habits, and to explain and schedule referrals for common tests. If this class can be held in an exam room, this may help you form kinesthetic memory cues and to think of the questions and expressions that you most frequently use in this setting.

Clarify the Chief Complaint

Vocabulario: El tiempo (*Time*)

el motivo de la consulta	the chief complaint
¿Qué le pasa?	What is happening (to you, him, her)?
¿Con qué frecuencia?	How often?
nunca, jamás	never
casi nunca	almost never
de vez en cuando	once in a while
a veces	at times
una o dos veces al día	once or twice a day
a menudo	often
frecuentemente	frequently
siempre	always
Es continuo.	It's continuous.
Va y viene.	It comes and goes.
¿Desde cuándo?	Since when?
desde esta mañana	since this morning
desde anoche	since last night
desde ayer	since yesterday
desde el lunes	since Monday
desde hace tres días	since three days ago
desde la semana pasada	since last week
¿Cuánto tiempo hace?	How long has it been?
Hace una hora.	It's been an hour.
Hace dos días.	It's been two days.
¿Cuánto tiempo dura el dolor?	How long does the pain last?
Dura de una a dos horas.	It lasts for one or two hours.
Dura varios días.	It lasts for several days.

 ## Estructura: ¿Cuánto tiempo hace?
(*How Long Has It Been?*)

• The verb *hacer* means "to do" and "to make." *Hacer* is irregular only in the first person singular (*yo*).

yo	**Hago** la cena a las ocho de la noche.
tú	¿**Haces** ejercicio todos los días?
él, ella, usted	Mi mamá **hace** una torta deliciosa.
nosotros/as	¿Qué **hacemos** hoy?
ellos, ellas, ustedes	Mis amigos no **hacen** nada hoy.

• The verb *hacer* is used in expressions of time. In such expressions, it is used in the third person singular.

¿Cuánto tiempo hace?	How long has it been?
Hace dos días.	It has been two days.
¿Hace mucho tiempo?	Has it been a long time?
Hace poco tiempo.	It has been a short time.

• Use *¿Cuánto tiempo hace que . . . ?* followed by a verb phrase to ask how long a symptom or condition has been going on.

¿Cuánto tiempo hace que usted tiene diabetes?
¿Cuánto tiempo hace que le duele el brazo?

• Use *hace* + period of time + *que* + verb phrase to declare how long the symptom or condition has been going on.

Hace dos años que tengo diabetes.
Hace una semana que me duele el brazo.

			dos horas				me duele la cabeza.
Hace	+		tres días	+	que	+	se me hinchan los tobillos.
			cuatro meses				tomo Lipitor.

HACIA FLUIDEZ

 ### 8.1 Actividad

Pregúntale a su compañero/a cuánto tiempo hace que tiene los siguientes síntomas. Responda ad líbitum (*respond ad lib*).

Modelo: Me duele la espalda.
—¿Cuánto tiempo hace que le duele la espalda?
—Hace tres días que me duele la espalda.

A. Tengo fiebre.
B. Estoy enfermo.
C. Tengo hipertensión.
D. Me duele la garganta.
E. Tengo rigidez en el cuello.

F. Toso mucho.
G. Estoy mareado.
H. Mi hijo tiene gripe.
I. Tengo dolor de cabeza.
J. Mi suegra vive con nosotros.

 ### 8.2 Actividad

Prepare un diálogo con un/a compañero/a para exponer a la clase. Pregúntale qué le pasa (el motivo de la consulta), la frecuencia del síntoma, cuánto tiempo hace, desde cuándo y cuánto tiempo duran los episodios. Use el formulario siguiente para organizar su presentación. Aquí hay ideas para el motivo de la consulta.

Tengo ardor en el estómago.	My stomach burns.
Tengo sudores por la noche.	I have night sweats.
Se me hinchan los tobillos.	My ankles get swollen.
Me duele el pecho.	My chest hurts.
Sangro por la nariz.	My nose bleeds.

1. Motivo de la consulta:

_____.

2. Frecuencia:

_____.

3. Cuánto tiempo hace:

_____.

4. Desde cuándo:

_____.

5. Duración:

_____.

Un chiste

Doctor:	¿Qué le pasa?
Paciente:	Tengo amnesia total.
Doctor:	¿Desde cuándo tiene amnesia?
Paciente:	Desde el sábado ocho de mayo del 2012 a las dos en punto de la tarde.
Doctor:	¡Caramba!

Vocabulario: ¿Qué le mejora? (*What Makes You Better?*)

ayudar	to help
mejorar	to improve
empeorar	to worsen

Preguntas útiles

¿Qué le ayuda?	What helps you?
¿Qué le mejora?	What makes you better?
¿Qué le empeora?	What makes you worse?
¿Qué le hace sentir mejor?	What makes you feel better?
¿Qué le hace sentir peor?	What makes you feel worse?

Expresiones útiles

El ibuprofeno me ayuda.	Ibuprofen helps me.
Comer fritura me empeora.	Eating fried food makes me worse.

Vocabulario: Las materias fecales (*Bowel Movements*)

heces, materias fecales	feces
defecar, evacuar, ensuciar	to move one's bowels
hacer pupú	to "go poop" (juvenile)
¿Tiene diarrea o estreñimiento?	Do you have diarrhea or constipation?
¿Con qué frecuencia evacua?	How often do you move your bowels?
¿De qué color es la materia fecal?	What color is the stool?
¿Hay sangre?	Is there blood?
¿Cómo son las heces (materias fecales)?	How are the stools?
¿Son . . .	Are they . . .
. . . blancas?	. . . white?
. . . verdosas?	. . . greenish?
. . . como la brea?	. . . like tar?
. . . flotantes?	. . . floating?
. . . blandas?	. . . soft?
. . . líquidas?	. . . liquid?
. . . mocosas?	. . . with mucus?
. . . duras y secas?	. . . hard and dry?

HACIA FLUIDEZ

 ### 8.3 Actividad

Prepare un diálogo con un/a compañero/a para presentar a la clase. Usted es gastroenterólogo y su compañero/a sufre de estreñimiento. Clarifique el problema por ejemplo cuánto tiempo hace y cómo son las heces fecales. Después hable de posibles remedios. Algunos remedios generales para el estreñimiento son:

comer papaya
hacer ejercicio todos los días
comer más frutas, verduras y granos porque son ricos en fibra
beber mucha agua u otros líquidos
tomar el tiempo necesario para evacuar
tomar laxantes solamente si el médico lo indica
tomar 2 cucharadas de hidróxido de magnesia y un vaso de agua al acostarse

 ### Video: *La pulmonía*

Vea la *Demostración* del capítulo 8, donde el Dr. Vargas le hace preguntas al Sr. Flores para clarificar su motivo de consulta. Después, haga el ejercicio 8.4.

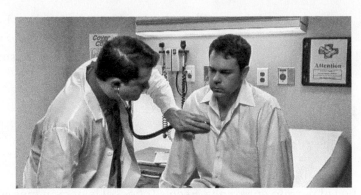

«Respire profundamente».

Sr. Flores:	Doctor, no me siento bien. Estoy enfermo.
Dr. Vargas:	¿Qué le pasa?
Sr. Flores:	Toso mucho.
Dr. Vargas:	¿Tiene dolor?
Sr. Flores:	Me duele el pecho cuando toso y cuando respiro profundamente.
Dr. Vargas:	¿Cuánto tiempo hace que tiene la tos?
Sr. Flores:	Hace tres o cuatro días.
Dr. Vargas:	¿Desde cuándo le duele el pecho cuando tose?
Sr. Flores:	Hoy es viernes. Desde el martes entonces.
Dr. Vargas:	Cuando tose, ¿hay flema?
Sr. Flores:	Sí, una flema verdosa.
Dr. Vargas:	¿Hay sangre cuando tose?
Sr. Flores:	No.
Dr. Vargas:	¿Tiene fiebre?
Sr. Flores:	Ayer tuve una fiebre de treinta y nueve grados.
Dr. Vargas:	¿Hay algo que mejora el dolor y la fiebre?
Sr. Flores:	No me gusta tomar los calmantes, pero ayer tomé un calmante.
Dr. Vargas:	¿Qué tomó?
Sr. Flores:	Dos ibuprofén.
Dr. Vargas:	Le quitó la fiebre el ibuprofén?
Sr. Flores:	Sí, me mejoró bastante pero en cuatro horas la fiebre y el dolor volvieron.
Dr. Vargas:	Usted tiene una tos con dolor y fiebre alta de hace tres días. El ibuprofén ayuda pero los síntomas vuelven. Tiene esputo verdoso. Puede ser una pulmonía. Voy a escucharle los pulmones ahora. Respire profundamente. Respire por favor. Respire. Otra vez. Otra vez. Y una vez más. Señor Flores, usted tiene pulmonía. Es una infección bacteriana del pulmón izquierdo. Voy a recetarle un antibiótico. Levofloxacino, quinientos miligramos, por la boca, una vez al día por diez días, número diez. Lleve esta receta a la farmacia. Es para un antibiótico. Tome

una pastilla todos los días por diez días. Es importante tomar todo el medicamento. Va a sentirse mejor pronto. Tenemos que hacer una radiografía del pecho hoy. Rosmery le va a hacer la cita.

HACIA PRECISIÓN

 8.4 Ejercicio

Lea el párrafo en voz alta. Escoja (*choose*) la opción más adecuada de las palabras en paréntesis.

El señor Flores está _____ (bien, enfermo). El problema es que

hace tres o cuatro días que le duele _____ (el pecho, la cabeza)

cuando _____ (evacua, tose). Cuando tose hay _____

(flema, sangre) y el pobre don Francisco tiene _____ (fiebre,

calor). El doctor Vargas dice que el señor Flores tiene _____ (un

virus, pulmonía) y que necesita _____ (esteroides, antibióticos)

y _____ (una sonografía, una radiografía del pecho). Tiene que

tomar los antibióticos _____ (por suero intravenoso, por vía oral).

Pronto el señor Flores va a estar _____ (peor, mejor).

 # Conduct a Physical Examination

 ## Estructura: El verbo *ir* para hablar del futuro
(*The Verb* Ir *to Talk about the Future*)

• The verb *ir* is an irregular verb and means "to go." These are the forms of the verb in the present tense.

yo	**Voy** a la clínica todos los viernes.
tú	¿**Vas** al dentista cada seis meses?

él, ella, usted	¿**Va** usted a la farmacia hoy?
nosotros/as	**Vamos** a la cafetería para comer.
ellos, ellas, ustedes	Mis hijos **van** a la casa de su abuela.

• Ask or tell what "is going to" happen, using the verb *ir* (conjugated in the present tense), the preposition *a,* and a verb infinitive. Note that the *a* does not translate literally.

| Usted va a estar bien. | You are going to be fine. |
| Voy a consultar con un cirujano. | I am going to consult with a surgeon. |

• *Vamos* also means "Let's." Its use highlights collaboration, without implying "talking down to" as it might in English.

Vamos a ver.	Let's see.
Vamos a esperar.	Let's wait; let's hope.
Vamos a tomarle la temperatura.	Let's take your temperature.

Estructura: Las contracciones *al* y *del*
(*The Contractions* al *and* del)

• The preposition *a* means "to." When followed by the definite article *el,* the two are contracted to form the word *al.* There is no contraction with *la, las,* or *los.*

| Voy a la clínica. | I go (I'm going) to the clinic. |
| Voy *al* hospital. | I go (I'm going) to the hospital. |

• The "personal a" also contracts with the definite article *el.*

| Examino al señor Ulloa ahora. | I'll examine Señor Ulloa now. |

• The preposition *de* means "of" or "from" and is used to express possession as well. When *de* is followed by the definite article *el,* the two are contracted to form the word *del.* There is no contraction with *la, las,* or *los.*

Le llamo de la clínica.	I'm calling (you, him, her) from the clinic.
Le llamo *del* hospital.	I'm calling (you, him, her) from the hospital.
¿Cuál es el teléfono del Sr. Vega?	What is Sr. Vega's telephone number?

HACIA FLUIDEZ

 ## 8.5 Actividad

Observe la foto de la Clínica Chan Aquino (página 190). ¿Cuáles servicios ofrecen? Su compañero/a va a la clínica esta tarde. Pregúntale a su compañero/a cuál es su propósito para ir a la clínica. Por ejemplo,

—Voy a la Clínica Chan Aquino.
— ¿Para qué va a la clínica?
—Voy a la clínica para una biopsia de la piel.

Algunos de los servicios incluyen:

cirugía cardiovascular   radiografía del pecho
evaluación psicológica   análisis de sangre
electrocardiograma   examen físico infantil

    ## 8.6 Actividad

La madre de su compañero/a tiene una cita en la clínica mañana. Pregúntale los detalles de sus planes. Por ejemplo,

—Mi mamá va a la clínica mañana.
—¿Por qué va ella a la clínica?
—¿Para qué va?
—¿Con quién va a ir?
—¿A qué hora va a regresar?

¿Por qué?	Why (cause)?
¿Para qué?	Why (purpose)?
regresar	to return

Vocabulario: El examen físico (*The Physical Exam*)

mirar	to look, to look at
escuchar, auscultar	to listen, to listen to, to auscultate
tocar, presionar, palpar	to touch, to press, to palpate
dar golpecitos, percutir	to tap, to percuss
el estetoscopio	stethoscope
medir al bebé (a la bebé)	to measure the baby
pesar al niño (a la niña)	to weigh the child
tomar la temperatura	to take the temperature
tomar la presión arterial	to take the blood pressure

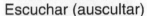
Escuchar (auscultar)   Tocar (palpar)   Dar golpecitos (percutir)

medir el oxígeno en la sangre	to measure the blood oxygen
escuchar los pulmones	to listen to the lungs
escuchar el corazón	to listen to the heart
mirar la garganta	to look at the throat
sacar sangre para un análisis	to draw blood for a test
hacer un electrocardiograma	to take an electrocardiogram
hacer un examen digital de la próstata	to do a digital exam of the prostate

Algunos tratamientos que van con *ir* + *a* + infinitivo

poner un suero	to put in an IV
poner una inyección	to give an injection
poner una venda, curita	to put on a bandage, Band-Aid
poner puntos	to suture
sacar puntos	to remove stitches

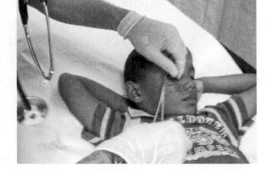

El doctor le pone puntos al niño.
La cortadura va a sanar bien.

Medir is an irregular verb (*mido, mides, mide, medimos, miden*). When treating a minor injury, a mother may say, *Sana, sana, culito de rana; si no sanas hoy, sanarás mañana* (Heal, heal, toad's little tail; if you don't heal today, you'll heal tomorrow). Many of these verbs use the indirect object to represent the patient. Recall that these may be placed either before the conjugated verb or as a suffix to the verb infinitive. It makes no difference which.

La doctora le va a mirar los ojos.   La doctora va a mirarle los ojos.

Video: *El examen físico*

Vea la *Trama* del capítulo 8, donde el
Dr. Vargas le haga un examen físico
al Sr. Flores.

Dr. Vargas: Su temperatura y presión arterial son excelentes. Vamos a
hacerle un examen físico ahora. ¿Está listo?

Sr. Flores: Sí.

Dr. Vargas: Muy bien. Primero voy a mirarle los ojos. Mire el punto de luz.
Bien. ¿Tiene problemas con la vista?

Sr. Flores: No tengo problemas con la vista. No uso lentes.

Dr. Vargas: Muy bien. Ahora, voy a mirarle los oídos. ¿Le duelen los oídos?

Sr. Flores: No.

Dr. Vargas: Ahora, voy a mirarle la nariz y la garganta. Abra la boca, saque
la lengua y diga a-a-a-h-h-h. Muy bien. Ahora voy a tocarle el
cuello. Bien. Ahora, voy a escucharle los pulmones y el corazón.
Respire profundamente por la boca. De nuevo. Muy bien.
Acuéstese por favor. Respire profundamente. Otra vez. Otra
vez. Y una vez más. Ahora voy a darle golpecitos en el pecho.
Ahora, voy a tocarle el abdomen. Dígame si le duele. Respire
profundamente. Otra vez. Muy bien. Ahora, por favor, levante las
piernas y trate de resistir cuando yo empujo. Muy bien. La otra
pierna. Perfecto. Ahora voy a hacerle un examen de la próstata a
través del ano. Por favor, póngase la bata.

la bata   robe

HACIA PRECISIÓN

8.7 Ejercicio

En la foto, la enfermera mide al bebé. ¿Qué más le hace al bebé en su primer examen físico? Escriba una «x» en las actividades que son parte del primer examen
físico infantil. Después comparta con la clase los resultados.

A. _____ ponerle puntos   C. _____ pesarle

B. _____ escucharle el corazón   D. _____ ponerle un suero

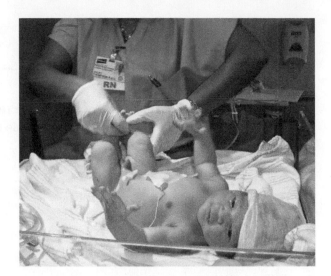

La enfermera mide al recién nacido. Es su primer examen físico. Foto cortesía de Otoniel Acevedo Medina.

E. _____ examinarle la próstata   G. _____ tomarle la temperatura

F. _____ escucharle los pulmones   H. _____ sacarle sangre para un análisis

8.8 Ejercicio

Identifique las oraciones de la columna «B» que van frecuentemente con las oraciones de la columna «A» durante un examen físico. Escriba en la columna «B» la letra que corresponde de la columna «A».

A	*B*
A. Voy a mirarle los ojos.	_____ Respire profundamente.
B. Voy a percutirle el pecho.	_____ ¿Le duele cuando lo presiono?
C. Voy a mirarle la garganta.	_____ Golpecitos.
D. Voy a tocarle el cuello.	_____ Mueva la cabeza hacia la derecha.
E. Voy a escucharle los pulmones.	_____ Acuéstese boca arriba por favor.
F. Voy a presionarle el abdomen.	_____ ¿Tiene problemas con la vista?
G. Voy a hacerle un electrocardiograma.	_____ Abra la boca y diga «a-a-a-a».

HACIA FLUIDEZ

 ### 8.9 Actividad

Usted es médico y su compañero/a es paciente. Pregúntale qué le pasa y cuando el/la paciente le dice un motivo de la consulta, use el vocabulario nuevo para decirle qué le va a hacer. Por ejemplo,

> —¿Qué le pasa?
> —Sufro del corazón. Tengo taquicardia.
> —Voy a escucharle el corazón.

Aquí hay unos motivos de consulta.

A. Tengo fiebre.
B. Tengo una cortadura.
C. Me duele mucho la garganta.
D. Sufro de asma y tengo la respiración corta.
E. Hace cinco días que tengo puntos en la pierna.
F. Necesito la vacuna antitetánica (*tetanus vaccine*).
G. Mi papá tiene pulmonía y necesita antibióticos.
H. Estoy aquí para chequearme la glucosa en la sangre.
I. Mi bebé no come mucho y está demasiado chiquito.
J. Sufro de la presión alta. Me duele la cabeza y estoy mareado.

 ### 8.10 Actividad

El profesor escribe cuatro columnas en la pizarra (*board*). Las columnas son: mirar, auscultar, palpar y percutir. Los estudiantes escriben palabras, frases y oraciones asociadas con cada columna. Por ejemplo, en la columna «auscultar» escriba *Voy a escucharle la arteria carótida* o *¿Toma medicamento para bajar el colesterol?*

HACIA FLUIDEZ

 ### 8.11 Actividad

Use esta guía (*guide*) para demostrar un examen físico con un/a compañero/a. Su compañero/a debe contestar las preguntas ad líbitum.

Motivo de la consulta

Favor de quitarse la ropa y ponerse la bata del hospital. Voy a volver pronto. ¿Qué le pasa? ¿Cuánto tiempo hace que usted tiene (el problema, los síntomas)? ¿Desde cuándo? ¿Con qué frecuencia? ¿Qué tiempo dura/n (el problema, los síntomas)? ¿Toma usted algún medicamento todos los días? ¿Es usted alérgico a algún medicamento o a alguna comida? ¿Qué mejora el problema? ¿Qué lo empeora?

El examen físico

Voy a mirarle los ojos. Míreme la nariz. Mire a ese punto de luz. ¿Tiene problema de la vista? ¿Usa lentes? Voy a mirarle los oídos. ¿Le duelen los oídos? Voy a mirarle la nariz y la garganta. Abra la boca, saque la lengua y diga «a-a-a-h». Voy a tocarle el cuello.

Voy a escucharle los pulmones y el corazón. Respire profundamente por la boca. Otra vez. Tosa. Tosa otra vez. ¿Hay flema cuando tose? ¿De qué color es la flema? ¿Es de un color claro, amarillo o verdoso? ¿Hay sangre cuando tose? ¿Le duele cuando tose? ¿Tiene dolor de pecho? ¿Es un dolor fuerte (punzante, quemante, pesado)? ¿Tiene a veces los tobillos hinchados?

Favor de acostarse (*lie down*). ¿Tiene dolor en el estómago? ¿Le duele la barriga? ¿Le duele cuando presiono aquí? ¿Tiene diarrea? ¿Tiene estreñimiento? ¿Hay sangre cuando orina? ¿Hay sensación de ardor? ¿Hay picazón? ¿Hay una secreción blanca? ¿Tiene relaciones sexuales? Tengo que examinarle la próstata a través del ano con el dedo, usando un guante. Levántese y ponga los codos en la camilla. Tengo que introducir un dedo para tocarle la próstata. Es un poco incómodo, pero terminamos rápido.

A Word That Says a Lot: *Así*

Boast that using only one Spanish word, you can teach someone how to tie shoelaces or to button a shirt. What word is that useful and versatile? When you are not sure how to verbalize an instruction, simply demonstrate the action you want the patient to perform and say the word *así*, which in this context means "in this way" or "like this."

Palpating the Breasts or Testes

Prior to palpating the breasts or testes, consider saying, *Tenemos que examinarle los senos (los testículos)*. The use of *tener que* highlights necessity as the motivator; *examinar* is a clinical term, and the first person plural demonstrates partnership. This expression helps you avoid a novice-speaker faux pas such as, *Quiero tocarle los senos* or *Voy a palparle los testículos*.

Schedule Follow-up Tests

Vocabulario: Algunos análisis y procedimientos
(*Some Tests and Procedures*)

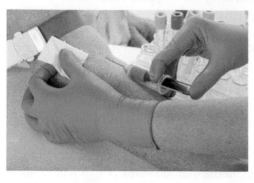

«Tengo que sacarle sangre para hacer un análisis».

El laboratorio (*The Laboratory*)

la biopsia	biopsy
el análisis de orina	urine test
el análisis de sangre	blood test
el análisis de glucosa en la sangre	blood glucose test
el cultivo de las heces fecales	stool culture
la concentración de alcohol en la sangre	blood alcohol level

Imágenes diagnósticos (*Diagnostic Imaging*)

la radiografía, los rayos equis	x-ray
la placa	film, x-ray
la tomografía computarizada	CT Scan
el ecograma, el sonograma, el ultrasonido	echogram, sonogram, ultrasound
el mamograma	mammogram
el angiograma	angiogram
las imágenes por resonancia magnética	MRI

Pruebas de los órganos (*Tests of the Organs*)

la broncoscopia	bronchoscopy
la espirometría	spirometry
el electrocardiograma	EKG
la prueba de estrés	stress test
la supervisión Holter	Holter monitor

el electroencefalograma	EEG
la colonoscopia	colonoscopy
la endoscopia	endoscopy

HACIA PRECISIÓN

8.12 Ejercicio

Identifique las pruebas por nombre después de leer las descripciones.

A. Es una radiografía, o una placa de una vena o arteria. Antes de hacerla, se introduce un catéter en una vena o arteria. Se inyecta una solución, o medio de contraste. La prueba es para descubrir si hay enfermedad en una vena, una arteria o un órgano.

_____

B. Es una grabadora portátil para grabar información del ritmo cardíaco durante un tiempo, como un electrocardiograma.

> **grabadora portátil** a portable recorder

_____

C. Son para hacer unas imágenes muy específicas de una parte del cuerpo sin usar rayos equis.

_____

D. Es un procedimiento en que se introduce un tubo o un catéter por la nariz o por la boca para examinar los bronquios o los pulmones.

_____

E. Es una prueba en la cual un patólogo examina una muestra de tejido con un microscopio para descubrir si hay cáncer u otra enfermedad.

> **muestra de tejido** tissue sample
>
> The word «*o*» changes to «*u*» before words that begin with *o* or *ho*.

_____

F. Es un examen de rayos equis de los senos para descubrir si hay tumores
o quistes.

| quiste   cyst |

_____

G. Es una prueba en la cual el paciente exhala en un instrumento que
mide cuanto aire entra y sale de los pulmones para medir la capacidad
respiratoria de los pulmones.

_____

H. Es una exploración del interior del intestino grueso con un colonoscopio.

_____

HACIA FLUIDEZ

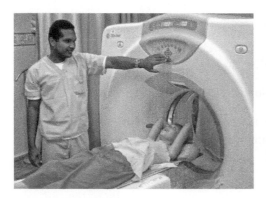 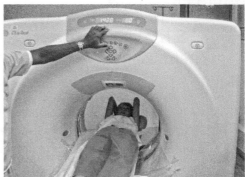

 ## 8.13 Drama imprevisto

Vea la foto de la niña que necesita una tomografía computarizada. Usted es técnico
de radiografía y su compañero/a es un paciente que sufre de dolores de cabeza
persistentes. Demuestre (*demonstrate*) una entrevista donde usted se presenta al
paciente y le explica el procedimiento.

Vocabulario: Haciendo citas (*Scheduling Appointments*)

de/por la mañana	in the morning
de/por la tarde	in the afternoon/evening
de/por la noche	in the nighttime
de una vez	at once
mañana	tomorrow
pasado mañana	the day after tomorrow
la semana que viene	next week

dentro de dos semanas	within two weeks
el mes que viene	next month
el año que viene	next year

Preguntas útiles

¿Puede venir el lunes a las cinco?   Can you come on Monday at five?

Expresiones útiles

Puedo (no puedo) venir a las cinco.   I can (cannot) come at five.

Note that *de* is used when a specific time is mentioned:

Puedo venir a las cinco de la tarde.

Por is used when a specific hour is not mentioned:

Necesito una cita por la tarde.

HACIA FLUIDEZ

 ### 8.14 Actividad

Vea el vocabulario de análisis y procedimientos. Usted es enfermero y su compañero/a es un paciente que necesita un análisis o procedimiento específico. Explíquele el procedimiento y después comparta su conversación con la clase. Por ejemplo,

análisis de glucosa en la sangre
—Usted necesita un análisis de glucosa en la sangre. Tenemos que sacarle una gota de sangre del dedo para determinar cuanta glucosa, o azúcar, hay en la sangre.

 ### 8.15 Actividad

Usted es recepcionista y su compañero/a es un paciente que necesita varios de los siguientes análisis o procedimientos. Haga una cita (*make an appointment*) para la fecha y la hora conveniente para la clínica y el paciente y dentro del tiempo especificado.

A. sacar los puntos   (dentro de dos semanas)
B. hacer un análisis de sangre   (dentro de una semana)

C. una endoscopia   (dentro de un mes)
D. un electroencefalograma   (mañana)
E. un angiograma   (la semana que viene)
F. un análisis de orina   (dentro de una semana)
G. un electrocardiograma   (dentro de dos semanas)

8.16 Reciclaje

Look at the illustration of four signs and answer the following questions.

A. ¿A qué hora es el grupo de autoayuda?
B. ¿Quién me puede operar las cataratas?
C. ¿Quién trabaja en el departamento de maternidad?
D. ¿Está abierto los martes el consultorio del Dr. Padilla Desgarennes?
E. ¿A qué hora cierra el consultorio del Dr. Blas Salinas?
F. ¿Cuál es el número de teléfono del gastroenterólogo?

8.17 Reciclaje

Historia clínica

Fecha de consulta: _____

Apellidos: _____ Nombres: _____

Fecha de nacimiento: _____ Lugar de nacimiento: _____

Sexo: _____ Nacionalidad: _____ Teléfono: _____

Motivo de la consulta: _____

Historia familiar: _____

Antecedentes médicos: _____

Medicamentos actuales: _____

Alergias: _____

Tabaco, alcohol, drogas: _____

Último uso: _____

PA _____ / _____ FC _____ FR _____ Altura _____ Peso _____

Pulmones: _____

Corazón: _____

Abdomen: _____

Impresión diagnóstica: _____

Tratamiento: _____

_____

_____

Firma

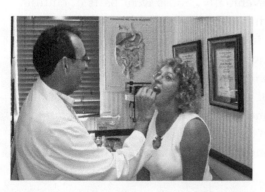

Vea la fotografía del doctor y su paciente. ¿Qué dice (*says*) el doctor? Use el formulario *Historia clínica* para demostrar el examen con un/a compañero/a. Note las siguientes abreviaturas: tensión arterial (TA), frecuencia cardíaca (FC) y frecuencia respiratoria (FR).

The *Historia Clínica* form is available for download from the Web site

Cultural Note: A Dynamic Process

Culture is dynamic, and frontiers are disappearing. Culture is imported and exported. Countries and cultures are interdependent, and no group is isolated. Groups are penetrated by outside cultures, for example via products and media, such as Internet, television, and advertisements. People export culture as they migrate. Then they acculturate gradually, generally in three generations, although children are fast. The host culture, or receiving culture, is changed also. Thus, an individual's culture of origin and the receiving mainstream culture are not always vastly different. As the world shrinks, flattens, and globalizes, cultures encounter situations that are easily assimilated and others that are not, forcing them to adapt.

Immigrants and others who have cross-cultural experiences may decide that there are aspects of both cultures that they like and dislike. They may either consciously or unconsciously cling to—or reject—specific aspects of their culture of origin while embracing aspects of the host culture. In the chapter 7 video, Sra. Flores says, *A Francisco le gusta comer su pollo frito y su salami. Sí, tienen mucha grasa, pero quiero hacerle la comida que a él le gusta.* She may have been experiencing conflict between a traditional gender role and the new information that she was learning about diets. In chapter 9, Rosmery compares Halloween and *El día de los muertos* and laments, *Mis hijos están americanizados.*

Language competency is an essential component of acculturation. Families may resist acculturation by recognizing that the way to preserve cultural views and traditions is to speak Spanish at home. Children, on the other hand, may resist speaking Spanish, as a way to avoid appearing different among peers. This may create intergenerational communication gaps. The same children may one day regret not speaking Spanish, and decide to take classes in order to rediscover their heritage or connect with elderly family members.

Children may be pressured to choose between cultures or may learn to skillfully navigate both worlds. Families eventually choose what parts of culture to preserve and what to leave behind in order to comfortably assimilate. With some experience, families and individuals may function very successfully in both cultures. For example, a wedding planned by a Latin American family might not begin at the time printed on the invitation. This is because it must begin when the bride is ready, and all guests have arrived. The same family, when scheduling a business appointment may insist, *"Empezamos a la una, hora americana* (We'll start at one o'clock, American time),"* to encourage punctuality. Some Latinos have commented that it seemed odd that the host culture not only sets the time for a celebration to begin, but also might set the time for it to end.

During the process of acculturation individuals may feel lonely, frustrated, and incompetent to function in the new society. Parents may struggle with communicating with their children's teachers or pediatrician. They may not understand why their children would rather play with friends than go to Tío Alfredo's birthday party, and wonder why neighbors do not collaborate in rearing each other's children. Elderly persons may feel less valued and respected than in their culture of origin. Temporary relief is available in enclaves, or neighborhoods that keep the cultural identity of their members while coexisting with the surrounding dominant culture. These enclaves also provide great opportunities for host culture members to have cross-cultural experiences.

Models for comparing health across ethnic groups have focused on genetics and racial differences, on cultural lifestyles (diet and exercise, for example), on socioeconomic status, and on proximity to pathogens (living in cities, for example). Although each view has merit, controlling socioeconomic factors in health care access (literacy, insurance, transportation, and the linguistic competency of the patient and provider) can ameliorate some of the measured health disparity between groups.

Chapter 9
«¿Qué pasó?»

Communication Goals

Vocabulary

Structure

Video

Cultural Note

I n this chapter you will learn to talk about things that occurred in the past. You will learn to ask, "What happened?" and "Did you take your medicine?" You will be able to ask, "When was the last time that you . . . ?" You'll also be able to ask about the context of the chief complaint: "What was going on when this happened?" Contextual themes will incorporate pre-surgical interviews, cardiac rehabilitation, and the work of visiting nurses and paramedics.

 ## Ask What Happened

Vocabulario: Tiempos pasados (*Times in the Past*)

esta mañana	this morning
hoy	today
anoche	last night
ayer	yesterday
anteayer	the day before yesterday
el jueves pasado	last Thursday
la semana pasada	last week
el mes pasado	last month
el año pasado	last year

lunes	martes	miércoles	jueves	viernes
anteayer	ayer	hoy	mañana	pasado mañana

 ### Estructura: El pretérito de los verbos regulares (*The Preterit of Regular Verbs*)

• Now you'll be able to describe actions that were completed in the past. Like the present tense, the preterit tense is formed by changing the form of the verb according to the subject (who or what is doing the action). The first and third persons have written accents that guide you to stress that syllable when speaking. The other forms are stressed on the next-to-last syllable. Here are the forms of the verb *tomar* in the preterit. Verbs ending in -*ar* that follow this pattern of endings are called "regular."

yo	**Tomé** la nitroglicerina esta mañana.
tú	**¿Tomaste** el antiácido antes de comer?
él, ella, usted	**¿Tomó** usted mucha agua con el medicamento?
nosotros/as	Raúl y yo **tomamos** el autobús para llegar.
ellos, ellas, ustedes	Mis hijos **tomaron** las vitaminas con el desayuno.

• The preterit of regular verbs ending in *-er* and *-ir* is formed similarly by changing the form of the verb according to the subject. Here are the forms of the verb *comer* in the preterit. Verbs ending in *-er* and *-ir* that follow this pattern are called "regular."

yo	**Comí** arroz con pollo anoche.
tú	**¿Comiste** bien?
él, ella, usted	Juan no **comió** nada.
nosotros/as	Ada y yo **comimos** mucho en la cafetería.
ellos, ellas, ustedes	Los niños **comieron** el almuerzo en la escuela.

• The first person plural, or *nosotros,* form is the same in both the present and the preterit tenses for verbs ending in *-ar* and *-ir*. Tell them apart by the context.

Nosotros siempre tomamos café por la mañana (*present tense*).
Ayer tomamos café antes de salir para el hospital (*past tense*).

HACIA PRECISIÓN

 ## 9.1 Ejercicio

Complete las siguientes oraciones con la forma correcta del verbo entre paréntesis. Use el pretérito del pasado.

A. Anoche mis tíos y mis primos nos _____ (visitar).

B. Ellos _____ (llegar) a las cinco de la tarde.

C. Mis padres _____ (cocinar) mucha comida deliciosa.

D. Mi hermano y yo _____ (comer) ensalada, carne y arroz.

E. Después de comer, (yo)_____ (estudiar) para la clase de español.

F. En la noche mi tía _____ (sufrir) de acidez.

G. A las ocho mi tío le _____ (comprar) un antiácido para mi tía.

H. Mi tía se _____ (tomar) el antiácido con un vaso de agua.

9.2 Ejercicio

Complete las siguientes preguntas con la forma correcta del verbo entre paréntesis. Después practique las preguntas con un/a compañero/a.

A. ¿En qué año _____ (nacer) usted?

nacer	to be born
tragar	to swallow

B. ¿A usted le _____ (escribir) la doctora una receta nueva?

C. ¿Por cuántos años _____ (vivir) sus padres con usted?

D. ¿Cuántas botellas de vino _____ (beber) los enfermeros en la fiesta?

E. ¿_____ (ver*) tú el accidente ayer?

F. ¿A qué hora _____ (salir) tú de tu casa esta mañana?

G. ¿_____ (cuidar) bien los enfermeros a tu padre en el hospital?

H ¿_____ (tragar) doña María la pastilla grande sin problema?

*When *ver* is used in the preterit, the accents are not written.

HACIA FLUIDEZ

 ## 9.3 Actividad

Usted es un enfermero que visita a sus pacientes en sus casas. Su compañero/a es su paciente. Vea la lista de «Quehaceres para hoy» y pregúntele al paciente **qué hizo** (what *he or she did*) o no hizo hoy.

Modelo: tomar el antibiótico
　　　　　—¿Tomó usted el antibiótico?
　　　　　—Sí, tomé el antibiótico.
　　　　　(o)
　　　　　—No, no lo tomé.

Quehaceres para hoy

Tomar el antibiótico ☑
Llamar a la farmacia ☑
Cambiar el vendaje ☑
Comer una banana ☐
Usar el oxígeno ☑
Leer el periódico ☐
Llamar a la clínica ☑
Comprar la medicina ☐
Medir la glucosa ☑

9.4 Actividad

Pregúntele a un/a compañero/a si las siguientes personas hicieron o no (*did or did not do*) lo que el doctor les recomendó.

> Modelo: el paciente, tomar el medicamento hoy
> —¿Tomó el paciente el medicamento hoy?
> —Sí, el paciente tomó el medicamento hoy.
> (o)
> —No, el paciente no tomó el medicamento hoy.

A. tú, tomar la aspirina esta mañana
B. su madre, tomar la codeína anoche
C. usted, usar la insulina
D. los niños, usar el inhalador
E. Maribel, comer cinco porciones de frutas hoy
F. el señor Vega, tomar el antibiótico hoy
G. ustedes, tomar las vitaminas con el desayuno
H. la paciente, usar el oxígeno
I. Juan, comprar el jarabe
J. la doctora, escribir la receta
   para mi hermano

Llámeme si me necesita. Mi teléfono es nueve-once.

 ## 9.5 Actividad

Es una novela y ustedes son actores de doblaje (*voice actors*). En esta novela, el protagonista Rafaelito toma una sobredosis de su medicamento, su novia Isabela llama al 9-11 y Pedro el paramédico es el héroe del día. Escoja tres actores y lea la novela en voz alta. **Exagere** las emociones. Mientras lee, tiene que conjugar los verbos (entre paréntesis) en el pretérito del pasado.

Isabela: Rafaelito es mi novio y lo amo. Lo amo mucho pero es un hombre difícil y no puedo vivir con él.
Rafaelito: Isabela es mi novia y la amo. La amo muchísimo pero ella dice

que no puede vivir conmigo. No puedo vivir sin ella. Quiero morir. Hace diez minutos que (tomar) una sobredosis de mis medicamentos.

Isabela: Ay, Rafaelito, mi amor, mi vida, mi corazón. (Tomar) una sobredosis porque no quieres vivir sin mí. Pero Rafaelito, no vas a morir, porque yo (llamar) al nueve-once y la ambulancia va a llegar pronto.

Pedro: Soy Pedro, el paramédico. Estoy aquí y todo va a estar súper bien. ¿Quién (llamar) al nueve once?

Isabela: Yo (llamar) porque mi novio (tomar) pastillas para quitarse la vida.

Pedro: Señor, ¿qué (tomar) usted?

Rafaelito: Pastillas. Aquí está la botella. Son para los nervios.

Pedro: ¿Cuántas pastillas (tomar) usted?

Rafaelito: (Tomar) todas. Como diez pastillas.

Pedro: ¿Cuánto tiempo hace que usted las (tomar)?

Rafaelito: Hace media hora, más o menos.

Pedro: ¿(Tomar) bebidas alcohólicas también?

Rafaelito: No. No bebo nunca.

Pedro: ¿(Vomitar)? ¿Tiene deseo de vomitar?

Rafaelito: No. No (vomitar), pero tengo mucho sueño.

Pedro: Vamos a llevarlo al hospital. Usted va a estar súper bien.

Isabela: Pedro, tú (salvar) a mi novio. Eres buenísimo. ¿Cuál es tu número de teléfono?

Pedro: Llámeme si me necesita. Mi teléfono es nueve-once. Con su permiso, en este momento tengo que salvar una vida. Hasta luego.

Estructura: El pretérito de algunos verbos irregulares
(*The Preterit of Some Irregular Verbs*)

• The verbs *ser, ir, estar, tener,* and *decir* are among those that have irregular morphology in the preterit past tense.

• The verbs *ser* and *ir* take the same form in the preterit. They are differentiated by the context of the sentence.

yo	**Fui** estudiante de medicina por un año. (Ser)
tú	¿**Fuiste** a la clínica ayer? (Ir)
él, ella, usted	Hoy es domingo. Ayer **fue** sábado. (Ser)
nosotros/as	**Fuimos** a la clínica para consultar con el neurólogo. (Ir)
ellos, ellas ustedes	Los niños no **fueron** pacientes de esta clínica. (Ser)

• Recall that the verb *estar* (to be) is used to talk about location, feelings, and conditions. Here are the forms of *estar* in the preterit.

yo	**Estuve** enfermo anoche.
tú	**Estuviste** en la clínica ayer.
él, ella, usted	Mi esposa **estuvo** en el hospital el lunes.
nosotros/as	**Estuvimos** en casa anoche.
ellos, ellas, ustedes	Los niños **estuvieron** enfermos con gripe.

• The verb *tener* (to have) takes forms that are very similar to the verb *estar*. Recall that *tener que* + infinitive means "to have to." In the preterit, we can talk about things that we *had* as well as things that we *had to do* in the past.

yo	**Tuve** fiebre anoche.
tú	**Tuviste** un ataque epiléptico.
él, ella, usted	Ana **tuvo** que tomar la aspirina para quitar el dolor.
nosotros/as	Mi hermano y yo **tuvimos** que cuidar a nuestro padre.
ellos, ellas, ustedes	Mis padres **tuvieron** que llamar una ambulancia.

• The verb *decir* (to say, to tell) normally requires the indirect object pronoun, which indicates to whom something was said.

yo	Le **dije** a la enfermera que mi mamá sufre de azúcar.
tú	¿Qué le **dijiste** a tu mamá anoche, Paquito?
él, ella, usted	El pediatra me **dijo** que el niño no tiene infección.
nosotros/as	Le **dijimos** a Rosa que ella debe ir al consultorio.
ellos, ellas, ustedes	Los pacientes **dijeron** que la cafetería debe servir arroz.

Cortesía del humorista Pepe Angonoa, used with permission.

HACIA PRECISIÓN

 ### 9.6 Ejercicio

Indique si los verbos en las siguientes oraciones son *ir* o *ser*.

A. Ayer fue miércoles.	Ir	Ser
B. La prueba de Pap fue negativa.	Ir	Ser
C. La semana pasada fui a la clínica.	Ir	Ser
D. Fui estudiante de medicina en el 2011.	Ir	Ser
E. El enfermero fue a la cafetería para comer.	Ir	Ser
F. El cirujano que me operó fue el doctor Pérez.	Ir	Ser
G. Mi madre y yo fuimos al consultorio el martes.	Ir	Ser

 ### 9.7 Ejercicio

Una madre pasó una noche difícil. Complete el párrafo con la forma correcta de los verbos *ser, ir, estar, tener* o *decir* en el pretérito del pasado.

Anoche el bebé _____ (estar) enfermo. Mi pobre bebé _____

(tener) una fiebre alta. Su temperatura _____ (estar) en cuarenta

grados. Nosotros _____ (ir) al hospital. El doctor que nos atendió

_____ (ser) el doctor Vargas. Yo _____ (estar) muy nerviosa. El

doctor _____ (decir) que _____ (ser) una infección de los oídos y

nos recetó un antibiótico.

 ### 9.8 Ejercicio

Estos son los planes que el doctor Aquino tuvo para el enero pasado. Haga oraciones para decir qué hizo (*what he did*) y cuándo. Por ejemplo, «El tres de enero el doctor Aquino y Ana comieron en la casa de Javier».

3 de enero	comer en la casa de Javier con Ana
5 de enero	visitar a doña Mercedes en Boston
11 de enero	trabajar en la clínica desde las ocho hasta las cinco

13 de enero	ir a la clase de inglés con don Máximo
14 de enero	consultar con el anestesiólogo
15 de enero	no comer nada; beber líquidos claros
16 de enero	tener una colonoscopia
17 de enero	ir al consultorio de la Dra. Muñoz de Jones para un examen físico
30 de enero	ir de vacaciones a Venezuela

HACIA FLUIDEZ

9.9 Actividad

Usted es un enfermero que visita a sus pacientes en sus casas. Su compañero/a es su paciente. Pregúntele al paciente si *tuvo que* hacer lo siguiente.

Modelo: tomar la nitroglicerina
—¿Tuvo usted que tomar la nitroglicerina?
—Sí, tuve que tomar la nitroglicerina.
(o)
—No, no tuve que tomar la nitroglicerina.

A. usar insulina
B. usar el oxígeno
C. cambiar el vendaje
D. tomar una pastilla para el dolor
E. llamar a la compañía de seguros médicos

9.10 Actividad

Lea la carta que doña Silvestrina le escribió a su hijo en los Estados Unidos y conteste las siguientes preguntas.

A. ¿Cómo se llama la madre de Felipe, y cómo está ella?
B. ¿Qué le pasó a doña Silvestrina?
C. ¿Tuvo fiebre?
D. ¿Cuál fue la temperatura?
E. ¿Cuántos días estuvo en el hospital?
F. ¿Qué tratamiento le dieron?
G. ¿Quién cuidó a doña Silvestrina?

9 de enero

Querido hijo,

¿cómo estás? Espero que bien. Yo estoy mejor, gracias a Dios. Estuve interna por 3 días. Tuve una fiebre de 40 grados. Fue una pulmonía. Me dieron antibióticos por suero y medicamento para el dolor. Los doctores y enfermeros me cuidaron bien. Hasta pronto, tu mamá que te quiere mucho, Silvestrina Robles

Give Test Results

El resultado de una prueba puede ser positivo o negativo. Como son adjetivos, tienen género y número. Por ejemplo,

> Su prueba de tuberculosis fue *positiva.*
> Las placas de su pecho fueron *negativas.*
> El resultado de su radiografía fue *negativo.*

HACIA PRECISIÓN

9.11 Ejercicio

Informe al paciente de sus resultados. Si todo está bien, añada (*add*) «Todo está bien. Gracias a Dios». Si no, añada «Tenga confianza. Todo va a estar bien».

> Modelo: la placa del pecho (negativa)
> —Tenemos el resultado de la placa del pecho. Fue negativa, gracias a Dios.

A. la biopsia	(positiva)
B. el análisis de sangre	(negativo)
C. la prueba de tuberculosis	(positiva)
D. la tomografía computarizada	(negativa)
E. la prueba del SIDA (*AIDS test*)	(negativa)
F. la prueba de embarazo (*pregnancy test*)	(positiva)
G. el sonograma de la vesícula biliar (*gall bladder*)	(negativo)

Conduct a Pre-surgery Interview

Vocabulario: Antes de la cirugía (*Pre-surgery*)

¿Cuándo fue la última vez que . . . ?	When was the last time that . . . ?
usar alcohol o drogas	to use alcohol or drugs
orinar	to urinate
evacuar, defecar	to move one's bowels
menstruar	to menstruate
empezar su período	to start your menses

beber algo	to drink something
comer algo	to eat something
¿Tiene/Usa usted . . . ?	Do you have / Do you use . . . ?
una peluca	a wig
un diente flojo	a loose tooth
una prótesis	a prosthesis
una dentadura postiza	dentures
lentes o lentes de contacto	glasses or contact lenses
problemas con el corazón	heart problems
problemas con los pulmones	lung problems

Preguntas útiles

¿Cuándo comenzó su último período?

¿Está usted alérgico a algún medicamento?

¿Cuándo fue la última vez que usted / el niño evacuó?

¿Fuma? ¿Cuánto bebe? ¿Cuándo fue la última vez que bebió alcohol?

¿Usa drogas? ¿Cuándo fue la última vez que usó heroína/cocaína/
marihuana?

HACIA FLUIDEZ

 ### 9.12 Actividad

Con un/a compañero/a, prepare y presente a la clase una entrevista pre-quirúrgica
(*pre-surgical interview*). Usted es cirujano y su compañero/a es un paciente que
llegó para tener una colecistectomía.

Nombre: _____   Alergias: _____

Historia médica: _____

Prótesis: _____

Alcohol/drogas: _____

La última vez que:

Bebió: _____   Evacuó: _____   Comenzó el período: _____

Vocabulario: Palabras tranquilizadoras
(Words of Reassurance)

Todo va a estar bien.	Everything is going to be fine.
Por favor, cálmese.	Please calm down.
No tenga miedo.	Don't be afraid.
Tenga confianza.	Have trust.
No se preocupe.	Don't worry (formal).
No te preocupes.	Don't worry (informal).
No va a doler.	It's not going to hurt.
Va a mejorar.	It's going to get better.
Hay que seguir adelante.	One must go on.

 ## Video: *Dolor terrible*

Vea la *Demostración* del capítulo 9, donde la Sra. Flores habla con Rosmery sobre un problema de salud.

Rosmery: Me gusta hablar de México.

Sra. Flores: Ya lo veo. Es difícil estar lejos de nuestros seres queridos. Rosmery, perdona, pero tengo que hacerte una pregunta.

Rosmery: Sí, como no.

Sra. Flores: Hace un mes Francisco y yo fuimos a un restaurante argentino, para celebrar nuestro aniversario de bodas. Lo hacemos todos los años. Bueno, la noche comenzó bien. El restaurante era muy elegante. Francisco pidió chorizo asado y yo pedí carne asada. Sabes que el asado es famoso en los restaurantes argentinos. La carne tenía un poco de grasa. Después de la comida pedimos un café y de repente me dolió el estómago. Fue algo terrible. Tenía náusea. Fui al baño y vomité. Francisco tuvo que llevarme a la casa de una vez. La pregunta es, ¿qué puede ser? No puedo estar embarazada.

Rosmery: ¿Fue la primera vez que te dio un dolor tan grande?

Sra. Flores: Sí, pero, A-A-A-Y-Y-Y-Y.

Rosmery: ¿Qué te pasa?

Sra. Flores: Me duele, qué dolor.

Rosmery: ¿Dónde? ¿Dónde te duele? Enséñame dónde.

Sra. Flores: Me duele aquí.

Rosmery: ¿Desde cuándo que te duele?
Sra. Flores: Hace más o menos un mes. Son como ataques.
Rosmery: ¿Cómo es el dolor?
Sra. Flores: Ay, es punzante, como un cuchillo.
Rosmery: Cuando te duele, ¿cuánto tiempo dura el dolor?
Sra. Flores: Más o menos de cinco a diez minutos, y a veces vomito.
Rosmery: Vamos a ver. Voy a poner mi mano allí. Respira profundamente.
Sra. Flores: A-y-y-y-y, allí me duele mucho.
Rosmery: Tenemos que hacerte una cita con el doctor.

La vesícula biliar

HACIA FLUIDEZ

 ### 9.13 Actividad

Escriba una nota clínica con un/a compañero/a para documentar el caso de la Sra. Flores. Después comparta su nota con la clase. Debe incluir la siguiente información:

El motivo de la consulta

_____

El problema específico

_____

La impresión diagnóstica

_____

El plan de tratamiento

_____

 ### 9.14 Actividad

Observe el dibujo de la sala de emergencias (página 218). Hable de los pacientes que esperan al doctor y decida a quién el doctor debe de atender primero y quién debe ser segundo y tercero. Después presenten entrevistas entre uno de los pacientes y el enfermero de clasificación (*triage nurse*) para identificar el motivo de la consulta y llegar a una definición del problema.

 9.15 Actividad _____

Usted es paramédico y su compañero/a es paciente. Con su compañero/a, prepare
y presente a la clase una entrevista donde el paramédico llega al lugar (*location*)
de una emergencia y determina qué pasó. Aquí hay posibles preguntas.

> ¿Qué le pasó?
> ¿Perdió la conciencia?
> ¿Tiene dificultad para respirar?
> ¿Es usted alérgico/a a algún medicamento?
> ¿Toma usted algún medicamento todos los días?
> ¿Qué otros problemas de salud tiene usted?
> ¿Cuál es el nombre de su doctor?

 ## Ask What Was Happening

 ### Estructura: El imperfecto del pasado
(*The Imperfect Mood of the Past Tense*)

• You have been practicing the preterit mood of the past tense, which is used to
narrate actions that were completed in the past. In contrast, the imperfect de-
scribes past conditions and actions without freezing them in time. For example,

¿Qué pasó?	What happened?
¿Qué pasaba cuando eso pasó?	What was going on when that happened?

• Here are the forms of the verbs in the imperfect. Verbs ending in -*er* and -*ir* share the same verb endings.

	Tomar	*Comer*	*Vivir*
yo	tomaba	comía	vivía
tú	tomabas	comías	vivías
él, ella, usted	tomaba	comía	vivía
nosotros/as	tomábamos	comíamos	vivíamos
ellos, ellas, ustedes	tomaban	comían	vivían

• Few verbs are irregular in the imperfect mood. Here are two of them.

	Ser	*Ir*
yo	era	iba
tú	eras	ibas
él, ella, usted	era	iba
nosotros/as	éramos	íbamos
ellos, ellas, ustedes	eran	iban

Cuando **era** niño, mi abuela me **hacía** té de manzanilla.
When I was a child, my grandmother made me chamomile tea.

Antes, yo **tomaba** una botella de cuarenta onzas de cerveza todas las noches.
I used to drink a 40-ounce bottle of beer every night.

Yo siempre **comía** fritura sin pensar en el colesterol.
I always would eat fried food without thinking about cholesterol.

Cuando **vivíamos** en Chile, **tomábamos** té de orégano para el estómago.
When we lived in Chile, we drank oregano tea for the stomach.

• Use the imperfect mood to tell the following.
  ○ Habitual actions in the past. These are not frozen in time.

   Antes, **fumaba** dos paquetes de cigarrillos todos los días.
   Cuando **me enfermaba** mi abuela **me preparaba** un té.

  ○ Actions that were in progress or in the background

   ¿Qué **hacía** usted cuando el dolor empezó?
   Mientras **caminaba** en el parque me **dolían** las rodillas.

  ○ How things *used to* be

   Mis padres **eran** estrictos con nosotros.
   Antes, los doctores **tenían** más tiempo para hablar con los pacientes.

○ Time and age in the past

>   **Eran** las cuatro de la mañana cuando tomé la nitroglicerina.
>   Cuando **tenía** cinco años me sacaron las amígdalas.

• The verb *ir* can indicate past intentions when used in the imperfect and combined with another verb.

>   **Iba a darle** aspirina al niño para el dolor, pero tenía fiebre también.

Un chiste

Una mujer murió y su esposo, el viudo, estaba en la funeraria con un amigo. El hombre lloraba inconsolablemente. Tenía mucha baba (mucho moco) en la barbilla. Cuando llegó otra persona su amigo le dijo, «Mira, la baba». El hombre le respondió, «Sí, lavaba y cocinaba».

HACIA PRECISIÓN

9.16 Ejercicio

Complete el párrafo con la forma correcta de los verbos. Use el modo imperfecto del pasado.

Cuando _____ (ser) niño, _____ (vivir) en Puerto Rico. Mis abuelos

_____ (vivir) con nosotros. Abuela _____ (saber) mucho de las plantas

medicinales. Cuando _____ (tener) gripe, me _____ (hacer) té de

hojas de limón y naranja. Cuando _____ (tener) gases en la barriga, me

_____ (preparar) té de anís. Mis padres no me _____ (dar) remedios

caseros. Ellos me _____ (llevar) a la farmacia, y el farmacéutico nos

_____ (vender) un jarabe o una pastilla. No me _____ (gustar) los

jarabes. _____ (preferir) las tisanas de mi abuelita.

HACIA FLUIDEZ

 ### 9.17 Actividad

Con un/a compañero/a haga y conteste las siguientes preguntas. Comparta con la clase información interesante.

A. Cuando tenías cinco años, ¿dónde vivías?
B. ¿Qué idiomas hablaban tus padres en casa?
C. ¿Qué te gustaba comer cuando eras niño?
D. ¿Te enfermabas mucho cuando eras niño?
E. ¿Sabía tu abuela mucho de remedios caseros?
F. Cuando eras joven, ¿te gustaban los jarabes para la tos?
G. Cuando eras estudiante, ¿te enfermabas de las enfermedades que estudiabas?

9.18 Actividad

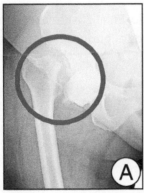 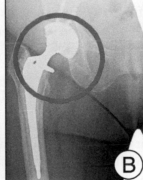 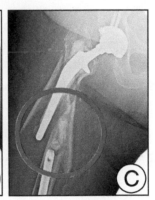

Vea las placas de caderas. Escoja una de las placas y explique la historia del paciente. Después comparta sus ideas con la clase. Por ejemplo,

¿Dónde estaba cuando se le fracturó la cadera?
¿Qué hacía? ¿Qué síntomas tenía?
¿Cuándo le reemplazaron la cadera?   **reemplazar** to replace
¿Qué pasó después del reemplazo?

 ### 9.19 Actividad

The scene from the *Centro de rehabilitación cardiovascular* shows that one's actual behavior may be healthier than one's thoughts. These patients are thinking about their old habits despite their changed behavior. Hold a cardiac rehabilitation group therapy session. Use the imperfect mood of the past tense to tell about

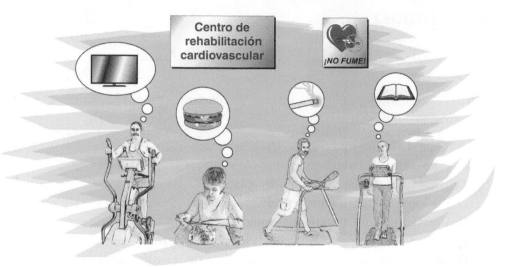

your former life as a heart attack waiting to happen; the preterit mood to recount your heart attack; and the present tense to tell about your new habits. Here's an example.

> Antes, comía mucha fritura y no hacía ejercicio. En el 2011 tuve un ataque al corazón. Ahora como ensalada con vinagre, voy al gimnasio todos los días y tomo una aspirina por la mañana.

Here are some things that may be associated with heart health either for good or for bad.

estar sobrepeso, estar obeso/a	bajar de peso
comer más frutas y verduras	hacer ejercicio regularmente
dejar de fumar	tomar una aspirina todos los días
controlar la diabetes	controlar la hipertensión
comer fritura, comer dulces	cocinar con mucha sal
quitar la grasa de la carne	lidiar (cope) con el estrés
mirar mucha televisión	pasar mucho tiempo en el sofá

Antes comía mucha fritura.
Anoche miraba la televisión.
En el 2007 tuve un ataque al corazón.
No hacía ejercicio.
Me dolía el pecho.
Fumaba.
Estaba en el sofá. El dolor corría por mi brazo.

The imperfect tells the background information (blue).
The preterit tells an event that was frozen in time (red).

9.20 Drama imprevisto

Create a meeting of a self-help group like Alcoholics Anonymous. Use discretion, as you'll not know who may be a member in real life. Use the imperfect mood to tell what your life was like before you made a commitment to sobriety, the preterit mood to say what happened to change your ways, and the present tense to describe your current behavior. Here is an example.

> Mi nombre es Barbara y soy alcohólica. Antes, bebía todas las noches y trasnochaba. No llegaba a mi casa hasta las cuatro de la mañana. No podía levantarme temprano para ir a trabajar. En el 2009 me enfermé de la diabetes y dejé de beber. Ahora voy a las reuniones de Alcohólicos Anónimos, paso más tiempo en la casa con mi familia y bebo café negro sin azúcar.

Here is a word bank to scaffold your communication.

trasnochar	to stay up all night
estar ebrio/a	to be intoxicated
estar borracho/a	to be drunk
manejar ebrio/a	to drive while intoxicated
sobrio/a	sober
pelear	to argue, fight
pasar tiempo en los bares	to spend time in bars
malgastar dinero	to spend money unwisely
dejar de beber	to give up drinking

 ## Video: *Memorias de México*

Vea la *Trama* del capítulo 9, donde Rosmery y la Sra. Flores hablan de sus abuelas y sus países de origen.

Sra. Flores:	Rosmery, ¿piensas mucho en México?
Rosmery:	Ay, sí, y me hace mucha falta.
Sra. Flores:	¿Qué te hace falta?
Rosmery:	Cuando era niña vivíamos con mi abuela. Mi papá trabajaba aquí en los Estados Unidos. Mi mamá trabajaba en el Distrito Federal. Pasaba mucho tiempo con mi abuela. Ella siempre sabía

	qué hacer cuando estaba enferma. Es posible que por mi abuela yo decidiera ser enfermera.
Sra. Flores:	Interesante. Tu abuela sabía mucho de los remedios caseros.
Rosmery:	Sí. Por ejemplo, cuando no me podía dormir, ella me hacía un té de manzanilla. Cuando estaba resfriada, me hacía un té de hojas de naranja y limón con canela, jengibre y miel de abeja.
Sra. Flores:	Mi abuelita también sabía mucho de remedios caseros. Cuando me dolía el estómago me hacía un té de orégano o un té de anís.
Rosmery:	No me gusta mucho el té de orégano pero me encanta el té de anís. Mi abuela también me preparaba eso. Ay, es bueno para sacar los gases del estómago.
Sra. Flores:	En mi casa cuando nos enfermábamos no íbamos al doctor. Primero mi abuelita nos hacía un té. Si el té no funcionaba, íbamos a la farmacia y el farmacéutico nos recomendaba algo. Si el remedio de la farmacia no funcionaba, íbamos al doctor.
Rosmery:	Hasta ahora lo hacen así en muchos países. Y déjame decirte que en muchos países el farmacéutico recomienda los medicamentos que aquí en los Estados Unidos son controlados.
Sra. Flores:	¿Está viva tu abuela?
Rosmery:	No, mi abuela murió cuando yo tenía doce años.
Sra. Flores:	Lo lamento mucho.
Rosmery:	Gracias. Fue un tiempo muy difícil. Mi mamá dejó su trabajo en el Distrito Federal y vino a vivir con nosotros. Cada año celebrábamos el día de los muertos.
Sra. Flores:	¿El día de los muertos?
Rosmery:	Íbamos a pasar la noche en el cementerio frente la tumba de mi abuela.
Sra. Flores:	¿No tenías miedo?
Rosmery:	¿Mande?
Sra. Flores:	Que si no tenías miedo.
Rosmery:	No, la verdad es que todo el mundo tiene miedo a la muerte, bueno, nadie se quiere morir antes de tiempo, pero cuando pasábamos la noche en el cementerio con mi abuela, nos sentíamos muy unidos como familia. Hacíamos la comida que a mi abuela le gustaba, chiles rellenos con queso, y llevábamos la comida al cementerio para comer. Llevábamos flores también, como ofrenda para mi abuela. No nos sentíamos tan solos, porque el espíritu de mi abuela estaba con nosotros. Hasta ahora creo que ella está siempre conmigo.
Sra. Flores:	Es una tradición muy bonita. Acá en los Estados Unidos todo es diferente. Acá celebran el día de las brujas, tú sabes, Halloween,

y no respetan de la misma manera a los muertos. Los niños van de casa en casa buscando dulces.

Rosmery: Los niños buscan dulces, y sus padres pagan al dentista.

Sra. Flores: Es verdad.

Rosmery: Ay, mis hijos están muy americanizados. Tenemos que visitar México pronto.

Se celebra el día de los muertos el 2 de noviembre. La foto es de una ofrenda en la tumba de un ser querido. Cortesía de Carlos Brito.

HACIA FLUIDEZ

 9.21 Actividad

Haga las siguientes preguntas a un/a compañero/a para comparar la vida de su compañero/a con la de Rosmery.

A. ¿Dónde vivía Rosmery cuando era niña?

B. ¿Qué tomaba Rosmery cuando era niña y estaba resfriada?

C. ¿Iba Rosmery al doctor frecuentemente?

D. ¿Dónde vivías tú cuando eras niño/a?

Flor de tilo (izquierda, para dormir); manzanilla (derecha, para los nervios); y anís (centro, para el estómago)

E. ¿Qué tomabas tú cuando eras niño/a y estabas resfriado/a?

F. ¿Con qué frecuencia ibas tú al doctor cuando eras niño/a?

 ## 9.22 Reciclaje

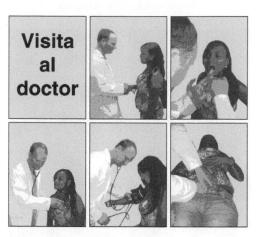

Observe las imágenes de la «Visita al doctor». Usted es la paciente. Use el vocabulario del examen físico y la gramática del tiempo pasado para decirle a un amigo
qué pasó en su visita al doctor. Si necesita ideas, estas preguntas le van a ayudar.

A. ¿Por qué fue usted al consultorio?   F. ¿Le tomó la temperatura?

B. ¿Qué síntomas tenía usted?   G. ¿Cómo estuvo su presión arterial?

C. ¿Le miró los oídos?   H. ¿Le escuchó el abdomen?

D. ¿Le percutió el pecho?   I.   ¿Qué fue el diagnóstico?

E. ¿Qué parte del cuerpo le palpó?   J.   ¿Le recetó un medicamento?

El romero (izquierda) alivia problemas
calientes. El eucalipto (derecha) puede tener
efectos mucolíticos. El aceite de eucalipto
puede ser tóxico cuando no está diluido.

El nopal (izquierda) y la sábila (derecha)
pueden tener efectos antihiperglicémicos
y aumentar los efectos de medicamentos
que bajan la glucosa.

Cultural Note: *Remedios caseros*

Pythagoras said, "Before calling the doctor, call a friend." A Latino might advise, *Antes que llamar al médico llame a la abuelita o al farmacéutico.* In the video for chapter 9, Rosmery and Sra. Flores reminisce about their grandmothers, who always knew what *remedio casero,* or home remedy, to recommend. When Abuela's *tisana* ("tea") did not work, then the family would consult with the pharmacist, who might have recommended and sold a drug that in many countries would be controlled. If that did not work, the family would consult a physician. This particular pathway may spring from tradition, finances, or the availability of a health care provider.

Herbal remedies are available at open-air markets, neighborhood grocers, and botanical shops (*botánicas*), although travelers may bring remedies when returning from abroad. Dried plants pass customs in a way that live plants with soil do not. In the United States herbal remedies are not regulated by the Food and Drug Administration. Although a remedy that is made from a fresh or dried plant is commonly referred to as *un té,* this is a generalization of "tea," which is the name of a more specific group of plants. The proper name for such remedies is *una tisana* or *una infusión.*

Baldo © 2007 Baldo Partnership. Dist. by Universal Press Syndicate. Reprinted with permission. All rights reserved.

The dawning of the age of antibiotics (which contributed significantly to longevity) and the widespread use of medications that either block or enhance (agonize) neurotransmitters led many to attribute illness to microbes or chemical imbalances. Another worldview attributes illness to an imbalance in the body or spirit. Forces that may be out of balance have been described as ying and yang and hot and cold among others. Many Latinos think of certain botanical remedies as being *hot* and others as *cold.* These are general terms that include a small percentage of botanical remedies. "Hot" remedies include ginger, cinnamon, and citrus leaves (*jengibre, canela y hojas de los árboles cítricos*) and help restore balance when we suffer from "cold" disorders such as a cold or a depressed affect. "Cold" remedies include anise, chamomile, linden flower, and oregano (*anís, manzanilla, flor de tilo y orégano*) and help restore balance when we suffer from "hot" disorders such as dyspepsia, "nerves," or insomnia.

In general, many home remedies are effective either for their own medicinal properties, for their placebo effect, for the comfort they conjure, or a combination of these. However, when there is a more effective agent available, the use of a home remedy as a first line of defense may delay medical care at the patient's risk. Although phytotherapy is generally considered safe and effective, it may be helpful to know what a patient is taking and to review a list of contraindications or possible herb-drug interactions. General knowledge of herb-drug interactions is sparse, although the World Health Organization has published monographs, and other books are becoming available in both traditional and alternative markets. Interactions may include the capacity of the herb to slow the absorption of a drug (suspected of fibrous herbs such as psyllium), to affect the drug's elimination, to synergize its effect, or to add to its hepatotoxicity. *Sábila* (aloe vera, more common in the Caribbean) and *nopal* (prickly pear cactus, more common in Mexico) may synergize other antihyperglycemic agents.

The availability of antibiotics over the counter in Latin America has been suspected of contributing to the emergence of antibiotic-resistant microbes. An antibiotic that loses its efficacy may have to be taken off the market for as long as 45 years prior to regaining its usefulness. Some people warn that we will move into a "post-antibiotic" age. Mexico recently banned the sale of antibiotics and antiviral drugs without a doctor's prescription. To adjust to this, some pharmacies have employed physicians who offer free consultations at the pharmacy. Unfortunately these consultations are not usually informed by laboratory and other tests, but the measure may help to prolong the efficacy of antibiotics.

Chapter 10
Padecimientos e historia médica

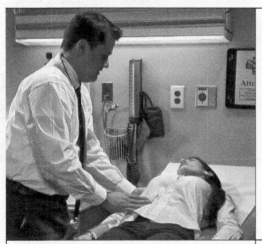

B y the end of this chapter you will know how to ask about medical history, including illnesses, surgeries, and immunizations. You will learn the names of internal organs, to talk about illnesses and diseases, and to prepare patients for various surgeries.

 ## Ask about Current Medical Conditions

Organization of vocabulary aids memorization. These terms are organized in the way that they may be elicited during a history and physical exam. We begin with an abbreviated history and proceed to a review of systems and a list of infectious and tropical diseases. Then we provide more elaborate practice by talking about cancer, tuberculosis, and pandemic flu. Let's begin with the abbreviated history. Some practitioners consider these diseases to be too dangerous to miss.

 ### Vocabulario: Padecimientos y la historia abreviada (*Illnesses and the Abbreviated History*)

la enfermedad cardiovascular	cardiovascular disease
la angina de pecho	angina pectoris
el ataque al corazón	heart attack
el infarto cardíaco	coronary infarction
la trombosis cardíaca	coronary thrombosis
la hipertensión, la presión alta	hypertension
la insuficiencia cardíaca	congestive heart failure
el asma	asthma
el cáncer	cancer
la diabetes	diabetes
la epilepsia	epilepsy
la convulsión, el ataque epiléptico	convulsion, seizure
la hepatitis	hepatitis
la herida en la cabeza	head injury
la ictericia, la piel amarillenta	jaundice, yellowish skin
los ojos amarillentos	yellowish eyes
problemas de los riñones	kidney problems
la insuficiencia renal	kidney failure
. . . aguda, crónica	. . . acute, chronic
la fiebre reumática	rheumatic fever
la tuberculosis	tuberculosis

Preguntas útiles

¿Padece del corazón?	Do you have heart problems?
¿Padece de los riñones?	Do you have kidney problems?
¿Ha tenido problemas con el hígado?	Have you had liver problems?
¿Tuvo alguna vez un golpe en la cabeza?	Have you had a head injury?

**Síntomas previos a
un derrame cerebral**

1. Entumecimiento o debilidad repentinos en la cara, un brazo o una pierna, particularmente en un lado del cuerpo.

2. Confusión y problemas para hablar, comprender, ver o caminar.

3. Dolor de cabeza severo.

**Si tiene alguno de
estos síntomas,
llame al 911 de inmediato.**

Estructura: El verbo *padecer* (*To Suffer From*)

• The verb *padecer* is used to speak of illnesses or conditions from which the patient suffers. In the present indicative tense *padecer* is irregular in only the first person singular (*yo*). It is used with the preposition *de*.

• These are the forms of the verb *padecer* in the present tense.

yo	**Padezco** de leucemia.
tú	**¿Padeces** de diabetes?
él, ella, usted	¿De qué **padece** usted?
nosotros/as	Mi hermano y yo **padecemos** de asma.
ellos, ellas, ustedes	Mis padres **padecen** del corazón.

• *Sufrir* can also be used to identify current medical conditions. Like *padecer*, it is used with the preposition *de. Sufrir* is a regular verb ending in *-ir.*

¿Sufre de alguna enfermedad o problema médico?
Hace cinco años que sufro de artritis reumatoide.

HACIA PRECISIÓN

 ## 10.1 Ejercicio

Haga oraciones completas usando sujetos de la columna «A», la forma correcta
del verbo *sufrir* o *padecer* y complementos de la columna «B».

Modelo: los niños / asma
—Los niños padecen de asma. Los niños sufren de asma.

A	B	*Oración*
los niños	artritis	_____.
los pacientes	asma	_____.
la paciente	angina	_____.
mis padres	anemia	_____.
mi hijo	diabetes	_____.
yo	enfisema	_____.
Rosaura y Filomena	hepatitis C	_____.
usted	cólera	_____.
mi hermana y yo	cataratas	_____.

 ## 10.2 Ejercicio

Seleccione las palabras entre paréntesis que mejor completen las oraciones.

A. La tuberculosis del pulmón es (un virus, una bacteria).
B. La piel amarillenta es un síntoma de (hepatitis, tuberculosis).
C. Los pacientes que sufren de (asma, epilepsia) tienen convulsiones.
D. Los pacientes con hiperglucemia padecen de (diabetes, angina de pecho).
E. Los tobillos hinchados son un síntoma de (diabetes, insuficiencia
   cardíaca).

F. Si un tumor es (benigno, maligno), el paciente tiene cáncer.

G. La causa principal de la enfermedad valvular del corazón es (la fiebre reumática, el infarto cardíaco).

Vocabulario: Enfermedades y el repaso de sistemas
(*Illnesses and Review of Systems*)

Another way to aid the process of memorization is to organize the information to be memorized. Some well-known methods suggest using "pegs" to organize the list to be memorized. For this we'll use the "review of systems."

El sistema neurológico

la espina bífida	spina bifida
la hemorragia cerebral, el derrame	cerebral hemorrhage
el infarto cerebral	cerebral infarct
la jaqueca, la migraña	migraine
la parálisis cerebral	cerebral palsy
el tumor cerebral	brain tumor

El sistema respiratorio

la amigdalitis	tonsillitis
la bronquitis crónica	chronic bronchitis
la enfermedad pulmonar obstructiva crónica (EPOC)	COPD
el enfisema	emphysema
la pulmonía, la neumonía	pneumonia
la tuberculosis	tuberculosis

El sistema cardiovascular

el aneurisma	aneurysm
la hipercolesterolemia	hypercholesterolemia
la hipertensión, la hipotensión	hypertension, hypotension
el soplo cardíaco	heart murmur

El sistema gastrointestinal

el cálculo biliar (la piedra biliar)	gallstone
la cirrosis hepática	cirrhosis of the liver
el cólico, el empacho	colic, indigestion
las hemorroides	hemorrhoids
el pólipo	polyp

el reflujo esofágico, la acidez	esophageal reflux
la úlcera	ulcer

El sistema genitourinario

el agrandamiento de la próstata	BPH
el cálculo (las piedras) en el riñón	renal calculus (stones)
la endometriosis	endometriosis
la infección del aparato urinario	bladder infection, urinary tract infection (UTI)
la nefritis	nephritis

El sistema endocrinológico

la diabetes	diabetes
la hiperglucemia, la hipoglucemia	hyperglycemia, hypoglycemia
el hipertiroidismo, el hipotiroidismo	hyperthyroidism, hypothyroidism
la obesidad	obesity

El sistema esqueletomuscular

la artritis reumatoide	rheumatoid arthritis
la distrofia muscular	muscular dystrophy
la esclerosis múltiple	multiple sclerosis
la ciática	sciatica
la osteoporosis	osteoporosis

La piel

la catarata	cataract
el eccema	eczema
la irritación del pañal	diaper rash
la melanoma	melanoma
los piojos	head lice
la psoriasis	psoriasis
la sarna	scabies

Problemas de la sangre

la anemia	anemia
la hemofilia	hemophilia
la leucemia	leukemia
el linfoma	lymphoma
la anemia drepanocítica	sickle cell anemia

Derrame refers to a leak or overflow. It is not a medical term, but is commonly used for hemorrhage. *Amígdala* is "tonsil" rather than a structure in the brain. A folk explanation attributes *empacho* to food sticking to the walls of the intestine. A parent may report, *El niño está empachado,* and pinch and pull at the abdomen to help "dislodge" the food.

HACIA FLUIDEZ

 ### 10.3 Actividad

Esta actividad se juega similar al *Jeopardy*. Diga en voz alta una definición para una de las enfermedades. La clase debe adivinar (*guess*) la enfermedad de la lista del vocabulario. Por ejemplo,

Es una inflamación del hígado.
—¿Qué es la hepatitis?
Durante un ataque debe poner una nitroglicerina debajo de la lengua.
—¿Qué es la angina de pecho?
Uno en quinientos africano-americanos lo tiene.
—¿Qué es la anemia drepanocítica?

Vocabulario: Las enfermedades infecciosas y tropicales (*Infectious and Tropical Diseases*)

To lead a more complete history-taking interview, you may want to ask about some of the following diseases. Venereal infectious diseases are included in chapter 12.

el cólera	cholera
la conjuntivitis	conjunctivitis
la culebrilla	herpes zoster, shingles
el dengue (clásico, hemorrágico)	dengue (classic, hemorrhagic)
la difteria	diphtheria
la disentería	dysentery
el estafilococo dorado	MRSA, golden staph
la fiebre tifoidea	typhoid fever
el pian, la frambuesa	yaws
la leptospirosis	leptospirosis
la meningitis	meningitis
la mononucleosis	mononucleosis
la paperas	mumps

el sarampión

la paperas

la rubéola	rubella (German measles)
el sarampión	rubeola, measles
el tétano, el tétanos	tetanus
la tos ferina	pertussis, whooping cough
la varicela, las viruelas locas	chicken pox

Los parásitos

la enfermedad de Chaga	Chaga's disease
la infección por giardias	giaradiasis
las lombrices	intestinal worms
el paludismo, la malaria	malaria
la teniasis, la infección por tenia	tapeworm
la toxoplasmosis	toxoplasmosis

Yaws is a nonvenereal form of syphilis that is present in the Americas and can cause a VDRL test to be positive, although the VDRL test is less common now, and more specific tests result in fewer false positives.

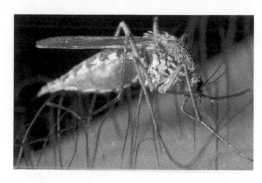

Un vector es un ser vivo que puede transmitir o propagar una enfermedad.

HACIA FLUIDEZ

 ## 10.4 Actividad

Usar el vocabulario en varios contextos le va a ayudar con la memorización. Use el vocabulario nuevo de enfermedades infecciosas y tropicales para contestar las siguientes preguntas.

A. ¿Cuáles de las enfermedades están causadas por un virus?

B. ¿Cuáles son enfermedades bacterianas?

C. ¿Para cuáles enfermedades hay vacuna?

D. ¿Cuáles se mejoran con los antibióticos?

E. ¿Cuáles están causadas por comida infectada?

F. ¿Cuáles enfermedades afectan el sistema neurológico?

G. ¿Cuáles son las enfermedades más comunes donde usted trabaja?

H. ¿Cuáles eran comunes en los niños que nacieron antes del 1956?

I. ¿Cuáles pueden ser transmitidas por vectores, como los mosquitos?

J. ¿Cuál puede ser transmitida por las heces de un gato (*cat*) infectado?

Lectura: El estafilococo dorado (*MRSA*)

Muchas personas saludables tienen la bacteria estafilococo dorado en la piel. En algunos casos la bacteria entra en el cuerpo y causa una infección en la sangre o una pulmonía. La meticilina es un antibiótico muy efectivo contra el estafilococo, pero algunos estafilococos son resistentes a la meticilina. Estos se llaman *estafilococo dorado o estafilococo resistente a la meticilina*. También se llama *MRSA* por su nombre en inglés.

Las infecciones serias son más comunes en los hospitales que en la comunidad. Una infección adquirida (*acquired*) en el hospital se llama *una infección nosocomial*. Para prevenir la infección es importante lavarse las manos. También es importante practicar las precauciones universales, no compartir toallas, lavar bien las sábanas y siempre cubrir las cortadas con un vendaje o una tirita (curita).

Lectura: La leptospirosis (*Leptospirosis*)

La leptospirosis es una infección grave y contagiosa causada por la bacteria *leptospira*. No es muy común en los Estados Unidos. Hay más casos en lugares tropicales. Ocurre cuando el agua o la comida está contaminada con orina o heces de ratas, ratones u otros animales. Los síntomas incluyen fiebre, fotofobia, dolor de cabeza, dolores abdominales y en las piernas y color amarillo en los ojos. El tratamiento normalmente incluye tomar penicilinas, tetraciclinas, cloramfenicol o eritromicina. Las medidas de prevención incluyen:

• Vacunar a los animales domésticos.
• Eliminar las ratas y los lugares donde se reproducen.
• Lavar los platos, vasos y otros utensilios de cocina antes de usarlos.
• Lavar las latas de comida antes de abrirlas o consumir la comida.

Lectura: El cólera (*Cholera*)

El cólera es una enfermedad intestinal infecciosa causada por una bacteria. Se transmite cuando se toma agua o comida contaminada con heces fecales. El síntoma principal del cólera es diarrea aguda. Otros síntomas incluyen vómito y calambres severos en el estómago. El cólera normalmente tiene una tasa de mortalidad (*mortality rate*) de un 1 por ciento. Para prevenir el cólera debe lavarse bien las manos con agua y jabón después de evacuar y orinar y antes de preparar comida y comer. Debe cocinar bien los alimentos y no comer los vege-

tales crudos. Es importante lavar las verduras y las frutas en agua purificada. Para purificar el agua debe hervirla por un minuto. Si no es posible hervir el agua, media cucharadita de cloro (Clorox) descontamina cinco galones de agua en treinta minutos.

hervir to boil
hervida boiled

El tratamiento más importante es la rehidratación por vía oral. Algunos antibióticos ayudan. Estos incluyen tetraciclina, eritromicina, trimetoprima, doxiciclina y ciprofloxacina. Cuando una persona tiene diarrea o vómitos, es urgente beber muchos líquidos para evitar la deshidratación. Tome las bebidas que normalmente toma. También las farmacias venden bebidas de rehidratación.

Para hacer una bebida de rehidratación donde no la puede comprar, use un litro de agua purificada y agregue una cucharadita—o menos—de sal (sal de mesa) y ocho cucharaditas de azúcar. Esta sal de rehidratación oral (SRO) reduce la necesidad de administrar líquidos intravenosos. Es importante no usar más de una cucharadita de sal por litro, porque cuando se incrementa la osmolaridad de la solución también incrementa los efectos adversos de la hipernatremia, como vómitos.

El jugo de fruta y la banana contienen potasio, un mineral que ayuda a combatir la deshidratación. Los adultos deben tomar tres o más litros de líquido diario. Los niños deben tomar un litro o más diario.

Para purificar el agua, hiérvala por un minuto.

HACIA FLUIDEZ

 ### 10.5 Actividad

Usted tiene un amigo que va de voluntario a un país donde hay un brote (*outbreak*) de cólera. Su amigo tiene varias preguntas. Prepare una conversación para presentar a la clase. Algunas preguntas incluyen por ejemplo:

A. ¿Qué es el cólera?
B. Si me enfermo de cólera, ¿voy a morir?
C. ¿Es posible prevenir el cólera? ¿Cómo?
D. ¿Qué hago si la farmacia no tiene bebidas de rehidratación?

 # Educate a Patient about Cancer

Vocabulario: El cáncer (*Cancer*)

el auto examen	self-exam
benigno/a	benign
la biopsia	biopsy
el cáncer de pulmón	lung cancer
el cansancio	fatigue
la célula	cell
la cirugía	surgery
maligno/a	malignant
la metástasis	metastasis
la pérdida de cabello	hair loss
la quimioterapia	chemotherapy
la radioterapia	radiation therapy
el sistema linfático	the lymph system
el tumor	tumor

Preguntas útiles

¿Ha tenido cáncer?	Have you had cancer?
¿Hay [historia de] cáncer en la familia?	Is there [a history of] cancer in the family?

Lectura: El cáncer

El cuerpo humano es un organismo dinámico. Nuevas **células** forman y células viejas mueren. En algunos casos, el cuerpo forma células nuevas y las células viejas no mueren. Las células adicionales a veces forman un **tumor**. Cuando hay un tumor, un oncólogo saca unas células para hacer una **biopsia**. Si la biopsia es negativa, el tumor es **benigno** y no es cáncer. Si la biopsia es positiva, el tumor es **maligno** y es cáncer.

La pérdida de cabello es un posible efecto secundario de la quimioterapia.

Usualmente el nombre de un cáncer específico depende de la parte del cuerpo afectada. Algunos ejemplos son, cáncer del pulmón, cáncer de la próstata y cáncer del cerebro. Si el cáncer de una parte del cuerpo afecta la sangre, el **sistema linfático** u otras partes del cuerpo, se llama la **metástasis**.

Los tratamientos para el cáncer son la cirugía, la radioterapia y la quimioterapia. La **cirugía** es para sacar un tumor maligno. La **radioterapia** usa radiación para destruir células cancerosas. La **quimioterapia** usa medicamentos para destruir células cancerosas. Los tratamientos destruyen células benignas también, pero el cuerpo forma nuevas células. Otros efectos secundarios son **cansancio**, náusea, vómitos, diarrea, estreñimiento y **pérdida de cabello**.

Para prevenir el cáncer, debe decirle a su médico si tiene una historia familiar de cáncer. No fume. No coma carne roja más de dos veces a la semana. Debe comer una dieta balanceada y hacer ejercicio regularmente. Aprenda a hacer un **auto examen** de los senos o los testículos. Dile a su doctor si algo es irregular.

HACIA FLUIDEZ

 ## 10.6 Actividad

Con un/a compañero/a, conteste las siguientes preguntas.

A. ¿Cuál es el nombre de la especialidad médica asociada con el cáncer?
B. Cuando hay cáncer en la garganta, ¿cómo se llama el cáncer?
C. ¿Qué es un tumor? ¿Son malignos todos los tumores?
D. ¿Qué hace un oncólogo para saber si un tumor es maligno?
E. ¿Hay tratamientos para el cáncer? ¿Cuáles son?
F. ¿Tienen efectos secundarios los tratamientos para el cáncer?
G. ¿Cómo se previene el cáncer?

H. ¿Cuáles son los cánceres que el uso de tabaco puede causar?

I. ¿Qué es un auto examen de los senos? ¿Quién lo hace y para qué?

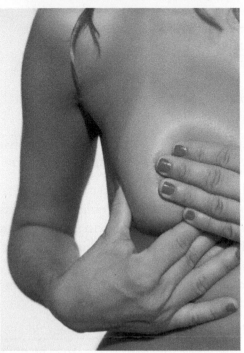

El auto examen de los senos.

Ask about Medical History

Estructura: El pretérito perfecto
(The Present Perfect Tense)

• Use the present perfect tense to speak about a past action that continues to affect the present. As in English, use the auxiliary verb "to have" (*haber*) and the past participle of the verb representing the past experience. To form the past participle of *-ar* verbs, add *-ado* to the stem. To form the participle of *-er* and *-ir* verbs, add *-ido* to the stem.

He consultado con el oncólogo.	I have consulted with the oncologist.
¿Has tenido varicela?	Have you had chicken pox?
¿Ha tenido alguna cirugía?	Have you ever had surgery?
Hemos llamado a la doctora.	We have called the doctor.
¿Han leído la radiografía?	Have they read the x-ray?

• This will be especially helpful during medical history–taking interviews, both for asking general questions and for asking about specific illnesses.

> ¿De qué enfermedades **ha sufrido** usted?
> ¿Cuáles enfermedades **ha tenido** usted?
> ¿**Ha padecido** de paludismo?

• The patient may respond using the present perfect, but it is likely that he or she will use the preterit form of the verb *tener*.

He tenido varicela.	I have had chicken pox.
Tuve paperas cuando era niño.	I had mumps when I was a child.

• Recall that in chapter 3 we used the past participle as an adjective with the verb *estar* to say, *El tobillo está hinchado.* When used as an adjective, the past participle must agree with the noun in number and gender. In the present perfect tense (with the verb *haber*), it is used as a verb, not as an adjective, so it always ends in *-o*.

• The following verbs are irregular in the formation of the past participle. You are already familiar with *muerto* and *roto*.

Infinitivo	*Participio*	*Ejemplo*
decir	dicho	Yo le **he dicho** que sí.
escribir	escrito	¿**Has escrito** tu nombre?
hacer	hecho	**He hecho** planes para la cirugía.
morir	muerto	Dos de mis tíos **han muerto** del corazón.
ver	visto	No **he visto** a la doctora.
romper	roto	¿Se **ha roto** usted un hueso?
poner	puesto	No me **han puesto** el suero.

Un chiste

Profesor:	¿Se escribe *dormido* o *durmido*?
Estudiante:	Se escribe *despierto* (*awake*).

HACIA PRECISIÓN

 ## 10.7 Ejercicio

Complete las oraciones con el presente perfecto de los verbos entre paréntesis para identificar experiencias que las siguientes personas han tenido.

A. Mi hermano _____ _____ (tener) piojos.

B. Yo _____ _____ (sufrir) de bronquitis crónica.

C. ¿_____ _____ (poner) tú la vacuna de la hepatitis B?

D. Mis padres _____ _____ (comprar) sus medicamentos.

E. Mi hermano y yo _____ _____ (consultar) con el urólogo.

F. El doctor me _____ _____ (hacer) el examen rectal digital de la próstata.

HACIA FLUIDEZ

10.8 Actividad

Circule en la clase para hacer una encuesta. Pregúnteles a sus compañeros/as si han tenido las siguientes enfermedades. Por ejemplo, pregunte *¿Ha tenido la conjuntivitis?* y conteste, *Sí, he tenido la conjuntivitis* (o) *No, no he tenido la conjuntivitis.* Después comparta sus resultados con la clase.

Enfermedades	*Nombres de compañeros/as*	
conjuntivitis	_____	_____
paludismo	_____	_____
jaquecas	_____	_____
paperas	_____	_____
varicela	_____	_____
amigdalitis	_____	_____
una gripe mala	_____	_____

10.9 Actividad

Con un/a compañero/a, practique una entrevista para tomar la historia médica. Primero, pregúntele de cuáles enfermedades ha padecido. Después busque más detalles, por ejemplo su edad y dónde vivía cuando se enfermó y si fue hospitalizado.

> Modelo: ¿Ha estado hospitalizado alguna vez?
> ¿De qué enfermedades ha padecido?
> ¿Ha tenido varicela?
> ¿Cuántos años tenía cuando tuvo varicela?
> ¿Dónde vivía en ese tiempo?

 ## 10.10 Actividad

Con un/a compañero/a prepare una entrevista para exponer a la clase. Usted es pediatra y su compañero/a es madre o padre de un niño que es un paciente nuevo de la clínica. Pregúntele al padre o a la madre sobre la historia médica de su hijo. El padre o madre contesta ad líbitum.
Por ejemplo,

> —¿De qué enfermedades ha padecido el niño?
> —Tuvo varicela el año pasado.

 ## 10.11 Drama imprevisto

Play the game *Afortunadamente, desafortunadamente.* One person suffers from an illness. The next student adds a statement that begins with *afortunadamente* and the following student adds a statement that begins with *desafortunadamente.* See how long you can carry a thread of conversation until you have to change topics. Here's an example.

> Padezco de diabetes. Afortunadamente, tengo una receta para la metformina. Desafortunadamente, la farmacia está cerrada. Afortunadamente, tengo metformina en la casa. Desafortunadamente, me gustan los dulces. Afortunadamente, no hay dulces en la casa. Desafortunadamente, hoy es el día de brujas (*Halloween*).

 ## 10.12 Drama imprevisto

Play the television talk show *Hipocondríaco competitivo* ("Competitive Hypochondriac"). You'll need four students to sit in front of the classroom, an emcee, and a studio audience. As members of the studio audience ask contestants about their medical history and current conditions, things get a little competitive, and dare we say, contagious. Audience members may add sympathetic comments such as, *¡Pobrecito! ¡Qué pena!* and *¡Qué calamidad!* The emcee gives points according to acuity, for example, *Mil puntos para Betty por tener la lengua infectada e hinchada.*

 Video: *La colecistitis*

Vea la *Trama* del capítulo 10 donde el Dr. Vargas le examina a la Sra. Flores para saber si tiene colecistitis.

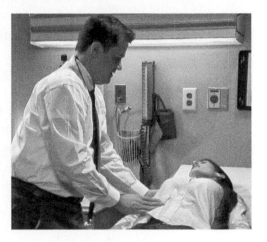

Dr. Vargas: Rosmery me dijo que tenía un fuerte dolor en el abdomen.

Sra. Flores: Sí, doctor, es un dolor terrible, pero va y viene.

Dr. Vargas: ¿Con qué frecuencia le duele?

Sra. Flores: Tres o cuatro veces por semana. Los ataques duran de cinco a diez minutos.

Dr. Vargas: ¿Cuándo empezó este problema?

Sra. Flores: Hace un mes.

Dr. Vargas: ¿Hay algo que lo empeora?

Sra. Flores: Sí, doctor. Está peor cuando como algo grasoso como los huevos o la carne de res.

Dr. Vargas: Cuando le duele el abdomen, ¿tiene náusea o vómitos?

Sra. Flores: Sí. Una vez estaba en un restaurante argentino con mi esposo, Francisco. Me sentí muy mal, y vomité, y él tuvo que llevarme a la casa.

Dr. Vargas: Vamos a hablar de su historia médica. ¿Ha tenido cirugías?

Sra. Flores: Tuve un parto por cesárea. Elsita nació por cesárea. Y cuando tenía diez años me sacaron las amígdalas.

Dr. Vargas: Una cesárea y una tonsilectomía. ¿Ha tenido otras cirugías?

Sra. Flores: No. Esas dos, nada más.

Dr. Vargas: ¿De qué enfermedades padece?

Sra. Flores: No tengo nada. Estoy saludable. Sólo el dolor de estómago.

Dr. Vargas: ¿Tiene diabetes?

Sra. Flores: No.

Dr. Vargas: ¿Ha tenido convulsiones o ataques epilépticos?

Sra. Flores: No.

Dr. Vargas: ¿Ha tenido asma, hipertensión o dificultad para respirar?

Sra. Flores: No.

Dr. Vargas: ¿Ha tenido problemas con el corazón?

Sra. Flores: No, gracias a Dios.

Dr. Vargas: Bien. Voy a tocarle el abdomen. Acuéstese por favor. Respira profundamente.

Sra. Flores: A-y-y-y-y, eso me duele.

Dr. Vargas: Lo siento. Perdone. Eso es un signo clásico de la colecistitis. La colecistitis es una inflamación de la vesícula biliar. La vesícula está al lado derecho, debajo del hígado. Le duele cuando la toco con la mano. Tenemos que hacer una sonografía para confirmar el diagnóstico.

Sra. Flores: ¿Es algo muy serio doctor?

Dr. Vargas: Primero vamos a hacer la cita para la sonografía. Rosmery le va a hacer la cita. Si usted tiene cálculos, o piedras en la vesícula, vamos a hacer una cita con un cirujano.

Sra. Flores: ¿La cirugía es peligrosa?

Dr. Vargas: No se preocupe. Es un procedimiento común. Va a estar en el hospital uno o dos días, pero todo va a estar bien.

HACIA FLUIDEZ

 ## 10.13 Actividad

Conteste las siguientes preguntas basadas en el video.

A. ¿Quién refirió a la Sra. Flores al doctor Vargas?
B. ¿Cuál fue el motivo de la consulta?
C. ¿Qué historia médica tiene la Sra. Flores?
D. ¿Qué empeora a la Sra. Flores?
E. ¿Cuál es la historia de este problema?
F. ¿Cuál es la impresión diagnóstica del Dr. Vargas?
G. ¿Qué otra prueba quiere el doctor?
H. ¿Cree usted que la Sra. Flores va a necesitar cirugía? ¿Por qué cree eso?

 ## Estructura: Pronombres indefinidos y negativos
(Indefinite and Negative Pronouns)

• Indefinite pronouns refer to people and things that we either cannot specify or do not want to specify. Negative pronouns work alone or in conjunction with the word *no* to make a negative statement. Here we also include useful positive and negative expressions that are not pronouns.

Pronombres indefinidos		*Pronombres negativos*	
algo	something	**nada**	anything, nothing
alguien	someone	**nadie**	no one
alguno/a/os/as	some, any	**ninguno/a**	none, not any
alguna vez	ever	**nunca, jamás**	never
algunas veces	sometimes	**siempre**	always
también	also, too	**tampoco**	neither

• Spanish often uses double negatives. *No necesito nada* means, "I don't need anything." The word *no* precedes the verb, and the negative pronoun follows it. The word *no* is omitted when the negative pronoun precedes the verb.

¿Necesita algo para el dolor?	No necesito nada.
¿Hay alguien en casa?	No hay nadie.
¿Ha tenido cirugía alguna vez?	Nunca he tenido cirugía.
¿Algunas veces le duele la mano?	No me duele nunca. / Nunca me duele.

• The pronouns *alguno* and *ninguno* drop their final -*o* when they are used before a masculine, singular noun. They become *algún* and *ningún*.

¿Toma usted algún medicamento?	No tomo ningún medicamento.
¿Le ayuda algún medicamento?	Ningún medicamento me ayuda.

HACIA PRECISIÓN

 ## 10.14 Ejercicio

Complete la siguiente conversación usando los pronombres indefinidos y negativos.

Dra. Ávila: ¿Sufre usted de _____ enfermedad?

Doña Rosa: No, no sufro de _____ enfermedad.

Dra. Ávila: ¿Toma usted _____ medicamento?

Doña Rosa: No tomo _____ medicamento.

Dra. Ávila: ¿Es usted alérgica a _____ alimento?

Doña Rosa: No soy alérgica a _____ alimento.

Dra. Ávila: En su familia, ¿_____ ha tenido cáncer?

Doña Rosa: No, en mi familia _____ ha padecido de cáncer.

Dra. Ávila: ¿Hay _____ en la casa para ayudarla?

Doña Rosa: Vivo sola. No hay _____ más en casa.

Ask about Symptoms

Vocabulario: Síntomas generales (*General Symptoms*)

Síntomas neurológicos

la confusión	confusion
el entumecimiento	numbness, tingling
el problema para hablar	problem speaking
el problema para ver, caminar	problem seeing, walking

Síntomas respiratorios

la dificultad para respirar	difficulty breathing
la falta de aire	shortness of breath
la fatiga, el cansancio	fatigue
los silbidos	wheezing
los sudores nocturnos	night sweats
la tos, toser	cough, to cough

Síntomas cardiovasculares

el desmayo	fainting
el dolor del pecho	chest pain
. . . que corre por el brazo	. . . that radiates to the arm
las manos y los pies fríos	cold hands and feet
el mareo	dizziness
la palpitación, temblor del pecho	palpitation
la taquicardia	tachycardia
los tobillos hinchados	swollen ankles (edema)

Síntomas gastrointestinales

el ardor	burning sensation
el gas abdominal	abdominal gas
la náusea	nausea
el vómito	vomiting
el estreñimiento	constipation
la diarrea	diarrhea
los calambres	cramps
la pérdida de peso	weight loss
la pérdida del apetito	loss of appetite

Síntomas genitourinarios

el flujo de orina débil	weak stream
la incapacidad para orinar	urinary retention
la incontinencia de orina	urinary incontinence
sangre en la orina	hematuria
la urgencia urinaria	urinary urgency
vaciado incompleto de la vejiga	incomplete bladder emptying

Síntomas del reumatismo

la inflamación	inflammation
la hinchazón	swelling
la rigidez	stiffness
el dolor en las articulaciones	joint pain

HACIA FLUIDEZ

 ### 10.15 Actividad

Muchas veces se recetan los medicamentos para aliviar síntomas. Después de estudiar el vocabulario de los síntomas generales, identifique algunas indicaciones comunes de los siguientes medicamentos.

Modelo: Dulcolax.
—Dulcolax es para aliviar el estreñimiento.

A. Mylanta
B. Compazine
C. Calamine
D. Benadryl
E. la nitroglicerina

F. Proventil
G. Prilosec
H. Afrin
I. Robitussin DM
J. la aspirina

 ### 10.16 Actividad

Identifique algunos de los síntomas de las siguientes enfermedades. Por ejemplo,

— ¿Cuáles son algunos de los síntomas de la depresión?
— Algunos de los síntomas de la depresión son la tristeza, la pérdida de peso y la pérdida del apetito.

A. el asma
B. la úlcera
C. la gripe
D. el hipotiroidismo
E. el enfisema

F. la artritis
G. la tuberculosis
H. el ataque al corazón
I. la hipertensión
J. la pulmonía

10.17 Actividad

En grupos pequeños, escriba información para educar a un paciente sobre una de las enfermedades que es común donde un miembro del grupo trabaja. Por ejemplo:

> La pulmonía es una inflamación en los pulmones. Hay una infección bacteriana o un virus que afecta una parte de un pulmón o hasta los dos pulmones. Los síntomas son fiebre, tos, dolor en el pecho y/o dolor cuando respira. El tratamiento es tomar antibióticos o medicamentos antivirales. A veces también el paciente necesita usar un inhalador de alivio rápido o recibir los medicamentos por suero intravenoso y tener terapia respiratoria.

10.18 Drama imprevisto

This is a guessing game. One student volunteers to be the patient, and the instructor secretly assigns him or her one of the illnesses to represent. The rest of the class asks questions about symptoms until someone can guess the illness that was assigned. For example,

—¿Qué síntomas tiene usted?
—Tengo mareos y desmayos.
—¿Tiene la presión baja?
—Sí, tengo la presión baja.

Educate a Patient about Tuberculosis

Lectura: La tuberculosis

La tuberculosis es una infección bacteriana. Usualmente afecta los pulmones y es contagiosa. Pasa de una persona a otra por medio del aire, por ejemplo cuando una persona con tuberculosis tose, estornuda o habla. Pero en un 15 por ciento de los casos es una infección que puede ocurrir en otras partes del cuerpo, tal como en el cerebro, los riñones, los huesos o la espina dorsal.

Hay dos pruebas comunes para la tuberculosis. Una es la prueba cutánea de la tuberculina. Para hacerla, un enfermero pone una inyección subcutánea (debajo de la piel) en el antebrazo usando una jeringuilla pequeña. Dentro de dos o tres días es necesario examinar el brazo para ver si hay una reacción. Si hay una reacción suficientemente grande y con hinchazón en el área afectada, el resultado es positivo. La otra prueba es una prueba de sangre para la tuberculosis. Para hacerla, un flebótomo toma una muestra de sangre. Esta prueba se llama la prueba QuantiFERON.

Si la prueba para la tuberculosis es positiva, la persona está infectada con la bacteria, pero la persona no está necesariamente enferma o contagiosa. Para determinar si tiene la enfermedad de tuberculosis de los pulmones hay que hacer una placa del pecho y/o análisis del esputo. Cuando una persona tiene un resultado positivo, pero la placa del pecho es negativa, la persona no tiene la enfermedad de la tuberculosis, porque en su cuerpo la bacteria está inactiva o no está presente en cantidades suficientes. Esto se llama la tuberculosis latente. La bacteria a veces dura algunas semanas o hasta muchos años sin causar enfermedad. Un doctor a veces receta un medicamento que baja las posibilidades de tener una infección activa. Hay personas que han tenido la vacuna para la tuberculosis (la vacuna BCG, o Bacilo de Calmette-Guerin). La vacuna puede causar un resultado positivo con la prueba cutánea, pero no afecta la prueba de sangre. La vacuna no es común en los Estados Unidos.

Algunos síntomas de la tuberculosis de los pulmones son cansancio, dolor del pecho, tos o tos con sangre, pérdida de peso, una fiebre leve y sudores nocturnos. Hay antibióticos que pueden curar la tuberculosis. Si toma los medicamentos para la tuberculosis es muy importante tomarlos por el tiempo indicado.

HACIA FLUIDEZ

 ## 10.19 Actividad

Hágale las siguientes preguntas a un/a compañero/a para reafirmar la comprensión de la lectura de tuberculosis.

A. ¿Es contagiosa la tuberculosis de los pulmones?
B. ¿Cómo pasa la tuberculosis de una persona a otra?
C. ¿Cuáles son los síntomas de la tuberculosis de los pulmones?
D. ¿Cómo se hace la prueba para la tuberculosis?
E. Si el resultado es positivo, ¿tiene tuberculosis el paciente?
F. ¿Cómo se confirma que el paciente tiene tuberculosis de los pulmones?
G. ¿Hay una vacuna para prevenir la tuberculosis?
H. ¿Hay tratamiento para curar la tuberculosis?

Ask about Surgical History

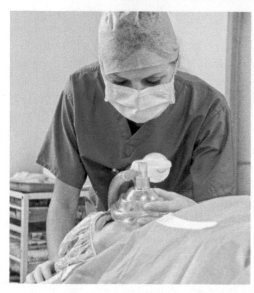

La cirugía (una intervención quirúrgica)

La historia quirúrgica (*Surgical History*)

Like English-speaking laypeople, Spanish-speaking laypeople may be more likely to describe a surgery or procedure than to know its medical name. The doctor might say, *Usted tiene cálculos en la vesícula. Hay que operarlo/la,* rather than *Usted necesita una colecistectomía.* Likewise the patient, giving his or her surgical history might say, *Me sacaron la vesícula biliar.*

Vocabulario: Los órganos internos y las glándulas (*Internal Organs and Glands*)

el cerebro	brain
la amígdala	tonsil
la glándula tiroidea, el tiroides	thyroid
el ganglio linfático	lymph gland
el corazón	heart
el pulmón	lung
el esófago	esophagus
el estómago	stomach
el duodeno	duodenum
el apéndice	appendix
el páncreas	pancreas
la vesícula biliar	gallbladder

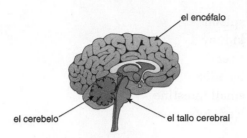

el encéfalo

el cerebelo

el tallo cerebral

El cerebro

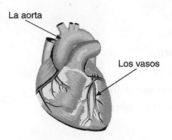

La aorta

Los vasos

El corazón

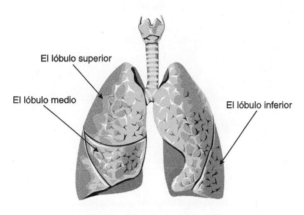

El lóbulo superior

El lóbulo medio

El lóbulo inferior

Los pulmones

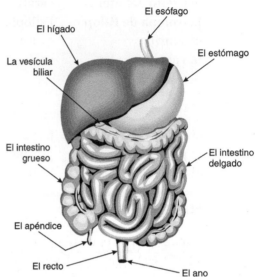

El esófago

El hígado

La vesícula biliar

El estómago

El intestino grueso

El intestino delgado

El apéndice

El recto

El ano

El sistema digestivo

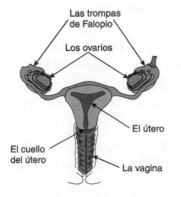

Las trompas de Falopio

Los ovarios

El útero

El cuello del útero

La vagina

El sistema reproductor

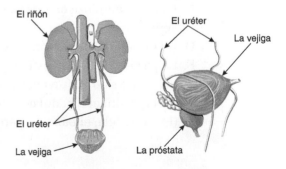

El riñón

El uréter

La vejiga

El uréter

La vejiga

La próstata

El sistema excretor

el bazo	spleen
el riñón	kidney
el hígado	liver
la vejiga	bladder
el intestino delgado	small intestine
el intestino grueso, el colon	large intestine

Mujeres

la matriz	womb
el útero	uterus
el cuello del útero	cervix
la trompa de Falopio	Fallopian tube
el ovario	ovary
la vagina	vagina

Hombres

el pene	penis
la próstata	prostate gland
el testículo	testicle

HACIA PRECISIÓN

 ## 10.20 Ejercicio

Seleccione la opción entre paréntesis que mejor complete las oraciones.

A. Los hombres deben hacerse autoexamen de (la próstata, los testículos).
B. La histerectomía es una cirugía para sacar (el útero, el tiroides).
C. La orina empieza en (los riñones, el hígado) y pasa a (la vesícula, la vejiga).
D. (El duodeno, el pulmón) es el órgano de la respiración.
E. La parte del tubo digestivo que llega al estómago es (el bazo, el esófago).
F. Un óvulo sale de (un ovario, el útero) y entra en la trompa de Falopio.
G. (El corazón, el hígado) es el órgano más grande en el cuerpo.
H. (La amígdala, el bazo) es parte del sistema linfático.

Vocabulario: Algunas cirugías y procedimientos
(*Some Surgeries and Procedures*)

la sala de operaciones, el quirófano	operating room
la sala de recuperación	recovery room
la unidad de cuidado intensivo	intensive care unit
la cirugía ambulatoria	ambulatory surgery
la cirugía con hospitalización	inpatient surgery
la artroscopia	arthroscopy
la cirugía láser	laser surgery
la laparoscopia	laparoscopy
el trasplante	transplant

La anestesia (*Anesthesia*)

la anestesia local	local anesthesia
la anestesia general	general anesthesia

Los procedimientos (*Procedures*)

la cirugía a corazón abierto	open-heart surgery
la cirugía de cataratas	cataract surgery
la cirugía de bypass gástrico	gastric bypass surgery
el amarre de las trompas	tubal ligation
la amigdalotomía, tonsilectomía	tonsillectomy
la apendectomía	appendectomy
el bypass de la arteria coronaria	coronary artery bypass
la cirugía exploratoria	exploratory surgery
la colecistectomía	cholecystectomy
la colostomía	colostomy
la cirugía de la arteria carótida	carotid artery surgery
la histerectomía	hysterectomy
el marcapasos	pacemaker
la nefrectomía	nephrectomy
la neumonectomía	pneumonectomy
el reemplazo de rodilla, cadera	knee, hip replacement

Preguntas útiles

¿Ha tenido alguna cirugía?	Have you ever had surgery?

Expresiones útiles

Enséñeme sus cicatrices.	Show me your scars.
Me sacaron la matriz.	They took out my womb.
Me operaron de la próstata.	They operated on my prostate.

HACIA PRECISIÓN

 ### 10.21 Ejercicio

Identifique las siguientes cirugías.

A. _____ Es un procedimiento quirúrgico usado por los cirujanos ortopédicos para visualizar, diagnosticar y tratar problemas en las articulaciones.

B. _____ Es una operación que se hace sin hospitalizar (internar) al paciente.

C. _____ Es un procedimiento quirúrgico para sacar un riñón.

D. _____ El cirujano hace varias incisiones pequeñas para introducir una cámara pequeña que el cirujano usa para observar la cirugía e introducir los instrumentos que el cirujano necesita para hacer la cirugía.

E. _____ Es un procedimiento quirúrgico para diagnosticar una enfermedad abdominal o para saber si la víctima de un trauma tiene heridas internas graves.

HACIA FLUIDEZ

 ### 10.22 Actividad

Usted es médico de cabecera y su compañero/a es un paciente nuevo. Prepare para presentar a la clase una entrevista donde le pregunta al paciente su historia quirúrgica. Identifique el nombre de la cirugía, el año y el nombre del cirujano.

 ### 10.23 Actividad

Usted es cirujano y su compañero/a es un paciente que necesita cirugía. Prepare para presentar a la clase una entrevista donde le explica al paciente la cirugía. Aquí hay algunas ideas.

Paciente	Diagnóstico	Cirugía
Señor Peña	Cáncer del pulmón izquierdo	Lobectomía
Señora Labredo	Apendicitis aguda	Apendectomía
Tito del Rosario	Amigdalitis frecuente	Amigdalotomía
Señora Garrido	Accidente automovilístico	Cirugía exploratoria

Educate a Patient about Vaccinations

Vocabulario: Las vacunas (*Vaccinations*)

hepatitis A	hepatitis A (HepA)
hepatitis B	hepatitis B (HepB)
difteria, tétanos y tos ferina	diphtheria, tetanus, and whooping cough (DTaP/Tdap)
poliomielitis (polio)	polio
neumocócica conjugada	pneumococcal infection (PCV)
rotavirus	rotavirus (RV)
sarampión, paperas y rubéola	measles, mumps, and rubella (MMR)
varicela	varicella
virus del papiloma humano	human papillomavirus (HPV)
meningocócica conjugada	meningococcal infection (MCV4)
influenza (gripe)	influenza

Estructura: El verbo *ponerse* y las vacunas
(*The Verb* Ponerse *and Vaccinations*)

• "I am going to give you an injection," is *Voy a ponerle una inyección*. To ask about vaccination history, we will need the preterit of the verb *ponerse* (to put). The verb *ponerse* is irregular in the preterit. Here it is used with reflexive objects.

yo	Me **puse** la vacuna para el tétanos.
tú	¿Te **pusiste** la vacuna para la hepatitis?
él, ella, usted	La enfermera me **puso** una inyección.
nosotros/as	Antes de viajar nos **pusimos** dos vacunas.
ellos, ellas, ustedes	Mis padres se **pusieron** la vacuna antigripal.

• Spanish *vacuna* and English "vaccination" are derived from the Latin word for cow (*vacca*), because the vaccine that eradicated smallpox was made from cowpox vesicles obtained from healthy vaccinated bovine animals.

—¿A usted le pusieron la vacuna para el tétanos?
—La enfermera me la puso ya.

- A booster vaccine is *una vacuna de refuerzo.*

    Debe tener una vacuna de refuerzo contra el tétanos, la difteria y la tos ferina cada diez años.

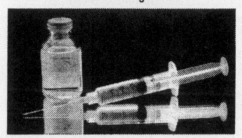

Una vacuna confiable

Gamma Globulina HUBBER Antitetánica (Humana) Liofilizada

Avisamos a todos los Médicos, Centros Médicos, Clínicas, Farmacias y clientes en general que ya tenemos disponibles en cantidades suficientes.
No necesita refrigeración.

EVITE LOS RIESGOS... UTILICE LO SEGURO.

Distribuye:

 CENTRAL DE MEDICAMENTOS, S.A.

Calle Hostos No.105, Sto. Dgo.
Tel. 685-2085 • Y desde el Interior sin cargos al Tel. 1-200-3744

HACIA FLUIDEZ

 <u>10.24 Actividad</u>

Pregúntele a su compañero/a si ha tenido las siguientes vacunas. Por ejemplo,

    —¿A usted le pusieron la vacuna para el tétanos?
    —Sí, me la pusieron
    (o)
    —No, no me la pusieron.

A. la meningitis   E. la pulmonía
B. la difteria   F. el sarampión
C. la varicela   G. la gripe
D. la poliomielitis   H. la hepatitis B

 ## 10.25 Actividad

Usted es asociado médico y su compañero/a es un paciente que tiene una corta-dura en la mano derecha. Pregúntele al paciente qué pasó y cuándo fue su última vacuna de refuerzo para el tétanos. Explíquele que necesita puntos para cerrar la herida.

Motivo de la consulta: «Abrí una lata de sopa y me corté la mano».
Impresión diagnóstica: Cortadura en la mano derecha
Plan de tratamiento: Vacuna para el tétanos; cinco puntos; crema
                            antibiótica; vendaje.

Lectura: La pandemia de gripe (*The Pandemic Flu*)

La gripe es una enfermedad de las vías respiratorias. Un virus la causa y la en-fermedad es contagiosa. Los síntomas de la gripe incluyen todos los síntomas de un resfriado común, más una fiebre alta, dolores musculares, y posibles sín-tomas gastrointestinales como náusea, vómito y diarrea. Las complicaciones serias de la gripe incluyen la pulmonía, la deshidratación y la insuficiencia cardiaca congestiva.

Muchas personas se enferman con la influenza cada año y muchos de ellos se mejoran sin problema. Otras personas son hospitalizadas por varios días y algunas mueren de las complicaciones de la gripe. Hay ciertas personas que no se enferman con la gripe porque sus cuerpos la combaten o porque se han vacunado. La mejor manera para prevenir la gripe es recibir una vacuna contra la gripe todos los años.

La gripe pandémica es una gripe que no tiene vacuna para prevenirla. Para prevenir una pandemia de gripe, debe lavarse las manos frecuentemente y no debe poner las manos cerca de los ojos, la nariz o la boca. Si está enfermo con la gripe o si hay una pandemia de gripe en la comunidad, no debe salir de la casa para ir a lugares públicos como las escuelas o los mercados.

 ## Video: *La sonografía*

Vea la *Demostración* del capítulo 10 donde la enfermera Rosmery le explica una sonografía a la señora Flores.

Rosmery: Tú necesitas una cita para un ecograma abdominal.

Sra. Flores: Perdón, el doctor me dijo que necesito una sonografía.

Rosmery: Ecograma y una sonografía son lo mismo. Es una prueba que tiene muchos nombres. Se dice ecograma, ecografía, sonograma, sonografía y ultrasonido. Son muchos nombres pero es lo mismo.

Sra. Flores: Estoy un poco nerviosa.

Rosmery: No te preocupes. La sonografía no duele. Tampoco es peligrosa. No usa rayos equis, y sí, podremos ver los órganos del cuerpo, para ver si tienes cálculos en la vesícula.

Sra. Flores: ¿Cómo debo prepararme para la prueba? ¿Puedo comer algo la noche anterior?

Rosmery: Debes comer alimentos sin grasa la noche antes de la prueba.

Sra. Flores: Es fácil evitar la comida grasosa, porque me duele mucho el estómago. Ahora como frutas, verduras y pan sin mantequilla.

Rosmery: Muy bien. Pero no debes comer nada diez horas antes del examen. Te van a dar una bata para ponerte durante el examen. Luego te van a poner una gelatina clara en el abdomen y el técnico que te va a hacer el examen va a presionarte en el abdomen con una maquinita que se llama transductor. Es muy rápido. ¿Entiendes?

Sra. Flores: Sí, gracias. Ahora me siento menos nerviosa.

Rosmery: ¿Está bien mañana a las nueve de la mañana para el examen?

Sra. Flores: Sí. No trabajo mañana. Puedo llegar a las nueve de la mañana.

Rosmery: Bien. Pero no olvides. No comas nada con grasa, y no comas nada después de las once de la noche.

Sra. Flores: Entendido. Gracias.

Rosmery: Nos vemos mañana, entonces.

Sra. Flores: Hasta entonces.

HACIA FLUIDEZ

   ## 10.26 Actividad

Usted es enfermero y su compañero/a es un paciente que necesita una sonografía de la vesícula biliar. Prepare una de las siguientes dos situaciones para presentar a la clase. En la presentación, usted va a explicarle la sonografía y la preparación para la sonografía al paciente, pero en estas dos opciones, todo es un poco diferente que en el video. Opción 1: el paciente está más nervioso que la Sra. Flores y hace muchísimas preguntas, por ejemplo si el procedimiento duele y si debe comer ciertas comidas específicas o no. Opción 2: el enfermero quiere estar seguro que el paciente comprende todo, y le hace muchas preguntas de comprensión.

 ## 10.27 Reciclaje

Practique el uso del pretérito e imperfecto del pasado. Observe la receta que escribió el doctor Loza para ayudar a un americano que viajaba en México y se enfermó de gastroenteritis. Conteste las siguientes preguntas.

Farmacias del **Ahorro**
Te queremos bien.

Dr. Rey Loza Gómez
Cedula profesional 2087606
Universidad Autónoma de Guerrero
Real de Cuauhtémoc No. 4

Nombre del paciente: ROBERT O.CHASE
Edad: 55a
Peso:
Presión Arterial:

ALERGIA MED.NO

Fecha: 30DIC10
Temperatura:
Talla:

FUROXONA CP.
1.- FURAZOLIDONA CAOLIN PECTINA SUSPEN.
        TOMAR DOS CUCH. C/12 HRS POR 2 DIAS.
2.- BACTRIM F. TAB. 400mg. 80mg.(TRIMETOPRIMA CON SULFA.)
        TOMAR 1 C/8 HRS POR 5 DIAS.
3.- BUSCAPINA COMP. TAB. (BUTILHIOSCINA METAMIZOL SODICO.)
        TOMAR 1 C/ 8 HRS EN CASO DE DOLOR ESTOMACAL

Súrtase esta receta en cualquier Farmacia del Ahorro

A. ¿Cuántos años tenía el paciente?
B. ¿Era el paciente alérgico a algún medicamento?
C. ¿Dónde estaba el paciente cuando se enfermó?
D. ¿Qué síntomas tuvo el paciente?
E. ¿Qué medicamentos recetó el doctor?
F. ¿Cuántas cucharadas de caolín pectina tenía que tomar el paciente en 24 horas?
G. ¿Cuántas tabletas de trimetoprima con sulfa necesitaba comprar el paciente para tomar el medicamento en la manera indicada?

10.28 Reciclaje

This is a popular improvisation. Practice symptoms and the imperfect mode. Two students face each other in front of the classroom. Student three stands a couple of meters behind student two and visible only to student one and the class. Student two asks student one, *¿Por qué llegaste tarde?* Student three mimes a symptom that student one then deciphers and uses as an excuse, for example, *Tenía alergia y estornudaba mucho.*

Cultural Note: Feeling at Home Somewhere Else

Think of another culture you have visited. Suppose you were living there and had to be institutionalized for a long convalescence. Considering your current cultural identity, what would help you to feel "at home?" Even if you were bilingual, would it be important for someone to speak with you in your primary language? What reading materials would you want to have available? Are there certain foods you would crave and others you would want to avoid? What sort of relationship would you want with your caretakers? How comfortable would you feel about being touched or bathed? Would the gender of your caretaker matter? How much of your personal information, treatment plan, and prognosis would you want caretakers to share with your family? Finally, how would you feel about caretakers writing in your medical record, "Patient unable to participate in treatment because of language barrier"?

Suppose a well-intentioned staff member were to treat you as a stereotypical person from your culture? For example, the dietitian arranges for you to have a special diet of hamburgers and hot dogs while the recreation therapist plays country and western music, but you actually have other preferences. Of course you'd be gracious about it, but would the stereotyping cancel the good intentions?

Now think about your current work setting. Does a receptionist greet patients and visitors in a familiar language? Do the magazines, newspapers, wall hangings, and dietary choices reflect the cultural diversity of the patients and their families? How diverse is the staff at various levels of the organization? Are health-education pamphlets and discharge instructions available in the languages that patients speak? How long does it usually take to find a qualified interpreter or translator when needed?

Of course Spanish-speakers themselves are culturally diverse to the extent that the large group is considered polycultural. They are heterogeneous with regard to cultural origin, religion, ethnicity, geographic origin, education, and socioeconomic position. We may describe North Americans that way, too, and acknowledge and celebrate the way diversity has enriched society. Such diversity challenges health care workers to learn the cultural traditions, worldviews, and practices of their own diverse patient population. However, even when you believe you are knowledgeable about a patient's culture of origin, you cannot safely assume that you are therefore knowledgeable about an individual's personal experience of his or her culture. General cultural knowledge must not promote the stereotyping of individuals.

In health care, there has been a tendency toward standardizing care along clinical pathways. This promotes consistent adherence to empirically proven methods. However, an obstetrician with volunteer experience abroad said about the delivery room, "The problem was that every time we turned our backs, the women would get out of the stirrups and squat in the corners of the room." There was apparent disagreement between care providers and patients about the best position in which to give birth. Health care workers are not necessarily trained to ask the patient his or her belief about treatment. Societies demonstrate varying degrees of expectation with regard to the extent to which newly arriving groups should assimilate.

Aside from the debate about the benefits of gravity-assisted childbirth, there are many areas in which a facility may work to become more "familiar-feeling" to a culturally diverse patient population. One hospital held a meeting between the chief cook, the dietitian, the owner of an ethnic restaurant, and hospital staff members who shared the cultural origins of many of the patients. Staff and patients contributed their favorite recipes from home. Then under the dietitian's guidance about what was nutritionally desirable, the cook was able to translate the recipes to prepare larger quantities of food. The restaurant owners shared information about suppliers of less common foods and spices. As a result, patients felt more welcome, and perhaps some were able to draw upon inner resources of comfort that had been instilled much earlier in life.

Chapter 11
Internamientos, odontología y la salud mental

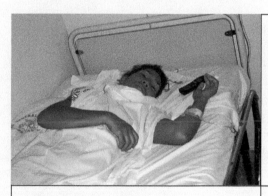

Communication Goals

Vocabulary

Structure

Video

Cultural Note

B y the end of this chapter you will know additional vocabulary to help you with hospital admissions and discharge planning. You will know the terms associated with dental prophylaxis and treatment. You will be able to ask about feelings. You will know phrases and cultural considerations pertinent to basic mental status exams and substance abuse assessment.

Announce a Hospitalization

Vocabulario: El internamiento
(Hospital Admission)

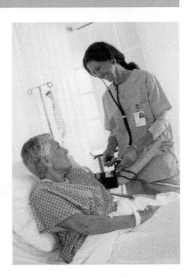

internar, hospitalizar	to admit, to hospitalize
quedarse interno/a	to remain inpatient
la hospitalización	hospitalization
la estadía	stay, length of stay
la habitación privada	private room
la habitación semiprivada	semiprivate room
dar de alta	to discharge

Preguntas útiles

¿Ha estado hospitalizado/a?	Have you been hospitalized?
¿Ha estado interno/a?	Have you been inpatient?

Expresiones útiles

Tiene que quedarse interno/a.	You/he/she must remain inpatient.
Le damos de alta mañana.	We'll discharge you/him/her tomorrow.

 ### Video: *La laparoscopia*

Vea la *Trama* del capítulo 11, donde el doctor Vargas le explica una colecistectomía a la señora Flores.

Dr. Vargas: Tenemos los resultados de la sonografía. Usted tiene cálculos en la vesícula biliar. Debemos hacer una cirugía para sacarle la vesícula.

Sra. Flores: ¿Una cirugía? Pero tengo que cuidar a mi hija, Elsita. ¿Cuánto tiempo voy a estar en el hospital, doctor?

Dr. Vargas: Uno o dos días. La colecistectomía es una cirugía
común. Ahora, hacemos
la colecistectomía laparoscópica. Hacemos cuatro
pequeñas incisiones en
el abdomen, y el paciente
vuelve a su casa el próximo
día.

Sra. Flores: ¿Por qué cuatro incisiones?

Dr. Vargas: Una es muy pequeña y debajo del ombligo, para introducir
una pequeña cámara que el cirujano usa para ver la vesícula
y observar la cirugía. Las otras tres son para introducir los
instrumentos que el cirujano usa en la cirugía.

Sra. Flores: Es increíble. La medicina está muy avanzada.

Dr. Vargas: Gracias a la cirugía laparoscópica, los pacientes pueden volver
a sus actividades normales más rápido.

Sra. Flores: Pero, ¿no necesito la vesícula para nada?

Dr. Vargas: Puede llevar una vida normal sin la vesícula. La cirugía,
como cualquier procedimiento médico, tiene sus beneficios y
riesgos. El primer beneficio es el quitar los síntomas, como el
dolor, la náusea y los vómitos. El segundo beneficio es el evitar
complicaciones con la vesícula, por ejemplo, sin tratamiento la
inflamación se puede empeorar o puede tener infección.

Sra. Flores: ¿Cuáles son los riesgos, doctor?

Dr. Vargas: Es una pregunta importante. En su caso, el riesgo de no hacer
la cirugía es peor que los riesgos de la cirugía. Pocas personas
tienen complicaciones con la cirugía, pero los riesgos incluyen
la posibilidad de sangrar, la posibilidad de tener infección o las
posibles complicaciones con la anestesia.

Sra. Flores: Está bien, doctor.

Dr. Vargas: El día después de la cirugía los pacientes se quitan los vendajes
y se bañan. Normalmente toman líquidos por uno o dos días.
Es importante caminar para evitar los coágulos de sangre en
las piernas. Dentro de una semana resumen sus actividades
normales.

Sra. Flores: ¿Cómo puedo saber si hay complicaciones?

Dr. Vargas: Llame al consultorio del cirujano si tiene fiebre o tiene color
amarillo en los ojos o en la piel. Llame si el dolor empeora, si el
abdomen se hincha, o si tiene náusea o vómitos persistentes o
secreción en las incisiones.

Sra. Flores: Doctor, ¿usted me puede hacer la cirugía? Yo lo conozco, y me siento más cómoda con usted.

Dr. Vargas: Gracias por la confianza, pero no soy cirujano. Hay una buena cirujana en la clínica. Ella se llama la doctora García. Ella la va a llamar para hacer una cita para hablar sobre la cirugía. En esa cita puede hablar con el anestesiólogo también.

Sra. Flores: Gracias.

Dr. Vargas: De nada. Suerte.

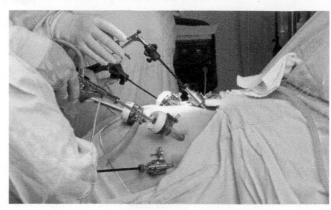

Con la colecistectomía laparoscópica, el paciente vuelve a su casa el próximo día.

HACIA PRECISIÓN

 ## 11.1 Ejercicio

Seleccione las palabras entre paréntesis que mejor completen el párrafo.

Mi madre tiene los tobillos hinchados y dificultad para respirar. El cardiólogo dice que la va a _____ (dar de alta, internar) para un ecograma y una cateterización cardíaca. Si todo va bien, le va a _____ (dar de alta, hospitalizar) en dos días. Ella está en la sala de emergencias y no quiere _____ (quedarse interno, quedarse interna), pero el cardiólogo dice que el corazón es el músculo más importante del cuerpo y hay que cuidarlo.

HACIA FLUIDEZ

 ## 11.2 Actividad

Usted es enfermero y su compañero/a es paciente. Explíquele que necesita quedarse interno para tener un procedimiento médico y contéstele sus preguntas. Aquí hay algunas ideas para comenzar.

Nombre	*Diagnóstico*	*Procedimiento*	*Estadía*
Doña Olga	colecistitis	colecistectomía	dos días
Juancito	amigdalitis	amigdalotomía	un día
Sra. Méndez	apendicitis	apendectomía	dos días
Señor Colón	angina de pecho	angiograma	dos días
Sr. Olivencia	artritis	reemplazo de rodilla	cuatro días

 ## 11.3 Drama imprevisto

En grupos de tres personas, preparen y expongan a la clase una reunión familiar de la familia Flores donde la señora Flores les explica a Francisco y Elsita la colecistectomía que va a tener. Elsita tiene muchas preguntas. Francisco y Marisol se las contestan.

Lectura: Las directivas avanzadas (*Advance Directives*)

Normalmente los hospitales hacen todo lo posible para curar a los pacientes. Cuando un paciente está gravemente enfermo y no hay posibilidad de recuperación, el paciente tiene derecho de aceptar o negar los tratamientos que no curan su enfermedad pero que lo mantienen con vida por

gravemente enfermo	critically ill
no hay posibilidad de recuperación	terminally ill
derecho de negar	right to refuse

más tiempo, por ejemplo, el ventilador y la reanimación cardiopulmonar. Hay personas que no les gusta la idea de mantenerse con vida con máquinas u otros sistemas artificiales. La directiva avanzada es un documento legal que le permite al paciente dar instrucciones a los doctores con relación al uso de los sistemas artificiales. El documento se llama *directiva* porque el paciente le da instrucción al doctor con respeto a los tratamientos que quiere o que no quiere recibir. Se llama *avanzada* porque es importante firmarlo antes de estar gravemente enfermo, en coma o permanentemente inconsciente. Aunque una persona se niegue al uso del ventilador o a la reanimación cardiopulmonar, puede aceptar el uso de fluidos intravenosos y/o medicamentos para el dolor que son designados solamente para mantenerlo confortable.

 ## Discuss Activities of Daily Living

 ### Estructura: Los verbos reflexivos (*Reflexive Verbs*)

• A verb is *reflexive* when a pronoun is used to indicate that an action is done to oneself. The subject and object of the verb are the same. The infinitive form appears with the pronoun *se* attached as a suffix. Thus the verb *bañar* means "to bathe," and *bañarse* means "to bathe oneself."

Baño al bebé diario.   I bathe the baby daily.
Me baño por la noche.   I bathe myself at night.

• *Lavarse* means "to wash oneself." The reflexive pronouns are *me, te, se, nos,* and *se.* Except for *se,* they are the same as the direct and indirect object pronouns.

yo	**Me lavo** las manos antes de examinar a los pacientes.
tú	¿**Te lavas** las manos después de toser o estornudar?
él, ella, usted	La enfermera **se lava** las manos frecuentemente.
nosotros/as	Cuando tenemos sueño **nos lavamos** la cara con agua fría.
ellos, ellas, ustedes	Los niños **se lavan** las manos antes de comer.

• In Spanish, the reflexive pronoun says whose hands are being washed. English uses the possessive pronoun. To use both would be redundant.

Me lavo las manos.   I wash **my** hands.

• Like the object pronouns, the reflexive pronouns are placed before a conjugated verb or a negative command; they are attached to a verb infinitive or an affirmative command. When attached to a command as a suffix, they may necessitate a written accent to mark the location of the oral stress. (Write the accent when two or more syllables follow the oral stress.)

Tiene que bañarse.   You must take a bath.
Se tiene que bañar.   You must take a bath.
¡Báñese!   Take a bath!
No se bañe hoy.   Don't bathe today.

• Verbs may be used in their reflexive form—or not—to indicate an individual's level of independence in activities of daily living.

Baño al Sr. Ramírez.   I bathe Sr. Ramírez.
La Sra. Vega se baña.   Sra. Vega bathes herself.

Vocabulario: Actividades de la vida cotidiana (*Activities of Daily Living*)

acostarse (o–ue)	to lie down, to go to bed
afeitarse	to shave oneself
bañarse	to bathe oneself
cepillarse	to brush oneself
despertarse (e–ie)	to awaken
ducharse	to shower oneself
levantarse	to get up
peinarse	to comb oneself
ponerse la ropa	to get dressed
quitarse la ropa	to take off one's clothes

vestirse (e–i)	to get dressed
desvestirse (e–i)	to take off one's clothes
virarse	to roll over

The notations *o–ue*, *e–ie* and *e–i* signal "stem-changing verbs," in which a vowel changes in all but the first person plural (*nosotros*). There are those in which an *o* changes to *ue*, those in which an *e* changes to *ie*, and those in which an *e* changes to *i*. In chapter 7 you learned the verb *preferir* (*e–ie*). Stem-changing verbs are treated

La niña no se baña. Su mamá la baña.

as regular verbs in the preterit, except for the verbs ending in *-ir*, which change only in the third person singular and plural (note *se vistió*, *se vistieron*, below).

acostarse (o–ue)	*despertarse (e–ie)*	*vestirse (e–i)*	
		Presente	*Pretérito*
me acuesto	me despierto	me visto	me vestí
te acuestas	te despiertas	te vistes	te vestiste
se acuesta	se despierta	se viste	**se vistió**
nos acostamos	nos despertamos	nos vestimos	nos vestimos
se acuestan	se despiertan	se visten	**se vistieron**

HACIA PRECISIÓN

 11.4 Ejercicio

Complete el párrafo con las formas correctas de los verbos entre paréntesis.

Buenos días. Me llamo Juan y mi esposa se llama Melania. Yo _____

_____ (levantarse) a las cinco de la mañana y _____ _____

(bañarse). Melania _____ _____ (levantarse) a las cinco y media y _____

_____ (bañarse). Yo _____ _____ (afeitarse) mientras Melania

_____ _____ (secarse) el cabello. Después, nosotros _____ _____

(vestirse), _____ (desayunar) y _____ (salir) de la casa a las siete.

HACIA FLUIDEZ

 ## 11.5 Actividad

Indique el orden en que usted hace estas actividades en un día típico. Después describa su día a la clase. Por ejemplo, *Me despierto muy temprano. Me levanto a las seis y media de la mañana.*

_____ desayunar con huevos y pan

_____ mirar la televisión y acostarse

_____ cenar

_____ llegar a la casa muy cansado/a

_____ despertarse muy temprano

_____ levantarse a las seis de la mañana

_____ cepillarse los dientes

_____ bañarse y vestirse

_____ salir a las ocho para trabajar

 ## 11.6 Actividad

Haga las siguientes preguntas a un/a compañero/a. Normalmente usamos el informal (*tú*) cuando hablamos con un/a compañero/a, pero aquí practicamos el formal (*usted*) para hablar con los pacientes.

Modelo: —¿Se baña usted por la mañana o por la noche?
　　　　—Me baño por la mañana.

A. ¿Se despierta usted antes de las seis de la mañana?
B. ¿A qué hora se levanta por la mañana?
C. ¿Se ducha por la mañana o por la noche?
D. ¿Se afeita todos los días?
E. ¿Se peina o se cepilla el cabello?

¿Se baña usted por la mañana o por la noche?

    F. ¿Se cepilla los dientes antes o después del desayuno?
    G. ¿Cuántas veces al día se cepilla los dientes?
    H. ¿Se acuesta temprano o tarde los domingos?

 ## 11.7 Actividad

Usamos los verbos reflexivos para hablar de los pacientes independientes, pero no para hablar de los pacientes dependientes. Observe la diferencia entre el Sr. Aquino Linares y la Sra. Silva de Palma.

> La señora Silva de Palma es independiente. Ella se baña sin ayuda. El Sr. Linares es dependiente. Necesita ayuda y depende completamente de un enfermero para cuidarlo. El enfermero baña al Sr. Linares. El enfermero peina al Sr. Linares, pero la Sra. Silva de Palma
>
> ____ _____ .

Ahora, identifique más diferencias entre los cuidados de los dos pacientes con respeto a sus actividades cotidianas.

 ## 11.8 Actividad

Mauricio y Karina son novios pero son muy diferentes. Mauricio es un hombre muy bueno pero tiene malos hábitos de higiene. Karina tiene buenos hábitos de higiene. Observe las fotos de Mauricio y Karina y hable de las diferencias. Agregue (*add*) otros detalles que no son obvios en las fotos.

Mauricio   Karina

11.9 Actividad

La rutina
de Paola

Observe la imagen de la rutina de Paola y hable de su rutina diaria.

 ## 11.10 Actividad

Practique los verbos reflexivos en el pretérito. Los verbos que cambian sus vocales de *o–ue, e–ie,* o *e–i* no cambian en el pretérito (excepto los que terminan en *-ir* en la tercera persona singular y plural). En esta actividad, use el pretérito para identificar cómo ayer fue diferente.

Modelo: Siempre me acuesto temprano, pero ayer fue diferente.
— Ayer me acosté tarde.

A. Siempre me despierto temprano, pero ayer fue diferente.
B. Siempre me levanto temprano, pero ayer fue diferente.
C. Maribel siempre se viste antes de las ocho pero ayer fue diferente.
D. Mis hijos siempre se cepillan después de desayunar pero ayer fue diferente.
E. Siempre me peino antes de salir pero ayer fue diferente.
F. Juan siempre se afeita antes de salir pero ayer fue diferente.
G. Siempre me ducho antes de acostarme, pero ayer fue diferente.

11.11 Drama imprevisto

Play "What's My Line?" Three students volunteer to sit in front of the class and answer questions designed to uncover each one's idiosyncrasy with regard to personal habits. These roles may be secretly assigned, or you may create your own. These ideas will get you started.

    A. Una persona que sufre de insomnio.
    B. Una persona que tiene buenos hábitos de higiene.
    C. Una persona que tiene malos hábitos de higiene.
    D. Un hombre que se afeitó ayer por primera vez en diez años.

 ## Estructura: *Se* y eventos imprevistos
(Se *and Unplanned Events*)

• The pronoun *se* is used with reflexive verbs. It is also used when announcing an unplanned event or one with no specific actor. Use the pronoun *se,* the indirect object (indicating to whom the event happened), and the third person singular or plural of the verb (because the event serves as the subject of the verb). For example,

Se me hinchan los tobillos.	My ankles swell.
Se le fracturó la pierna.	His/her/your leg fractured.

• Perhaps this constitutes a cultural-linguistic pardon that recognizes that some unfortunate events are nobody's fault. *Rompí mi pierna* (I broke my leg) would sound intentional to a Spanish-speaker. *Se me rompió la pierna* (My leg broke) was accidental.

• This construction is commonly used with verbs including *olvidar* (to forget), *perder* (*e–ie*) (to lose, to misplace), and *caer* (to drop, to fall); and with injuries including *quemarse, fracturarse,* and *hincharse* among others. For example,

Se me olvidó.	I forgot.
Se me olvidan las cosas.	I forget things.
Se me perdieron las recetas.	The prescriptions got lost.
Se me cayó la botella y se rompió.	The bottle fell and broke.

HACIA PRECISIÓN

 ## 11.12 Ejercicio

Exprese las siguientes oraciones para enfocar más en el evento que en el actor.

Modelo: Olvidé la cita.
—Se me olvidó la cita.

A. Rompí un hueso.   _____.

B. Olvidé ponerme la insulina.   _____.

C. Fracturaste el dedo.   _____.

D. Quemaste la mano.   _____.

E. ¿Perdió usted la receta?   _____.

F. Tengo los tobillos hinchados.   _____.

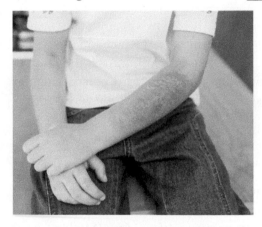

Al niño se le quemó el antebrazo.

 ## Estructura: Los verbos *dormir* y *poder*
(*The Verbs* To Sleep *and* To Be Able)

• The verb *dormir* (to sleep) is an *o–ue* stem-changing verb in the present tense. In the preterit it has a stem change only in the third person singular and plural.

	Presente	*Pretérito*
yo	duermo	dormí
tú	duermes	dormiste
él, ella, usted	duerme	**durmió**
nosotros/as	dormimos	dormimos
ellos, ellas, ustedes	duermen	**durmieron**

¿Duerme bien por la noche?	Do you sleep well at night?
¿Durmió bien anoche?	Did you sleep well last night?

• The reflexive form *dormirse* means "to nod off" or "to fall asleep."

Me duermo aquí en la silla.   I fall asleep here in the chair.

• The verb *poder* (to be able) is an *o–ue* stem-changing verb as well. It is often used before another verb, with that verb's infinitive form.

yo	**Puedo** respirar mejor ahora.
tú	¿Me **puedes** decir qué pasó?
él, ella, usted	Juan no **puede** caminar.
nosotros/as	**Podemos** ayudar a su madre.
ello, ellas, ustedes	Los niños no **pueden** abrir la botella.

• After greeting a person, you may want to continue,

¿En qué le puedo ayudar?   How can I help you?

HACIA FLUIDEZ

 ## 11.13 Ejercicio

Haga las siguientes preguntas a un/a compañero/a. Use la forma correcta del verbo entre paréntesis.

A. ¿_____ (poder) usted dormir sin tomar una pastilla para dormir?

B. ¿Cuánto tiempo hace que usted no _____ (dormir) bien?

C. ¿Cuántas horas _____ (dormir) usted anoche?

D. ¿_____ (poder) usted abrir la botella?

E. ¿_____ (poder) usted tragar (*swallow*) la pastilla grande sin problema?

F. ¿_____ (poder) usted llegar mañana a las siete de la mañana?

G. La enfermera dijo que anoche usted no _____ (dormir) bien. ¿Tiene sueño?

HACIA FLUIDEZ

 11.14 Actividad

Usted es psicólogo y su compañero/a es un paciente que sufre de depresión. Prepare y exponga a la clase una entrevista donde ustedes dos hablan de la dificultad para dormir y la pérdida de apetito (*loss of appetite*). Por ejemplo, en capítulo 7 aprendieron a preguntar *¿Ha bajado de peso?*

 ## Plan a Hospital Discharge

The odd phrase *dar de alta* appears to have its origin in military service. When a soldier was injured, he was sent to the hospital with the orders *dar de baja,* because his movement reduced the number of soldiers. He was returned to the ranks with the orders *dar de alta,* because his presence augmented the fighting force. In hospitals, the designation *dar de alta* refers to the doctor's order proclaiming the patient appropriate to return home.

 ### Vocabulario: Planear los cuidados posteriores (*Discharge Planning*)

dar de alta	to discharge from the hospital
¿Cuándo me dan de alta?	When do they discharge me?
A usted le dan de alta mañana.	They discharge you tomorrow.
¿Necesita ayuda en la casa?	Do you need help at home?
¿Cocina usted para si mismo/a?	Do you cook for yourself?
¿En qué piso vive usted?	On what floor do you live?
¿Hay escalera?	Are there stairs?
¿Hay ascensor?	Is there an elevator?
¿Quién lo/la va a llevar a la casa?	Who is going to take you home?
¿Tiene oxígeno en la casa?	Do you have oxygen at home?

Preguntas útiles

¿Tiene usted familiares o amigos que lo/la ayudan en la casa?
¿Tiene o ha tenido un enfermero que lo/la visita en la casa?
¿De qué agencia es/fue el enfermero?
¿Cuál es el número de teléfono de la agencia de enfermería?

HACIA FLUIDEZ

 ### 11.15 Actividad

Usted es un enfermero que planea los cuidados posteriores para los pacientes hospitalizados. Su compañero/a es paciente. El doctor le va a dar de alta al paciente mañana. El paciente sufre de hipertensión y necesita ayuda de una agencia de enfermería para evaluar su presión sanguínea en la casa todos los días por una semana. Explíquele el plan de tratamiento. También debe preguntarle al paciente los datos personales necesarios para inscribirle con la agencia.

A. nombre, dirección y número de teléfono
B. familiares que viven en la casa
C. información del plan médico
D. agencia de enfermería preferida

 ## Teach about Dental Hygiene

Vocabulario: El odontólogo
(The Dentist)

La boca

el diente	tooth
las encías	gums
los dientes de leche	baby teeth
la muela	molar
la muela del juicio (el cordal)	wisdom tooth
la dentadura postiza	false teeth
la corona	crown
de oro	gold
de porcelana	porcelain

La higiene bucal *(Oral Hygiene)*

el/la higienista dental	dental hygienist
la limpieza	cleaning
la crema dental	toothpaste
el hilo dental	dental floss
el fluoruro	fluoride

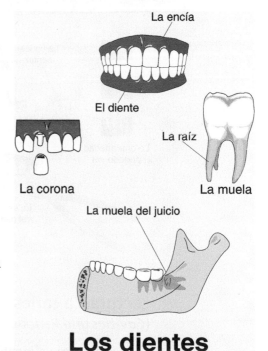

La encía

El diente

La raíz

La corona

La muela

La muela del juicio

Los dientes

el enjuague	rinse
el sarro, la placa	plaque
prevenir	to prevent

Los padecimientos y los tratamientos

la caries dental	dental cavity
la gingivitis	gingivitis
la periodontitis	periodontitis
el empaste	filling
el sellador (sellante*)	sealant
la extracción de diente	tooth extraction
el tratamiento de canal	root canal treatment
enjuagarse la boca	to rinse one's mouth

Sellante is not in the official Spanish dictionary but is often used in this context.

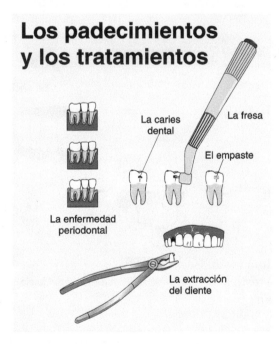

Lectura: La caries y las enfermedades de las encías
(*Cavities and Periodontal Disease*)

Las bacterias que normalmente están en la boca pueden causar las caries. Primero, las bacterias forman placa en los dientes. Las bacterias en la placa transforman en ácidos el azúcar que comemos o bebemos. Estos ácidos hacen las caries. Los bebés que duermen con el biberón pueden tener caries por el azúcar que hay en la leche. Por eso, los bebés no deben dormir con un biberón en la boca. Para prevenir las caries debe comer y beber menos alimentos dulces. También, hay que cepillarse los dientes dos veces al día y usar el hilo dental. Debe usar una crema dental con fluoruro. El fluoruro protege los dientes. Hay suplementos de fluoruro en forma de tabletas, gotas y enjuagues. Debe de ir al consultorio del dentista dos veces al año para una limpieza profesional. El dentista puede ponerle selladores (sellantes) en los dientes para prevenir las caries.

La gingivitis es una inflamación de las encías. Algunos de los síntomas de la gingivitis son las encías rojas e hinchadas, dolor cuando toma bebida o comida fría, caliente o dulce, y sangre en las encías cuando se cepilla. Sin tratamiento adecuado la gingivitis puede causar la periodontitis. La periodontitis es cuando hay infección entre la encía y el diente. Para evitar las enfermedades de las encías es importante limpiarse la boca diario con hilo dental y cepillo, usar una crema dental con fluoruro y tener exámenes regulares por un dentista o higienista dental.

HACIA FLUIDEZ

 11.16 Actividad

Haga las siguientes preguntas a un/a compañero/a para confirmar la comprensión de la lectura.

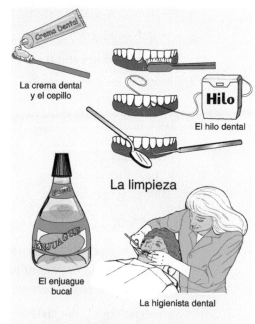

La crema dental y el cepillo

Hilo

El hilo dental

La limpieza

El enjuague bucal

La higienista dental

La higiene bucal

A. ¿Qué causa las caries?
B. ¿Cómo se previene las caries?
C. ¿Por qué no deben de dormir los bebés con un biberón en la boca?
D. Si quiero prevenir las caries, ¿cuál es una buena merienda?
E. ¿Qué es la gingivitis y cuáles son los síntomas?
F. ¿Quién puede explicarme el uso correcto del hilo dental?

 11.17 Actividad

Usted es higienista dental y su compañero/a es paciente. Use estas preguntas para comenzar una entrevista con su paciente. Después enseñe al paciente cómo evitar las caries y la gingivitis.

A. ¿Cuándo fue la última vez que usted vio a un dentista?
B. ¿Cuándo fue la última vez que usted tuvo una limpieza dental?

C. ¿Le duele un diente? ¿Le duele cuando come o toma algo frío o caliente?

D. ¿Hay sangre cuando se cepilla los dientes y las encías?

Conduct a Mental Status Exam

Estructura: El verbo *sentirse* (*To Feel*)

• Until now we have used the verb *estar* to talk about feelings and the verb *tener* to talk about drive states.

—¿Cómo está usted?   —Estoy bien, gracias.

—¿Tiene usted hambre?   —Sí, tengo hambre.

• *Sentirse* is often used to talk about feelings as well.

—¿Cómo se siente usted?   —Estoy cansado pero me siento bien.

• *Sentirse* is a stem-changing reflexive verb like *despertarse* because it goes with reflexive pronouns and the *e* changes to *ie* except in the first person plural (*nosotros*).

yo	**Me siento** cansado.
tú	¿Cómo **te sientes**?
él, ella, usted	Mi papá **se siente** solo sin mi mamá.
nosotros/as	**Nos sentimos** bien aquí en México.
ellos, ellas, ustedes	Los niños **se sienten** mejor hoy.

Vocabulario: Los sentimientos (*Feelings*)

The following adjectives represent feelings. They must agree with their corresponding nouns in both gender and number. For example, *Juan se siente dichoso*, and *Ana y Luisa se sienten contentas*.

aborrecido	disgusted	**celoso**	jealous
agitado	agitated	**contento**	content
agobiado	overwhelmed	**culpable**	guilty
agotado	drained	**deprimido**	depressed
agradable	pleasant	**descorazonado**	disheartened
agradecido	thankful	**desesperado**	desperate
alegre	happy	**dichoso**	lucky
aliviado	relieved	**disgustado**	disgusted
ansioso	anxious	**encantado**	pleased
asustado	frightened	**enfadado**	annoyed
avergonzado	ashamed	**enfermo**	sick

enfogonado	enraged (*slang*)	**preocupado**	worried
enojado	angry	**rechazado**	rejected
frustrado	frustrated	**satisfecho**	satisfied
furioso	furious	**solitario**	lonely
interesado	interested	**soñoliento**	sleepy
molesto	uncomfortable	**sorprendido**	surprised
nervioso	nervous	**tímido**	shy
ofendido	offended	**traicionado**	betrayed
orgulloso	proud	**triste**	sad

These are also used with the verb *estar,* as in *Estoy disgustado,* and *Marisol está ansiosa.* Recall that the choice of *ser* communicates more stable traits.

La niña es tímida.   The girl is always shy.
La niña está tímida.   The girl is feeling or acting shy right now.

The reflexive verb *ponerse* may be used when a situation is perceived to cause an emotional response. For example, *Me pongo nervioso cuando estoy donde el dentista.* Now there's an opening for cognitive behavioral therapy!

HACIA PRECISIÓN

11.18 Ejercicio

Seleccione las palabras entre paréntesis que mejor completen las oraciones.

A. Tomar mucho café me pone (avergonzado, agitado).
B. Cuando estoy resfriado, me siento (molesto, satisfecho).
C. Cuando trabajo mucho llego a la casa muy (agotado, ofendido).
D. Estoy (ansioso, dichoso) cuando tengo una cita con el odontólogo.
E. Me pongo (agobiado, orgulloso) cuando hay mucho trabajo y poco tiempo.
F. Me siento muy (aliviado, soñoliento) cuando paso la noche sin dormir bien.

11.19 Ejercicio

Hay mucho vocabulario nuevo. Vamos a organizarlo para recordarlo bien. De la lista de palabras que expresan sentimientos, escriba tres palabras en las siguientes cinco categorías básicas: alegría (*joy*), tristeza (*sadness*), enojo (*anger*), miedo (*fear*) y vergüenza (*shame*).

la alegría   la tristeza

_____   _____

_____   _____

_____   _____

el enojo   el miedo   la vergüenza

_____   _____   _____

_____   _____   _____

_____   _____   _____

HACIA FLUIDEZ

 ## 11.20 Actividad

Con un compañero/a, identifique los sentimientos asociados con las siguientes situaciones. No se olvide que los adjetivos deben concordar (*agree*) con el género del compañero que contesta la pregunta.

> Modelo: Tengo un trabajo nuevo.
> —¿Cómo te sientes?
> —Me siento *nervioso/a*.

A. Tengo cáncer.   F. Tuve una biopsia ayer.
B. Me voy a casar.   G. Voy a tener cirugía.
C. Hablo español muy bien.   H. Tengo doscientos dólares.
D. El paciente está mejor.   I. Tengo el día libre mañana.
E. Necesito una inyección.   J. Mi amiga está muy enferma.

 ## 11.21 Actividad

Observe las caras e identifique el sentimiento que usted asocia con la expresión de la cara. Adivine por qué la persona se siente así o qué le pasó recientemente. Por ejemplo, *Ella se siente alegre porque su mamá estaba enferma pero ahora está mejor.*

Las emociones

Vocabulario: Las enfermedades mentales y sus síntomas (*Mental Illnesses and Symptoms*)

Los trastornos de ansiedad (*Anxiety Disorders*)

El retraso, el retraso mental	delay, mental retardation

la fobia social	social phobia
el trastorno de pánico	panic disorder
el trastorno de estrés postraumático	post-traumatic stress disorder
el trastorno obsesivo compulsivo	obsessive-compulsive disorder

Los trastornos del estado de ánimo (*Mood Disorders*)

la enfermedad bipolar	bipolar disorder
la depresión	depression
la manía	mania

Los trastornos sicóticos (*Psychotic Disorders*)

la sicosis	psychosis
la esquizofrenia	schizophrenia
el trastorno esquizoafectivo	schizoaffective disorder

Los síntomas (*Symptoms*)

las palpitaciones	palpitations
el insomnio	insomnia

la irritabilidad	irritability
la falta de apetito	lack of appetite
la tristeza	sadness
el llanto	crying jag
el delirio	delusion
la paranoia	paranoia
la alucinación	hallucination
las voces	voices

El suicidio (*Suicide*)

suicidarse, quitarse la vida, matarse	to commit suicide
hacerse daño	to harm oneself

Preguntas útiles

¿Cómo está su estado de ánimo?	How is your mood?
¿Piensa en suicidarse?	Do you think of committing suicide?
¿Tiene planes de quitarse la vida?	Do you have a plan to commit suicide?
¿Tiene deseo de hacerse daño?	Do you want to hurt yourself?
¿Hay voces que le molestan?	Are there voices that bother you?
¿Oye voces que otra persona no puede oír?	Do you hear voices that others cannot hear?

oír *to hear*
oigo
oyes
oye
oímos
oyen

HACIA FLUIDEZ

 11.22 Actividad

Usted es un enfermero psiquiátrico y su compañero/a es su paciente. Practique estas partes de un examen mental abreviado.

A. ¿Cómo se llama usted?

B. ¿Qué día es? (¿En qué año estamos? ¿En qué mes estamos? ¿Cuál es la fecha de hoy?)

C. ¿Dónde estamos? (¿En qué país estamos? ¿En qué ciudad estamos? ¿Cómo se llama el lugar donde nosotros estamos?)

D. ¿Cómo se siente usted? ¿Cómo está su estado de ánimo?

E. ¿Duerme bien? (¿Cuánto tiempo hace que no duerme bien?)

F. ¿Come bien? (¿Tiene un buen apetito?)

G. ¿Oye voces que otra persona no puede oír? (¿Qué dicen las voces?)

H. ¿Tiene deseo de suicidarse o de hacerse daño?

I. Escuche estas tres palabras: *cama, manzana, brazo*. Repítalas.

J. ¿Cuánto es cien menos siete? ¿Cuánto es noventa y tres menos siete?

K. ¿Cuáles fueron las tres palabras que yo le dije y que usted me repitió hace unos momentos?

 ## 11.23 Actividad

En grupos de tres personas prepare para exponer a la clase una entrevista entre el señor Peinado, su hijo Emilio y un profesional de salud mental. La familia vino a la clínica porque hace dos semanas Emilio ha estado *hablando solo* (*talking to himself*).

 ## 11.24 Drama imprevisto

Doña Isabel

Observe la foto de doña Isabel. Ella vivió en Argentina casi toda la vida pero vino a los Estados Unidos para vivir con sus hijos mayores (*grown children*) porque no tenía nadie para cuidarla en Argentina. Ahora tiene síntomas de depresión. Quiere trabajar y sentirse útil (*useful*). Ella no puede comunicarse con sus nietos porque ellos hablan inglés. En grupos pequeños prepare para exponer a la clase una entrevista entre doña Isabel, sus hijos mayores y un profesional de salud mental.

 ## Address Addictions

Vocabulario: Adicciones (*Addictions*)

la abstinencia	abstinence
síntomas de abstinencia	withdrawal symptoms
la adicción	addiction
el apoyo	support
dejar de beber/fumar/usar	to quit drinking/smoking/using
la dependencia física	physical dependence
desintoxicación	detoxification
ebrio/a, borracho/a	intoxicated, drunk
la recaída	relapse
la recuperación	recovery

sobrio/a   sober
la tolerancia   tolerance

Preguntas útiles

¿Toma bebidas alcohólicas?

¿Alguien le ha dicho que bebe mucho?

¿Bebe mucho más que antes?

¿A veces toma muy temprano para comenzar el día?

¿Ha tenido problemas en el trabajo por el alcohol?

¿Tiene ansiedad, nauseas, sudor o temblores cuando deja de beber?

¿Ha recibido tratamiento en un centro de desintoxicación?

¿Usa drogas como cocaína, heroína o marihuana?

¿Con qué frecuencia usa la cocaína (la heroína, la marihuana)?

¿Cuándo fue la última vez que usted bebió (usó cocaína)?

Lectura: El alcoholismo y el abuso de drogas
(*Alcoholism and Drug Abuse*)

aunque
although

Aunque muchas personas no tienen problemas cuando toman bebidas alcohólicas, hay grupos que no deben beber. Los niños, las mujeres embarazadas y las personas que sufren de alcoholismo no deben beber. El consumo de alcohol en exceso puede causar problemas de salud tales como enfermedades del hígado, el corazón y el páncreas. Beber en exceso también puede provocar problemas sociales y familiares tales como accidentes, problemas legales y problemas en el trabajo.

Los tres síntomas principales del alcoholismo son **dificultad para dejar de beber**, **tolerancia**, y **dependencia física**. La tolerancia es cuando necesita beber más alcohol que antes para sentirse **ebrio**. Las personas que tienen dependencia física normalmente necesitan tratamiento médico para dejar de beber.

La cocaína es un estimulante que causa una adicción seria.

Este tratamiento se llama **desintoxicación** e incluye vitaminas, tranquilizantes y observación para controlar síntomas tales como sudor, náusea, temblores, convulsiones y alucinaciones visuales. Para seguir **la recuperación** y evitar una **recaída** es importante tener los servicios de un consejero personal o familiar y de un grupo de **apoyo**, como Alcohólicos Anónimos.

El abuso de drogas es un problema de salud pública. Las drogas más frecuentemente abusadas incluyen cocaína, heroína, marihuana, anfetaminas, esteroides anabólicos y drogas de receta médica. La cocaína es un estimulante que causa una **adicción** seria. Las personas que usan cocaína la inhalan o la fuman. El abuso de cocaína puede causar problemas serios de salud tales como problemas cardíacos, insuficiencia respiratoria y derrame cerebral. La heroína es una droga que proviene de la morfina. El abuso de heroína puede provocar problemas como muertes por sobredosis y enfermedades infecciosas tales como hepatitis y VIH/SIDA transmitidas por jeringuillas compartidas. El consumo habitual de la heroína puede causar **tolerancia** y **dependencia física**. Cuando una persona con adicción **deja de usar** heroína, puede tener **síntomas de abstinencia**. Estos síntomas incluyen agitación, dolores musculares, diarrea, vómitos y escalofríos.

HACIA FLUIDEZ

11.25 Actividad

Usted es médico de cabecera y su compañero/a es un paciente que hace poco tiempo estaba ebrio y tuvo un accidente automovilístico. Prepare y exponga a la clase una evaluación para descubrir si el paciente tiene síntomas de tolerancia y dependencia física y si debe internarse en un centro de desintoxicación.

 Video: *At the Drop of a Hat*

Vea la *Atracción especial* de capítulo 11. Después vamos a participar en un juego.

Dr. Vargas:	Okay, contestants. We are going to play, "At the Drop of a Hat." Draw an emotion from the hat and then repeat a line while acting—or overacting—that emotion. Later we'll identify the emotions for points. The line is *Tengo una cita con el gastroenterólogo.*
Rosmery:	Tengo una cita con el gastroenterólogo.
Marisol:	Tengo una cita con el gastroenterólogo.
Francisco:	¿Qué quieres decir con eso?
Marisol:	Relájate, mi amor, es un juego.
Francisco:	Tengo una cita con el gastroenterólogo.

Dr. Vargas: Okay, for one thousand points, who can identify all the emotions?

Elsita: ¡Yo! ¡Yo! Rosmery estuvo asustada, Mamá estuvo enamorada, y Papá estuvo furioso.

Dr. Vargas: ¡Perfecto! Let's play another round. The line is, *La doctora va a volver pronto.*

Rosmery: La doctora va a volver pronto.

Marisol: La doctora va a volver pronto.

Francisco: La doctora va a volver pronto.

Dr. Vargas: Okay, for one thousand points, who can identify the emotions?

Elsita: ¡Yo lo sé! ¡Yo lo sé!

Dr. Vargas: Okey, Elsita, ¿Cómo se sintieron?

Elsita: Rosmery estuvo deprimida, Mamá estuvo aliviada, y Papá estuvo preocupado.

Dr. Vargas: ¡Mil puntos para Elsita!

HACIA FLUIDEZ

 ## 11.26 Drama imprevisto

Now it is your turn to play "At the Drop of a Hat," a game in which you draw an emotion from a hat and then overact a line of script demonstrating that emotion. The instructor will prepare a container with slips of paper identifying emotional states. Students take turns drawing an emotion and reading a line "in character." The "studio audience" then attempts to identify the emotions for points. Here are a few examples of possible lines, but feel free to make up your own.

A. Tengo que trabajar en el hospital mañana.
B. El profesor / La profesora va a cocinar esta noche.
C. Tenemos un examen en la clase de español esta noche.

Cultural Note: *Los nervios*

Mental health assessment and treatment are affected by language and by factors beyond language. A marginally bilingual patient who is being interviewed in his or her second language may demonstrate psychomotor retardation and thought blocking that appear similar to depression; or may use neologisms or have word-finding problems that appear similar to cognitive decline. The same patient may exhibit tangential speech or talk in a circumstantial rather than linear logic that appear similar to hypomania. Recall that in the chapter 9 *Demostración* video segment, Marisol told Rosmery about her cholecystitis pain. However, before arriving at a description of the pain, she spoke of the anniversary, the restaurant, and the food that she and Francisco ordered. Clinicians face the danger of mistakenly attributing artifacts of speaking a second language to psychopathology, and also the danger of mistakenly attributing mental health symptoms to linguistic or cultural causes.

The versatile *sábila* (aloe vera) was hung on this door to keep evil spirits away. Its use for burns is well known, and some studies have shown that aloe juice can produce an additive effect with antihyperglycemic agents.

Beyond language, many patients have unique psychosocial stressors. For example, a few immigrants have mortgaged family homesteads to unscrupulous opportunists for money to pay a "coyote" for passage abroad. This substantially increases the pressure to work and send money home to repay the debt. Others may greatly miss their homeland but not have paperwork that permits round-trip travel. Some feel caught between the desire to return and the embarrassment of not having achieved economic goals they had originally set off to accomplish.

Patients may have limited experience in describing psychiatric problems. When asked about his or her condition, the patient may say, *Padezco de los nervios* or *Sufro de los nervios,* terms related to traditional beliefs that nerves are central to psychiatric distress. When asked what medication he or she takes, the patient may respond, *Tomo una pastilla para los nervios.* Furthermore, while some Latinos may "psychologize" stressors and emotional problems, others may attribute them to physical or spiritual causes. Some patients retain folk explanations for their problems, including a belief in *el espiritismo,* which is related to communication with spirits. Auditory hallucinations may be attributed to *seres,* or "beings." Clinicians are careful to educate a psychotic patient and his or her support system about the anticipated risks and benefits of pharmacotherapy. At the same time, nonpsychotic patients of Caribbean origin have reported hearing the voice of a separated loved one.

A *chamán* is a folk healer who is believed to have supernatural powers to heal illness, tell the future, or invoke or exorcise spirits.

It is important to assess the degree to which a patient has retained original and traditional cultural beliefs and values. Some clues are elicited by asking whom the patient has consulted about the problem: *¿Con quién ha consultado usted?* This may include a doctor, a priest (*sacerdote*), a pastor (*pastor*), or even a folk healer (*espiritista, santero, curandero, chamán*). It is helpful to know what the helpers have said about the problem (*¿Qué le dijo el sacerdote?*) Because of the primacy of family in a patient's support system, it is beneficial to know how the family interprets the meaning of the distress. Considering the influence of religion, it will be advantageous to discover what the priest, pastor, or church believes about taking medications. Clinicians must assess and respect the current values and beliefs of the patient as a starting point before suggesting an alternative approach. Would you be willing to ally with a folk healer?

There are aspects of the mental status exam that are not helpful when literally translated from English. Clinicians sometimes assess the patient's general fund of information in order to get a sense of the patient's overall intelligence. It would be unfair to ask a recent immigrant to name the past five United States presidents, the distance from New York to California, or the accomplishments of Samuel Clemons. It may be more appropriate to ask, *¿Quién fue Cristóbal Colón?, ¿Cuál es la capital de su país?*, or *¿Cuándo se celebra el día de independencia en su país?*

Sometimes the higher mental functions are estimated by assessing the patient's capacity for abstract thinking. Often this is done by asking the patient to interpret proverbs. There is some controversy over whether a proverb should be one with which the patient is expected to be familiar. Even so, it is probably not as helpful to translate "Men who live in glass houses should not throw stones" as it would be to provide a saying that is more commonly known in the patient's community. Here are several of the more common Spanish proverbs:

1. De tal palo, tal astilla (similar to "A chip off the old block").
2. Casa de herrero, cuchillo de palo (The blacksmith's house has a wooden knife).
3. Todo lo que brilla no es oro (All that shines is not gold).
4. Más vale pájaro en mano que cien volando (A bird in hand is worth a hundred flying).
5. No hay rosa sin espinas (There is no rose without thorns).
6. El día más claro llueve (It rains on the clearest day).
7. No hay mal que por bien no venga (similar to "Every cloud has a silver lining").

For an interpretation, ask: *¿Qué significa eso?* (What does that mean?), or *¿Qué quiere decir eso?* (What does that express?).

Ataque de nervios is a culture-bound syndrome that constitutes an accepted—and sometimes expected—behavioral reaction to overwhelming psychosocial distress such as loss, bereavement, or sudden bad news. It appears in some non-Latino cultures as well. The symptoms resemble those of panic attack, except that unlike panic, *ataque de nervios* has an easily identifiable precipitant. In addition to panic symptoms, sufferers may complain of a sensation of heat rising to the head, may fall to the floor as if having a seizure, or may become aggressive. Although sometimes sufferers are brought to medical attention, *ataque de nervios* is primarily dealt with in the community and without medical intervention. In some cases, herbal remedies and brief, intensive family support may rival the efficacy of benzodiazepines. Often, the sufferer will resume his or her premorbid functioning within a day. When the *ataque* takes place outside of the cultural context, medical intervention is more likely. If the practitioner determines that hospitalization is indicated, care should be taken not to isolate the patient from his or her primary support system.

Chapter 12
Maternidad y la protección sexual

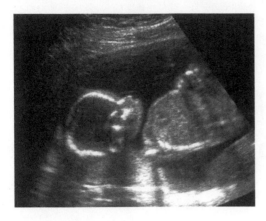

¿Es femenino o masculino? ¿Qué prefieren los padres? Prefieren un bebé saludable.

B y the end of this chapter you will know vocabulary that is helpful in labor and delivery. You will be able to use informal commands to make direct requests on a more personal basis. You will have had some practice educating patients about safer sex and sexually transmitted diseases.

Confirm a Pregnancy

Vocabulario: El embarazo (*Pregnancy*)

La menstruación (*Menstruation*)

menstruar	to menstruate
el periodo, el período, la regla	period
la ovulación	ovulation
el calambre	cramp
el coágulo	clot
la menopausia, el cambio	menopause, the change

El embarazo (*Pregnancy*)

estar embarazada, estar encinta*	to be pregnant
embarazo ectópico	ectopic pregnancy
el aborto provocado	abortion
el aborto natural, el aborto espontáneo	miscarriage

Las pruebas (*Tests*)

la prueba del embarazo	pregnancy test
la sonografía, el ultrasonido, el ecograma	ultrasound
la prueba de Papanicolaou	Pap smear test

Preguntas útiles

¿Menstrua usted?	Do you menstruate?
¿Menstrua usted todavía?	Do you still menstruate?
¿Cuándo comenzó su último período?	When did your last period start?
¿Son regulares sus períodos?	Are your periods regular?
¿Tiene relaciones sexuales?	Are you sexually active?
¿Sangra más que lo normal?	Do you bleed more than usual?
¿Ha estado embarazada anteriormente?	Have you been pregnant before?
¿Cuántos embarazos ha tenido?	How many pregnancies have you had?
¿Ha subido de peso?	Have you gained weight?

*Although you may hear the slang *preñada*, it is generally reserved for livestock.

La prueba de Papanicolaou

Para detectar el cáncer del cuello del útero todas las mujeres que tienen treinta años de edad o menos y son activas sexualmente deben hacerse la prueba de Pap anualmente. Las mujeres que no son activas sexualmente deben hacerse la prueba de Pap antes de cumplir los veintiún años. Las mujeres mayores de treinta años deben tener la prueba de Pap anualmente o cada dos o tres años dependiendo de sus factores de riesgo.

HACIA PRECISIÓN

 ## 12.1 Ejercicio

Escriba las preguntas que obtienen (*elicit*) las siguientes respuestas.

A. _____

—Mi ginecóloga es la doctora Hernández Mejía.

B. _____
—Mi último período comenzó el primero de julio.

C. _____
—Mis períodos duran de tres a cuatro días.

D. _____
—Sí, son regulares.

E. _____
—A veces me duele el primer día.

F. _____
—Tuve una prueba de Pap el año pasado en septiembre.

G. _____
—Me hicieron un ultrasonido el mes pasado.

H. _____
—Hace como tres meses que no tengo la menstruación.

I. _____
—Antes pesaba cincuenta y cinco kilos. Ya peso como sesenta.

J. _____
—Nunca he usado drogas. No fumo tampoco.

HACIA FLUIDEZ

 ## 12.2 Actividad

Usted es enfermero en una clínica obstétrica y su compañero/a es una paciente que vino para hacerse una prueba de embarazo. La prueba fue positiva y la paciente está embarazada. Hágale las siguientes preguntas a la paciente. La paciente debe contestar ad líbitum.

A. ¿Cuándo comenzó su último período?
B. ¿Es su primer embarazo? (¿Ha estado embarazada anteriormente?)
C. ¿Cuántos embarazos ha tenido? (¿Cuántas veces ha estado embarazada?)
D. ¿Cuántos hijos tiene?
E. ¿Cuándo fue su último parto (*delivery*)?
F. ¿Ha tenido abortos espontáneos?
G. ¿Ha tenido abortos provocados?
H. ¿Ha tenido parto por operación cesárea?

12.3 Actividad

Entreviste a un/a compañero/a en español para confirmar los siguientes datos. Después comparta su entrevista con la clase.

A. Nombre de paciente: _____

B. Nombre de pediatra: _____

C. Primer día del último período: _____

D. Duración de períodos: _____

E. Aumento de peso durante este embarazo: _____

F. Uso de tabaco, alcohol y drogas: _____

G. Fecha de última prueba de Pap: _____

H. Fecha del último ultrasonido: _____

12.4 Actividad

Usted es un enfermero obstétrico y su compañero/a es una paciente que tuvo una prueba de embarazo. La prueba fue positiva. Hable con la paciente para explicar el resultado. Estas preguntas pueden ayudarle a empezar la entrevista.

A. ¿Cómo se siente? ¿Está sorprendida?
B. ¿Cuándo empezó su último período?
C. ¿Ha estado embarazada anteriormente?
D. ¿Cuántos embarazos ha tenido?
E. ¿Qué pasó con su primer embarazo?
F. ¿Cuántos años tenía usted?
G. ¿Cuántos hijos tiene actualmente?
H. ¿Ha tenido abortos provocados o espontáneos?
I. ¿Cuándo fue su último embarazo?
J. ¿Ha tenido parto por operación cesárea?

12.5 Drama imprevisto

Tres estudiantes dramatizan una visita al doctor. Hay un esposo ansioso, su esposa y un/a obstetra. El esposo dice que él ha notado cambios en su esposa que le hace pensar que ella está embarazada. La esposa cree que el esposo está equivocado y dice, *¡No puede ser!*

 ## 12.6 Drama imprevisto

Grupos de tres estudiantes dramatizan una visita al doctor en la cual la Sra. Peña lleva a su hija a la clínica después de descubrir que Marisol está embarazada hace seis o siete meses pero ha escondido (*hidden*) el embarazo de su familia hasta hoy.

 ## Teach about Possible Complications

Vocabulario: Posibles complicaciones (*Possible Complications*)

la fiebre
los tobillos o pies hinchados
el dolor de cabeza severo
el vómito persistente
la secreción vaginal
las contracciones del útero

la hinchazón
la cara o manos hinchadas
los problemas con la vista
el dolor cuando orina
el sangramiento vaginal

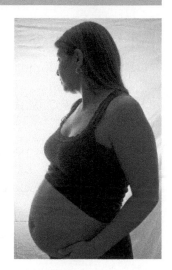

Foto cortesía de Otoniel Acevedo Medina

 ## 12.7 Actividad

Usted es obstetra en una clínica obstétrica y su compañero/a está embarazada. Explique a la paciente cuáles son las posibles complicaciones del embarazo y cómo llamar a la clínica para hacer una cita urgente.

12.8 Actividad

Usted es un enfermero obstétrico en una clínica obstétrica y su compañero/a es una paciente embarazada que le ha llamado para informarle que tiene una complicación del embarazo. Pregúntele si tiene o ha tenido otras complicaciones también, por ejemplo si ha tenido o tiene secreciones vaginales, y hágale una cita urgente.

 ## Coach a Delivery

Vocabulario: El parto (*Delivery*)

nacer	to be born
la presentación pelviana, de nalgas	breech position
romper fuente, romper la bolsa de agua	to break water
las contracciones del útero	contractions
el monitoreo fetal	fetal monitor
dar a luz, parir, alumbrar	to deliver
el parto, el alumbramiento	delivery
el parto vaginal, el parto espontáneo	vaginal delivery, spontaneous delivery (NSVD)
la operación cesárea	cesarean section
los dolores del parto	labor pains
la episiotomía	episiotomy
la placenta	placenta
el medicamento epidural para el dolor	epidural medication for pain
el medicamento para adelantar el parto	medication to advance the delivery
dar el seno, dar el pecho, amamantar*	to breast-feed
la unidad para cuidados intensivos neonatales	neonatal intensive care unit (NICU)
¡Es un niño! ¡Es una niña!**	It's a boy! It's a girl!
¡Felicidades!	Congratulations!

*For those who choose not to breast-feed, *la mamadera, el biberón, la mamilla,* and *la tetera* are all words for the baby's bottle, depending on the country of origin.

**In Puerto Rico and the Dominican Republic, many say, *¡Es varón!* and *¡Es hembra!* but these terms refer to livestock in Peru and other countries.

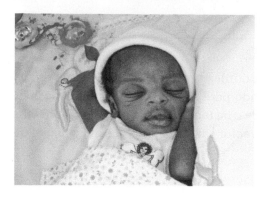

¡Felicidades! ¡Es una niña!

HACIA PRECISIÓN

 ## 12.9 Ejercicio

Seleccione las palabras entre paréntesis que mejor completen las oraciones.

A. La (operación cesárea, episiotomía) es una incisión en la vulva para facilitar el parto del feto.

B. La (operación cesárea, episiotomía) es necesaria cuando el parto vaginal no es posible.

C. La (placenta, bolsa de agua) es un órgano que está entre la superficie interior del útero y el cordón umbilical.

D. Cuando no hay (contracciones, placenta) se usa medicamento para adelantar el parto.

E. El embarazo (ectópico, inesperado) es un embarazo anormal porque el óvulo fertilizado no está en el útero.

 ## Estructura: El imperativo informal
(*Informal* [tú] *Commands*)

• In chapter 6 you learned to make requests using *favor de, hay que,* and *tener que,* and you learned formal (*usted*) commands; in chapter 7 you used the verb *deber* to say what a person ought to do. Here you'll learn to make direct requests of persons with whom you may relate on a less formal basis. Use the informal (*tú*) command when addressing children and persons with whom you are on a first-name basis.

tutear to address informally

• Affirmative (Do it!) commands are formed by using the third person singular.

| tomar | ¡Toma el medicamento! |
| comer | ¡Come más vegetales! |

• Negative (Don't do it!) commands are formed like the formal (*usted*) commands, and an *s* is added. That is, remove the *-o* from the first person singular form of the present tense and add *-es* for verbs that end in *-ar* and *-as* for verbs that end in *-er* and *-ir.*

tomar	¡No tomes el medicamento!
comer	¡No comas nada!

• Commands are direct and to the point, and as such may be useful during labor and delivery.

empujar	¡Empuja!	¡No empujes!
respirar	¡Respira!	¡No respires!
mirar	¡Mira!	¡No mires!

• When reflexive or object pronouns are used with commands, the pronouns are suffixes to affirmative commands and placed before negative commands as a separate word. When the use of a pronoun results in the spoken stress being prior to the penultimate syllable, an accent mark is written.

acostarse	¡Acuéstate!	¡No te acuestes!
	—boca arriba (*face up*)	
	—boca abajo (*face down*)	
bañarse	¡Báñate!	¡No te bañes!
lavarse	¡Lávate las manos!	¡No te laves las manos!
levantarse	¡Levántate!	¡No te levantes!
moverse	¡Muévete!	¡No te muevas!
virarse	¡Vírate!	¡No te vires!

• Here are eight commonly used irregular verbs.

decir	¡Di!	¡No digas!
hacer	¡Haz!	¡No hagas!
ir	¡Ve!	¡No vayas!
poner	¡Pon!	¡No pongas!
salir	¡Sal!	¡No salgas!
ser	¡Sé!	¡No seas!
tener	¡Ten!	¡No tengas!
venir	¡Ven!	¡No vengas!

HACIA PRECISIÓN

 ## 12.10 Ejercicio

Complete las dos columnas con los imperativos afirmativos y negativos que faltan.

Imperativo informal afirmativo	*Imperativo informal negativo*
A. ¡_____!	A. ¡No te muevas!
B. ¡Levántate!	B. ¡_____!
C. ¡_____!	C. ¡No te vires!
D. ¡_____!	D. ¡No te bañes hoy!
E. ¡Come!	E. ¡_____!
F. ¡Acuéstate!	F. ¡_____!
G. ¡_____!	G. ¡No levantes el brazo!
H. ¡Respira!	H. ¡_____!

12.11 Ejercicio

Escriba los imperativos informales que mejor completen las siguientes oraciones afirmativas y negativas.

A. (hacer)   No _____ la cita para hoy. _____ la cita para mañana.

B. (salir)   _____ temprano de la casa. No _____ tarde.

C. (irse)   _____ al consultorio. No _____ al hospital.

D. (bañar)   No _____ al bebé hoy. _____ al bebé mañana.

E. (bañarse)   No _____ hoy. _____ mañana.

F. (ponerse)   _____ la bata del hospital. No _____ ropa interior.

G. (comer)   No _____ nada después de las once. _____ bien mañana.

12.12 Ejercicio

Complete los siguientes imperativos que se escuchan frecuentemente en el área de partos.

A. ¡No _____ _____ (preocuparse)!

B. ¡_____ (relajarse)!

C. ¡No _____ (comer) nada!

D. Si tienes sed, ¡_____ (comer) pedacitos de hielo (*ice chips*)!

E. ¡_____ (empujar)!

F. ¡No _____ (empujar)!

G. ¡_____ (respirar)!

H. ¡No _____ (respirar)!

HACIA FLUIDEZ

12.13 Actividad

Vamos a jugar *Simon Says*. El profesor va a decir—o no—*Simón dice* antes de dar un imperativo. La clase obedece (*obeys*)—o no—según las instrucciones. Note que ¡Muévete! significa *Move!* pero ¡Mueve el brazo! no es reflexivo. Aquí hay algunos imperativos para empezar el juego.

A. ¡Levántate!   E. ¡Abre la boca!
B. ¡No te levantes!   F. ¡Cierra los ojos!
C. ¡Siéntate!   G. ¡No muevas el dedo!
D. ¡Mueve la mano derecha!   H. ¡Levanta el pie izquierdo!

Lectura: Después del parto

Después del parto es normal sangrar por la vagina por dos o hasta tres semanas. Pero si sangra mucho o la sangre es muy roja, acuéstese con los pies elevados por dos o tres horas. Si la sangre continua, llame a su médico. No tenga relaciones sexuales por las primeras seis semanas después del parto o hasta

Dar el seno es dar amor.

que su obstetra, ginecólogo o partera le dé el permiso. Si tiene relaciones durante este tiempo, puede quedarse embarazada otra vez.

Si amamanta al bebé debe de amamantarlo en el principio de ocho a doce veces en veinticuatro horas. No se ponga a dieta. Necesita calorías y fluidos para lactar (producir leche). Coma una dieta balanceada y siga tomando las vitaminas prenatales.

Promote Safer Sex

Vocabulario: Las enfermedades transmitidas sexualmente (*Sexually Transmitted Diseases*)

Las enfermedades

la clamidia	chlamydia
la gonorrea	gonorrhea
la hepatitis B, C	hepatitis B, C
el herpes	herpes
la enfermedad de VIH	HIV disease
el SIDA	AIDS
la sífilis	syphilis

la verruga venérea   genital wart, papiloma
el virus del papiloma humano   papiloma virus

Los síntomas

el ardor   burning sensation
las ampollas   blisters
el dolor al orinar   painful urination
el goteo   dripping
las lesiones   lesions
la orina oscura   dark-colored urine

Las prevenciones

abstenerse   to abstain (conjugate like *tener*)
el condón de látex   latex condom
la educación   education
el examen pélvico   pelvic exam

La abstinencia es la única forma de evitar las enfermedades de transmisión sexual. Si no puede abstenerse, debe tener una relación sexual monógama con un compañero sano. Los condones de látex son efectivos contra el VIH.

Lectura: EL SIDA (*AIDS*)

El Síndrome de Inmunodeficiencia Adquirida (SIDA) es una enfermedad muy grave que daña las defensas del cuerpo. Daña la capacidad   **dañar** to damage
que tiene el cuerpo para combatir infecciones. Hay un virus llamado VIH (uve-i-hache) que causa el SIDA. Una persona puede tener el virus por muchos años sin estar enfermo o tener los síntomas del SIDA. Una persona infectada que no tiene síntomas del SIDA puede transmitir el virus a otra persona. Esta persona es *un portador sano* del SIDA. Algunos de los síntomas del SIDA son inflamación de los ganglios linfáticos, fiebre persis-   **ganglios linfáticos** lymph glands
tente sin explicación, sudores nocturnos, una pérdida rápida de peso, fatiga constante, diarrea persistente y manchas blancas en la boca (infección por hongos, o *thrush* en inglés). Hay otras enfermedades que pueden causar estos síntomas y no es necesariamente el SIDA. Si tiene algunos de estos síntomas sin una buena explicación, llame al médico.

La educación es la mejor defensa contra el SIDA. Es importante saber cómo defenderse del SIDA. La manera más segura es abstenerse, o no tener relaciones sexuales. Si tiene relaciones, es importante tenerlas con una sola persona y saber que esa persona es una persona sana. La comunicación entre parejas es esencial. Hay que hablar con la pareja acerca del SIDA y acerca de su historia sexual. Es muy peligroso tener relaciones sexuales con una persona que se inyecta drogas, o con varias personas. Es importante usar un condón de látex. Debe tener una prueba del VIH antes de planear el embarazo. Una madre infectada puede transmitir el virus al bebé.

> 1. Hable con la pareja sobre el SIDA.
> 2. Use un condón de látex cada vez que tiene contacto sexual.
> 3. No use drogas. Si usa drogas, no comparta jeringuillas. Lávelas con una solución de cloro y agua y enjuáguelas con agua.

Es peligroso inyectarse con drogas. Para estar saludable, deje de usar las drogas. Si no puede dejar de usar las drogas, no use las jeringuillas de otra persona y no comparta las jeringuillas. Si va a usar una jeringuilla más de una vez, lávela con una solución de cloro (Clorox) y agua y después enjuáguela con agua. Hágalo cada vez que la usa.

 abrazarse to hug

El SIDA no puede ser transmitido por contacto casual. Compartir comida, usar baños públicos, o abrazarse con una persona infectada no es peligroso.

No hay todavía cura para el SIDA pero hay tratamiento. Hay drogas anti-virales que pueden extender la vida de algunas personas. Si tiene síntomas del SIDA, es muy importante hablar con el médico o ir a una clínica.

HACIA FLUIDEZ

12.14 Actividad

Con un/a compañero/a confirme su comprensión de la lectura. Conteste las preguntas usando oraciones completas.

A. ¿Qué es el SIDA, y qué lo causa?

B. ¿Cuáles son los síntomas del SIDA?

C. ¿Cuál es la mejor defensa contra el SIDA?

D. ¿Con quién se debe hablar sobre el SIDA?

E. ¿Por qué se debe usar un condón de látex?

F. Si se inyecta drogas, ¿cómo debe lavar la jeringuilla?

G. ¿Se puede transmitir el SIDA al usar baños públicos?

H. ¿Hay cura para el SIDA?

I. ¿Cuándo debe consultarse con un doctor?

12.15 Actividad

Con un/a compañero/a haga y conteste las siguientes preguntas y así practique cómo educar a un paciente sobre la protección sexual.

A. ¿Cuál es la manera más segura de evitar las enfermedades de transmisión sexual?

B. ¿Tienen siempre síntomas las enfermedades transmitidas sexualmente?

C. ¿Cuáles son algunos de los síntomas de las enfermedades de transmisión sexual?

D. ¿Qué debe hacer si se tiene algunos de los síntomas?

E. ¿Quién debe ir al médico o a una clínica regularmente para hacerse un análisis de sangre?

F. Si tengo relaciones sexuales con varias personas, ¿qué protección debo usar?

 ## 12.16 Actividad

Usted es enfermero en una clínica del Departamento de Salud Pública. Su compañero/a es un paciente que pide una prueba de VIH. Prepare y presente a la clase una entrevista educativa.

12.17 Drama imprevisto

Un/a estudiante dramatiza la vida de Víctor L. Virus, y la clase lo entrevista sobre su vida interesante. Aquí hay algunas posibles preguntas, pero la clase puede inventar sus proprias preguntas. Víctor contesta ad líbitum.

A. ¿Eres introvertido o extrovertido?

B. ¿Conoces a mi hermano?

C. ¿Tienes una personalidad contagiosa?

Víctor L. Virus

D. ¿Qué te gusta hacer?

E. ¿Te gustan las personas que beben? ¿Por qué?

F. ¿Con qué frecuencia te lavas las manos? ¿Debo lavarme las manos frecuentemente?

G. Dicen que tu primera novia no era lo que esperabas. ¿Qué pasó?

H. Si tú y yo salimos una noche, ¿qué debo esperar? ¿Hay algo que no debemos usar?

I. ¿Es verdad que a veces usted duerme por mucho tiempo y al despertarse quiere reproducir?

 ## Video: *Mi hermano tiene SIDA*

Vea la *Trama* del capítulo 12 donde Marisol y Francisco hablan de cómo cuidar a Raúl el hermano de Marisol que sufre de VIH y ya no puede vivir solo.

Francisco: Marisol, me siento muy contento. Tu cirugía salió bien. Pero me dijiste que querías hablar algo conmigo.

Marisol: Sí. Quiero hablar contigo sobre mi hermano Raúl. Francisco, estoy muy preocupada por él. Ya no puede vivir solo. Él necesita ayuda. Creo que tiene que venir a vivir con nosotros ahora.

Francisco: ¿Qué ayuda necesita?

Marisol: Sabes que él vive en un quinto piso y no puede subir la escalera. Siempre se siente cansado. Y a veces no se toma el medicamento.

Francisco: Mi amor, Raúl tiene SIDA.

Marisol: Sí, yo entiendo que Raúl tiene SIDA, y la hepatitis B también.

Francisco: Raúl usa drogas.

Marisol: Raúl usaba drogas. Él está limpio hace dos años. Tú lo sabes.

Francisco: Tienes razón. Usaba drogas. Usó drogas por varios años, hasta que le diagnosticaron con el virus VIH. Dejó de usar drogas hace dos años. Es verdad. No le fue fácil, pero lo hizo. Mira, no quiero discutir contigo. Simplemente estoy preocupado por Elsita. Tenemos que pensar en Elsita primero.

Marisol: Yo siempre pienso en Elsita. Creo que podemos cuidar a mi hermano sin ponerla en riesgo.

Francisco: ¿Dijiste sin ponerla en riesgo? El SIDA es contagioso, ¿no?

Marisol: He leído mucho acerca del SIDA. Y hablé con el trabajador social de Raúl. El SIDA es contagioso, sí, pero no puede ser transmitido por contacto casual. Se puede vivir juntos, compartir la comida, hasta usar el mismo baño. El SIDA se transmite de una persona a otra a través de la sangre, el semen, las secreciones vaginales y por amamantar. Para protegernos, si tenemos una cortada, tenemos que cubrirla con un curita, y tenemos que lavarnos las manos frecuentemente.

Francisco: Y la hepatitis, ¿no es contagiosa también?

Marisol: Raúl tiene la hepatitis B. Como el SIDA, la hepatitis B se transmite a través de la sangre y otros fluidos del cuerpo. La diferencia es que hay una vacuna que nos puede proteger de la hepatitis B. Nos podemos vacunar.

Francisco: Es mucho trabajo, trabajar, cuidar a Elsita y cuidar a tu hermano. ¿Por qué Raúl no va a un asilo? En los asilos saben cuidar a las personas con SIDA.

Marisol: No me hables de un asilo. Él es mi hermano. En el asilo muy pocas personas hablan español. No le hacen la comida que a él le gusta. No hacen arroz todos los días. Tratan a los enfermos como números, o como pacientes; no como personas.

Francisco: Sí, tienes razón. Va a cambiar nuestra rutina, pero él va a sentirse mejor. Estoy de acuerdo contigo. Él puede vivir con nosotros.

Marisol: ¿Sabes por qué te amo Francisco?

Francisco: Dímelo.

Marisol: Porque siempre sabes qué debemos hacer.

HACIA FLUIDEZ

12.18 Drama imprevisto

Form appropriately sized groups to improvise the following situations. You may take a few moments to plan your role-play, but your skit should be unscripted.

A. Enact a Flores family meeting in which Marisol and Francisco explain to Elsita just what she needs to know about *tío* Raúl coming to live with them.

B. Enact a meeting between Marisol, Francisco, and Raúl in which Marisol and Francisco attempt to convince Raúl, who is an independent person with medical and home-care needs, that he should live with them.

C. Enact a home-care evaluation conducted by a visiting nurse at the Flores's home with Raúl, Marisol, and Francisco present.

Video: *What's My Line—What's Your Temperature?*

Vea la *Atracción especial* del capítulo 12. Después usted va a tener una oportunidad para jugar *What's My Line—What's Your Temperature?*, también.

Dr. Vargas: Okay, contestants. We are going to play "What's My Line— What's Your Temperature?" Draw a medical specialty from the hat and then act that role by asking about symptoms. Later, we'll identify the specialties for points. Have fun! To begin this round, everyone draw a card from the hat, and then circulate asking questions and performing examinations.

Rosmery: Déjame ver la boca. ¿Te cepillaste hoy? ¿Usas hilo dental todos los días? Dos veces por día, ¿ah? Tienes muchas caries. Aparte de eso, una sonrisa muy bonita.

Marisol: ¿Te sientes triste? ¿Escuchas voces? ¿Cómo te sientes cuando estás enojado?

Francisco: ¿Evacuaste hoy? ¿Tienes diarrea? ¿Estás estreñida? Tengo que introducir una cámara por el ano.

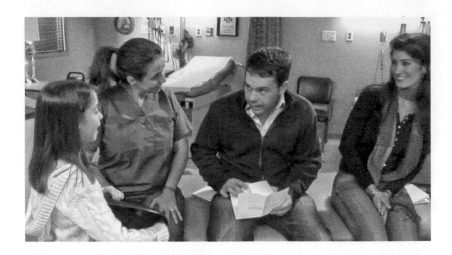

Dr. Vargas: Okay, for one thousand points, who can identify all the specialties?

Elsita: ¡Yo! ¡Yo! Rosmery es odontóloga, Mamá es psicóloga y Papá es gastroenterólogo.

Dr. Vargas: ¡Ah, perfecto! Let's play another round. All players draw another card.

Rosmery: Vamos a escucharte el corazón. U-u-y-y, estás enamorado. Está latiendo mucho. Vamos a ver los tobillos si están hinchados. Están hinchados. Te voy a dar una receta para la nitroglicerina.

Marisol: ¿Cuánto pesas? ¿Usas drogas? ¿Tomas alcohol?

Francisco: ¿Me oyes bien? ¿Tienes una tos seca? ¿Te duele la garganta?

Dr. Vargas: Okay, for ten thousand points, who can identify all the specialties?

Elsita: ¡Yo lo sé! ¡Yo lo sé!

Dr. Vargas: ¿Quiénes son, Elsita?

Elsita: Rosmery es cardióloga. Mamá es anestesióloga y Papá es otorrinolaringólogo.

Dr. Vargas: ¡Diez mil puntos para Elsita!

HACIA FLUIDEZ

 ## 12.19 Drama imprevisto

Now it is your turn to play "What's My Line—What's Your Temperature?" The instructor will prepare a container with slips of paper identifying medical specialties. Several students will take a paper and then ask each other the questions that a person with that role would likely ask during an examination. The "studio audience" then attempts to identify the medical specialties for points. Have fun!

12.20 Reciclaje

Now that you know the informal commands, list things that various specialists may wish to say to a patient. Then include your own specialty if it is not already listed.

El ortopedista: Mantén la pierna elevada.   No le hagas peso.

El radiólogo: _____

El nutricionista: _____

El farmacéutico: _____

El higienista dental: _____

Su especialidad: _____

12.21 Reciclaje

Consolidate your learning. Make an algorithm that integrates many of your new skills and will be useful for medical assessment in a variety of settings. (These are in the order presented in the book, and chapter numbers appear in parentheses.) Order your questions in the way that works best for you.

> ¿Qué le pasa? (3)
> ¿Están vivos sus padres? ¿De qué murieron? (5)
> ¿Qué enfermedades hay en su familia? (5)
> ¿Toma algún medicamento o remedio casero todos los días? (6)
> ¿Es usted alérgico a algún medicamento? (6)
> ¿Con qué frecuencia . . . ? ¿Desde cuándo . . . ? (8)
> ¿Cuánto tiempo hace que . . . ? ¿Cuánto tiempo dura . . . ? (8)
> ¿Qué le ayuda? ¿Qué le mejora? ¿Qué le empeora? (8)
> ¿Qué pasó? ¿Qué ocurría cuando eso pasó? (9)
> ¿Cuándo fue la última vez que . . . ? (9)
> ¿De qué enfermedades padece usted? (10)
> ¿Ha tenido (enfermedad)? ¿Ha tenido cirugía? (10)
> ¿Ha estado hospitalizado alguna vez? ¿Para qué? (11)
> ¿Ha estado embarazada? (12)

Cultural Note: Fathers and Childbirth

Manuel Franjul Peña cuida a su hija
Ana Camila Franjul Medina.

The birthing process has changed greatly in the United States during the past two generations. Most hospitals teach childbirth classes to couples using techniques designed by the French physician Fernand Lamaze. These include training the father or a friend to give support to the mother during childbirth. Through these changes over the past twenty years we have practically eradicated the medicated birth, especially the use of twilight and general anesthesia during birth. Latinos are generally eager to participate as couples in this preparation. However, not all do so because the classes are not always available in Spanish when needed, and because the practice is not yet as widespread in many of the countries from which the patients have emigrated. In poorer areas the presence of several deliveries in one room contraindicates the participation of fathers because of modesty.

Some Latinas do not communicate to their partner the expectation that he will take part in the delivery, and some men do not feel comfortable with the idea. Sexual topics are not traditionally discussed in the home. One man standing outside the room in which his wife was in labor admitted that he wanted to be in the room but would not enter because there were female relatives inside who would presumably know more about what to do.

At times the difference in participation between non-Latino and Latino men is not fully understood by health care providers as a difference in tradition. Assessing and understanding the individual family's cultural norms will enable the health care provider to begin the educational process from the perspective of the patient, her partner, and the family. This increases empathy, and may alleviate a father's discomfort in the delivery room.

Cultural Note:
Communication about Sexual Matters

At times, patients do not easily embrace the goals of health professionals in their teaching about safer sex. Many Latino families do not speak openly about sexual matters. The Catholic Church has disapproved of most forms of contraception. When educating patients about sex, the health care provider should assess and then respect the values of the patient prior to presenting new information in a nonjudgmental manner. Such respect is crucial.

Discussion of sexual and gender roles can uncover conflict in the individual and in his or her family. Many adults heard during childhood the refrain, *La mujer es de la casa y el hombre de la calle* (the woman is of the house and the man is of the street). This traditional double standard may pressure women to live at home until marriage, to remain chaste, and to value childbearing more than higher education and a career. The first- or second-generation female immigrant may feel caught between her traditional values and what she perceives to be a different norm in the United States. She may feel guilty over seeking sexual fulfillment as a single woman and insecure about asserting herself in business. She may not speak openly about being sexually active, except when confidentiality is assured. Other required yet sometimes taboo topics in sex education include homosexual behavior, alcoholism, and substance abuse. Raise these in a private setting, and do so only after establishing rapport with the patient.

Appendix 1
El abecedario
(The Spanish Alphabet)

Knowing the alphabet in Spanish (also called *el alfabeto*) will help you spell words aloud and conduct vision exams. To ask how the name Baldemira is spelled, use *¿Cómo se escribe Baldemira?* or *¿Cómo se deletrea Baldemira?* Currently there are 27 letters in the Spanish alphabet.

Letra	Nombre	Letra	Nombre	Letra	Nombre
a	a	j	jota	r	ere
b	be	k	ka	s	ese
c	ce	l	ele	t	te
d	de	m	eme	u	u
e	e	n	ene	v	uve
f	efe	ñ	eñe	w	doble uve
g	ge	o	o	x	equis
h	hache	p	pe	y	ye
i	i	q	cu	z	ceta

Some grammars include *rr* in the alphabet. The fourth edition of the *Diccionario académico* (1803) included *ch* and *ll* in the alphabet. Although these letters are digraphs (comprised of two letters each), they are considered letters because each represents a single sound. Words beginning with these two digraphs occupied their own sections in Spanish dictionaries until 1994, when La Asociación de Academias de la Lengua Española reordered those words into their places in the universal Latin alphabet. Now, words beginning with *ch* are found between words that begin with *ce* and those that begin with *ci,* and words beginning with *ll* are placed between words that begin with *li* and those that begin with *lo.* In 2010 the Real Academia Española changed the name of the letter *y* from *i griega* (Greek *i*) to *ye.* This eliminated the need to call the letter *i* by the name *i latina* (Latin *i*).

Appendix 2
A Guide to Some Irregular and Stem-Changing Verbs

Most of these verbs and morphologies have been introduced in the text. They are included here as a reference and for further study. The future tense expresses action that will happen in the future, as in *Me acostaré temprano el domingo* (I shall go to bed early on Sunday). Recall that in the text you learned to use expressions with *ir + a + infinitivo* to tell the near future, as in *Voy a acostarme temprano esta noche.*

acostarse (o–ue)   to lie down, go to bed

present	me acuesto, te acuestas, se acuesta, nos acostamos, se acuestan
preterit	me acosté, te acostaste, se acostó, nos acostamos, se acostaron
imperfect	me acostaba, te acostabas, se acostaba, nos acostábamos, se acostaban
future	me acostaré, te acostarás, se acostará, nos acostaremos, se acostarán
usted command	¡Acuéstese! ¡No se acueste!
tú command	¡Acuéstate! ¡No te acuestes!
past participle	acostado

almorzar (o–ue)   to eat lunch

present	almuerzo, almuerzas, almuerza, almorzamos, almuerzan
preterit	almorcé, almorzaste, almorzó, almorzamos, almorzaron
imperfect	almorzaba, almorzabas, almorzaba, almorzábamos, almorzaban
future	almorzaré, almorzarás, almorzará, almorzaremos, amorzarán
usted command	¡Almuerce! ¡No almuerce!
tú command	¡Almuerza! ¡No almuerces!
past participle	almorzado

comenzar (e–ie)   to begin

present	comienzo, comienzas, comienza, comenzamos, comienzan
preterit	comencé, comenzaste, comenzó, comenzamos, comenzaron
imperfect	comenzaba, comenzabas, comenzaba, comenzábamos, comenzaban
future	comenzaré, comenzarás, comenzará, comenzaremos, comenzarán
usted command	¡Comience! ¡No comience!
tú command	¡Comienza! ¡No comiences!
past participle	comenzado

dar   to give

present	doy, das, da, damos, dan
preterit	di, diste, dio, dimos, dieron
imperfect	daba, dabas, daba, dábamos, daban
future	daré, darás, dará, daremos, darán
usted command	¡Dé! ¡No dé!
tú command	¡Da! ¡No dés!
past participle	dado

decir   to say, to tell

present	digo, dices, dice, decimos, dicen
preterit	dije, dijiste, dijo, dijimos, dijeron
future	diré, dirás, dirá, diremos, dirán
imperfect	decía, decías, decía, decíamos, decían
usted command	¡Diga! ¡No diga!
tú command	¡Di! ¡No digas!
past participle	dicho

despertarse (e–ie)   to wake up

present	me despierto, te despiertas, se despierta, nos despertamos, se despiertan
preterit	me desperté, te despertaste, se despertó, nos despertamos, se despertaron
imperfect	me despertaba, te despertabas, se despertaba, nos despertábamos, se despertaban
future	me despertaré, te despertarás, se despertará, nos despertaremos, se despertarán
usted command	¡Despiértese! ¡No se despierte!
tú command	¡Despiértate! ¡No te despiertes!
past participle	despierto

dormir (o–ue)   to sleep

present	duermo, duermes, duerme, dormimos, duermen
preterit	dormí, dormiste, durmió, dormimos, durmieron
imperfect	dormía, dormías, dormía, dormíamos, dormían
future	dormiré, dormirás, dormirá, dormiremos, dormirán
usted command	¡Duérmase! ¡No se duerma!
tú command	¡Duérmete! ¡No te duermas!
past participle	dormido

estar   to be

present	estoy, estás, está, estamos, están
preterit	estuve, estuviste, estuvo, estuvimos, estuvieron
imperfect	estaba, estabas, estaba, estábamos, estaban
future	estaré, estarás, estará, estaremos, estarán
usted command	¡Esté! ¡No esté!
tú command	¡Está! ¡No estés!
past participle	estado

hacer   to do, to make

present	hago, haces, hace, hacemos, hacen
preterit	hice, hiciste, hizo, hicimos, hicieron
imperfect	hacía, hacías, hacía, hacíamos, hacían
future	haré, harás, hará, haremos, harán
usted command	¡Haga! ¡No haga!
tú command	¡Haz! ¡No hagas!
past participle	hecho

ir   to go

present	voy, vas, va, vamos, van
preterit	fui, fuiste, fue, fuimos, fueron
imperfect	iba, ibas, iba, íbamos, iban
future	iré, irás, irá, iremos, irán
usted command	¡Vaya! ¡No vaya!
tú command	¡Ve! ¡No vayas!
past participle	ido

poder (o–ue)   to be able

present	puedo, puedes, puede, podemos, pueden
preterit	pude, pudiste, pudo, pudimos, pudieron
imperfect	podía, podías, podía, podíamos, podían
future	podré, podrás, podrá, podremos, podrán
past participle	podido

poner   to put, to place

present	pongo, pones, pone, ponemos, ponen
preterit	puse, pusiste, puso, pusimos, pusieron
imperfect	ponía, ponías, ponía, poníamos, ponían
future	pondré, pondrás, pondrá, pondremos, pondrán
usted command	¡Ponga! ¡No ponga!
tú command	¡Pon! ¡No pongas!
past participle	puesto

preferir (e–ie)   to prefer

present	prefiero, prefieres, prefiere, preferimos, prefieren
preterit	preferí, preferiste, prefirió, preferimos, prefirieron
imperfect	prefería, preferías, prefería, preferíamos, preferían
future	preferiré, preferirás, preferirá, preferiremos, preferirán
usted command	¡Prefiera! ¡No prefiera!
tú command	¡Prefiere! ¡No prefieras!
past participle	preferido

querer (e–ie)   to want, to like

present	quiero, quieres, quiere, queremos, quieren
preterit	quise, quisiste, quiso, quisimos, quisieron
imperfect	quería, querías, quería, queríamos, querían
future	querré, querrás, querrá, querremos, querrán
past participle	querido

saber   to know

present	sé, sabes, sabe, sabemos, saben
preterit	supe, supiste, supo, supimos, supieron
imperfect	sabía, sabías, sabía, sabíamos, sabían
future	sabré, sabrás, sabrá, sabremos, sabrán
usted command	¡Sepa! ¡No sepa!
tú command	¡Sabe! ¡No sepas!
past participle	sabido

sentarse (e–ie)   to sit down

present	me siento, te sientas, se sienta, nos sentamos, se sientan
preterit	me senté, te sentaste, se sentó, nos sentamos, se sentaron
imperfect	me sentaba, te sentabas, se sentaba, nos sentábamos, se sentaban
future	me sentaré, te sentarás, se sentará, nos sentaremos, se sentarán
usted command	¡Siéntese! ¡No se siente!
tú command	¡Siéntate! ¡No te sientes!
past participle	sentado

sentirse (e–ie)   to feel

present	me siento, te sientes, se siente, nos sentimos, se sienten
preterit	me sentí, te sentiste, se sintió, nos sentimos, se sintieron
imperfect	me sentía, te sentías, se sentía, nos sentíamos, se sentían
future	me sentiré, te sentirás, se sentirá, nos sentiremos, se sentirán
usted command	¡Siéntase! ¡No se sienta!
tú command	¡Siéntete! ¡No te sientas!
past participle	sentido

ser   to be

present	soy, eres, es, somos, son
preterit	fui, fuiste, fue, fuimos, fueron
imperfect	era, eras, era, éramos, eran
future	seré, serás, será, seremos, serán
usted command	¡Sea! ¡No sea!
tú command	¡Sé! ¡No seas!
past participle	sido

tener   to have

present	tengo, tienes, tiene, tenemos, tienen
preterit	tuve, tuviste, tuvo, tuvimos, tuvieron
imperfect	tenía, tenías, tenía, teníamos, tenían
future	tendré, tendrás, tendrá, tendremos, tendrán
usted command	¡Tenga! ¡No tenga!
tú command	¡Ten! ¡No tengas!
past participle	tenido

venir   to come

present	vengo, vienes, viene, venimos, vienen
preterit	vine, viniste, vino, vinimos, vinieron
imperfect	venía, venías, venía, veníamos, venían
future	vendré, vendrás, vendrá, vendremos, vendrán
usted command	¡Venga! ¡No venga!
tú command	¡Ven! ¡No vengas!
past participle	venido

vestirse (e–i)   to dress oneself

present	me visto, te vistes, se viste, nos vestimos, se visten
preterit	me vestí, te vestiste, se vistió, nos vestimos, se vistieron
imperfect	me vestía, te vestías, se vestía, nos vestíamos, se vestían
future	me vestiré, te vestirás, se vestirá, nos vestiremos, se vestirán
usted command	¡Vístase! ¡No se vista!
tú command	¡Vístete! ¡No te vistas!
past participle	vestido

English to Spanish Glossary

The translations in this glossary are generally limited to the context in which the words are used in the book. The abbreviation (*v*) indicates a verb.

a

abdomen **el abdomen**

able (to be able) (*v*) **poder** (o–ue)

abortion **el aborto (provocado, espontáneo)**

about **sobre**

abrasion **la abrasión**

abstain (*v*) **abstener**

abstinence **la abstinencia**

accident **el accidente**

accuracy **la precisión**

acetaminophen **el acetaminofén**

ache **el dolor sordo**

ache (*v*) **doler** (o–ue)

active **activo/a**

acute **agudo/a**

addict **el/la adicto/a**

addiction **la adicción**

address **la dirección**

admission (to a hospital) **el internamiento, la estadía**

admit (*v*) **internar, hospitalizar, dar de baja**

adrenaline **la adrenalina**

advance (*v*) **adelantar**

aerosol **el aerosol**

after **después de**

afternoon **la tarde**

afterward **después**

age **la edad**

agitated **agitado/a**

AIDS **el SIDA**

ailment **el padecimiento, la enfermedad**

air **el aire** (*palabra femenina*)

  —pollution **la contaminación del aire**

alcohol **el alcohol**

alive **vivo/a**

allergen **el alérgeno**

allergic **alérgico/a**

allergy **la alergia**

aloe vera **la sábila**

also **también**

always **siempre**

ambulance **la ambulancia**

ambulatory **ambulatorio/a**

American **americano/a**

americanized **americanizado/a**

amount **la cantidad**

analgesic **el analgésico, el calmante**

analysis **el análisis**

anaphylactic shock **el shock anafiláctico**

anaphylaxis **la anafilaxis**
and **y**
anemia **la anemia**
anesthesia **la anestesia**
anesthesiologist **el/la anestesiólogo/a**
aneurysm **el aneurisma**
anger (*v*) **enojar(se), enfadar(se)**
anger **el enojo, el enfado**
angina pectoris **la angina de pecho**
angiogram **el angiograma**
angry **enojado/a, enfadado/a**
animal **el animal**
animal dander **la caspa de animal**
anise **el anís**
ankle **el tobillo**
annoy (*v*) **molestar**
annoyance **la molestia**
annoyed **enfadado/a**
answer (*v*) **contestar**
antacid **el antiácido**
antibiotic **el antibiótico**
antibody **el anticuerpo**
anticholinergic **el anticolinérgico**
anticoagulant **el anticoagulante**
anticonvulsant **el anticonvulsante**
antidepressant **el antidepresivo**
antidiarrheal **el antidiarreico**
antihistamine **el antihistamínico**
antihyperglycemic **el antihiperglucémico**
antiinflammatory **el antiinflamatorio**
antipyretic **el antipirético**
antispasmodic **el antiespasmódico**
anus **el ano**
anxiety **la ansiedad**
anxious **ansioso/a, nervioso/a**
anyone **alguien**
apoplexy **la apoplejía**
appendectomy **la apendectomía**
appendicitis **la apendicitis**
appendix **el apéndice**
appetite **el apetito**
apple **la manzana**
apply (*v*) **aplicar**
appointment **la cita**
April **abril**

area **la área**
argue (*v*) **discutir, pelear**
arise (*v*) **levantar(se)**
arm **el brazo**
arrive (*v*) **llegar**
arthritis **la artritis**
arthroscopy **la artroscopia**
as, like **como**
ashamed **avergonzado/a**
ask (*v*) **preguntar**
ask for (*v*) **pedir** (e–i)
aspirin **la aspirina**
asthma **el asma** (*palabra femenina*)
attack **el ataque**
audiologist **el/la audiólogo/a**
audiology **audiología**
August **agosto**
aunt **la tía**
avocado **el aguacate**
avoid (*v*) **evitar**
awake **despierto/a**
awaken (*v*) **despertar(se)** (e–ie)

b

baby **el/la bebé**
baby teeth **los dientes de leche**
back **la espalda**
bacterial **bacteriano/a**
bacterium **la bacteria**
bad **malo/a**
badly **mal**
banana **la banana, el plátano, el guineo**
bandage **el vendaje, la tirita, la curita**
barbiturate **el barbitúrico**
bath **el baño**
bathe (*v*) **bañar(se)**
bathroom **el cuarto de baño**
be (*v*) **ser** (*irregular*), **estar** (*irregular*)
bean **el frijol, la habichuela, la judía**
because **porque**
bed **la cama**
bedpan **la silleta, el pato de cama**
beef **la carne de res**
beer **la cerveza**
before **antes de**

behind **detrás de**
believe (*v*) **creer**
benefit **el beneficio**
benign **benigno/a**
betrayed **traicionado/a**
better **mejor**
better (to get better) (*v*) **mejorar**
beverage **la bebida**
bilingual **bilingüe**
biopsy **la biopsia**
birth **el nacimiento, el parto, el
alumbramiento**
black **negro/a**
blackboard **la pizarra**
bladder **la vejiga**
blanket **la frazada**
bleed (*v*) **sangrar**
blind **ciego/a**
blister **la ampolla**
blond **rubio/a**
blood **la sangre**
blood pressure **la presión sanguínea,
la presión arterial, la presión de la
sangre**
board **la tabla**
body **el cuerpo**
bone **el hueso**
bore (*v*) **aburrir**
bottle **la botella, el frasco; el biberón, la
tetera** (*baby's bottle*)
brain **el cerebro**
bread **el pan**
break (*v*) **quebrar, romper**
break water (*v*) **romper fuente**
breakfast (*v*) **desayunar**
breakfast **el desayuno**
breast **el seno**
breast-feed (*v*) **amamantar, dar el seno,
dar el pecho**
breathe (*v*) **respirar**
breathing **la respiración**
breech position **la presentación pelviana,
la presentación de nalgas**
broccoli **el brócoli**
bronchia **el bronquio**

bronchial **bronquial**
bronchoscopy **la broncoscopia**
broth **el caldo**
brother **el hermano**
brother-in-law **el cuñado**
bruise **el moretón**
bruit **el soplo**
brunette **moreno/a**
brush (*v*) **cepillar(se)**
brush **el cepillo**
bump (*v*) **golpear(se)**
bump **el golpe**
burn (*v*) **quemar(se)**
burn **la quemadura**
burned **quemado/a**
burning sensation **el ardor**
butter **la mantequilla**
buttock **el gluteo, la nalga, el pompis**
buy (*v*) **comprar**

C

cake **la torta, el bizcocho, el pastel**
calcium **el calcio**
calf **la pantorrilla**
call (*v*) **llamar**
call **la llamada**
calorie **la caloría**
can **la lata**
can (to be able) (*v*) **poder** (o–ue)
cancer **el cáncer**
candy **el dulce**
canned **enlatado/a**
capsule **la cápsula, la gragea**
car **el coche, el carro, el automóvil**
carbohydrate **el carbohidrato**
card **la tarjeta**
cardiac **cardíaco/a**
cardiologist **el/la cardiólogo/a**
cardiology **la cardiología**
cardiovascular disease **la enfermedad
cardiovascular**
care **el cuidado**
care for (*v*) **cuidar**
carpal **carpiano/a**
carpet **la alfombra**

carpus **el carpo**
carrier (asymptomatic) **el portador (sano)**
carrot **la zanahoria**
carry (*v*) **llevar**
cast **el yeso**
cataract **la catarata**
catheter **la sonda, el catéter**
catheter (urinary) **la algalia, la sonda**
cavity **la caries, la caries dental**
cell **la célula**
cereal **el cereal**
cerebral **cerebral**
cerebral palsy **la parálisis cerebral**
cervix **el cuello del útero, el cuello de la matriz**
cesarean section **la operación cesárea**
chair **la silla**
cheek **la mejilla, el cachete**
cheekbone **el pómulo**
cheese **el queso**
chemotherapy **la quimioterapia**
chest **el pecho**
chest pain **el dolor del pecho**
chew (*v*) **masticar**
chewable **masticable**
chicken **el pollo**
chicken pox **la varicela, la viruela loca**
child **el/la niño/a, el/la muchacho/a**
chill **el escalofrío**
chin **la barbilla**
Chinese **el chino** (*lang.*)
chlamydia **la clamidia**
chocolate **el chocolate**
cholecystectomy **la colecistectomía**
cholera **el cólera**
chronic **crónico/a**
cigarette **el cigarrillo**
cinnamon **la canela**
cirrhosis **la cirrosis, la cirrosis hepática**
city **la ciudad**
class **la clase**
classic **clásico/a**
clavicle **la clavícula**
clean **limpio/a**
cleaning **la limpieza**

clear **claro/a**
clinic **la clínica**
close (*v*) **cerrar** (e–ie)
closed **cerrado/a**
clot **el coágulo, el émbolo**
clothes **la ropa**
clothing **la ropa**
cocaine **la cocaína**
coccyx **el cóccix**
cockroach **la cucaracha, el bicho**
coconut **el coco**
codeine **la codeína**
cold **frío/a**
cold (common cold) **el resfriado, el resfrío, el catarro, la monga** (*slang*)
colic **el cólico, los cólicos**
collide (*v*) **chocar**
collision **el choque**
colon **el colon**
colonoscopy **la colonoscopia**
color **el color**
colostomy **la colostomía**
comb (*v*) **peinar(se)**
comb **el peine**
come (*v*) **venir** (*irregular*)
comfortable **cómodo/a, confortable**
common **común**
complication **la complicación**
condom **el condón, el preservativo**
confirm (*v*) **confirmar**
congestion **la congestión, el catarro**
congestive heart failure **la insuficiencia cardíaca**
congratulations **felicidades**
conscious **consciente**
constant **constante, continuo/a**
constipation **el estreñimiento**
consult (*v*) **consultar**
consult **la consulta**
content **contento/a**
contraceptive **el contraceptivo, el anticonceptivo**
contraction **la contracción**
convulsion **la convulsión**
cook (*v*) **cocinar**

cook **el/la cocinero/a**
COPD **la enfermedad pulmonar obstructiva crónica, el enfisema**
cough (*v*) **toser**
cough **la tos**
cough suppressant **el antitusígeno**
counselor **el/la consejero/a**
CPR **la reanimación cardiopulmonar**
cramp **el calambre**
cranium **el cráneo**
crash (*v*) **chocar**
crash **el choque**
crazy **loco/a**
cream **la crema, el ungüento**
crisis **la crisis**
crown **la corona**
crush (*v*) **polvorizar**
crushing **pesado/a**
crutch **la muleta**
cry (*v*) **llorar**
crying jag **el llanto**
CT scan **la tomografía computarizada**
culture (laboratory) **el cultivo**
curious **curioso/a**
current **actual**
custodian **el/la tutor/a**
custody **la custodia**
cut (*v*) **cortar(se)**
cut **la cortada, la cortadura, el tajo**
cyst **el quiste**

d

damage (*v*) **dañar**
dangerous **peligroso/a**
dark **oscuro/a**
date **la fecha**
daughter **la hija**
daughter-in-law **la nuera, la yerna**
day **el día**
dead **muerto/a**
deaf **sordo/a**
death **la muerte**
decaffeinated **descafeinado/a**
December **diciembre**
decongestant **el descongestionante**

deep **profundo/a**
dehydration **la deshidratación**
deliver (a baby) (*v*) **dar a luz, parir, alumbrar**
delivery (of a baby) **el parto, el alumbramiento**
delusion **el delirio**
demonstrate (*v*) **demostrar**
dengue **el dengue**
dental floss **el hilo dental**
dental hygienist **el/la higienista dental**
dentist **el/la dentista, el/la odontólogo/a**
dentistry **la odontología**
denture **la dentadura postiza**
dependence **la dependencia**
depressed **deprimido/a**
depression **la depresión**
dermatologist **el/la dermatólogo/a**
dermatology **la dermatología**
description **la descripción**
desk **el escritorio**
desperate **desesperado/a**
dessert **el postre**
diabetes **la diabetes**
diagnosis **el diagnóstico**
dialysis **la diálisis**
diarrhea **la diarrea**
die (*v*) **morir** (o–ue)
diet **la dieta, el plan de alimentación**
dietician **el/la dietista**
dilute (*v*) **diluir**
dine (*v*) **cenar**
dinner **la comida, la cena**
diphtheria **la difteria**
disabled **incapacitado/a, el/la inválido/a, con capacidades diferentes**
discover (*v*) **descubrir**
disease **la enfermedad**
disgusted **disgustado/a, aborrecido**
disheartened **descorazonado/a**
disorder **el trastorno**
distressed **angustiado/a**
diuretic **el diurético**
divorce (*v*) **divorciarse**
divorce **el divorcio**

divorced **divorciado/a**
dizziness **el mareo**
dizzy **mareado/a**
do, make (*v*) **hacer** (*irregular*)
doctor **el doctor, la doctora, el/la médico/a**
doctor's office **el consultorio**
doll **la muñeca**
door **la puerta**
drain (*v*) **drenar**
drain **el drenaje**
drained **agotado/a**
draw blood (*v*) **sacar sangre**
drill **la fresa dental, el taladro**
drink (*v*) **beber**
drink **la bebida**
drip (*v*) **gotear**
dripping **el goteo**
drive (*v*) **manejar**
drop **la gota**
drug **la droga**
drunk **ebrio/a, borracho/a**
dry (*v*) **secar(se)**
dryness **la sequedad**
dust **el polvo**
dust mite **el ácaro del polvo**
dysentery **la disentería**

e

each, every **cada**
ear **el oído** (*inner*), **la oreja** (*outer*)
early **temprano**
eat (*v*) **comer**
echogram **el ecograma**
ectopic pregnancy **el embarazo ectópico**
eczema **el eccema**
egg **el huevo**
eighth **el/la octavo/a**
elbow **el codo**
elderly **mayor, anciano/a**
electrocardiogram **el electrocardiograma**
electroencephalogram **el electroencefalograma**
elevator **el ascensor**
eliminate (*v*) **eliminar**

elixir **el elixir**
embolism **la embolia, el émbolo**
emergency **la emergencia, la urgencia**
emergency room **la sala de urgencias**
emphysema **el enfisema**
enchanted **encantado/a**
end (*v*) **terminar**
end **el fin**
endocrinologist **el/la endocrinólogo/a**
endometriosis **la endometriosis**
endoscopy **la endoscopia**
English **el inglés** (*lang.*)
enrage (*v*) **enojar(se), enfadar(se), enfogonar(se)** (*slang*)
enraged **enojado/a, enfadado/a, enfogonado/a** (*slang*)
ENT **el/la otorrinolaringólogo/a**
epilepsy **la epilepsia**
epinephrine **la epinefrina**
episiotomy **la episiotomía**
esophageal reflux **el reflujo esofágico**
esophagus **el esófago**
eucalyptus **el eucalipto**
ever **alguna vez**
every **cada**
exam **el examen**
examination **la examinación**
examine (*v*) **examinar**
exhale (*v*) **exhalar**
expectorant **el expectorante**
explain (*v*) **explicar**
exploratory **exploratorio/a**
extraction **la extracción**
eye **el ojo**
eyeglasses **los lentes, los anteojos**

f

face **la cara**
faint (*v*) **desmayar(se)**
fall (*v*) **caer**
Fallopian tube **la trompa de Falopio**
false teeth **los dientes postizos, la dentadura, la caja de dientes, el puente** (*bridge*)
fan **el ventilador, el abanico** (Carib.)

far **lejos**
fascinate (*v*) **fascinar**
fast (*v*) **ayunar**
fast **rápido/a**
fat **gordo/a**
fat **la grasa**
fat-free **descremado/a**
father **el padre**
father-in-law **el suegro**
fatigue **el cansancio, la fatiga**
fear **el miedo**
February **febrero**
feces **la materia fecal, las heces, el excremento**
feed (*v*) **alimentar, dar de comer**
feel (*v*) **sentir(se)** (e–ie)
female **femenino/a, hembra**
femur **el fémur**
fetus **el feto**
fever **la fiebre**
fiber **la fibra**
fibula **el peroné**
fifth **el/la quinto/a**
fight (*v*) **luchar, pelear**
filling (dental) **el empaste**
film **la placa**
find (*v*) **encontrar** (o–ue)
fine **bien**
finger **el dedo**
fingernail **la uña**
first **el/la primero/a**
fish (*v*) **pescar**
fish **el pescado**
floor **el piso**
flow **el flujo**
flu **la gripe, la influenza**
fluid **el fluido**
fluoride **el fluoruro**
foam **la espuma**
folk healer **el/la espiritista, el/la curandero/a, el/la chamán**
follow (*v*) **seguir** (e–ie)
food **el alimento, la comida**
foot **el pie**
forearm **el antebrazo**

forehead **la frente**
forget (*v*) **olvidar**
foster child **el/la hijo/a de crianza**
fourth **el/la cuarto/a**
fracture **la fractura**
    comminuted— **la fractura conminuta**
    compound— **la fractura compuesta**
    multiple— **la fractura múltiple**
    open— **la fractura abierta**
    simple— **la fractura simple**
    spiral— **la fractura espiral**
    transverse— **la fractura oblicua**
French **el francés** (*lang.*)
french fries **las papas fritas**
frequency **la frecuencia**
frequent **frecuente**
frequently **frecuentemente**
Friday **el viernes**
friend **el/la amigo/a**
frightened **asustado/a**
from **de**
(in) front of **delante de, enfrente de**
frozen **helado/a**
fruit **la fruta**
frustrated **frustrado/a**
furious **furioso/a**

g

gallbladder **la vesícula biliar**
gallstone **el cálculo en la vesícula**
gasp (*v*) **jadear**
gasping **el jadeo**
gastritis **la gastritis**
gel **el gel**
gelatin **la gelatina**
generalist **el/la médico/a general, el/la generalista, el/la médico/a de cabecera**
generous **generoso/a**
genital wart **la verruga venérea**
geriatric **geriátrico/a**
geriatrician **el/la geriatra**
geriatrics **la geriatría**
German **el alemán** (*lang.*)
giardiasis **la infección por giardias**
ginger **el jengibre**

gingivitis **la gingivitis**
give (*v*) **dar** (*irregular*)
gland **la glándula**
glass **el vaso**
glaucoma **la glaucoma**
glove **el guante**
go (*v*) **ir** (*irregular*)
go to bed (*v*) **acostarse** (o–ue)
God **Dios**
godchild **el/la ahijado/a**
godfather **el padrino**
godmother **la madrina**
gold **el oro**
golden **dorado/a**
gonorrhea **la gonorrea**
good **bueno/a**
good-bye **adiós**
gout **la gota**
grain **el grano**
grandchild **el/la nieto/a**
grandparent **el/la abuelo/a**
grape **la uva**
grapefruit **la toronja**
grease **la grasa**
great aunt **la tía abuela**
great grandchild **el/la bisnieto/a**
great grandfather **el bisabuelo**
great grandmother **la bisabuela**
great uncle **el tío abuelo**
green **verde**
greenish **verdoso/a**
grind (*v*) **moler** (o–ue)
ground **molido/a, majado/a**
guilt **la culpa**
guilty **culpable**
gum (anat.) **la encía**
gunshot wound **la herida de bala**
gynecologist **el/la ginecólogo/a**
gynecology **la ginecología**

h

hair **el cabello**
half-brother **el hermano de madre, el hermano de padre**

half-sister **la hermana de madre, la hermana de padre**
hallucination **la alucinación**
hallway **el pasillo**
hand **la mano**
handsome **guapo/a**
happen (*v*) **pasar**
happiness **la felicidad, la alegría**
happy **feliz, contento/a, alegre**
hard **duro/a**
harm (*v*) **dañar**
harm **el daño**
have (*v*) **tener** (*irregular*)
he **él**
head **la cabeza**
head injury **la herida en la cabeza**
headache **el dolor de cabeza**
health **la salud**
hear (*v*) **oír**
hearing **el oído**
heart **el corazón**
    —attack **el ataque al corazón**
    —murmur **el soplo en el corazón**
height **la altura**
helicopter **el helicóptero**
hello **hola**
help (*v*) **ayudar**
help **la ayuda**
hemophilia **la hemofilia**
hemorrhage **la hemorragia**
hemorrhagic **hemorrágico/a**
hemorrhoids **las hemorroides**
hepatitis **la hepatitis**
here **aquí**
hernia **la hernia**
heroin **la heroína, la manteca** (*slang*)
herpes **el herpes**
herpes zoster **la culebrilla**
hip **la cadera**
history **la historia**
HIV **el VIH**
hives **las ronchas, el sarpullido, la urticaria**
Holter monitor **la supervisión Holter**
honey **la miel de abeja**

hope (*v*) **esperar**
hope **la esperanza**
hopeless **desesperado/a**
hopelessness **la desesperación**
hospital **el hospital**
hospitalization **la hospitalización, el internamiento**
hour **la hora**
how? **¿cómo?**
how many? **¿cuántos/as?**
how much? **¿cuánto/a?**
humerus **el húmero**
hunger **el hambre**
hurt (*v*) **doler** (o–ue)
hypercholesterolemia **la hipercolesterolemia**
hyperglycemia **la hiperglucemia**
hypertension **la hipertensión, la presión alta**
hyperthyroidism **el hipertiroidismo**
hypoglycemia **la hipoglucemia**
hypotension **la hipotensión, la presión baja**
hypothyroidism **el hipotiroidismo**
hysterectomy **la histerectomía**

i

I **yo**
ibuprofen **el ibuprofeno, el ibuprofén**
ice **el hielo**
ice cream **el helado, el mantecado**
ilium **el íleon**
ill **enfermo/a**
illness **la enfermedad, el padecimiento**
implant (*v*) **implantar**
implant **el implante**
in front of **delante de, enfrente de**
inch **la pulgada**
incontinence **la incontinencia**
infarct **el infarto**
infect (*v*) **infectar**
infection **la infección**
inflame (*v*) **inflamar**
inflammation **la inflamación**
influenza **la influenza**

inhale (*v*) **inhalar**
inhaler **el inhalador, la pompa** (*slang*)
inject (*v*) **inyectar**
injection **la inyección**
injure (*v*) **lastimar, herir**
injury **la herida**
insomnia **el insomnio**
insufficiency **la insuficiencia**
insurance **el seguro**
    medical— **el plan médico**
intelligent **inteligente, listo/a**
intensive care **el cuidado intensivo**
intensive care unit **la unidad de cuidados intensivos**
interest (*v*) **interesar**
interested **interesado/a**
interesting **interesante**
internist **el/la médico/a internista**
intestinal **intestinal**
    —worm **la lombriz intestinal**
    —bug **el bicho intestinal**
intestine **el intestino**
    large— **el intestino grueso**
    small— **el intestino delgado**
intravenous **intravenoso/a**
iron (Fe) **el hierro**
irritability **la irritabilidad**
Italian **el italiano** (*lang.*)
itch (*v*) **picar, sentir comezón, sentir picazón**
itch **la picazón, la comezón**
IV fluid **el suero**

j

January **enero**
Japanese **el japonés** (*lang.*)
jaundice **la ictericia**
jaundiced **amarillento/a**
jaw **la mandíbula**
jealous **celoso/a**
job **el trabajo**
joint **la articulación, la coyuntura**
juice **el jugo, el zumo**
July **julio**
June **junio**

k

kidney **el riñón**

kidney stone **el cálculo en el riñón, la piedra en el riñón**

kill (*v*) **matar**

kilogram **el kilogramo**

kind **amable, simpático/a**

kitchen **la cocina**

knee **la rodilla**

kneecap **la patela, la rótula**

know (*v*) **saber** (*irregular*), **conocer** (*irregular*)

knuckle **el nudillo**

l

labor **el parto**

—pain **el dolor del parto**

to be in— **estar de parto**

laboratory **el laboratorio**

laceration **la laceración, la cortadura**

language **el idioma, la lengua, el lenguaje**

laparoscopy **la laparoscopia**

lard **la manteca**

large **grande**

large intestine **el intestino grueso**

laser **el láser**

late **tarde**

later **luego**

latex **el látex**

laxative **el laxante**

learn (*v*) **aprender**

left **el/la izquierdo/a**

leg **la pierna**

lemon **el limón**

length of stay **la estadía**

leptospirosis **la leptospirosis**

leukemia **la leucemia**

lice **los piojos**

like (*v*) **gustar, querer** (e–ie)

like, as **como**

like this **así**

lime **el limón**

lip **el labio**

liquid **el líquido**

listen (*v*) **escuchar**

listen with a stethoscope (*v*) **auscultar**

lithium **el litio**

live (*v*) **vivir**

liver **el hígado**

lonely **solitario/a**

long **largo/a**

look (*v*) **mirar**

lose (*v*) **perder** (e–ie)

loss **la pérdida**

luck **la suerte**

good— **la buena suerte**

lucky **dichoso/a**

lukewarm **tibio/a**

lump **la bolita, la pelotita**

lumpectomy **la lumpectomía**

lunch (*v*) **almorzar** (o–ue)

lunch **el almuerzo**

lung **el pulmón**

lymph gland **el ganglio linfático**

m

machine **la máquina**

make, do (*v*) **hacer** (*irregular*)

malaise **el malestar general**

malaria **el paludismo**

male **masculino/a, el varón**

malignant **maligno/a**

man **el hombre**

mania **la manía**

manic-depressive **maníacodepresivo/a**

March **marzo**

married **casado/a**

marry (*v*) **casar(se)**

mash (*v*) **majar**

maternal **materno/a**

matter (*v*) **importar**

May **el mayo**

meal **la comida**

measles **el sarampión**

German— **la rubéola**

meat **la carne**

medical record **el expediente médico, la historia médica**

medication **el medicamento, la medicina**

medicine **la medicina**

meningitis **la meningitis**

menopause **la menopausia, el cambio de vida**

menstruate (v) **menstruar**

menstruation **la menstruación, la regla, el período, el periodo**

mental illness **la enfermedad mental**

mental retardation **el retraso mental**

metabolism **el metabolismo**

metacarpal **metacarpiano/a**

metacarpus **el metacarpo**

metastasis **la metástasis**

metatarsus **el metatarso**

midwife **la comadrona, la partera**

migraine **la jaqueca, la migraña**

milk **la leche**

milligram **el miligramo**

milliliter **el mililitro**

mine **mío/a/os/as**

miscarriage **el aborto natural, la pérdida**

miss (v) **hacer falta** (irregular)

molar **la muela**

mold **el moho**

mole **el lunar**

Monday **el lunes**

money **el dinero, la plata**

monitor (v) **monitorear**

monitor **el monitor**

mononucleosis **la mononucleosis**

month **el mes**

monthly **mensual, mensualmente**

more **más**

more or less **más o menos**

morning **la mañana**

mother **la madre**

mother-in-law **la suegra**

mouth **la boca**

move (v) **mover** (o–ue)

move up (v) **adelantar**

MRI **las imágenes por resonancia magnética**

MRSA **el estafilococo resistente a la meticilina, el estafilococo dorado**

mucolytic **el mucolítico**

mucus **el moco**

multiple sclerosis **la esclerosis múltiple**

mumps **la paperas**

muscle **el músculo**

my **mi, mis**

n

name (v) **nombrar**

name **el nombre, el apellido** (surname)

natural **natural**

nausea **la náusea**

nebulize (v) **nebulizar**

neck **el cuello**

need (v) **necesitar**

need **la necesidad**

needle **la jeringuilla, la aguja**

negative **negativo/a**

neither **tampoco**

neonatal intensive care **el cuidado intensivo neonatal**

nephrectomy **la nefrectomía**

nephritis **la nefritis**

nerve **el nervio**

nervous **nervioso/a**

neurologist **el/la neurólogo/a**

neurology **la neurología**

never **nunca, jamás**

next **próximo/a**

night **la noche**

night sweats **los sudores nocturnos**

ninth **el/la noveno/a**

nitroglycerine **la nitroglicerina**

nobody, no one **nadie**

nose **la nariz**

nosocomial **nosocomial**

nothing **nada**

noun **el sustantivo**

November **noviembre**

now **ahora**

numbness **el entumecimiento**

nurse **el/la enfermero/a, la norsa** (slang)

nurse practitioner **enfermero/a con licencia para diagnosticar y tratar padecimientos y recetar medicamentos**

nurse's aide **el/la ayudante de enfermero**

nursing **la enfermería**
nutritionist **el/la nutricionista**

o

oatmeal **la avena**
obese **obeso/a**
obesity **la obesidad**
obstetrician **el/la obstetra**
obstetrics **la obstetricia**
October **octubre**
odor **el olor**
offend (*v*) **ofender**
offended **ofendido/a**
offer (*v*) **ofrecer** (*irregular*)
offering **la ofrenda**
office **la oficina**
    doctor's office **el consultorio**
oil **el aceite**
ointment **el ungüento, la crema**
old **viejo/a, anciano/a**
on (top of) **encima de**
oncologist **el/la oncólogo/a**
oncology **la oncología**
open (*v*) **abrir**
open **abierto/a**
operating room **la sala de operaciones, el quirófano**
ophthalmologist **el/la oftalmólogo/a**
ophthalmology **la oftalmología**
or **o**
oral **oral**
orange **la naranja, la china**
    —juice **el jugo de naranja, el jugo de china**
oregano **el orégano**
orthopedic **ortopédico/a**
orthopedic surgeon **el/la cirujano ortopédico/a**
orthopedics **la ortopedia**
orthopedist **el/la ortopedista**
osteoporosis **la osteoporosis**
otorhinolaryngologist (ENT) **el/la otorrinolaringólogo/a**
otorhinolaryngology **la otorrinolaringología**

ought (*v*) **deber**
our **nuestro/a**
outpatient **ambulatorio/a**
ovary **el ovario**
overdose **la sobredosis**
overweight **sobrepeso/a**
overwhelmed **agobiado/a**
ovulate (*v*) **ovular**
ovulation **la ovulación**
owe (*v*) **deber**
oxygen **el oxígeno**

p

pacemaker **el marcapasos**
pain (*v*) **doler** (o–ue)
pain **el dolor**
    burning— —**quemante**
    dull— —**latente, sordo**
    sharp— —**agudo, punzante**
pale **pálido/a**
palpate (*v*) **palpar, tocar**
palpitation **la palpitación**
palsy **la parálisis**
pancreas **el páncreas**
pandemic **la pandemia**
pandemic **pandémico/a**
pant (*v*) **jadear**
panting **el jadeo**
Pap smear test **la prueba de Papanicolau, el examen de Papanicolau**
paper **el papel**
papilloma **el papiloma**
paralysis **la parálisis**
paramedic **el/la paramédico/a**
paranoia **la paranoia**
paranoid **paranoico/a**
parents **los padres**
patch **el parche**
paternal **paterno/a**
paternity **la paternidad**
patient **el/la paciente**
peanut butter **la mantequilla de cacahuate, la mantequilla de maní**
pediatric **pediátrico/a**
pediatrician **el/la pediatra**

pediatrics **la pediatría**
pen **el bolígrafo, la pluma, el lapicero**
penis **el pene**
pepper **el ají, el pimiento**
percuss (*v*) **percutir, dar golpecitos**
period **el período, el periodo, la regla, la menstruación**
periodontitis **la periodontitis**
permission **el permiso**
persistent **persistente**
personal **personal**
pertussis **la tos ferina**
phalange **la falange**
pharmacist **el/la farmacéutico/a**
pharmacy **la farmacia**
phlegm **la flema**
phobia **la fobia**
physical exam **el examen físico**
physical therapist **el/la terapeuta físico/a**
physician **el/la médico/a, el/la doctor/a**
physician's assistant **el/la asociado/a médico/a**
piece **el pedazo**
pill **la pastilla, la píldora, la tableta, el comprimido**
pillow **la almohada**
place **el lugar**
placenta **la placenta**
plain **sencillo/a**
plaque (dental) **el sarro**
plastic surgeon **el/la cirujano/a plástico/a**
pleasant **agradable**
please (*v*) **gustar, encantar**
please **por favor**
pleasure **el placer**
pneumonectomy **la neumonectomía, la pulmonectomía**
pneumonia **la pulmonía, la neumonía**
podiatrist **el/la podiólogo/a**
podiatry **la podiología**
pole **el palo**
polio **la polio, la poliomelitis**
pollen **el polen**
polyp **el pólipo**
poor **pobre**

porcelain **la porcelana**
portion **la porción**
Portuguese **el portugués** (*lang.*)
positive **positivo/a**
potato **la papa**
pound **la libra**
practice (*v*) **practicar**
precaution **la precaución**
pregnancy **el embarazo**
pregnant **embarazada, encinta**
prescribe (*v*) **recetar**
prescription **la receta**
press (*v*) **palpar, presionar, oprimir**
pressure **la presión**
prevent (*v*) **prevenir** (*irregular*)
preventative **preventivo/a**
prevention **prevención**
prickly pear cactus **el nopal**
private **privado/a**
procedure **el procedimiento**
prognosis **el pronóstico**
prolapse **el prolapso**
prostate **la próstata**
prostatitis **la prostatitis**
prosthesis **la prótesis**
protein **la proteina**
proud **orgulloso/a**
provoke (*v*) **provocar**
prune **la ciruela**
psoriasis **la psoriasis**
psychiatric **psiquiátrico/a**
psychiatrist **el/la psiquiatra**
psychiatry **la psiquiatría**
psychologist **el/la psicólogo/a**
psychology **la psicología**
psychosis **la psicosis**
psychotic **psicótico/a**
pulmonologist **el/la neumonólogo/a**
pulsating **latente**
pulse **el pulso**
punctual **puntual**
puree **puré**
push (*v*) **empujar**
put (*v*) **poner** (*irregular*)
pyramid **la pirámide**

q

quarter **cuarto/a**

question (*v*) **preguntar** (*to ask*),
    cuestionar (*to doubt, wonder*)

question **la pregunta**

quick **rápido/a**

quinine **la quinina**

r

radiation therapy **la radioterapia**

radio **el radio**

radiologist **el/la radiólogo/a**

radiology **la radiología**

rash **la erupción, la irritación**

reach **el alcance**

reaction **la reacción**

read (*v*) **leer**

receive (*v*) **recibir**

receptionist **el/la recepcionista**

record (*v*) **grabar**

recorder **la grabadora**

recovery room **la sala de recuperación,
    la sala de restablecimiento**

rectum **el recto**

red **rojo/a, colorado/a**

refrigerator **el refrigerador, la nevera**

regular **regular**

reject (*v*) **rechazar**

rejected **rechazado/a**

rejection **el rechazo**

relieved **aliviado/a**

remain (*v*) **quedar(se)**

remedy **el remedio**

    home remedy **el remedio casero**

remember (*v*) **recordar** (o–ue)

remove (*v*) **sacar, quitar(se)**

renal calculus **el cálculo en el riñón,
    las piedras en el riñón**

renal failure **la insuficiencia renal**

replacement **el reemplazo**

resistant **resistente**

respiratory therapist **el/la terapeuta
    respiratorio/a**

rest (*v*) **descansar**

rest **el descanso**

result **el resultado**

resuscitate (*v*) **resucitar**

resuscitation **la resucitación**

return (*v*) **volver** (o–ue), **regresar**

rheumatic fever **la fiebre reumática**

rheumatologist **el/la reumatólogo/a**

rheumatology **la reumatología**

rib **la costilla**

rice **el arroz**

rich **rico/a**

right **el/la derecho/a**

right **derecho/a**

rinse (*v*) **enjuagar**

rinse **el enjuague**

risk **el riesgo**

robe **la bata**

roll over (*v*) **virar(se)**

room **el cuarto, la habitación**

root canal **el tratamiento de canal**

rosemary **el romero**

rubella **la rubéola**

rum **el ron**

run (*v*) **correr**

s

sacrum **el sacro**

sad **triste**

sadness **la tristeza**

salad **la ensalada**

salmon **el salmón**

salt **la sal**

same **igual**

sample **la muestra**

sandwich **el emparedado, el sándwich**

satisfied **satisfecho/a**

Saturday **el sábado**

sausage **la salchicha, el chorizo**

say (*v*) **decir** (*irregular*)

scabies **la sarna**

scapula **el omóplato**

scare (*v*) **asustar**

scare **el susto**

scared **asustado/a**

schizophrenia **la esquizofrenia**

schizophrenic **esquizofrénico/a**

school **la escuela**
sciatic **ciático/a**
sciatica **la ciática**
scrotum **el escroto**
sealant **el sellador, el sellante**
seat belt **el cinturón de seguridad**
second **segundo/a**
secretary **el/la secretario/a**
secretion **la secreción**
sedative **el sedante, el calmante**
see (*v*) **ver** (*irregular*)
self exam **el autoexamen**
sensation **la sensación**
September **septiembre**
seventh **el/la séptimo/a**
severe **severo/a**
sew (*v*) **coser**
sexually transmitted disease **la enfermedad transmitida sexualmente**
shake (*v*) **agitar**
shame **la vergüenza**
share (*v*) **compartir**
shave (*v*) **afeitar(se)**
she **ella**
sheet **la sábana**
shine (*v*) **brillar**
shingles **la culebrilla**
shoe **el zapato**
shop (*v*) **hacer compras** (*irregular*)
shop **la tienda**
short **bajo/a** (*height*), **corto/a** (*length*)
shortness of breath **la dificultad para respirar, la falta de aire, la fatiga**
should (*v*) **deber**
shoulder **el hombro**
shy **tímido/a**
sick **enfermo/a**
sickness **la enfermedad**
side **el lado**
side effect **el efecto secundario**
sight **la vista**
single **soltero/a**
sister **la hermana**
sister-in-law **la cuñada**
sit (*v*) **sentar(se)** (e–ie)

sixth **el/la sexto/a**
skeleton **el esqueleto**
skin **la piel**
skinny **flaco/a**
sleep (*v*) **dormir** (o–ue)
sleeping pill **la pastilla para dormir**
slow **despacio, lento/a**
small **pequeño/a, chiquito/a**
small intestine **el intestino delgado**
smallpox **la viruela**
smell (*v*) **oler** (*irregular*)
smell (*sense of*) **el olfato**
smell **el olor**
smoke (*v*) **fumar**
smoke **el humo**
smoke detector **el detector de humo**
snack **la merienda**
sneeze (*v*) **estornudar**
sneeze **el estornudo**
sober **sobrio/a**
social **social**
social work **el trabajo social**
social worker **el/la trabajador/a social**
soda pop **el refresco**
soft **blando/a**
soft drink **la gaseosa, el refresco**
some **algún, alguno/a**
someone **alguien**
something **algo**
sometimes **a veces**
son **el hijo**
son-in-law **el yerno**
sonogram **el sonograma, el ecograma**
sonograph **la sonografía, el ecograma**
soup **la sopa**
soybean **la soja**
Spaniard **el/la español/a**
Spanish **el español** (*lang.*)
speak (*v*) **hablar**
specialty **la especialidad**
speech therapist **el/la terapeuta de lenguaje, el/la terapeuta del habla**
spend (money) **gastar**
spend (time) **pasar**
spice **la especia**

spina bifida **la espina bífida**
spine **la espina dorsal**
spirit **el ánimo, el espíritu**
spirometry **la espirometría**
spit (*v*) **escupir**
spleen **el bazo**
spontaneous **espontáneo/a**
sprain (*v*) **torcer(se)** (o–ue)
sprain **la torcedura**
sprained **torcido/a**
spray (*v*) **rociar**
spray **el aerosol**
sputum **el esputo**
squash **la calabaza**
stab wound **la puñalada**
stain (*v*) **manchar**
stain **la mancha**
staphylococcus **el estafilococo**
starch **el almidón**
start (*v*) **empezar** (e–ie)
start **el principio, el comienzo**
stepbrother **el hermanastro**
stepfather **el padrastro**
stepmother **la madrastra**
stepsister **la hermanastra**
sternon **el esternón**
steroid **el esteroide**
stethoscope **el estetoscopio**
stiffness **la rigidez**
stitch (*v*) **coser**
stitch **el punto**
stomach **el estómago**
straight **derecho/a**
street **la calle**
stress **el estrés**
stretcher **la camilla**
stroke **la apoplejía, la embolia cerebral,
    la hemorragia vascular**
strong **fuerte**
student **el/la estudiante**
study (*v*) **estudiar**
study **el estudio**
sudden **repentino/a, de repente**
suffer (*v*) **sufrir**
suffer (from an illness) (*v*) **padecer**

sugar **el azúcar** (*palabra femenina*)
suicide, to commit (*v*) **suicidarse,
    matarse, quitarse la vida**
suicide **el suicidio**
Sunday **el domingo**
supper **la cena**
suppository **el supositorio**
surgeon **el/la cirujano/a**
surgery **la cirugía**
surname **el apellido**
suspension **la suspención**
swallow (*v*) **tragar**
swallow **el trago**
sweat (*v*) **sudar**
sweat **el sudor**
sweet **dulce**
swell (*v*) **hinchar**
swelling **la hinchazón**
swollen **hinchado/a**
symptom **el síntoma**
syndrome **el síndrome**
syphilis **la sífilis**
syringe **la jeringa, la jeringuilla**
syrup **el jarabe** (*medicine*), **el
    almíbar**
system **el sistema**

 t

tablespoon **la cuchara**
tablespoonful **la cucharada**
tachycardia **la taquicardia**
take (*v*) **tomar**
take out (*v*) **sacar**
talk (*v*) **hablar**
tall **alto/a**
tapeworm **la teniasis**
tarsus **el tarso**
taste (*v*) **probar** (o–ue)
taste **el gusto, el sabor**
tea **el té, la infusión, la tisana**
tear (secretion) **la lágrima**
teaspoon **la cucharita**
teaspoonful **la cucharadita**
technician **el/la técnico/a**
telephone **el teléfono**

tell (*v*) **decir** (*irregular*)
temperature **la temperatura**
tenth **el/la décimo/a**
test **la prueba**
testicle **el testículo**
tetanus **el tétano, el tétanos**
thank you **gracias**
thankful **agradecido/a**
that **ese, esa, aquel, aquella**
the **el, la**
then **entonces**
therapist **el/la terapeuta**
there **allí, allá**
thermometer **el termómetro**
they **ellos, ellas**
thigh **el muslo**
thin **delgado/a**
third **el/la tercero/a**
thirst **la sed**
this **este, esta**
those **esos, esas, aquellos, aquellas**
throat **la garganta**
thrombosis **la trombosis**
thrush **una infección en la boca producida por hongos**
Thursday **el jueves**
thus **así**
thyroid **el tiroides, la glándula tiroidea**
time **el tiempo, la hora**
tibia **la tibia**
tire (*v*) **cansar**
tired **cansado/a**
toast (*v*) **tostar**
toast **la tostada, el pan tostado**
today **hoy**
toe **el dedo del pie**
tolerance **la tolerancia**
tomato **el tomate, el jitomate**
tomorrow **mañana**
tongue **la lengua**
tongue-twister **el trabalengua**
tonsil **la amígdala**
tonsillectomy **la tonsilectomía, la tonsilotomía, la amigdalectomía**
tonsillitis **la amigdalitis**

too **también**
tooth **el diente**
toothpaste **la crema dental**
(on) top of **encima de**
topical **tópico/a**
tormented **mortificado/a**
touch (*v*) **tocar**
touch **el tacto**
toward **hacia**
towel **la toalla**
toxoplasmosis **la toxoplasmosis**
tradition **la tradición**
tranquilizer **el calmante**
transplant (*v*) **trasplantar**
transplant **el trasplante**
treat (*v*) **tratar**
treatment **el tratamiento**
triglyceride **el triglicérido**
true **verdadero, cierto**
truth **la verdad**
tuberculosis **la tuberculosis**
Tuesday **el martes**
tumor **el tumor**
tuna **el atún**

u

ulcer **la úlcera**
ulna **el cúbito**
ultrasound **la sonografía, el ecograma**
umbilical cord **el cordón umbilical**
uncle **el tío**
under **debajo de**
unit **la unidad**
United States **los Estados Unidos**
until **hasta**
urgency **la urgencia**
urinate (*v*) **orinar**
urine **la orina**
urine sample **la muestra de orina**
urologist **el/la urólogo/a**
urology **la urología**
us **nosotros, nosotras**
useful **útil**
useless **inútil**
uterus **el útero, la matriz**

V

vaccinate (v) **vacunar**
vaccination **la vacuna**
vagina **la vagina**
vaginal **vaginal**
varicela **la varicela**
vegetable **el vegetal, la verdura, la legumbre**
vehicular **automovilístico/a**
vein **la vena**
vertebra **la vértebra**
very **muy**
victim **la víctima**
virus **el virus**
visit (v) **visitar**
visit **la visita**
visitor **el/la visitante**
vitamin **la vitamina**
voice **la voz**
vomit (v) **vomitar**
vomit **el vómito**

W

wait (v) **esperar**
walk (v) **caminar**
want (v) **querer** (e–ie)
wash (v) **lavar(se)**
we **nosotros, nosotras**
weak **débil**
weakness **la debilidad**
wear (v) **llevar**
Wednesday **el miércoles**
week **la semana**
weekend **el fin de semana**
weekly **semanal, semanalmente**
weeping (crying) **el llanto**
weigh (v) **pesar**
weight **el peso**
well **bien, sano/a**
what? **¿qué?, ¿cuál?**
wheelchair **la silla de ruedas**
wheeze **el silbido**
when **cuando**
when? **¿cuándo?**

where **donde**
where? **¿dónde?**
  from where? **¿de dónde?**
  to where? **¿adónde?**
which? **¿cuál?**
white **blanco/a**
who **quien**
who?, whom? **¿quién?**
whole **entero/a**
  —grain **integral**
to whom? **¿a quién?**
whooping cough **la tos ferina**
why? **¿por qué?**
widow **la viuda**
widower **el viudo**
wife **la esposa, la mujer**
window **la ventana**
wine **el vino**
wisdom **la sabiduría**
wisdom tooth **el cordal, la muela del juicio**
withdraw (v) **retirar**
woman **la mujer**
womb **la matriz**
word **la palabra**
work (v) **trabajar**
worse **peor**
worsen (v) **empeorar**
wound **la herida**
wrist **la muñeca**
write (v) **escribir**
written **escrito/a**

X

x-ray **la radiografía, los rayos equis, la placa**
x-ray technician **el/la técnico/a de radiografía**

y

yaws **el pian, la frambuesa**
year **el año**
yellow **amarillo/a**
yellowish **amarillento/a**

yesterday **ayer**
yogurt **el yogur**
you **tú, usted, ustedes**
young **joven**
your **tu, su**

yours **tuyo/a, suyo/a**
yucca **la yuca**

Z

zero **el cero**

Spanish to English Glossary

The translations in this glossary are generally limited to the context in which the words are used in the book.

a

el **abanico** fan
el **abdomen** abdomen
aborrecido disgusted
el **aborto espontáneo** miscarriage
el **aborto natural** miscarriage
el **aborto provocado** abortion
la **abrasión** abrasion
abril April
abrir to open
abstener to abstain
la **abstinencia** abstinence
la **abuela** grandmother
el **abuelo** grandfather
aburrido/a bored; boring
aburrir to bore
el **ácaro del polvo** dust mite
el **accidente** accident
el **aceite** oil
el **acetaminofén** acetaminophen
acostar(se) (o–ue) to lie down, to go to bed
activo/a active
actual current
adelantar to advance, to move up
la **adicción** addiction

el/la **adicto/a** addict
adiós good-bye
¿**adónde?** to where?
la **adrenalina** adrenaline
el **aerosol** aerosol
afeitar(se) to shave
agitado/a agitated
agitar to agitate
agobiado/a overwhelmed
agosto August
agotado/a drained
agradable pleasant
agradecido/a thankful
el **aguacate** avocado
aguantar to bear, to endure
agudo/a acute
la **aguja** needle
el/la **ahijado/a** godson, goddaughter
ahora now
el **aire** (*palabra femenina*) air
el **alcance** reach
el **alcohol** alcohol
alegre happy
la **alegría** happiness
el **alemán** German
el **alérgeno** allergen

la alergia allergy
alérgico/a allergic
la alfombra rug, carpet
la algalia urinary catheter
algo something
alguien someone, anyone
algún, alguno/a some
alguna vez ever
algunas veces sometimes
alimentar to feed
el alimento food
aliviado/a relieved
el alivio relief
allá there
allí there
el almíbar syrup
el almidón starch
la almohada pillow
almorzar (o–ue) to eat/have lunch
el almuerzo lunch
alto/a tall
la alucinación hallucination
el alumbramiento birth
alumbrar to give birth
amable kind, nice
amamantar to breast-feed
amarillento/a yellowish, jaundiced
amarillo/a yellow
la ambulancia ambulance
ambulatorio/a ambulatory, outpatient
la amígdala tonsil
la amigdalitis tonsillitis
la amigdalotomía tonsillectomy
el/la amigo/a friend
la ampolla blister
la anafilaxis anaphylaxis, anaphylactic shock
el analgésico analgesic
el análisis analysis
anciano/a elderly
la anemia anemia
la anestesia anesthesia
la anestesiología anesthesiology
el/la anestesiólogo/a anesthesiologist
la aneurisma aneurysm

la angina de pecho angina pectoris
el angiograma angiogram
angustiado/a distressed
el animal animal
el ánimo spirit
el anís anise
el ano anus
anoche last night
la ansiedad anxiety
ansioso/a anxious
el antebrazo forearm
antes de before
el antiácido antacid
el antibiótico antibiotic
el anticoagulante anticoagulant
el anticonvulsante anticonvulsant
el anticuerpo antibody
el antidepresivo antidepressant
el antidiarreico antidiarrheal
el antiespasmódico antispasmodic
el antihiperglucémico antihyperglycemic
el antihistamínico antihistamine
el antiinflamatorio antiinflammatory
el antipirético antipyretic
el antitusígeno antitussive
el año year
el apellido surname
la apendectomía appendectomy
el apéndice appendix
la apendicitis appendicitis
el apetito appetite
aplicar to apply
la apoplejía apoplexy
aprender to learn
aquel, aquella that
aquellos, aquellas those
aquí here
el ardor burning sensation
la área area
el arroz rice
la articulación joint
la artritis arthritis
la artroscopia arthroscopy
el ascensor elevator
así thus, in this way, like this

asilo asylum, nursing home
el asma (*palabra femenina*) asthma
el/la asociado/a médico/a physician's assistant
la aspirina aspirin
asustado/a scared, frightened
asustar to scare, to frighten
atacar to attack
el ataque attack
el atún tuna
la audiología audiology
el/la audiólogo/a audiologist
auscultar to listen with a stethoscope
automovilístico/a vehicular
la avena oatmeal
avergonzado/a ashamed
ayer yesterday
la ayuda help
el/la ayudante assistant, helper
ayudar to help
ayunar to fast
el azúcar (*palabra femenina*) sugar
azucarado/a sugar-added

b

la bacteria bacterium
bacteriano/a bacterial
bajo/a short (height)
bañar(se) to bathe
el baño bath, bathroom
la barbilla chin
el barbitúrico barbiturate
la bata robe, hospital gown
el bazo spleen
el/la bebé baby
beber to drink
la bebida beverage
el beneficio benefit
benigno/a benign
el biberón baby's bottle
bien well
bilingüe bilingual
la biopsia biopsy
el/la bisabuelo/a great grandfather, great grandmother

el/la bisnieto/a great grandson, great granddaughter
blando/a soft
la boca mouth
el bolígrafo pen
la bolita lump
borracho/a drunk
la botella bottle
el brazo arm
el brócoli broccoli
la broncoscopia bronchoscopy
bronquial bronchial
el bronquio bronchial tube
buenmozo handsome
bueno/a good

C

el cabello hair
la cabeza head
cada each, every
la cadera hip
caer (*irregular*) to fall
la calabaza squash
el calambre cramp
el calcio calcium
el cálculo en el riñón kidney stone
el caldo broth
la calle street
el calmante tranquilizer, analgesic
calmar(se) to calm, to calm down
el calor heat
la caloría calorie
la cama bed
la camilla stretcher, gurney
caminar to walk
el cáncer cancer
la canela cinnamon
cansado/a tired
el cansancio fatigue
cansar to tire, to grow tired
la cantidad amount
la cápsula capsule
la cara face
cardíaco/a cardiac
la cardiología cardiology

el/la cardiólogo/a cardiologist
la caries cavity
la carne meat
   —de res beef
casado/a married
casar(se) to marry
la caspa dandruff
   —de animal animal dander
la catarata cataract
el catarro congestion, common cold
el catéter catheter
celoso/a jealous
la célula cell
la cena supper, dinner
cenar to eat/have supper
cepillar(se) to brush
el cereal cereal
   —cocido cooked cereal
   —seco dry cereal
cerebral cerebral
el cerebro brain
el cero zero
la cerveza beer
el/la chamán folk healer
el chino Chinese
chiquito/a small
chocar to collide, to crash
el chocolate chocolate
el choque collision, crash
la ciática sciatica
ciático/a sciatic
la cicatriz scar
ciego/a blind
el cinturón de seguridad seat belt
la cirrosis cirrhosis
la ciruela plum, prune
la cirugía surgery
el/la cirujano/a surgeon
   —ortopédico/a orthopedic surgeon
   —plástico/a plastic surgeon
la cita appointment
la ciudad city
la clamidia chlamydia
la clase class
clásico/a classic

la clavícula clavicle
la clínica clinic
clínico/a clinical
el coágulo clot
la cocaína cocaine
el cóccix coccyx
el coche car
la cocina kitchen
cocinar to cook
el/la cocinero/a cook
el coco coconut
la codeína codeine
el codo elbow
la colecistectomía cholecystectomy
la colecistitis cholecystitis
el cólera cholera
el cólico, los cólicos colic
el colon colon
la colonoscopia colonoscopy
el color color
colorado/a red
la colostomía colostomy
la comadrona midwife
combatir to fight
comer to eat
la comezón itch, itching
la comida meal
como like, as
¿cómo? how?
cómodo/a comfortable
compartir to share
la complicación complication
comprar to buy
el comprimido pill
común common
el condón condom
confirmar to confirm
la congestión congestion
congestionado/a congested
consciente conscious
el/la consejero/a counselor
constante constant
consultar to consult
el consultorio doctor's office
la contaminación contamination

—del aire air pollution
contento/a happy, contented
contestar to answer
la contracción contraction
el contraceptivo contraceptive
la convulsión convulsion
el corazón heart
    el ataque al corazón heart attack
    el soplo en el corazón heart murmur
el cordal wisdom tooth
el cordón umbilical umbilical cord
la corona crown
    —de oro / —porcelano gold / porcelain
correr to run
corriente regular, everyday
la cortadura cut
cortar(se) to cut
cortés polite
la cortesía politeness
corto/a short (length)
coser to sew
la costilla rib
la coyuntura joint
el cráneo cranium
creer to believe
la crema cream, ointment
    —dental toothpaste
la crisis crisis
crónico/a chronic
¿cuál? which?
cuando when
¿cuándo? when?
¿cuánto/a? how much?
¿cuántos/as? how many?
cuarto/a quarter part
el cuarto room
el cúbito ulna
la cuchara tablespoon
la cucharada tablespoonful
la cucharadita teaspoonful
la cucharita teaspoon
el cuello neck
    —del úturo, —de la matriz cervix
el cuerpo body
el cuidado intensivo intensive care

    —neonatal neonatal intensive care
cuidar to care for
la culebrilla herpes zoster, shingles
la culpa guilt
culpable guilty
el cultivo culture (laboratory)
el/la cuñado/a brother-in-law, sister-in-law
curioso/a curious
la curita small bandage
la custodia custody

d

dañar to damage, to harm
el daño damage, harm
dar (*irregular*) to give
dar a luz to give birth
dar de alta to discharge
de of, from
¿de dónde? from where?
debajo de under
deber ought, should, to owe
débil weak
la debilidad weakness
el/la décimo/a tenth
decir (*irregular*) to say, to tell
el dedo finger
el dedo del pie toe
defecar to move one's bowels
dejar to leave behind
delante de (in) front of
delgado/a thin
el delirio delusion
demasiado/a too much
demostrar (o–ue) to demonstrate
el dengue dengue
la dentadura teeth, set of teeth
    —postiza dentures, false teeth
el/la dentista dentist
la dependencia dependence
la depresión depression
deprimido/a depressed
derecho/a right, straight
el/la dermatólogo/a dermatologist
la dermatología dermatology

el derrame leak, spill, hemorrhage
desayunar to eat/have breakfast
el desayuno breakfast
descafeinado/a decaffeinated
descansar to rest
el descanso rest
el descongestionante decongestant
descorazonado/a disheartened
descremado/a fat-free
la descripción description
descubrir to discover
desesperado/a hopeless, desperate
la deshidratación dehydration
desmayar(se) to faint
despacio/a slow, slowly
despertar(se) (e–ie) to awaken
despierto/a awake
después afterward
después de after
detrás de behind
el día day
la diabetes diabetes
el diagnóstico diagnosis
la diálisis dialysis
la diarrea diarrhea
dichoso/a lucky
diciembre December
el diente tooth
    —de leche baby tooth
la dieta diet
el/la dietista dietician
la difteria diphtheria
diluir to dilute
el dinero money
la dirección address
discapacitado/a disabled
la disentería dysentery
disgustado/a disgusted
el diurético/a diuretic
divorciado/a divorced
divorciar(se) to divorce, to get divorced
el divorcio divorce
el doctor, la doctora doctor
doler (o–ue) to ache, to hurt
el dolor pain

    —agudo, punzante sharp—
    —del parto labor—
    —latente, sordo dull—
    —quemante burning—
el domingo Sunday
donde where
¿dónde? where?
    ¿adónde? to where?
    ¿de dónde? from where?
dorado/a golden
dormir (o–ue) to sleep
el drenaje drain, drainage
drenar to drain
la droga drug
duchar(se) to shower
dulce sweet
el dulce candy
durar to last, endure
duro/a hard

e

ebrio/a drunk
el eccema eczema
el ecograma sonogram, sonograph
ectópico/a ectopic
la edad age
el efecto secundario side effect
el the
él he
el electrocardiograma electrocardiogram
el electroencefalograma
    electroencephalogram
eliminar to eliminate
el elixir elixir
ella she
ellos/as they
embarazada pregnant
el embarazo pregnancy
la embolia embolism
    —cerebral stroke
la emergencia emergency
el empacho indigestion
el emparedado sandwich
el empaste filling (dental)
empeorar to worsen

empezar (e–ie) to start, begin
empujar to push
encantado/a pleased
encima de on (top of)
encinta pregnant
encontrar (o–ue) to find
la endocrinología endocrinology
el/la endocrinólogo/a endocrinologist
la endometriosis endometriosis
la endoscopia endoscopy
enero January
enfadado/a annoyed
enfadar(se) to become annoyed
la enfermedad sickness, illness
　　—**cardiovascular** cardiovascular
　　　disease
　　—**de Chaga** Chaga's disease
　　—**pulmonar obstructiva crónica**
　　　COPD
　　—**transmitida sexualmente** sexually
　　　transmitted disease
la enfermería nursing
el/la enfermero/a nurse
enfermo/a sick, ill
la enfisema emphysema
enfogonado/a enraged (*slang*)
enfogonar(se) to enrage (*slang*)
el enjuague rinse
enjuagar to rinse
enlatado/a canned
enojado/a angry
enojar to anger
enojar(se) to get angry
el enojo anger
la ensalada salad
enseñar to teach, to show
entero/a whole
el entumecimiento numbness
la epilepsia epilepsy
la epinefrina epinephrine
la episiotomía episiotomy
la erupción rash
esa that
el escalofrío chill
la esclerosis múltiple multiple sclerosis

escribir to write
escrito/a written
el escritorio desk
el escroto scrotum
escuchar to listen
la escuela school
escupir to spit
ese that
el esófago esophagus
la espalda back
el español Spanish, Spaniard
la especia spice
la especialidad specialty
la esperanza hope
esperar to wait, to hope
la espina bífida spina bifida
la espina dorsal spine
el espíritu spirit
la espirometría spirometry
espontáneo/a spontaneous
la espuma foam
el esputo sputum
el esqueleto skeleton
la esquizofrenia schizophrenia
esquizofrénico/a schizophrenic
esta this
la estadía length of stay
los Estados Unidos the United States
el estafilococo staphylococcus
el estafilococo dorado MRSA
estar (*irregular*) to be
la estatura height
este this
el esternón sternum
el esteroide steroid
el estetescopio stethoscope
el estómago stomach
estornudar to sneeze
el estornudo sneeze
el estreñimiento constipation
el estrés stress
el/la estudiante student
estudiar to study
el estudio study
el eucalipto eucalyptus

evacuar to move one's bowels
evitar to avoid
el examen exam
la examinación examination
examinar to examine
exhalar to exhale
el expectorante expectorant
el expediente médico medical record
explicar to explain
exploratorio/a exploratory
la extracción extraction

f

la falange phalange
la falta de aire shortness of breath
el/la farmacéutico/a pharmacist
la farmacia pharmacy
fascinar to fascinate
la fatiga fatigue, shortness of breath
febrero February
la fecha date
las felicidades congratulations
feliz happy
el fémur femur
el feto fetus
la fibra fiber
la fiebre fever
la fiebre reumática rheumatic fever
el fin de semana weekend
firmar to sign
flaco/a skinny
la flema phlegm
el fluido fluid
el flujo flow
el fluoruro fluoride
la fobia phobia
la fractura fracture
    —abierta open fracture
    —compuesta compound fracture
    —conminuta conminuted fracture
    —espiral spiral fracture
    —oblicua transverse fracture
    —simple simple fracture
la frambuesa yaws; raspberry
el francés French

el frasco bottle
la frazada blanket
la frecuencia frequency
frecuente frequent
frecuentemente frequently
la frente forehead
la fresa dental drill; strawberry
el frío cold (temperature)
frío/a cold
frustrado/a frustrated
la fruta fruit
fuerte strong
fumar to smoke
furioso/a furious

g

el ganglio linfático lymph gland
la garganta throat
la gaseosa soft drink
gastar to spend money
la gastritis gastritis
el gel gel
la gelatina gelatin
generoso/a generous
el/la geriatra geriatrist
la geriatría geriatrics
geriátrico/a geriatric
la ginecología gynecology
ginecológico/a gynecologic
el/la ginecólogo/a gynecologist
la gingivitis gingivitis
la glándula gland
        —tiroide thyroid—
la glaucoma glaucoma
el gluteo buttock
el golpe bump
golpear(se) to bump, hit
el golpecito tap
la gonorrea gonorrhea
gordo/a fat
la gota drop, gout
gotear to drip
el goteo dripping
la grabadora recorder
grabar to record

gracias thank you
la gragea capsule
el grano grain
la grasa fat, grease
la gripa common cold
la gripe flu, common cold
el guante glove
guapo/a handsome (with *ser*), angry (with
    estar)
el guineo banana
gustar to please
el gusto taste

h

la haba, la habichuela bean
la habitación room
hablar to talk, to speak
hacer (*irregular*) to do, to make
hacer falta to miss
hacia toward
el hambre hunger
hambriento/a hungry
hasta until
hay there is, there are
las heces fecales feces
helado/a frozen
el helado ice cream
el helicóptero helicopter
la hembra female
la hemofilia hemophilia
la hemorragia hemorrhage
hemorrágico/a hemorrhagic
las hemorroides hemorrhoids
la hepatitis hepatitis
la herida wound, injury
    —de bala gunshot wound
herir to injure
el/la hermanastro/a brother-in-law, sister-
    in-law
el/la hermano/a brother, sister
el/la hermano/a de madre half-brother,
    half-sister
el/la hermano/a de padre half-brother,
    half-sister
la hernia hernia

la heroína heroin
el herpes herpes
el hielo ice
el hierro iron (Fe)
el hígado liver
higiénico/a hygienic
el/la higienista dental dental hygienist
el/la hijastro/a stepson, stepdaughter
el/la hijo/a son, daughter
el/la hijo/a de crianza foster child
el hilo dental dental floss
hinchado/a swollen
hinchar to swell
la hinchazón swelling
la hipercolesterolemia
    hypercolesterolemia
la hiperglucemia hyperglycemia
la hipertensión hypertension
el hipertiroidismo hyperthyroidism
la hipoglucemia hypoglycemia
la hipotensión hypotension
el hipotiroidismo hypothyroidism
la histerectomía hysterectomy
la historia history
hola hello
el hombre man
el hombro shoulder
la hora hour
el hospital hospital
la hospitalización hospitalization
hospitalizar hospitalize
hoy today
el hueso bone
el huevo egg
el húmero humerus
el humo smoke

i

el ibuprofeno, el ibuprofén ibuprofen
la ictericia jaundice
el idioma language
igual equal, same
igualmente equally, same here, same to
    you
el íleon ilium

implantar to implant
el implante implant
importar to matter
incluir (*irregular*) to include
la incontinencia incontinence
el infarto infarct
la infección infection
    —por giardias giardiasis
    —por tenia tapeworm
infectar to infect
la inflamación inflammation
inflamado/a inflamed
inflamar to inflame
la influenza influenza
la infusión infusion, tea
el inglés English
el inhalador inhaler
el insomnio insomnia
la insuficiencia insufficiency
    —cardíaca congestive heart failure
    —renal renal failure
integral whole-grain
inteligente intelligent
interesado/a interested
interesante interesting
interesar to interest
el internamiento hospitalization
internar to admit (to an institution)
el intestino intestine
    —delgado small intestine
    —grueso large intestine
inútil useless
inválido/a disabled
la inyección injection
ir (*irregular*) to go
la irritabilidad irritability
la irritación rash
el italiano Italian
izquierdo/a left

j

jadear to gasp, to pant
el jadeo gasping, panting
jamás never
el japonés Japanese

la jaqueca migraine, headache
el jarabe syrup (medicine)
el jengibre ginger
la jeringa, la jeringuilla syringe
el jitomate tomato
joven young
el jueves Thursday
el jugo juice
    —de naranja orange juice
    —de manzana apple juice
    —de ciruela prune juice
julio July
junio June

k

el kilogramo kilogram

l

la the
el labio lip
la laceración laceration
el lado side
la lágrima tear (secretion)
la laparoscopia laparoscopy
largo/a long
el láser laser
lastimar to injure, to wound
latente pulsating
el látex latex
lavar(se) to wash (oneself)
el laxante laxative
la leche milk
leer to read
lejos far
la lengua tongue, language
el lenguaje language
los lentes eyeglasses
lento/a slow
la leptospirosis leptospirosis
la leucemia leukemia
levantar(se) to get up, to arise, to raise
leve light, slight, minor
la libra pound
el libro book
el limón lemon, lime

la limpieza cleaning
limpio/a clean
el líquido liquid
el litio lithium
la llamada call
llamar to call
llamar(se) to be named, to call oneself
el llanto crying jag
la llegada arrival
llegar to arrive
llevar to carry, wear
llorar to cry
loco/a crazy
la lombriz intestinal intestinal worm
luego later
el lugar place
la lumpectomía lumpectomy
el lunar mole
el lunes Monday
la luz light

m

la madrastra stepmother
la madre mother
la madrina godmother
majado/a mashed
majar to mash
mal badly
el malestar general malaise
maligno/a malignant
malo/a bad
la mancha stain
manchar to stain
la mandíbula jaw
manejar to drive, to manage
la manía mania
maníacodepresivo/a manic-depressive
la mano hand
la manteca lard; heroin (*slang*)
la mantequilla de cacahuate, la
    mantequilla de maní peanut butter
la mantequilla butter
la manzana apple
la mañana morning
mañana tomorrow

la máquina machine
el marcapasos pacemaker
mareado/a dizzy
el mareo dizziness
la marihuana marijuana
el martes Tuesday
marzo March
más more
más o menos more or less
masticable chewable
matar to kill
matarse to suicide
la matriz womb
mayo May
mayor older, elderly
el medicamento medication
la medicina medicine
el/la médico/a doctor
    —de cabecera, —generalista general
        practitioner
    —internista internist
la mejilla cheek
mejor better
mejorar to get better
la meningitis meningitis
la menopausia menopause
la menstruación menstruation
menstruar to menstruate
mensual, mensualmente monthly
la merienda snack
el mes month
la metástasis metastasis
el miedo fear
la miel de abeja honey
el miembro penis
el miércoles Wednesday
la migraña migraine
el miligramo milligram
el mililitro milliliter
mirar to look
el moco mucus
el moho mold
moler (o–ue) to grind
molestar to bother, to annoy
la molestia bother, annoyance

molesto/a uncomfortable, annoyed
molido/a ground
la monga common cold, flu (*slang*)
el monitor monitor
la mononucleosis mononucleosis
moreno/a dark, brunette
el moretón bruise
morir (o–ue) to die
mortificado/a tormented
mover(se) (o–ue) to move
el/la muchacho/a child
el mucolítico mucolytic
la muela molar
la muela del juicio wisdom tooth
la muerte death
la muestra sample
la mujer woman
la muleta crutch
la muñeca wrist, doll
el músculo muscle
el muslo thigh
muy very

n

nacer (*irregular*) to be born
el nacimiento birth
nada nothing
nadie nobody, no one
la nalga buttock
la nariz nose
natural natural
la náusea nausea
nebulizar to nebulize
el nebulizador nebulizer
la necesidad need
necesitar to need
la nefrectomía nephrectomy
la nefritis nephritis
negativo/a negative
el nervio nerve
nervioso/a nervous
la neumonectomía pneumonectomy
la neumonía pneumonia
el/la neumonólogo/a pulmonologist
la neurología neurology

el/la neurólogo/a neurologist
la nevera refrigerator
ningún, ninguno/a none, not any
el/la niño/a child
la nitroglicerina nitroglycerine
la noche night
nombrar to name
el nombre name
el nopal prickly pear cactus
la norsa nurse (*slang*)
nosocomial nosocomial
nosotros/as we, us
noveno/a ninth
noviembre November
el nudillo knuckle
la nuera daughter-in-law
nuestro/a our, ours
nunca never
el/la nutricionista nutritionist

o

o or
la obesidad obesity
obeso/a obese
el/la obstetra obstetrician
la obstetricia obstetrics
obstétrico/a obstetric
octavo/a eighth
octubre October
la odontología dentistry
el/la odontólogo/a dentist
ofender to offend
ofendido/a offended
ofrecer (*irregular*) to offer
la ofrenda offering
la oftalmología ophthalmology
el/la oftalmólogo/a ophthalmologist
el oído ear (inner), hearing
oír to hear
¡Ojalá! I hope so!
ojalá que . . . I wish that . . .
el ojo eye
oler (*irregular*) to smell
el olfato smell
el olor odor, smell

olvidar to forget
el omóplato scapula
la oncología oncology
el/la oncólogo/a oncologist
oprimir to press
oral oral
el orégano oregano
la oreja ear (outer)
orgulloso/a proud
la orina urine
orinar to urinate
el oro gold
la ortopedia orthopedics
ortopédico/a orthopedic
el/la ortopedista orthopedist
oscuro/a dark
la osteoporosis osteoporosis
la otorrinolaringología ENT
el/la otorrinolaringólogo/a ENT doctor
el ovario ovary
la ovulación ovulation
ovular to ovulate
el oxígeno oxygen

p

el/la paciente patient
padecer (*irregular*) to suffer (from an
   illness)
el padecimiento illness
el padrastro stepfather
el padre father
los padres parents
el padrino godfather
la palabra word
pálido/a pale
el palo pole, stick
palpar to palpate
la palpitación palpitation
el paludismo malaria
el pan bread
   —integral whole grain—
   —tostado toast
el páncreas pancreas
la pandemia pandemic
pandémico/a pandemic

la pantorrilla calf (anat.)
la papa potato
las papas fritas French fries
la paperas mumps
el papiloma papilloma
la parálisis paralysis, palsy
   —cerebral cerabral palsy
el/la paramédico/a paramedic
la paranoia paranoia
paranoico/a paranoid
el parche patch
la pareja partner, couple
parir to give birth
el/la partero/a midwife
el parto birth
pasar to happen, to pass
el pasillo hallway
la pastilla pill
la patela kneecap
la paternidad paternity
paterno/a paternal
el pato de cama bedpan
el pecho chest
el pedazo piece
el/la pediatra pediatrician
la pediatría pediatrics
pediátrico/a pediatric
pedir (e–i) to ask for, to beg
peinar(se) to comb
el peine comb
pelear to argue, to fight
el peligro danger
peligroso/a dangerous
el pelo hair
la pelotita lump
el pene penis
peor worse
pequeño/a small
percutir to percuss
perder (e–ie) to lose
la pérdida loss
el perico cocaine (*slang*)
el período, el periodo period
la periodontitis periodontitis
el permiso permission

el peroné fibula
persistente persistent
persistir to persist
personal personal
pesado/a crushing, heavy
pesar to weigh
el pescado fish
pescar to fish
el peso weight
el pian yaws
picar to itch
la picazón itch, itching
el pie foot
la piel skin
la pierna leg
la píldora pill
el pimiento bell pepper
los piojos lice
la pirámide pyramid
el piso floor
la pizarra blackboard
la placa film, x-ray; plaque
la placenta placenta
el placer pleasure
el plan de alimentación diet
el plan médico health insurance
la plata silver, money
pobre poor
poder (o–ue) to be able
la podiología podiatry
el/la podiólogo/a podiatrist
el polen pollen
la polio, la poliomielitis polio
el pólipo polyp
el pollo chicken
el polvo dust
polvorizar to crush
la pompa inhaler (*slang*)
la pompis buttock
el pómulo cheekbone
poner (*irregular*) to put
¿por qué? why?
la porcelana porcelain
la porción portion

porque because
el portador (sano) (asymptomatic) carrier
el portugués Portuguese
positivo/a positive
el postre dessert
practice practicar
la precaución precaution
la precisión accuracy, precision
la pregunta question
preguntar to ask a question
la presentación pelviana, la presentación de nalgas breech position
la presión pressure
   —arterial blood pressure
   —de la sangre blood pressure
   —sanguínea blood pressure
presionar to press
la prevención prevention
prevenir to prevent
preventivo/a preventive
primero/a first
el/la primo/a cousin
privado/a private
probar (o–ue) to test, taste, try
el procedimiento procedure
profundo/a deep
el prolapso prolapse
el pronóstico prognosis
la próstata prostate
la prostatitis prostatitis
prostético/a prosthetic
la proteína protein
la prótesis prosthesis
provocar to provoke
el/la próximo/a next
la prueba test
   —de Papanicolaou Pap smear test
la psicología psychology
el/la psicólogo/a psychologist
la psicosis psychosis
psicótico/a psychotic
el/la psiquiatra psychiatrist
la psiquiatría psychiatry
psiquiátrico/a psychiatric

la **psoriasis** psoriasis
el **pueblo** town
la **puerta** door
la **pulgada** inch
el **pulmón** lung
la **pulmonía** pneumonia
el/la **pulmonólogo/a** pulmonologist
el **pulso** pulse
el **punto** stitch, period, dot, point
puntual punctual
punzante stabbing
la **puñalada** stab wound
puré puree

q

que that
¿qué? what?, how?
quebrado/a broken
quedar(se) to remain
quemado/a burned
la **quemadura** burn
quemar(se) to burn
querer (e–ie) to want, to like
el **queso** cheese
quien who, whom
¿quién? who?, whom?
la **quimioterapia** chemotherapy
la **quinina** quinine
quinto/a fifth
el **quirófano** operating room
el **quiste** cyst
quitar(se) to remove

r

el **radio** radio
la **radiografía** x-ray
la **radiología** radiology
el/la **radiólogo/a** radiologist
la **radioterapia** radiotherapy
rápido/a quick
la **raquiña** itch, itching (*slang*)
la **reacción** reaction
la **reanimación cardiopulmonar** CPR
el/la **recepcionista** receptionist

la **receta** prescription
recetar to prescribe
rechazado/a rejected
rechazar to reject
el **rechazo** rejection
recibir to receive
el **recibo** receipt
recordar (o–ue) to remind, to remember
el **recto** rectum
el **reemplazo** replacement
el **reflujo esofágico** esophageal reflux
el **refresco** soda pop, soft drink
el **refrigerador** refrigerator
la **regla** period, menstruation
regresar to return
regular regular, O.K.
el **remedio** cure
 —**casero** home remedy
repentino/a, de repente sudden
la **res, la carne de res** beef
el **resfriado** common cold
el **resfrío** common cold
resistente resistant
la **respiración** respiration
respirar to breathe
la **resucitación** resuscitation
resucitar to resuscitate
el **resultado** result
retirar to withdraw
el **retraso mental** mental retardation
la **reumatología** rheumatology
el/la **reumatólogo/a** rheumatologist
rico/a rich
el **riesgo** risk
la **rigidez** stiffness
el **riñón** kidney
rociar to spray
la **rodilla** knee
el **romero** rosemary
romper to break
 —**fuente** to break water
el **ron** rum
las **ronchas** hives
la **ropa** clothes, clothing

la rubéola rubella, German measles
rubio/a blond, fair

S

el sábado Saturday
la sábana sheet
saber (*irregular*) to know
la sábila aloe vera
sacar to take out
el sacro sacrum
la sal salt
la sala de
 —**emergencia** emergency room
 —**espera** waiting room
 —**operaciones** operating room
 —**recuperación** recovery room
 —**urgencias** emergency room
la salchicha sausage
la salud health
sanar to heal
sangrar to bleed
la sangre blood
sano/a healthy, healed
el sarampión measles
la sarna scabies
el sarpullido hives
el sarro plaque (dental)
satisfecho/a satisfied
secar(se) to dry
la secreción secretion
el/la secretario/a secretary
la sed thirst
el sedante sedative
seguir (e–i) to follow
segundo/a second
el seguro insurance
seguro/a safe, sure
el sellador sealant
el sellante sealant
la semana week
sencillo/a plain, easy
el seno breast; sinus
 —**frontal** frontal sinus
 —**paranasal** paranasal sinus
la sensación sensation

sentar(se) (e–ie) to sit
sentir(se) (e–ie) to feel
septiembre September
séptimo/a seventh
la sequedad dryness
ser (*irregular*) to be
severo/a severe
sexto/a sixth
el shock anafiláctico anaphylactic shock
la sicosis psychosis
sicótico/a psychotic
el SIDA AIDS
siempre always
la sífilis syphilis
el silbido wheeze
la silla chair
la silla de ruedas wheelchair
la silleta bedpan
simpático/a kind
el síndrome syndrome
el síntoma symptom
el sistema system
sobre on, about, around
la sobredosis overdose
sobrepeso/a overweight
sobrio sober
la soja soybean
solitario/a alone
la sonda catheter
la sonografía ultrasound
la sopa soup
el soplo bruit
 —**cardíaco** heart murmur
sordo/a deaf
sorprendido/a surprised
su your, his, her, their
sudar to sweat
el sudor sweat
los sudores nocturnos night sweats
la suegra mother-in-law
el suegro father-in-law
el sueño dream, sleep
el suero IV fluid
la suerte luck
suicidarse to commit suicide

el **suicidio** suicide
el **supositorio** suppository
la **suspensión** suspension
el **susto** fright
suyo/a/os/as yours, his, hers, theirs

t

la **tabla** board
el **tacto** touch
el **tajo** cut
también also, too
tampoco neither
la **taquicardia** tachycardia
tarde late
la **tarde** afternoon
la **tarjeta** card
el **té** tea
el/la **técnico/a** technician
el **teléfono** telephone
la **temperatura** temperature
temprano early
tener (*irregular*) to have
la **teniasis** tapeworm
la **tensión arterial** blood pressure
el/la **terapeuta** therapist
    —**de lenguaje** speech therapist
    —**del habla** speech therapist
    —**físico/a** physical therapist
    —**respiratorio/a** respiratory therapist
tercero/a third
el **termómetro** thermometer
el **testículo** testicle
el **tétano, el tétanos** tetanus
la **tía** aunt
la **tía abuela** great aunt
la **tibia** tibia
tibio/a lukewarm
el **tiempo** time, weather
tímido/a shy
el **tío** uncle
el **tío abuelo** great uncle
la **tirita** small bandage
el **tiroides** thyroid
la **tisana** infusion (drink), tea
la **toalla** towel

el **tobillo** ankle
tocar to touch
la **tolerancia** tolerance
tomar to take
el **tomate** tomato
la **tomografía computarizada** CT scan
la **tonsilectomía** tonsillectomy
la **tonsilotomía** tonsillotomy
tópico/a topical
la **torcedura** sprain
torcer(se) (o–ue) to sprain
torcido/a sprained
la **toronja** grapefruit
la **torta** cake
la **tos** cough
la **tos ferina** pertussis, whooping cough
toser to cough
la **tostada** toast
la **toxoplasmosis** toxoplasmosis
el/la **trabajador/a social** social worker
trabajar to work
el **trabajo** job
    —**social** social work
el **trabalengua** tongue-twister
la **tradición** tradition
tragar to swallow
el **trago** swallow
traicionado/a betrayed
trasnochar to stay up all night
trasplantar to transplant
el **trasplante** transplant
el **trastorno** disorder
el **tratamiento** treatment
    —**de canal** root canal
tratar to treat
los **triglicéridos** triglycerides
triste sad
la **tristeza** sadness
la **trombosis** thrombosis
la **trompa de Falopio** Fallopian tube
tu your
tú you
la **tuberculosis** tuberculosis
el **tumor** tumor
tutear to address informally

el/la tutor/a custodian
tuyo/a/os/as yours

u

la úlcera ulcer
el ungüento ointment
la unidad unit
la uña fingernail
la urgencia urgency, emergency
la urología urology
el/la urólogo/a urologist
la urticaria urticaria, hives
usted you
el útero uterus
útil useful
la uva grape

v

la vacuna vaccination
vacunar to vaccinate
la vagina vagina
la varicela varicella, chicken pox
el varón male
el vaso glass
el vegetal vegetable
la vejiga bladder
la vena vein
el vendaje bandage
venir (*irregular*) to come
la ventana window
el ventilador fan
ver to see
la verdad truth
verdadero/a true
verde green
verdoso/a greenish
la verdura vegetable (green)
la vergüenza shame
la verruga venérea genital wart

la vértebra vertebra
la vesícula biliar gallbladder
la vez time (occurrence, occasion)
la víctima victim
viejo/a old
el viernes Friday
el VIH HIV
el vino wine
virar(se) to roll over
la viruela smallpox
las viruelas locas chicken pox
el virus virus
la visita visit
el/la visitante visitor
visitar to visit
la vista sight
la vitamina vitamin
la viuda widow
el viudo widower
vivir to live
vivo/a alive
volver (o–ue) to return
vomitar to vomit
el vómito vomit
la voz voice

y

y and
ya already, at last, right now
el/la yerno/a son-in-law, daughter-in-law
el yeso cast
yo I
el yogur yogurt

z

la zanahoria carrot
el zapato shoe
el zumo juice

Answer Key to *Ejercicios*

We have excluded those exercises whose responses may vary.

Chapter 1

1.1 Ejercicio

A. Hola. Buenos días. Buenas tardes. Buenas noches.
B. Adiós. Hasta luego.
C. Soy el doctor Vargas. Me llamo Francisco Flores.
D. Me alegro. Lo siento.
E. Mucho gusto. Encantado/a.

1.2 Ejercicio

1. Dr. Vargas: —Buenos días. Soy el doctor Vargas.
2. Sr. Flores: —Buenos días, doctor. Soy Francisco Flores.
3. Dr. Vargas: —Mucho gusto.
4. Sr. Flores: —El gusto es mío. ¿Cómo está usted?
5. Dr. Vargas: —Muy bien, gracias, ¿y usted?
6. Sr. Flores: —Bien, bien, gracias. Doctor, le presento a mi esposa Marisol García de Flores.
7. Dr. Vargas: —Encantado.
8. Sra. Flores: —Igualmente. Usted habla español. ¿De dónde es usted?
9. Dr. Vargas: —Soy de Puerto Rico.

1.6 Ejercicio

A. El doctor Colón es neurólogo.   La doctora Palma es neuróloga.
B. El doctor Aquino es odontólogo.   La doctora Valenzuela es odontóloga.
C. Ana es trabajadora social.   Tomás es trabajador social.
D. El señor García es consejero.   La señora Marques es consejera.
E. Leomara es farmacéutica.   Alfredo es farmacéutico.
F. El doctor Mena es psiquiatra.   La doctora Mariano es psiquiatra.

G. La doctora López es cardióloga.   El doctor López es cardiólogo.
H. La doctora Negrón es dentista.   El doctor José Peña Ortiz es dentista.

1.7 Ejercicio

A. la clínica   las clínicas
B. la puerta   las puertas
C. el monitor   los monitores
D. la cama   las camas
E. la sábana   las sábanas
F. la frazada   las frazadas
G. la almohada   las almohadas
H. el doctor   los doctores
I. el hospital   los hospitales

1.8 Ejercicio

A. tú   D. usted
B. tú   E. tú
C. usted   F. usted

1.9 Ejercicio

A. el Sr. Romero   él es
B. Juan y yo   nosotros somos
C. Sergio y Ana   ellos son
D. las enfermeras   ellas son
E. la familia   (la familia) es
F. la clase y yo   nosotros somos
G. los doctores   ellos son
H. el doctor y el enfermero ellos son
I. la clínica   (la clínica) es
J. usted, usted y usted   ustedes son

1.10 Ejercicio

A. Necesito una inyección.   Usted necesita un enfermero.
B. Sufro de problemas cardíacos.   Usted necesita un cardiólogo.
C. Sufro de diabetes.   Usted necesita un endocrinólogo,
                                          nutricionista, dietista, oftalmólogo.

D. Necesito una operación.   Usted necesita un cirujano.
E. Sufro de cáncer de los pulmones.   Usted necesita un oncólogo, cirujano.
F. Sufro de cataratas.   Usted necesita un oftalmólogo.
G. Necesito una dieta especial.   Usted necesita un dietista, nutricionista.
H. Sufro de problemas emocionales.   Usted necesita un psicólogo, psiquiatra,
                                          trabajador social.

I. Sufro de artritis.   Usted necesita un reumatólogo.
J. Tengo la clavícula fracturada.   Usted necesita un ortopedista.
K. Sufro de psoriasis.   Usted necesita un dermatólogo.
L. Mi bebé tiene fiebre.   Usted necesita un pediatra.

1.17 Ejercicio

A. La esposa del Sr. Flores se llama Marisol.

B. El doctor Vargas es de Puerto Rico.

C. La familia Flores es de la República Dominicana.

D. El doctor Vargas es médico generalista.

E. El cardiólogo trabaja con problemas del corazón.

F. Necesitas un urólogo si tienes problema con la próstata.

G. Si te duele el oído, necesitas consultar con un otorrinolaringólogo.

1.19 Ejercicio

A. alto   bajo

B. delgado   gordo

C. bajo   alto

D. anciano   joven

E. grande   pequeño

F. corto   largo

G. largo   corto

H. feo   bonito, guapo

I. gordo   delgado, flaco

1.20 Ejercicio

A. La doctora es inteligente.   Sí, es una doctora inteligente.

B. Los estudiantes son interesantes.   Sí, son unos estudiantes interesantes.

C. La enfermera es joven.   Sí, es una enfermera joven.

D. El profesor es guapo.   Sí, es un profesor guapo.

E. El médico es alto.   Sí, es un médico alto.

F. Los pacientes son delgados.   Sí, son unos pacientes delgados.

G. Los doctores son mayores.   Sí, son unos doctores mayores.

H. El neurólogo es simpático.   Sí, es un neurólogo simpático.

1.21 Ejercicio

A. Pedro es feo. ¿Cómo es Estrella?   Estrella no es fea, es bonita.

B. Marta es gorda. ¿Cómo es Juan?   Juan no es gordo. Es delgado.

C. Miguel es alto. ¿Cómo es Rosa?   Rosa no es alta. Es baja.

D. Ana es baja. ¿Cómo es Marco?   Marco no es bajo. Es alto.

E. Doña María es anciana. ¿Cómo es José?   José no es anciano. Es joven.

F. Carlos es guapo. ¿Cómo es Ana?   Ana no es guapa. Es fea.

G. Luis es delgado. ¿Cómo es Estrella?   Estrella no es delgada. Es gorda.

H. Juana es joven. ¿Cómo es Timoteo?   Timoteo no es joven. Es anciano.

Chapter 2

2.1 Ejercicio

A. Mi mamá **está** enferma.

B. ¿**Estás** bien?

C. **Estoy** mucho mejor, gracias a Dios.

D. Mis pacientes **están** mejores.

E. Marisol y yo **estamos** preocupados por Elsita.

F. La clínica **está** en la Main Street.

2.5 Ejercicio

A. **Estoy** en casa.

B. ¿Dónde **está** usted?

C. ¿**Estás** en el baño?

D. Mis hijos y yo **estamos** en la cafetería.

E. El pediatra **está** en el consultorio hoy.

F. El doctor y la enfermera **están** en la clínica con un paciente.

2.12 Ejercicio

Buenos días. Me llamo Hilda Rodríguez Portocarrero. **Soy** enfermera en el hospital Nuestra Señora de la Altagracia. El hospital **es** grande y famoso. El hospital **está** en Lima, Perú. Trabajo con la doctora Kathi Collins. La doctora Collins **es** norteamericana. Ella **está** en el hospital todos los días, pero yo no. Los sábados **estoy** en la clínica y los domingos **estoy** en casa. Los domingos la clínica **está** cerrada. La doctora **es** alta y delgada. Yo **soy** baja y no muy delgada. La doctora y yo **estamos** muy contentas.

2.13 Ejercicio

A. Originalmente soy de Phoenix, Arizona.
   ¿De dónde **es usted**?

B. Estoy en el hospital de lunes a viernes.
   ¿Cuándo **está usted** en el hospital?

C. Soy doctor de cabecera.
   ¿Cuál **es** su profesión?

D. La enfermera es alta, morena y muy simpática.
   ¿Cómo **es la enfermera**?

E. Estoy muy cansado.
   ¿Cómo está usted?

F. La doctora Marcelina Allende de Oviedo es la pediatra.
   ¿Quién es la pediatra?

2.22 Ejercicio

A. fácil

B. difícil

C. abril

D. café

E. peroné

F. sábado

G. oncólogo

H. final

Chapter 3

3.8 Ejercicio

A. Una cama es buenísima cuando tengo sueño.

B. Un carro deportivo es buenísimo cuando tengo prisa.

C. Una frazada es buenísima cuando tengo sueño / frío.

D. Un osito de peluche es buenísimo cuando tengo miedo.

E. Una hamburguesa es buenísima cuando tengo hambre.

F. Un ventilador es buenísimo cuando tengo calor.

G. Un vaso de agua es buenísimo cuando tengo sed / calor.

H. Una discusión es buenísima cuando tengo razón.

Ejercicio 3.21

A. Usted tiene la clavícula quebrada. La clavícula está quebrada.

B. Usted tiene el cúbito / el antebrazo quebrado. El cúbito / el antebrazo está quebrado.

C. Usted tiene el metacarpo / la mano quebrado/a. El metacarpo / la mano está quebrado/a.

D. Usted tiene el húmero quebrado. El húmero está quebrado.

E. Usted tiene el metatarso / el pie quebrado. El metatarso / el pie está quebrado.

F. Usted tiene el peroné y la tibia quebrados. El peroné y la tibia están quebrados.

G. Usted tiene el tobillo quebrado. El tobillo está quebrado.

H. Usted tiene el radio / el antebrazo derecho quebrado. El radio / el antebrazo derecho está quebrado.

Ejercicio 3.22

A. La rodilla no está quebrada, gracias a Dios; está torcida.

B. Los tobillos no están quebrados, gracias a Dios; están torcidos.

C. El cuello no está quebrado, gracias a Dios; está torcido.

D. Las muñecas no están quebradas, gracias a Dios; están torcidas.

E. El dedo no está quebrado, gracias a Dios; está torcido.

F. La espalda no está quebrada, gracias a Dios; está torcida.

G. El tobillo izquierdo no está quebrado, gracias a Dios; está torcido.

H. La muñeca derecha no está quebrada, gracias a Dios; está torcida.

Ejercicio 3.23

A. La encía está hinchada, pero no está infectada.

B. Los labios están hinchados, pero no están infectados.

C. La rodilla está hinchada, pero no está infectada.

D. Los tobillos están hinchados, pero no están infectados.

E. El dedo del pie está hinchado, pero no está infectado.

F. El codo izquierdo está hinchado, pero no está infectado.

G. La lengua está hinchada, pero no está infectada.

H. El ojo derecho está hinchado, pero no está infectado.

Chapter 4

4.1 Ejercicio

A Tengo veinticuatro costillas.

B. Tengo diez dedos.

C. Tengo veinticuatro vértebras.

D. Tengo dos orejas.

    E. Tengo diez dedos de los pies.

    F. Tengo (#) hermanos.

4.2 Ejercicio

    A. Su temperatura está en noventa y ocho grados.

    B. Su temperatura está en ciento punto ocho grados.

    C. Su temperatura está en noventa y siete punto cuatro grados.

    D. Su temperatura está en ciento tres grados.

    E. Su temperatura está en ciento cuatro punto dos grados.

    F. Su temperatura está en noventa y ocho punto nueve grados.

    G. Su temperatura está en ciento uno punto dos grados.

    H. Su temperatura está en ciento punto tres grados.

4.3 Ejercicio

    A. Su presión arterial está en ciento diez sobre sesenta y ocho.

    B. Su presión arterial está en ciento sesenta y seis sobre ciento diez.

    C. Su presión arterial está en ciento treinta y cuatro sobre ochenta.

    D. Su presión arterial está en ciento veintiocho sobre setenta.

    E. Su presión arterial está en ciento veintidós sobre ochenta y cuatro.

    F. Su presión arterial está en ciento dieciocho sobre noventa y dos.

    G. Su presión arterial está en ciento seis sobre setenta y cuatro.

    H. Su presión arterial está en ciento veinte sobre ochenta.

4.10 Ejercicio

    A. sus sábanas

    B. su cama

    C. nuestras frazadas

    D. sus camas

    E. su silla

    F. su consultorio

    G. mi estetoscopio

4.13 Ejercicio

    A. Son las tres.

    B. Son las doce y quince. Son las doce y cuarto. Son las doce quince.

    C. Son las diez y media. Son las diez treinta.

    D. Es la una menos veinticinco. Son las doce treinta y cinco.

4.14 Ejercicio

    A. Son las once menos quince de la mañana. Son las once menos cuarto de la mañana. Son las diez cuarenta y cinco de la mañana.

    B. Son las seis y quince de la mañana. Son las seis y cuarto de la mañana. Son las seis quince de la mañana.

    C. Son las ocho y media de la noche. Son las ocho treinta de la noche.

   D. Son las doce menos cinco de la noche. Son las once cincuenta y cinco de la noche.

   E. Son las cuatro menos cuatro de la tarde. Son las tres cincuenta y seis de la tarde.

   F. Son las seis y cinco de la tarde. Son las seis cinco.

4.15 Ejercicio

   A. Usted tiene una cita con el dentista (el odontólogo) el jueves catorce de diciembre a las tres y media de la tarde.

   B. Usted tiene una cita en la clínica el martes veintidós de enero a las diez y quince (cuarto) de la mañana.

   C. Usted tiene una cita con el doctor Contreras Medina el viernes veintiocho de febrero a las siete menos quince de la tarde.

   D. Su madre tiene una cita con el neurólogo, el Dr. Solano, el miércoles 30 de mayo a la una de la tarde.

Chapter 5

5.1 Ejercicio

   A. la esposa de mi hermano — mi cuñada
   B. el hijo de mi hijo — mi nieto
   C. el hijo de mi padrastro — mi hermanastro
   D. la hermana de mi madre — mi tía
   E. el hijo de mi tía — mi primo
   F. la hermana de mi primo — mi prima
   G. la madre de mi esposa — mi suegra
   H. el hijo de mi esposa y su exesposo — mi hijastro

5.2 Ejercicio

Hola. Me llamo Arturo. Mi **papá** se llama Juan Martínez. Él tiene una **hermana** que se llama Carmen y es mi **tía**. También tiene un **hermano** que se llama Pedro y es mi **tío**. Soy el **sobrino** de mi tía Carmen y mi tío Pedro. Tío Pedro tiene dos hijos. Ellos son mis **primos**. El padre de mi padre es mi **abuelo** Javier Martínez. La esposa de mi abuelo es mi **abuela**.

5.7 Ejercicio

   A. llegar — a las seis
   B. recetar — medicina para el colesterol
   C. caminar — en el parque
   D. leer — las instrucciones
   E. comprar — el medicamento
   F. escribir — una receta
   G. cocinar — vegetales
   H. sufrir de — una enfermedad

5.9 Ejercicio

A. Mi abuelo **cocina** vegetales para la familia.
B. Juan Miguel **camina** al hospital para trabajar todos los días.
C. Tú **lees** libros en inglés y español.
D. Los doctores **recetan** los medicamentos.
E. Marisol y su hermana **hablan** por teléfono todos los sábados.
F. Yo **como** mucha ensalada porque tiene fibra y muchas vitaminas.
G. Una enfermera **visita** a mi abuela en su casa una vez a la semana.
H. Luisito **toma** un vaso de **leche** porque tiene **sed**.
I. Miguelina **compra** libros por Internet con su tarjeta de crédito.

5.10 Ejercicio

Me llamo Shawn. **Soy** enfermero y **trabajo** en la clínica de lunes a viernes. No **vivo** lejos de la clínica y **camino** a la clínica todos los días. La clínica **abre** a las ocho de la mañana. La doctora Valerio **trabaja** en la clínica también. Ella y yo **cuidamos** a nuestros pacientes. La doctora **examina** a los pacientes y receta los medicamentos. Yo **enseño** a los pacientes cómo tomar sus medicamentos. Los pacientes **compran** sus medicamentos en la farmacia y **visitan** la clínica cuando están enfermos o **necesitan** más medicamento.

5.17 Ejercicio

A. Aprendo español rápidamente.
B. Enseño inglés **a** mis padres.
C. Mi esposa y yo hablamos español en casa.
D. Cuido **a** mis padres en la casa.
E. Visito **a** mi mamá todas las semanas.
F. Llamo **a** mi hermana por teléfono los domingos.
G. Mi hermano come una hamburguesa al mediodía.
H. Mi tío bebe tres tazas de café por la mañana.

Chapter 6

6.1 Ejercicio

A. la nicotina: parche, dulce, chicle (goma de masticar) y aerosol
B. la leche de magnesia: suspensión
C. el Pepto Bismol: suspensión, tabletas
D. la Visene: gotas
E. la insulina: inyección
F. el albuterol: inhalación
G. la guaifenesina: jarabe, cápsulas
H. la hidrocortisona 2%: crema, ungüento
I. el paregórico: elíxir, líquido
J. la compazina: supositorio, pastillas, inyección
K. la vacuna para la varicela: inyección
L. el ibuprofeno: pastilla, cápsula, suspensión, gotas, inyección

6.2 Ejercicio

A. toma

B. toma

C. tomas

D. tomamos

E. toma

F. toman

G. toman

6.5 Ejercicio

Quiero enseñarles cómo usar el inhalador para recibir el máximo beneficio del medicamento. Primero, **agite** bien el inhalador. Así. **Quite** la tapa protectora. **Exhale** completamente a través de su nariz y **mantenga** la boca cerrada. **Abra** la boca completamente y **ponga** la boquilla a una o dos pulgadas de su boca. Así. **Inhale** lentamente y profundamente y, al mismo tiempo, **oprima** la parte de abajo del envase para rociar el medicamento en la boca. Así. **Contenga** el aliento durante cinco a diez segundos, **retire** el inhalador y **exhale** lentamente a través de la nariz o boca. Así. **Ponga** la tapa protectora en el inhalador. Después de cada tratamiento, **enjuague** su boca con agua o enjuague bucal.

6.6 Ejercicio

A. Tome 1 pastilla cada 4 horas.

B. Tome 1 cucharadita por la mañana y 2 al acostarse.

C. Tome el medicamento con leche.

D. Tome 1 pastilla 4 veces al día por 10 días.

E. Tome mucha agua con el medicamento.

F. Tome 1 cucharada por la mañana.

G. Tome 2 pastillas cada 4 horas cuando sea necesario para el dolor.

H. Ponga 2 gotas en cada ojo 2 veces al día.

I. Aplique la crema por la mañana y por la noche.

J. Inyecte 2 cc por vía intramuscular 1 vez al mes.

6.7 Ejercicio

A. Tome el medicamento todos los días sin falta.

B. Amoxicilina (250 mg/5 ml), tome 1 cucharadita 3 veces al día por 5 días.

C. Guaifenesina, tome 1 cucharada 4 veces al día para la congestión.

D. Salbutamol, tome 1 inhalación cada 4 a 6 horas cuando sea necesario para la fatiga.

E. Donepezilo, tome 10 mg por la boca (por vía oral) 1 vez al día (diario) por la mañana.

F. Acetaminofén, tome 2 tabletas cada 4 a 6 horas cuando sea necesario para el dolor.

G. Mylanta, tome 2 cucharadas al acostarse.

H. Isoniazid, tome 1 tableta todos los días por la mañana.

I. Phenytoin 100 mg, tome 1 cápsula 3 veces al día.

    J. Loperamide, tome 1 cápsula cada 2 a 3 horas cuando sea necesario para la diarrea.

6.8 Ejercicio

    A. Lisinopril 5 mg, tome 1 pastilla por vía oral 2 veces al día.
    B. Hidroclorotiazida 25 mg, tome 2 pastillas por vía oral por la mañana.
    C. Metformina 500 mg, tome 1 pastilla por vía oral dos veces al día.
    D. Salbutamol, 1 inhalación cuando sea necesario para la fatiga.

6.10 Ejercicio

    A. Advil es una pastilla (tableta, comprimido). Es un antiinflamatorio no esteroide.
    B. Proventil es un aerosol. Es un broncodilatador.
    C. Bactrim es una pastilla. Es un antibiótico.
    D. Coumadin es una pastilla. Es un anticoagulante.
    E. Tylenol es una pastilla. Es analgésico y antipirético.
    F. Valium es una pastilla. Es un tranquilizante.
    G. Ex-Lax es una pastilla. Es un laxante.
    H. Benadryl es una pastilla o un líquido. Es antihistamínico (antialérgico).
    I. One-a-Day es una pastilla (cápsula). Es una vitamina.
    J. Pepto Bismol es una suspensión. Es un antiácido. Es un antidiarreico.
    K. Robitussin DM es un jarabe. Es un expectorante y un antitusígeno.
    L. La crema hidrocortisona 2 por ciento es una crema o un ungüento. Es antiinflamatorio.

6.12 Ejercicio

Don Ignacio, es muy importante usar **estos** medicamentos en la manera indicada. **Esta** crema es para aliviar el dolor de la quemadura. En caso de fiebre, **estas** pastillas son para quitar la fiebre. Si tiene mucho dolor, **estas** pastillas son para el dolor. **Este** jarabe es para la tos. Si está peor mañana, favor de llamar a **este** número de teléfono. Finalmente, **estas** recetas son para comprar más medicamentos.

6.15 Ejercicio

    A. Les receto un medicamento para sus hijos.
    B. Le escribo una carta a usted.
    C. Le llamo una ambulancia para la paciente.
    D. Les enseño español a los estudiantes.
    E. Le contesto el teléfono por la secretaria.
    F. Le leo el libro a usted.
    G. La doctora nos contesta la pregunta.

6.16 Ejercicio

    A. El doctor le receta un medicamento para Juan.
    B. La doctora le pregunta su historia médica a él.

C. Yo le escribo una carta al plan médico.

D. La anestesióloga me explica el procedimiento.

E. El enfermero les habla español a los pacientes.

F. Usted les compra la medicina a sus padres.

G. La pediatra le receta un antibiótico para mi bebé.

Chapter 7

7.1 Ejercicio

A. La carne de res es carne roja.

B. El pescado es del océano.

C. El mantecado es rico en calcio.

D. La avena es buena para la picazón.

E. Para consumir bacteria beneficiosa, coma yogur.

F. Para tener más fibra en la dieta, coma pan integral.

G. Para tener más vitamina A, coma zanahoria.

H. Un ingrediente principal de la ensalada es lechuga.

I. El huevo es posible futuro madre o padre de familia.

7.2 Ejercicio

A. A mí **me aburre** trabajar en una oficina.

B. A mis padres **les fascina** cuidar a su nieto.

C. A mí **me interesa** cocinar sin mucha grasa.

D. A los estudiantes **les fascina** aprender el español.

E. A nuestro profesor **le importa** hablar dos idiomas.

F. A mi mejor amigo **le gusta** comer arroz con pollo y ensalada.

7.8 Ejercicio

A. No, no debe cocinar con manteca.

B. Sí, debe comer pollo y pescado.

C. No, no debe comer mucho coco.

D. Sí, debe tomar leche baja en grasa.

E. Sí, debe comer queso bajo en grasa.

F. No, no debe comer papas fritas.

G. Sí, debe usar aceite de maíz.

H. En vez de la carne de res, debe comer (**answers will vary**).

I. **Answers will vary.**

7.9 Ejercicio

A. No, no debe usar mucha azúcar cuando cocina.

B. Sí, debe comer ensalada.

C. No, no debe beber vino.

D. No, no debe comer muchos dulces.

E. Sí, debe comer frijoles.

F. No, no debe usar leche condensada.

G   Sí, debe tomar refrescos dietéticos.

H. Sí, debe usar azúcar artificial.

7.11 Ejercicio

Su colonoscopia es el (**answers will vary**). No **tome** aspirina después del (**answers will vary**). El día anterior, **tome** bisacodilo 5 mg, 4 comprimidos por vía **oral** a las ocho de la mañana y siga una dieta de **líquidos claros**. No **coma** nada y no **tome** ningún producto lácteo. A las seis de la tarde, **tome** diez onzas de citrato de magnesio. A las nueve de la noche, tome otras diez onzas de **citrato** de **magnesio**. Siga una dieta de **líquidos claros** toda la **noche**. No tome nada por dos horas antes de la colonoscopia.

Chapter 8

8.4 Ejercicio

El señor Flores está **enfermo**. El problema es que hace tres o cuatro días que le duele **el pecho** cuando **tose**. Cuando tose hay **flema** y el pobre don Francisco tiene **fiebre**. El doctor Vargas dice que el señor Flores tiene **pulmonía** y que necesita **antibióticos** y una **radiografía del pecho**. Tiene que tomar los antibióticos **por vía oral**. Pronto el señor Flores va a estar **mejor**.

8.7 Ejercicio

A. _____ ponerle puntos

B. __X__ escucharle el corazón

C. __X__ pesarle

D. _____ ponerle un suero

E. _____ examinarle la próstata

F. __X__ escucharle los pulmones

G. __X__ tomarle la temperatura

H. __X__ sacarle sangre para un análisis

8.8 Ejercicio

A. Voy a mirarle los ojos.	__E__	Respire profundamente.
B. Voy a percutirle el pecho.	__F__	¿Le duele cuando lo presiono?
C. Voy a mirarle la garganta.	__B__	Golpecitos.
D. Voy a tocarle el cuello.	__D__	Mueva la cabeza hacia la derecha.
E. Voy a escucharle los pulmones.	__G__	Acuéstese boca arriba por favor.
F. Voy a presionarle el abdomen.	__A__	¿Tiene problemas con la vista?
G. Voy a hacerle un electrocardiograma.	__C__	Abra la boca y diga «a-a-a-a».

8.12 Ejercicio

A. Angiograma

B. Supervisión Holter

C. Imágenes por resonancia magnética

D. Broncoscopia

E. Biopsia

F. Mamograma
G. Espirometría
H. Colonoscopia

Chapter 9

9.1 Ejercicio

A. Anoche mis tíos y mis primos nos **visitaron**.
B. Ellos **llegaron** a las cinco de la tarde.
C. Mis padres **cocinaron** mucha comida deliciosa.
D. Mi hermano y yo **comimos** ensalada, carne y arroz.
E. Después de comer, yo **estudié** para la clase de español.
F. En la noche mi tía **sufrió** de acidez.
G. A las ocho mi tío le **compró** un antiácido para mi tía.
H. Mi tía se **tomó** el antiácido con un vaso de agua.

9.2 Ejercicio

A. ¿En qué año **nació** usted?
B. ¿A usted le **escribió** la doctora una receta nueva?
C. ¿Por cuántos años **vivieron** sus padres con usted?
D. ¿Cuántas botellas de vino **bebieron** los enfermeros en la fiesta?
E. ¿**Viste** tú el accidente ayer?
F. ¿A qué hora **saliste** tú de tu casa esta mañana?
G. ¿**Cuidaron** bien los enfermeros a tu padre en el hospital?
H. ¿**Tragó** doña María la pastilla grande sin problema?

9.6 Ejercicio

A. Ayer fue miércoles.	Ser
B. La prueba de Pap fue negativa.	Ser
C. La semana pasada fui a la clínica.	Ir
D. Fui estudiante de medicina en el 2011.	Ser
E. El enfermero fue a la cafetería para comer.	Ir
F. El cirujano que me operó fue el doctor Pérez.	Ser
G. Mi madre y yo fuimos al consultorio el martes.	Ir

9.7 Ejercicio

Anoche el bebé **estuvo** enfermo. Mi pobre bebé **tuvo** una fiebre alta. Su temperatura **estuvo** en cuarenta grados. Nosotros **fuimos** al hospital. El doctor que nos atendió **fue** el doctor Vargas. Yo **estuve** muy nerviosa. El doctor **dijo** que **fue** una infección de los oídos y nos recetó un antibiótico.

9.8 Ejercicio

El tres de enero el doctor Aquino y Ana **comieron** en la casa de Javier.
El cinco de enero el doctor Aquino **visitó** a doña Mercedes en Boston.

El once de enero el doctor Aquino **trabajó** en la clínica desde las ocho hasta las cinco.

El trece de enero el doctor Aquino y don Máximo **fueron** a la clase de inglés.

El catorce de enero el doctor Aquino **consultó** con el anestesiólogo.

El quince de enero el doctor Aquino no **comió** nada y **bebió** líquidos claros.

El dieciséis de enero el doctor Aquino **tuvo** una colonoscopia.

El diecisiete de enero el doctor Aquino **fue** al consultorio de la Dra. Muñoz de Jones para un examen físico.

El treinta de enero el doctor Aquino **fue** de vacaciones a Venezuela.

9.11 Ejercicio

A. La biopsia fue positiva.
B. El análisis de sangre fue negativo.
C. La prueba de tuberculosis fue positiva.
D. La tomografía computarizada fue negativa.
E. La prueba del SIDA fue negativa.
F. La prueba de embarazo fue positiva.
G. El sonograma de la vesícula biliar fue negativo.

9.16 Ejercicio

Cuando **era** niño, **vivía** en Puerto Rico. Mis abuelos **vivían** con nosotros. Abuela **sabía** mucho de las plantas medicinales. Cuando **tenía** gripe, me **hacía** té de hojas de limón y naranja. Cuando **tenía** gases en la barriga, me **preparaba** té de anís. Mis padres no me **daban** remedios caseros. Ellos me **llevaban** a la farmacia, y el farmacéutico nos **vendía** un jarabe o una pastilla. No me **gustaban** los jarabes. **Prefería** las tisanas de mi abuelita.

Chapter 10

10.2 Ejercicio

A. La tuberculosis del pulmón es **una bacteria**.
B. La piel amarillenta es un síntoma de **hepatitis**.
C. Los pacientes que sufren de **epilepsia** tienen convulsiones.
D. Los pacientes con hiperglucemia padecen de **diabetes**.
E. Los tobillos hinchados son un síntoma de **insuficiencia cardíaca**.
F. Si un tumor es **maligno**, el paciente tiene cáncer.
G. La causa principal de la enfermedad valvular del corazón es **la fiebre reumática**.

10.7 Ejercicio

A. Mi hermano **ha tenido** piojos.
B. Yo **he sufrido** de bronquitis crónica.
C. ¿**Has puesto** tú la vacuna de la hepatitis B?
D. Mis padres **han comprado** sus medicamentos.

E. Mi hermano y yo **hemos consultado** con el urólogo.

F. El doctor me **ha hecho** el examen rectal digital de la próstata.

10.14 Ejercicio

Dra. Ávila:	¿Sufre usted de **alguna** enfermedad?
Doña Rosa:	No, no sufro de **ninguna** enfermedad.
Dra. Ávila:	¿Toma **algún** medicamento?
Doña Rosa:	No tomo **ningún** medicamento.
Dra. Ávila:	¿Es usted alérgica a **algún** alimento?
Doña Rosa:	No soy alérgica a **ningún** alimento.
Dra. Ávila:	En su familia, ¿**alguien** ha tenido cáncer?
Doña Rosa:	No, en mi familia **nadie** ha padecido de cáncer.
Dra. Ávila:	¿Hay **alguien** en la casa para ayudarla?
Doña Rosa:	Vivo sola. No hay más **nadie** en casa.

10.20 Ejercicio

A. Los hombres deben hacerse autoexamen de los testículos.

B. La histerectomía es una cirugía para sacar el útero.

C. La orina empieza en los riñones y pasa a la vejiga.

D. El pulmón es el órgano de la respiración.

E. La parte del tubo digestivo que llega al estómago es el esófago.

F. Un óvulo sale de un ovario y entra en la trompa de Falopio.

G. El hígado es el órgano más grande en el cuerpo.

H. La amígdala es parte del sistema linfático.

10.21 Ejercicio

A. la artroscopia

B. la cirugía ambulatoria

C. la nefrectomía

D. la laparoscopia

E. la cirugía exploratoria

Chapter 11

11.1 Ejercicio

Mi madre tiene los tobillos hinchados y dificultad para respirar. El cardiólogo dice que la va a **internar** para un ecograma y una cateterización cardíaca. Si todo va bien, le va a **dar de alta** en dos días. Ella está en la sala de emergencias y no quiere **quedarse interna**, pero el cardiólogo dice que el corazón es el músculo más importante del cuerpo y hay que cuidarlo.

11.4 Ejercicio

Buenos días. Me llamo Juan y mi esposa se llama Melania. Yo **me levanto** a las cinco de la mañana y **me baño**. Melania **se levanta** a las cinco y media y **se baña**.

Yo **me afeito** mientras Melania **se seca** el cabello. Nosotros **nos vestimos, desayunamos** y **salimos** de la casa a las siete.

11.12 Ejercicio

A. Se me rompió un hueso.
B. Se me olvidó ponerme la insulina.
C. Se te fracturó el dedo.
D. Se te quemó la mano.
E. ¿Se le perdió la receta?
F. Se me hinchan los tobillos.

11.13 Ejercicio

A. **¿Puede** usted dormir sin tomar una pastilla para dormir?
B. ¿Cuánto tiempo hace que usted no **duerme** bien?
C. ¿Cuántas horas **durmió** usted anoche?
D. **¿Puede** usted abrir la botella?
E. **¿Puede** usted tragar la pastilla grande sin problema?
F. **¿Puede** usted llegar mañana a las siete de la mañana?
G. La enfermera dijo que anoche usted no **durmió** bien. ¿Tiene sueño?

11.18 Ejercicio

A. Tomar mucho café me pone **agitado**.
B. Cuando estoy resfriado, me siento **molesto**.
C. Cuando trabajo mucho llego a la casa muy **agotado**.
D. Estoy **ansioso** cuando tengo una cita con el odontólogo.
E. Me pongo **agobiado** cuando hay mucho trabajo y poco tiempo.
F. Me siento muy **soñoliento** cuando paso la noche sin dormir bien.

Chapter 12

12.1 Ejercicio

A. ¿Quién es su ginecólogo?
B. ¿Cuándo comenzó su último período?
C. ¿Cuánto tiempo duran sus períodos?
D. ¿Son regulares sus períodos?
E. ¿Le duelen los períodos?
F. ¿Cuándo fue su última prueba de Papanicolaou?
G. ¿Cuándo fue su último ultrasonido?
H. ¿Cuánto tiempo hace que no tiene la menstruación?
I. ¿Ha subido de peso?
J. ¿Usa drogas? ¿Fuma?

12.9 Ejercicio

A. La **episiotomía** es una incisión en la vulva para facilitar el parto del feto.
B. La **operación cesárea** es necesaria cuando el parto vaginal no es posible.

C. La **placenta** es un órgano que está entre la superficie interior del útero y el cordón umbilical.

D. Cuando no hay **contracciones** se usa medicamento para adelantar el parto.

E. El embarazo **ectópico** es un embarazo anormal porque el óvulo fertilizado no está en el útero.

12.10 Ejercicio

A. ¡Muévete!	A. ¡No te muevas!
B. ¡Levántate!	B. ¡No te levantes!
C. ¡Vírate!	C. ¡No te vires!
D. ¡Báñate!	D. ¡No te bañes hoy!
E. ¡Come!	E. ¡No comas!
F. ¡Acuéstate!	F. ¡No te acuestes!
G. ¡Levanta el brazo!	G. ¡No levantes el brazo!
H. ¡Respira!	H. ¡No respires!

12.11 Ejercicio

A. No hagas la cita para hoy. Haz la cita para mañana.

B. Sal temprano de la casa. No salgas tarde.

C. Vete al consultorio. No vayas al hospital.

D. No bañes al bebé hoy. Baña al bebé mañana.

E. No te bañes hoy. Báñate mañana.

F. Ponte la bata del hospital. No te pongas ropa interior.

G. No comas nada después de las once. Come bien mañana.

12.12 Ejercicio

A. ¡No te preocupes!

B. ¡Relájate!

C. ¡No comas nada!

D. Si tienes sed, ¡come pedacitos de hielo!

E. ¡Empuja!

F. ¡No empujes!

G. ¡Respira!

H. ¡No respires!

Illustration Credits

Karrie McCarter provided digital bone images.

The comic strips that appear on pages 155 and 227 are © 2007 Baldo Partnership. Reprinted by permission of Universal Uclick. All rights reserved.

The comics that appear on pages 49 and 211 are courtesy of humorist Pepe Angonoa and used with permission.

The food pyramid *Mi Pirámide* that appears on page 160 and the illustration *Mi Plato* that appears on page 160 are public domain resources provided by the United States Department of Agriculture. The *Pilón nutricional* on page 160 is courtesy of *Ministerio de Salud Pública, República Dominicana.*

Truth-Function of Aiken, South Carolina, provided the companion video still shots that appear throughout the book.

Dr. Jorge Amarante, *Nutriólogo Clínico,* shot the photos of his daughter Naura on pages 157 and 158 and contributed the *Pilón nutricional* of the *Ministerio de Salud Pública de la República Dominicana* that appears on page 160.

Carlos Brito of *Ideal Escuela de Español, Cuernavaca, Morelos, México* shot the photo of the offering for the Day of the Dead on page 225.

Otoniel Acevedo Medina took the photos of a pregnant woman and a newborn physical exam on pages 300 and 193.

The following photos were downloaded from Thinkstock.com: woman with headache on page 56; woman with cold on page 60; blood draw, page 196; mosquito on page 236; water boiling on page 238; woman with head scarf on page 240; nurse and patient on page 266; laparascopy on page 268; woman shampooing on page 272; woman with towel on page 273; man with poor hygiene on page 273; burned arm on page 276; cocaine user on page 288; and breastfeeding on page 306.

Frank Dlugoleski of DartZ Business Solutions LLC provided the icons that distinguish goals and classroom activities. DartZ also provided the following drawings: nurses, page 6; clinic, page 7; nurses, page 8; specialists, page 11; body forms, page 21; hot water bottle, page 31; bedside, page 32; pain scale, pages 32, 34, and 79; elevator bank, page 36; man soaking feet, page 54; head and head and body, pages 65 and 66; skeleton front and back, pages 68 and 69; broken bones, page 76; two men on telephone, page 88; clock faces, page 93; family trees, pages 105 and 107; action words, page 113; Alfredo and Mercedes, page 123; medication forms, page 129; *sarpullido,* page 146; pill reminder, page 153; food pyramid, page 160; breakfast, page 164; fruits and vegetables, page 166; physical exam, page 191; gall bladder, page 217; emergency room patients, page 218; hip replacements, page 221; cardiac rehabilitation, page 222; *visita al doctor,* page 226; measles and mumps, page 235; various internal organs, page 253; morning routine, page 274; teeth, page 279; dental conditions and treatments, page 280; dental hygiene, page 281; and feeling states, page 285.

Robert O. Chase created the remaining drawings and illustrations and shot the following photographs: Dr. Cordova on page 14; woman with pot on page 21; elderly man on page 21; woman with head scarf on page 21; pyramid on page 27; grandparents and child on page 28; hospital signage on pages 44, 45, and 48; man mixing concrete on page 51; sutured arm and leg on page 74; women hugging on page 81; family on page 102; three generations of women on page 104; birthday party on page 125; men at pharmacy on page 128; IV bag on page 129; woman at pharmacy on page 131; pharmacy wall on page 144; herbs and herbs with vegetables on page 154; various fruits and vegetables on pages 159, 169, 170, 178, and 180; hospital signs on pages 183, 190, and 197; doctor suturing boy on page 191; CT scan on page 198; throat exam on page 200; multiple signs on page 201; ambulances on pages 205 and 209; cemetery on page 225; herbs and cacti on pages 225 and 226; hospitalized woman on page 265; mother bathing baby on page 271; elderly aunt on page 287; aloe vera on page 291; *chamán* on page 292; family on page 295; and man with baby on page 314.

Index